W9-BWZ-981

Ute Dieckmann (ed.)
Mapping the Unmappable?

Ute Dieckmann (PhD) is an anthropologist at the University of Cologne with more than two decades of research experience (ethnographic, archival, oral history and livelihoods enquiry) in Namibia. She worked both in academia and for Namibian and international non-governmental organisations.

Ute Dieckmann (ed.)

Mapping the Unmappable?

Cartographic Explorations with Indigenous Peoples in Africa

[transcript]

This publication was made possible by the precious time and dedication of the authors, and was funded by the Deutsche Forschungsgemeinschaft (DFG, German Research Foundation) – Project number 57444011 – SFB 806.

Bibliographic information published by the Deutsche Nationalbibliothek
The Deutsche Nationalbibliothek lists this publication in the Deutsche Nationalbibliografie; detailed bibliographic data are available in the Internet at http://dnb.d-nb.de

Cover layout: Maria Arndt, Bielefeld
Cover illustration: Franz ||Hoëb and Noag Ganaseb at ||Oeb, Hoanib River, 2015. Composite image by Sian Sullivan and Mike Hannis, with aerial photographs from Survey Dept., Windhoek. Full attribution, page 7.
Proofread by Mary Chambers
Printed by Majuskel Medienproduktion GmbH, Wetzlar
Print-ISBN 978-3-8376-5241-3
PDF-ISBN 978-3-8394-5241-7
https://doi.org/10.14361/9783839452417

Contents

Acknowledgements

The contributions to this volume emerged from the international workshop *Mapping the unmappable? African hunter-gatherer relations with their environment and cartography*, organized within the framework of the E3 Project (*Anthropological Models for a Reconstruction of the First African Frontier*) of the Collaborative Research Centre 806 *Our Way to Europe*, funded by the German Research Foundation (Deutsche Forschungsgemeinschaft). It was held at the Thyssen Foundation in Cologne in December 2019.

I would like to express my special thanks to the German Research Foundation and the Collaborative Centre 806, the Competence Area IV (Cultures and Societies in Transition, University of Cologne) and the Thyssen Foundation for their support for the workshop. The workshop would not have been possible without the support of many people, including Thomas Widlok, Stephan Henn, Werner Schuck, Jürgen Richter, Anna Schreiber, Meike Meerpohl, among others.

Developing a volume out of this workshop was an inspiring task. First of all, I would like to thank the contributors and the reviewers for their commitment, compliance with deadlines and procedures and the productive exchange of ideas. For their invaluable help with editorial work and proofreading, I would like to express my gratitude to Celina Horev and Mary Chambers. Again, I would like to thank the CRC 806 for their considerable support for the volume. I also highly appreciate the support of the Global South Study Centre at the University of Cologne and of the DFG-AHRC project *Etosha-Kunene Histories* (www.etosha-kunene-histories.net).

I would also like to express my sincere gratitude to Sian Sullivan and Mike Hannis for the cover image, which is one of a series of images made for the exhibition *Future Pasts: Landscape, Memory and Music in West Namibia*, available to view online at https://www.futurepasts.net/exhibition.

Furthermore, I thank transcript for accepting this volume and for the frictionless process of publishing it.

Last but not least, I owe particular thanks to Hugh Brody and James Suzman, and to Bill Kemp (who died in January 2020), who drew me into cartographic explorations with indigenous people.

Introduction: Cartographic explorations with indigenous peoples in Africa[1]

Ute Dieckmann

Prologue

He took his wand, touched the parchment lightly and said, 'I solemnly swear that I am up to no good.' And at once, thin ink lines began to spread like a spider's web from the point that George's wand had touched. They joined each other, they crisscrossed, they fanned into every corner of the parchment; then words began to blossom on the top, great, curly green words, that proclaimed:

> *Messrs. Moony, Wormtail, Padfoot and Prongs*
> *Purveyors of Aids to Magical Mischief-Makers are proud to present*
> *THE MARAUDER'S MAP*

It was a map showing every detail of the Hogwarts castle and grounds. But the truly remarkable thing was the tiny ink dots moving around it, each labelled with a name in minuscule writing. Astounded, Harry bent over it. A labelled dot in the top left corner showed that Professor Dumbledore was pacing his study; the care-taker's cat, Mrs. Norris, was prowling the second floor, and Peeves, the poltergeist, was currently bouncing around the trophy room. And as Harry's eyes travelled up and down the familiar corridors, he noticed something else. This map showed a set

1   This research was undertaken within the framework of the Collaborative Research Cen-
     tre 806 *Our Way to Europe*, funded by the German Research Foundation. Support was
     also provided by the DFG-AHRC project *Etosha-Kunene-Histories* (www.etosha-kunene-
     histories.net). I would like to thank all the contributors for their inspiring input that
     has influenced my own thinking around the topic. I owe my special thanks to Thomas
     Widlok, Stephan Henn, Mara Jill Goldman, Saskia Vermeylen and Margaret Wickens
     Pearce for their invaluable comments on earlier drafts of this introduction.

of passages he had never entered.
(Harry Potter and the Prisoner of Azkaban by J.K. Rowling 2011 [1999]: 143-144)

Imagine this miraculous map, not static, timeless and 'dead', but with agents moving around (including animals and spirits), and with hitherto undiscovered paths.

When I re-read Harry Potter, it was not just this map that excited me, but I also discovered many aspects that reminded me of what I have read about or experienced of hunter-gatherer being-in-the-world (in the sense of experiencing, apprehending and acting in the world),[2] e.g. the agency of non-human beings or agency evolving from relations between different beings (e.g. wands and wizards), ontological hybridity, the possibilities of ontological transformations, sharing substances or essences, the power of imagination, dreams, prophecies, and so on.[3]

The incredible success of the Harry Potter novels gives proof that these ideas are not untranslatable or incomprehensible for a 'western'[4] public, but are apparently highly appealing.

Yet, this volume is not about novels and whimsical maps therein, and their potential to mediate non-western experiences of the world. We are looking at actual maps as a medium through which to visualize relational ontologies and other issues related to hunter-gatherers' being-in-the-world. That's where I start my introduction. This volume endeavors to bring two rather different strands of research and practices, namely cartography/mapping and relational anthropology/writing, into a closer dialogue and aims to explore their potential for integration.

---

2   The hyphenated phrase being-in-the-world was introduced by Heidegger. Ingold took it up to describe the organism-in-its-environment, and to stress its active engagement with the world (2011 [2000]: 76; 2018b: 221). I draw here on Ingold's use of the term.

3   Of course, there are also many differences, e.g. the wizard- and muggle-centrism (as opposed to an ecological integrated world with every entity playing its own role in the ecology). I do not mean to draw a direct analogy, but rather find the parallels useful to think through.

4   I am aware that I use the term 'western' as a "foil against which to contrast the particularity of experience for people living someplace, sometime" (Ingold 2018a: 49).

Cartography, mapping and counter-mapping

It is widely acknowledged nowadays that maps are powerful (Harley 1989; Wood 1992; Wood/Fels/Krygier 2010; Dodge 2011; Glaze 2009; Monmonier 2018). For centuries, cartography and the production of maps were under the control of powerful elites, states and their allies in the west and – albeit to a lesser degree – of academics who used maps as tools to categorize, to designate, to (re)produce and to propagate certain conceptions of the world (Crampton/Krygier 2005: 12; Glaze 2009: 181). Maps defined empires and helped to maintain control over indigenous peoples (Chapin/Lamb/Threlkeld 2005: 620).

Since the late 1980s, critical cartography has played a strong role in critically scrutinizing maps both methodologically and theoretically, initially drawing mainly from semiotics, deconstructivism and discourse analysis (e.g. Harley 1989; Wood 1992). Studies in this field revealed how particular worldviews are privileged by particular mapping practices (Harris 2015: 51), and how perspectives and interests were turned into 'knowledge' through maps. Later, the ontological focus shifted from the map as representation towards the process of mapping (Dodge/Perkins 2015: 38; Rose-Redwood 2015: 4; Kitchin/Gleeson/Dodge 2013: 480), a shift which was also called a "processual turn" (Halder/Michel 2018: 13). These post-representational analyses looked at the numerous practices and actors bringing mapping into being and at the effect that maps have for users (e.g. Harris 2015; Perkins 2008; Del Casino Jr./Hanna 2005; Harris/Hazen 2005).

Maps for/of the less privileged: Using the master's tool

As Nietschmann put it: "More indigenous territory has been claimed by maps than by guns" (Nietschmann 1994: 36). Since the 1970s, indigenous peoples have started to counteract with their own mapping projects, with the goal "to appropriate the state's *techniques* and *manners of representations* to bolster the legitimacy of 'customary' claims to resources" (Peluso 1995: 384, original emphasis). In other words, indigenous people appropriated the "master's tool" in order to challenge and to protest against the prevalent representations promulgated by governments and their allies. The rise of an international indigenous peoples' movement in the second half of the last century, the realization that maps were sources of power for the powerful (cf. Wood 1992), and the rapid development of new mapping technology (cf. Crampton/Krygier 2005), were all factors which played a role in this regard. Hunter-gatherer communities have been involved worldwide in indigenous mapping projects in which geospatial technologies (e.g. digital maps, satellite images, geographic information systems [GIS], and global positioning systems [GPS]) are increasingly employed in order to bring indigenous or local perspectives to the attention of those in power, who usually hold control over (official) maps (Crawhall 2009: 5-7).

The maps produced in these projects are known under different labels, also due to their slightly different foci, from "participatory tenure maps", "community maps" and "counter-maps" (coined by Peluso 1995) to "cultural maps" (e.g. used by UNESCO) or "indigenous maps" (see Chapin/Lamb/Threlkeld 2005, for more details of the terminology).[5] Under the broad umbrella of human ecology mapping, other often similar approaches have been used, e.g. "tenure and resource use mapping", "local ecological knowledge mapping" or "sense of place mapping" (see McLain et al. 2013: 651-652 and references therein).

The maps are almost as diverse as the actors involved and the methodologies applied, and can be categorized in different ways. Rocheleau, for example, lists cadastral maps; political/administrative maps (to claim property or contest boundaries); thematic maps; sketch maps; GIS-Generated Geo-References Maps of Land Use and Cover, Resources, Demography; and integrated and expanded GIS (combining multimedia records with geo-referenced maps, to combine qualitative and quantitative data on culture and ecology) (Rocheleau 2005: 337).

Cultural mapping was included in the support programs of UN Organizations, other internationally operating organizations (e.g. World Wildlife Fund for Nature, the Technical Centre for Agricultural and Rural Co-operation, the Forest Peoples Programme, the Rainforest Foundation), and national or local non-governmental organizations (NGOs). For example, the United Nations Educational, Scientific, and Cultural Organization (UNESCO) held "cultural-resource mapping" seminars in Bangkok and UNESCO also worked with the Indigenous Peoples of Africa Coordination Committee IPACC) on "participatory mapping" to foster the capacity of Africa's Indigenous Peoples to protect their cultural and biological resources. The Ford Foundation, the World Wildlife Fund and several Indonesian NGOs in Indonesia jointly published a

---

5   All the terms bear their specific problems. I will mostly use the terms "cultural maps", "indigenous maps" and "counter-maps" for maps made with/for indigenous communities. For a critical assessment of the term "cultural maps", see Dieckmann, this volume.

manual that included summaries of seven pioneering case studies of "community-mapping projects" in Kalimantan, Sulawesi and Sumatra (Rundstrom 2009: 316). Manuals on cultural mapping/participatory mapping have also been developed in many other regions (e.g. Tobias 2000; Cook/Taylor 2013; Rainforest Foundation UK 2015a; CTA 2010).

Cultural mapping was praised as possessing manifold advantages and benefits. UNESCO Bangkok, for example, lists these as: documentation of cultural resources, community empowerment, effective cultural resource management, community economic development, transmission of local knowledge and promotion of intercultural dialogue (Cook/Taylor 2013: 25-26).

Tobias listed the following purposes in his guidebook for First Nations in Canada on "land use and occupancy mapping, research design and data collection":

- "Documenting elders' oral history before more knowledge is lost.
- Determining shared use areas and reconciling boundary conflicts between neighboring aboriginal communities.
- Providing evidence for court cases involving aboriginal rights and title; settling treaty and claims under federal land claims processes; supporting compensation claims.
- Negotiating co-management agreements.
- Negotiating protective measures and benefits from industrial development.
- Determining probable impacts of development; supporting injunctions to stop unwanted development.
- Providing baseline data for long-term community planning and resource management.
- Supporting administrative programs such as land use permitting.
- Developing education curricula." (Tobias 2000: xii)

According to Alcorn, "community-based maps" could:

- "reveal areas where rights and responsibilities are cloudy;
- serve as evidence in courts of law;
- build consensus and mass support for policy reforms;
- renew local commitment to governing resources;
- promote community cohesion and self-actualisation;
- develop new links with administrative agencies;

- clarify rights over natural resources;
- promote cross-generational communication;
- renew cultural heritage;
- help control development." (Alcorn 2000: 11)

In an overview report for UNESCO, Poole summarized the various purposes of "cultural mapping" under the rubrics of tenure security and cultural revitalization (Poole 2003: 13), which seem to cover most but not all of the manifold purposes listed above.

It appears from these long lists that cultural mapping has been appreciated at times as an almost magical instrument in finding solutions for the diverse issues that indigenous peoples around the world are struggling with. It has been undertaken in many different contexts, with different agendas and different actors, at times with a top-down approach, at times more with a bottom-up approach (Rundstrom 2009: 316). In their review on indigenous mapping worldwide, Chapin et al. considered it as "a powerful tool for indigenous peoples in their struggles to defend and claim their ancestral lands, manage their resources, plan economic development, and preserve their cultures" (Chapin/Lamb/Threlkeld 2005: 630).

"Cartographic chainsaw massacres"[6] or strategically selected tools?

Despite the above discussed acceptance of indigenous/cultural/counter-mapping, there has also been far-reaching critique by mapping practitioners, activists, geographers, anthropologists and other academics. As Rocheleau pointed out, "[t]he new wave of community-based resource mapping and counter-mapping risks using the master's (blunt) tools to frame the infinite complexity of local places and peoples on the planet within a two-dimensional global grid of property rights and political authority" (Rocheleau 2005: 327). There is a danger, therefore, that maps may fix people, resources, habitats and territories in the Cartesian grid, "the iron grid of Descartes", and thereby reduce the multi-dimensional, dynamic and complex realities to a two-, or three-dimensional static construct (Rocheleau 2005: 328). In the mapping process, indigenous ontologies need to be translated into dominant cartographic tools, which brings the risk of distortion of original meanings and therefore the risk of appropriation by those in power (Halder/Michel

---

6   I borrow the term from Rocheleau (2005: 339).

2018: 16). And finally, indigenous maps might be "double-edged", functioning as tools both of political and territorial empowerment and of cultural and technical assimilation (Hirt 2012: 117).

The lack of theory and critical reflection in the indigenous mapping craze is of major concern. Due to the pragmatic origins of indigenous/counter-mapping rooted in empowerment and activism, the emphasis has mostly been on praxis over theory, action over reflection (Duxbury/Garrett-Petts/Mac Lennan 2015: 17). The approaches within the field of critical cartography have been employed for indigenous/counter-mapping to a rather limited degree. In 2009, Rundstrom stated: "With only a few exceptions, experienced scholars have considered counter-mapping a pragmatic exercise. They have tended to focus on establishing an empirical record of successes and failures, the reasons for the outcomes, and what practices do and do not work in the regional contexts in which they have worked. Theorizing their work in a broader context has been of secondary or no concern, perhaps understandably so." (Rundstrom 2009: 315)

Other points of critique have concerned the issue of participation in counter-mapping projects (e.g. Rocheleau/Edmunds 1997; Abbot et al. 1998), the social and cultural implications of technology transfer (e.g. Aporta/Higgs 2005), the risk of increasing conflicts within or between communities (Fox et al. 2005: 1; Taylor 2008), the (re)production of boundaries (e.g. Sletto 2009; Thom 2009; Hodgson/Schroeder 2002; Vermeylen/Davies/van der Horst 2012; Boden 2007), the tendency to treat or represent communities as homogeneous and static entities, or to fix dynamic systems within static representations (Roth 2009: 208), and the production of new property regimes (Bryan 2011: 41).

The implications and consequences of participatory mapping have been described, for example, as the "counter-mapping dilemma" (Roth 2009), the "ironic effects of counter mapping" (Fox et al. 2005), a "contradictory pursuit" (Rundstrom 2009: 316) or – referring to participatory GIS – questioned as being an "oxymoron" (Abbot et al. 1998). These critiques confront the actors, anthropologists and cartographers, as well as communities and their individual members, with the question of whether to map or not to map. Roth stated in 2009 that the majority answer to this question was at the time that the benefits of mapping would outweigh the costs (Roth 2009: 208).

Despite the well-known contradictions and side effects, I agree with those who would not entirely abandon maps for the purpose of making indigenous perspectives visible. First, it would mean to leave mapping and maps to those in power, which would strengthen their hegemony via the representation of their 'reality'. Second, maps are a seminal tool to convey 'information', one possible medium of communication. Maps tend to be more accessible and can be more easily understood than texts by anyone with the basic ability to read such graphical representation (Eide 2015: 183).

The English adage "A picture is worth a thousand words", becoming popular in the early 20th century with regard to promoting images in advertisements in the United States, summarizes a notion which is even more broadly applicable today. Our "lives are now determined by visuality and its screens to a degree that was unimaginable until recently" (Alloa 2016: 2). Some scholars have detected a "pictorial turn", although it not always clear if this 'turn' only refers to the objects (images) of enquiry or to the enquiry itself, a new way of thinking about the objects (ibid.).

Maps are images, though they have more similarities with texts than photographs do. It is much easier nowadays to design and publish maps online (or on paper) and, as Halder and Michel have put it: "Maps are probably more present in many people's everyday life than ever before" (Halder/Michel 2018: 13).[7] For some time now, there have been new ways of producing, distributing and using maps that lend them new weight as a medium for communication; there is a growing presence and relevance of maps in art, activism and social movements. The ubiquity of spatial information technology, GIS, low cost GPS and remote sensing image analysis software and the spread of participatory mapping techniques offer new opportunities, such as the production of a multiplicity of maps and the possibilities of combining them with multimedia and multilingual content (see e.g. Fox et al. 2005; Rocheleau 2005).

Thus, in a nutshell, maps and the technologies linked to them provide a multifaceted field for communication. As Eide has pointed out, each medium can be seen as a tool, and in order to build something, one can choose a combination of tools suited to the task (Eide 2015: 187).

However, the task must be well-defined and the tools must be chosen consciously: mapping and maps are not an end in themselves but a means to achieve 'something'.

---

7   The ubiquity of digital maps on the temporal distribution and occurrence of the coronavirus (Covid-19), updated daily or several times a day, is a vivid proof of this at the time of writing.

It is therefore necessary to identify, beforehand, what exactly is to be achieved by making a map.[8] Rocheleau's 2005 notion is still relevant today: "To avoid cartographic chainsaw massacres we need to stop, look, listen, think, and then map carefully." (Rocheleau 2005: 339) I would add that even before stopping, looking and thinking, we first need to respond to the why, what and for whom questions. Maps are *not* representations of reality but media to convey certain information, knowledges, practices, experiences and messages; we therefore need to be clear about what information, knowledges, experiences, practices and messages we would like to convey, for what reason and for/to whom. That is where I draw on recent scholarship within anthropology.

Ontologies, relationality, animism and ecology

During the last two decades, anthropology, like other disciplines, has (re)turned to questions of ontologies, from different perspectives and in different theoretical frameworks. This trend includes "ontological approaches to anthropology" (Eide/McCarty 2018: 209), "ontological anthropology" (Bird-David 2018: 307), "anthropology of ontologies" (Kohn 2015: 311) and "anthropology *as* ontology" (Holbraad/Pedersen/Viveiros de Castro 2014, n.p.). Within this broad field, the understanding and usage of the term "ontology" varies. Kohn, for instance, defines ontology as the study of "reality", which encompasses but is not limited to humanly constructed worlds. Others understand it as the study of "being" or "becoming" (Kohn 2015: 312). Holbaard et al. define the anthropological concept of ontology as "the multiplicity of forms of existence enacted in concrete practices, where politics becomes the non-sceptical elicitation of this manifold of potentials for *how things could be* – what Elizabeth Povinelli (2012), as we understand her, calls 'the otherwise'" (Holbraad/Pedersen/Viveiros de Castro 2014, n.p.). Notably, in the original (Greek) meaning, ontology referred to the *discourse* about the nature of being

---

8   The mapping of the coronavirus (Covid-19) comes to my mind again: while, in the initial stages of the pandemic, the maps were easy to read for people familiar with these kind of maps and the maps themselves provided an overview about where (and how much) the virus was present, later in time, the globe (and at times countries) seemed to be covered in frightening and overwhelming clouds (and the where and how much became much more difficult or impossible to grasp). What did the maps achieve then?

(Graeber 2015: 15). Some detect an "ontological turn" in anthropology[9] (mainly associated with the writings of Philippe Descola, Eduardo Viveiros de Castro and Bruno Latour – what Kohn calls the "narrow ontological turn" (2015: 316).[10] The wider ontological field would encompass works which rely on Latour's actor-network theory, the "ecological phenomenology" of Ingold (Eide/McCarty 2018: 209) and many others (cf. Kohn 2015: 315-316).

However one defines it, and despite all the differences, the common denominator within this otherwise broad field is the questioning of previously seemingly fundamental ontological certainties in order to generate new and different insights into 'the world' or 'the worlds'. It is, as Course pointed out, a "dual movement towards, on the one hand, exploring the basis of the western social and intellectual project and, on the other, of exploring and describing the terms in which non-western understandings of the world are grounded" (Course 2010: 248). The concept of ontology, or rather, the plurality of ontologies, invites both a reflection on our own 'reality' and an exploration of how other people and non-humans (e.g. Kohn 2013) configure their world, how things could be otherwise than we know them to be (Bird-David 2018: 307). Ontological anthropology sets out to open us up to other kinds of experiencing and thinking of and in the world, of other ways of being-in-the-world.

It is not the scope of this introduction to philosophically analyze the arguments and counterarguments within the context of the ontological turn. The debate has been productive in as much as it has (again) increased awareness of our own certainties by "destabilising our own forms of classification" (Heywood 2017: 4), or as Astor-Aguilera and Harvey put it: "In contrast to force-fitting the 'other' into our academic logics – regardless of archaeological, historical and ethnographic contexts demonstrating different world engagements – the world of 'others' is often a world not composed by and for humans but one in which humans are part of a larger relational community where a multitude of agents, seen and unseen, interact." (Astor-Aguilera/Harvey 2019: 3). Nevertheless, like many others, I have a number of concerns about the concept of

---

9   It is not the scope of this introduction to discuss whether it can in fact be considered as a 'turn', especially in anthropology. Furthermore, I am suspicious about as well as disoriented by all these so-called intellectual 'turns'. For critiques of the ontological turn see e.g. Pedersen 2012; Graeber 2015; Heywood 2017, 2012; Laidlaw/Heywood 2013.

10   Others might conceive of it as just filtering new wine into old bottles; see Guenther 2019b: 155.

ontology. Most importantly, originating as a concept with its partner epistemology, isn't this conceptual duo based on our own ontological assumptions,
namely that there is a world out there which can be apprehended through different epistemologies, an idea which many ontologists would clearly reject?
Doesn't ontology still imply something constructed in the mind, and therefore
perpetuates a body-mind dichotomy? Barad stated:

> The separation of epistemology from ontology is a reverberation of a
> metaphysics that assumes an inherent difference between human and
> nonhuman, subject and object, mind and body, matter and discourse. Onto-
> epistem-ology – the study of practices of knowing in being – is probably a
> better way to think about the kind of understandings that are needed to
> come to terms with how specific intra-actions matter. (Barad 2003: 829)[11]

I also endorse Ingold's suggestion of exploring "ontogenesis" and "ontogenetic multiplicity" as "open-ended pathways of becoming within one world
of nevertheless continuous variation", rather than a multiplicity of ontologies
(Ingold 2016: 303).[12]

Another, partly overlapping, inspiring field of research in the present
context is that of the ecological (also environmental) humanities. This "inter-
discipline" (with sub-disciplines like environmental literature, environmental philosophy, environmental history, environmental anthropology,
feminist/queer/indigenous science and technology studies) addresses much
more explicitly the current ecological crisis, including climate change, loss
of biodiversity, water degradation and many other anthropogenic events,
as well as the fact, that we are, from this point of view, no longer "able to
sustain the idea that humans are separate from nature" (Rose 2015: 1).[13] This
interdisciplinary field emerged from the acknowledgment across humanities
and the social and environmental sciences of the need for a more integrated

---

11   I am grateful to Mara Jill Goldman for reminding me of the writings of Karen Barad in
      this context.
12   Personally, I would simply prefer the term "the study of *being-in-the-world*". Although
      being-in-the-world is also burdened with some scientific-historical baggage, it em-
      braces experience, apprehension and activity, evades dichotomies and can be under-
      stood without an intensive pre-occupation with philosophy and phenomenology.
13   Although some scholars promulgating the ontological turn in anthropology, e.g. Kohn,
      consider the ontological turn in anthropology as a reaction to certain conceptual prob-
      lems arising from the specter of the global environmental crisis (Kohn 2015: 312), I
      doubt that all ontological anthropologists would subscribe to this.

and conceptually sensitive approach to environmental issues, rethinking the ontological exceptionality of the human. Ecological humanities seek to position humans "as participants in lively ecologies of meaning and value, entangled within rich patterns of cultural and historical diversity that shape who we are and the ways in which we are able to 'become with' others" (Rose et al. 2012: 2). In this regard, anthropological studies on ontologies which reveal the diverse ways in which humans made themselves at home in the wider ecology, and which also reveal the particularity of the nature/culture conceptualization as embedded and plausible only within the framework of the western history (e.g. Sullivan/Hannis 2016: 5), are vital for the approaches of ecological humanists in their re-positioning of humans (in general) in the ecology of life. The Australian philosopher Val Plumwood identified two tasks of ecological humanities: first, to (re)situate the human in ecological terms, and second, to (re)situate non-humans in ethical terms (Plumwood 2002: 8-9). It becomes evident that the political ambitions (in case we consider ethical claims as political ambitions) of ecological humanities are far more outspoken than those of many ontological anthropologists. However, from my point of view, all of them are (at least implicitly) political as well, as they challenge the dominant view of "being-on-top of the world" (Ingold 2011 [2000]: 76; see also Sullivan 2017).[14]

Relevant for the topic of this volume, both fields also share an interest in the "relational ontologies" or "connectivities" (as it is rather called within ecological humanities) of indigenous peoples (e.g. hunter-gatherers, hunter-pastoralists and hunter-herders), an interest which is also linked to the insight that there is something to be learned from their direct involvement with the non-human environment (see e.g. Sullivan 2017). Some scholars call for "relational politics" (Castree 2003).

In relational ontologies, beings (including non-humans) are regarded as persons[15] in relationships and they are constituted by these relationships, not because of any taxonomic designation (as in the western world) or according

---

14   Ingold is explicitly not one of the scholars of the "narrow" ontological turn (e.g. 2016: 303), but his works have much to say about ontologies and are generally referred to under the rubric of ontological anthropology or the new animism, e.g. Eide/McCarty 2018; Guenther 2015.

15   See Bird-David 2018: 307, for a brief critique of the concept of "person". I prefer "actors", "beings" or "others", who are endowed with their own subjectivity. "Person" is, from my point of view, too burdened with its western philosophical history, starting from "persona" in Latin, which referred to masks worn by actors on stage.

to my understanding of what Ingold describes as "populational thinking", as opposed to a "relational thinking" (Ingold 2018a: 103-104). This understanding implies the agency of non-human others as a fact of life and that sociality and historicity are indisputably inclusive of non-human others (Poirier/Dussart 2017: 9). Non-human others may include any other 'entities' in the environment, including rocks, mountains, rivers, other animals, plants, artefacts, thunder, winds or spirits.

The concept of animism is fundamental within relational ontologies. Graham Harvey defines animists as "people who recognise that the world is full of persons, only some of whom are human, and that life is always lived in relationship to others" (Harvey 2006: xi). The understanding of the concept has radically changed since Taylor introduced the term in the late 19th century (Bird-David 2018: 306; Willerslev 2013) and animism is no longer regarded as mistaken belief but as a mode of being that implies a set of ontological assumptions distinct from those on which a Cartesian understanding of the world is based – an understanding which still dominates large parts of science and public domains (Kohn 2015: 317; Bird-David 1999). This rather recent approach to animism has come to be known as the "new animism".

Another concept brought into the discussion on relational ontologies is kin, understood not as genealogical ties but as relational bonds. Following this understanding, kin is not restricted to humans but includes all beings with whom one entertains (inter-subjective) relationships (Bird-David 2017; Haraway 2015).

Relational ontologies and animism are widespread in hunter-gatherer societies. Based on Hallowell's work with Ojibwa in Northern Canada (Hallowell 1960), "new animism" flourished in South America (e.g. Descola 2013; Costa/Fausto 2010; Descola/Palsson 1996; Viveiros de Castro 1998), but spread over to North America (e.g. Scott 2006; see also contributions in Poirier and Dussart 2017; Brightman/Grotti/Ulturgasheva 2012), Siberia (Willerslev 2007; Pedersen 2001; Brightman/Grotti/Ulturgasheva 2012) and South Asia (Bird-David 1999; Århem/Sprenger 2016). Though not under the label "new animism" (Descola (2013) subsumed Australian indigenous ontologies under "totemism"), studies along this line were also conducted in Australia (see contributions in Poirier/Dussart 2017; Rose 2000; Povinelli 1995).

Of course, countless other anthropologists have earlier published relevant material all over the world in this regard, from different theoretical backgrounds and with different labels, e.g. "worldviews", "belief systems", "cosmology", or "religion", feeding into the more recent analytical frameworks.[16]

Mapping relational ontologies?

Relational ontologies have a clear reference to space. Indeed, I would argue that spatiality is an indispensable component of relational ontologies and maps are the medium par excellence to convey spatial information. However, the discussion above on ontologies, relations and ecologies remained somehow abstract. What do the insights within these fields exactly imply for mapping and what exactly could be mapped?

I point to some of the issues with regard to cartographic visualization which came to my mind when engaging with relational ontologies, the "new animism" and ecological humanities. These are certainly extensible and should be read as suggestions for further exploration. Furthermore, these are only general ideas; case studies of different groups living in different landscapes would raise different cartographic questions. Some of the issues will be addressed in this volume, while others might still have to wait for provisional or definitive answers.

Animism: If we take seriously the insight that people living with relational ontologies do not consider humans as ontologically particular but as being incorporated in a wider ecology of a variety of beings, we need to consider how to integrate people into maps. If I am not mistaken, most conventional maps do not depict people (people are the subjects who look at the map, not the objects to be looked at).[17] Occasionally, on colonial maps, there might be 'native' groups depicted on the map (rather as 'objects'). On indigenous/countermaps, plants and animals are mostly represented as resources but people are absent *on* the map. At times, people appear on photographs to pay honor to their participation in the mapping project or to indicate that it is based on their knowledge; the map might be said to be the map *of* a specific community, but the people are hardly integrated into the map itself.[18] Certainly, there

---

16   See e.g. Descola 2013 and Ingold 2011 [2000] (especially chapters 4, 7, 8) for references.

17   Some maps might present accumulated data referring to "people", like population density or coronavirus infections, or, in short, "objects of knowledge".

18   I am aware that I am generalizing here and in the following when I point out to the shortcomings on existing maps. There are exceptions. For example, some maps produced in the area of the Kgalagadi Transfrontier Park in Southern Africa (unpublished)

is the risk, according to the western subject-object separation, that people are objectified when put on the map. Is there any way to circumvent this?

Linked to this, can non-human beings become de-objectified on maps? How can animals and plants turn from resources or cultural heritage items into agential subjects?[19] How can less tangible agents, like ancestors, spirits, potency or winds be depicted on maps? Even more challenging, how can ontological mutability, ambiguity or hybridity be captured on maps? I would presume that GIS and cybercartography (see below) with dynamic visualization has much to offer in this regard.

Relationality: If relations are the constituting part of many hunter-gatherer ontologies, how can their meaning be visualized? I cannot imagine simple lines or double-pointed arrows doing justice to their significance and qualities. This refers both to human-human relationships and human-human networks (including inter-ethnic relations, which are often excluded from indigenous/cultural maps), but also to other kinds of relations, between human and non-human beings and between non-human and other non-human beings. The same goes for kinship (including between human and non-human beings) as relationships with specific qualities. Is there a way to visually weave social networks and relations into the landscape? Relationality also refers to the land. Are there no better ways to convey people's relations to the land and to places than putting indigenous place names (at times with explanations of their meaning) on the map?

Perspectivism: As maps are not the representation of one overall agreed upon reality, multi-mapping from different perspectives (see e.g. Rocheleau 2005: 358) becomes an imperative. This would include mapping from the perspectives of different human groups or individuals (e.g. women, men, children, elders, hunters, shamans, etc.) but it could also include mapping from the perspective of non-human agents (as perceived from the human perspective).[20] It would also imply leaving the conventional bird-eye's, panoptic view for various perspectives from within.

---

on family territories or maps in Etosha (unpublished) on the lifelines of specific individuals clearly depict people on the maps.

19   The pleonasm is deliberately chosen to stress the point.

20   What would Amazonians think the world would look like from the jaguar's perspective? How would lions perceive the world according to San? How would ancestors and spirits conceive of their world?

Mapping for whom?

As mentioned above, one needs to consider the *what* questions (which I have attempted above), as well as the question of the target group, the beholders of the map. Indigenous mapping projects often target policy makers, judges or decision-makers in the field of nature conservation in order to gain land rights, participation in nature conservation management for indigenous people and/or recognition of their cultural heritage. These indigenous maps are produced for quick results, sometimes in urgent political situations. Maybe integrating relational ontologies into the maps would have a rather longer-term impact, although they would not go smoothly with policy makers at first as they are used to the "Cartesian grid".[21] I imagine that the relational and animated maps ask for a new cartographic literacy. Thom, in the Canadian context, hoped for:

> The idea of this 'radical cartography' could well lead to the recognition of kin, the flexibility of group membership, and the protection of customary property rights in the kinds of powerful reconciliation arrangements being negotiated at treaty and self-government tables throughout the indigenous world. Reframing territories according to these less familiar references (at least to a western Cartesian cartography) will not undermine territorial land claims. Rather, it is likely to produce and sustain more harmonious political relations between related communities in a contemporary world of treaty settlements and self-determination. (Thom 2009: 201)

The "radical cartography" could avoid squeezing indigenous ontologies into Cartesian straitjackets. It could counter the risk of political empowerment being gained only by means of 'cultural' assimilation: using the master's language eventually leads to the loss of the mother tongue.

And on the other hand, to stay with that metaphor, it might help 'us'[22] to understand 'their' mother tongues a bit better. From my point of view, the unprecedented ecological crisis requires re-conceptualizations of the human within his/her environment. Relational ontologies could help us to re-think our being-in-the-world. I suggest that maps could help us to at least *imagine*[23] relational thinking (in the sense of "not kind but kin", adopted from Haraway

---

21   They might have an immediate impact within legal negotiations though.

22   'Us' refers to 'us westerners' here.

23   I don't use imagination as opposed to knowledge here, but as one kind of experience.

(2015: 161) – less anthropocentric and less anthropo-hubristic) with the potential of regarding and experiencing other-than-humans as agents and beings. This could contribute to an understanding that living *with* the environment instead of living *off* the environment might be a viable option.

Ingold suggested:

> [T]hat we reverse the order of primacy [of western ontology, the 'givenness' of nature and culture], and follow the lead of hunter-gatherers in taking the human condition to be that of a being immersed from the start, like other creatures, in an active, practical and perceptual engagement with constituents of the dwelt-in-world. This ontology of dwelling, I contend, provides us with a better way of coming to grips with the nature of human existence than does the alternative, Western ontology whose point of departure is that of a mind detached from the world, and that has literally to formulate it – to build an intentional world in consciousness – prior to any attempt at engagement. (Ingold 2011 [2000]: 42)

Two decades later, his proposal is even more relevant. However, as long as academic analyses and debates are mostly carried out in academic journals and publications, but are hardly accessible and incomprehensible for a general – even if sympathetic and interested – public, the political and environmental potential of this vision risks evaporating.

That's where maps can come in, not exclusively, but as one tool amongst many others, including other visual art, documentaries, novels, and whatever media one would like to explore for the purpose of unsettling 'our' own certainties while proposing new ways of apprehending and acting in the world. Maps are important to consider because they are easier to read than texts and thus more accessible to people from different linguistic and educational backgrounds (Lewis 2012: 40). Last but not least, they are the tool *par excellence* for expressing spatial interrelationships and therefore the spatiality of relational ontologies.

Why Africa?

The reasons for the regional focus of the book, namely Africa, are twofold, one referring to relational ontologies and the other to cartography.

In terms of relational ontologies, Africa was not on the radar of "new animists" or of scholars focused on relational ontologies until recently, and, as already mentioned, a one-size-fits-all approach to relational ontologies and animism did not prove productive. Guenther stresses: "[A]nimism is not some monolithic schema or cosmologico-religious complex but something diverse and multiplex, structurally varied, ecologically and historically contingent" (Guenther 2019a: ix). Some works on Khoe-San groups of Southern Africa (e.g. Sullivan 2017; Low 2014; Guenther 2015, 2019a, 2019b) have recently been published, and Skaanes has worked on the cosmology of the Hadza in Tanzania, though with a different theoretical approach (Skaanes 2015, 2017). These studies reveal similarities and differences from the "new animism" in other parts of the world which would need further examination. In Southern Africa, for example, ontological mutability, the significance of transformations (Guenther 2019a, 2019b), the relevance, transmission and sharing of "potency" (Low 2007), the agency of ancestors and of rain (Sullivan/Hannis 2016) seem to be important features of "San-imism" (Guenther 2019a: ix). This volume aims, therefore, at contributing to the spectrum of studies of relational ontologies.

As for cartography, indigenous/counter-mapping has been more prominent on other continents for a number of interconnected reasons: a) the movements and self-organization of indigenous peoples began earlier than in Africa (Niezen 2003, pp.72-86); b) indigenous/counter-mapping started earlier there (Chapin/Lamb/Threlkeld 2005); and c) indigenous peoples in other countries launched and won important land claims earlier (see e.g. Barume 2010), in which indigenous maps often played a significant role (see e.g. Wainwright/Bryan 2009; Thom 2009; Peterson 2017).

In Africa, indigenous mapping projects only began in the 1990s and were, to begin with, mainly conducted with agriculturalists (Chapin/Lamb/Threlkeld 2005: 625); later, hunter-gatherer groups and other indigenous peoples also became part of mapping projects (e.g. different San groups, Baka, Bagyeli, Ogiek). Projects were conducted in Central Africa,[24] Eastern Africa[25] and Southern Africa.[26] Critical anthropological analyses of these projects are rather limited to date (Hodgson/Schroeder 2002; Boden 2007; Taylor 2008; Vermeylen/Davies/van der Horst, 2012). Most of the indigenous mapping

---

24   E.g. Lewis 2012; Rainforest Foundation UK 2015b; Defo/Njounan Tegomo 2008; Nelson 2008; Njounan Tegomo/Defo/Usongo 2012.

25   E.g. Rambaldi et al. 2007; Muchemi/Kiteme 2015; Hodgson and Schroeder 2002; Adaptation Consortium 2015.

26   E.g. Crawhall 2009; Taylor 2002; Taylor and Murphy 2006; Xoms |Omis 2018; Boden 2007; Future Pasts 2015-2019.

projects in Africa have, by and large, followed rather conventional cartographic routes, based on western Cartesian ontology; that is, they represent plants and animals as resources to be exploited and complex land use patterns of hunter-gatherers as territories marked by fixed boundaries, i.e. indigenous being-in-the-world is transformed into a representation within the Cartesian grid and those issues not fitting into it (e.g. animistic experiences) are silenced.[27] What remain largely invisible are social relationships (with human and non-human others), 'potency', non-human agents and the dimension of time.

However, a number of examples, mainly from other continents, though not dealing explicitly with relational ontologies, illustrate that maps, and the cartographic techniques and technologies involved, are not inherently inappropriate to mediate indigenous ontologies. In a case study in India, Robbins (2003) demonstrated that satellite images can be classified according to land cover categories used by different local groups instead of following the classification system of the GIS/ecological analyst. Pearce and Louis (2008) reincorporated the seasonal and cyclical variations into maps of Nu'alolo Kai (Haiwaii) for a better portrayal of the "depth of place" knowledge of Hawai'ians. Developing a place name map in the Penobscot territory (Maine, US), Pearce (2014) transformed the conventional map design using tools of narrativity and translation for the purpose of expressing the depth of meaning of the place names. Participatory three-dimensional (3D) modelling (P3DM), as promoted by Rambaldi et al. (2010), is another promising method, because it brings the geographic information technology closer to local people.

Furthermore, cybercartography is used in a number of indigenous cases outside Africa (see contributions in Taylor/Lauriault 2014; Anoby/Murasugi/Dominguez 2018; Geomatics and Cartographic Research Centre and University 2011a, 2011b). Cybercartography and cybercartographic atlases allow for a more comprehensive type of documentation and communication of spatially referenced information, including indigenous relational ontologies. Cybercartography uses multimedia formats, is interdisciplinary and highly interactive, and also explores "the possibilities of using all five senses in its

---

27   This is not to say that the 'conventional' maps produced cannot yield any success. In fact, they can be appropriate for securing land rights or for participating in conservation. However, the side-effects would need to be thoroughly explored, e.g. that this kind of cartographic representation risks perpetuating hegemonic notions of environment and human 'users'.

representations in order to make cybercartographic atlases as reflective as possible of sensory realities" (Taylor 2014: 2-3). It allows for story-telling and story-building beyond the limits of the traditional maps and is a promising instrument complementing two-dimensional paper maps (Aporta et al. 2014: 241).

Also, the concept or rather "discursive frame of reference" (Roberts 2016: 4) of *deep mapping* used e.g. in the Digital Humanities, might also be worthy of further exploration for the current purpose. Deep mapping refers to the development of more complex maps of "the personalities, emotions, values, and poetics, the visible and invisible aspects of a place". Deep maps integrate a "reflexivity that acknowledges how engaged human agents build spatially framed identities and aspirations out of imagination and memory and how the multiple perspectives constitute a spatial narrative that complements the verbal narrative traditionally employed by humanists" (Bodenhamer/Harris/Corrigan 2013: 174). Roberts identifies some common threads in this wide field, "a concern with narrative and spatial storytelling; a multi-scalar and multilayered spatial structure; a capacity for thick description; a multimedial navigability; a spatially intertextual hermeneutics; an orientation towards the experiential and embodied; a strongly performative dimension; an embrace of the spatiotemporally contingent; a compliance with ethnographic and auto-ethnographic methods and frameworks; an 'undisciplined' interdisciplinary modality; a time-based cartographics; an open and processual spatial sensibility; and, perhaps most telling, a reflexive – yet 'aspirational' – sense of the fundamental unmappability of the world the 'deep map' sets out to map." (Roberts 2016: 5)

Contributions

The two strands of enquiry and praxis outlined above, loosely lumped together as counter-mapping/cultural mapping/community mapping/indigenous mapping on the one hand and relational ontologies/animism/being-in-the-world on the other, provide the basis for the contributions to this volume. The authors (all of them presenters at the workshop *Mapping the unmappable? African hunter-gatherer relations with their environment and cartography*) were invited to explore the potential of cartography and spatial technologies in mediating African relational ontologies and animism(s), thereby both contributing to the field of indigenous cartography and relational anthropology. While some of them apply a general scope or present cartographic examples from outside Africa, most of the contributions build on case studies in Africa.

As a conceptual opening, **Øyvind Eide**'s chapter can be read as an invitation to reflect on the concept of maps. Although many if not all of us have clear ideas about what maps are, these ideas are rarely spelled out. The chapter makes evident that it is worthwhile reflecting on our own concepts of maps and to state clearly how we understand maps. He further discusses the purpose of maps and draws attention to the relationship between maps and control, maps and politics, and pinpoints the distinction between topological and topographical maps. He suggests considering maps – one kind of spatial media product – as models, which allows us to focus more on their function than on their essential attributes.

In a thematic opening, **Hugh Brody** takes us back to the very beginning of cultural mapping projects, to Canada in the 1970s. He was involved in one of the first major mapping projects, the Inuit Land Use and Occupancy Project. This and subsequent mapping projects played a major role in indigenous land claims. Brody explains both the difficulties in representing multi-dimensional ways of using and occupying the land on two-dimensional maps and the challenges of using indigenous conceptualizations in western courts at the time, a topic also taken up by Saskia Vermeylen in this volume (see below). From Canada, Brody takes us to South Africa around two decades later, where he was involved in another cultural mapping project related to a potential land claim. This project was different in that the community involved, the ǂKhomani, [28] had experienced land dispossession for centuries and had therefore disappeared from official South African maps, an experience which they share with many Khoekhoegowab-speaking groups all over Southern Africa and which Sullivan, who worked with another group of Khoekhoe-gowab-speaking people in Namibia, addresses in her chapter as well (see below). The large-scale land dispossession left ǂKhomani living dispersed over large parts of the region. Unlike the maps produced in the Inuit Land Use and Occupancy Project, the ǂKhomani maps had to be built around memories of living far away from their ancestral homelands and around the experience of marginalization and loss of home, language and, partly, identity. However, despite their differences, both mapping projects, the Inuit and the ǂKhomani

---

28   In Khoekhoegowab (including the languages of ǂKhomani, Hai||om and Damara), some consonants that sound like clicks are written with the symbols |, ||, ! and ǂ (for information on pronunciation, see Footnote 3 in Sullivan's contribution).

case, arose from threats to land, subsistence practices, heritage, cosmologies and identity. Despite all the challenges involved in cultural mapping projects and associated land claims, Brody strongly calls for a continuation of mapping efforts within indigenous peoples' struggles for land and other rights and recognition.

Ute Dieckmann was involved in a similar project to the ǂKhomani project (in fact, Hugh Brody was involved as well), which was carried out with the Hai∣∣om in Namibia at the turn of the millennium. The Hai∣∣om have been evicted from their ancestral land (including the famous Etosha National Park). Unlike the ǂKhomani maps, whose main purpose was documentation for the purposes of the land claim (this seemed impossible in Namibia at the time), the Hai∣∣om maps were developed for the documentation of cultural heritage of the Hai∣∣om within the National Park, and for use in tourism, as the existence and history of the former inhabitants had been erased for the sake of Etosha as an African "untamed wilderness". Dieckmann critically assesses the Hai∣∣om maps in retrospect with regard to both academic discussions on relational ontologies and loosely connected fields of enquiry, and to her own research on Hai∣∣om-being-in-relations and being-in-Etosha. The concerns she raises for this particular case study also pertain – in her view – to many other (African) cultural mapping projects. She urges researchers working with indigenous communities in mapping projects to continuously reflect on their own ontological bias and stresses the risk of (unintentionally) reinforcing the primacy of western ontology. She suggests a new approach to mapping Hai∣∣om being-in-Etosha which might come closer to their own epistemiology and ontology.

Sian Sullivan and **Welhemina Suro Ganuses** have conducted a mapping project with neighboring groups (Damara / ǂNūkhoen and ∣∣Ubun) to the Hai∣∣om in north-west Namibia, who have also suffered from a long history of land dispossession and marginalization. The project aimed at (re)inscribing the (former) presence and connection of these people to the land, which had disappeared from official maps. In their chapter, they describe the history of land dispossession and focus on three 'un-mappable' dimensions of cultural significance, whose significance was brought to light during the project, namely genealogies, ancestral agencies, and song-dances, all highlighting the deep connection of the people to the land. Sullivan and Ganuses therefore argue against the observed *de*coupling of indigenous/local cultures from nature which has been undertaken in the colonial and (partly) post-colonial creation of 'wild' African landscapes in the name of nature conservation, tourism and trophy hunting. They call instead for a stronger integration of 'cultural heritage' into conservation activities in the area.

Leaving Southern Africa, we continue our cartographic explorations in Eastern Africa. **Mara Jill Goldman** conducted a mapping project with Maasai in Tanzania. Like the research of Dieckmann and Sullivan/Ganuses, Goldman's project was related to the nature conservation activities in the area. Her cartographic attempts with Maasai had grown from frustration with existing 'participatory' land-use mapping project in the region, which generally silenced Maasai multiple ways of being-in and knowing the landscape and in which 'participation' was very limited, while colonial practices of land exploitation and knowledge extractions were reinforced. She calls for a decolonization of mapping and – drawing on Mol and Law (2002) – suggests *mapping multiple*, a concept she elaborates in her chapter using Maasai place name practices and their dealings with boundaries, which were introduced by various players, including colonial administrators, nature conservationists and the state. With mapping multiple, she hopes to reconcile various epistemologies and ontologies without hierarchizing one over the other (and thus decreasing the tension between mapping and counter-mapping), with an acknowledgement that all these ontologies and epistemologies are more than one and less than many.

With **Thea Skaanes,** we stay in the same geographical region but she invites us to a very different exploration. She worked with Hadza in northern Tanzania. She takes us to three specific material objects – what she calls power objects – belonging to individual Hadza women. She argues that these objects cannot be assessed adequately within a discourse of property and socio-economic value. Instead, she reveals how these objects are materializations of social relations, how they are entwined around identity and names, kinship, time and ritual. The objects are linked to the spirit of women and their kin relations in the past and in the future. Skaanes argues that since there are conceptual intersections between objects and land, it is promising to look at land and places as materializations of social relations too. She illustrates this with the example of various mountains/gods within the Hadza homeland. Drawing on Appadurai (1996), she suggests comprehending land as different 'scapes', e.g. cosmoscapes, kinscapes or transactionscapes, all of which imply social relations. Like the objects she analyzes in her chapter, the maps produced should also be inherently multiple, flexible and shadowy. She imagines a hodological perspective – connecting kinship, places, and time – as a promising way forward. This kind of mapping, in her view, would allow us a look at the land from within, from the point of view of its inhabitants.

Saskia Vermeylen not only takes us to another region (Australia) but also invites us to deeper reflections on the relationship between law and cartography and on the (conceptual) connection between maps and art. She sketches the joint history of law and mapping and reflects on the problematic consequences of this joint history when indigenous peoples are asked to provide evidence of their ancestral connection to land in court cases. She argues that western cartographic practices reinforce a legal culture that allowed for the dispossession of indigenous peoples from their land by silencing alternative ways of being-in-the-landscape. She argues that mapping practices, in order to be helpful in native title claims, need to show the tension between the different legal cultures that come together. Two case studies of Aboriginal art, used in native title claims, illustrate her arguments and provide vivid examples of alternative ways of mapping the land, of *mapping the unmappable*.

Frederik von Reumont uses a phenomenological approach to start his cartographic enquiry. He asks how maps can communicate the experience and therefore meaning of places and spatiality. He points to the power of narration and visual art for the communication of meaning and suggests a multimodal approach to the communication of meaning. He introduces us to the world of comics – as a combination of visual art and narrative – and reveals the multiple potentials of fusing maps with comics. With comics, humans can (re)enter the map through various ways: their perspectives on, experiences of, relations to and interactions with the land (and other human and non-human agents) can be visualized and narrated. Furthermore, and equally important, comics within maps offer the possibility of taking a meta-look at the map. The map-making process and the map-viewing process can be communicated, and the map can become populated not only with inhabitants or beings-in-relation-to-the-land but by the authors and readers of the map as well. Merging comics and maps can illustrate that the meaning of land and places only evolves from the interaction and relationship between different agents (including the land). Therefore, the use of comics within maps can help to de-objectify the (conventional) map.

Finally, **Margaret Wickens Pearce** lets us participate in her personal journey of cartographic endeavors to map the unmappable. She rejects the idea that the map is an explanatory scientific document, the reader only being a passive consumer, but looks at cartography as a mode of creative expression, similar to creative languages of music and architecture and sharing qualities with speech and writing, a view which is also expressed by Vermeylen and von Reumont (this volume). Her work is cartographic art; she takes the common cartographic language and conventions apart and experiments with new forms of cartographic expressions. With her collaborative mapping projects, she provides inspiring practices and techniques of – *inter alia* – mapping the emotional depth of the landscape; of introducing dialogism and heteroglossia on maps; of the expression of Indigenous[29] ontologies (e.g. Indigenous concepts of time, space and perspective); of following Indigenous methodologies; of mapping the (epistemological) meaning of place names; of mapping stories as portals to Indigenous ontologies; of mapping relational ontologies; and last but not least of the deliberate representation of silences. Her chapter also reveals that cartography and the use of maps is an embodied experience: e.g. by retracing journeys on paper and travelling in the landscape, through choices about the format and layout of the map, through the need to look at the other side of the map in order for meaning to be disclosed, etc. Her chapter also reminds us that there are no universal techniques that can be used in order to map Indigenous relations to the land and its agents, and that mapping with Indigenous People is a long process of deep involvement, of careful and respectful listening while engaging in the map making process. With her approach to cartography, there is no reason left to believe that the unmappable cannot be mapped.

An introductory epilogue

This introduction deliberately did not offer any definition of "map". When I started the project leading to this book, I had a rather conventional concept of maps, maps fortified with "the iron grid of Descartes" (Rocheleau 2005: 328), depicting the land and its objects in a certain order. During the course of the project and thanks to the inspiring contributions, my reading of a "map" changed significantly: while being occupied with contemplating maps *on* relational ontologies, I started to see maps *through* the gaze of a relational ontology. I began to think about maps as expressions of specific *relationships* – first

---

29   In this volume, it is deliberately left to the individual authors to decide whether to capitalize or not to capitalize "indigenous" and related words. For my own part, I use a capitalized form only when clearly referring to a political category of people identifying with a global version of Indigenous Peoples.

and foremost, the relationship between the mapmakers and the environment, the space, the land (and the spatial agents therein), but also as expression of the relationship between the different collaborating/participating parties in the mapping project; between the map maker and the materials used, the paper, the so-called data, the colors or computers, etc. In this perspective, western (conventional) maps are manifestations of a rather *detached* relationship with the land: the viewer looks *upon* the land, from above, with *objects* on the map, signified by symbols or icons; authors (the cartographers) are mostly invisible (as in many scientific texts). The (conventional) map constitutes a de-personalized representation of an 'objective' reality, and is thereby a manifestation of a Cartesian worldview with a positivist/essentialist ontology. At the other end of the spectrum, the Aboriginal art that Vermeylen discusses in her chapter provides a very different example of a visualized expression of relations to the land, though this art would hardly be considered as maps at the first glance. Social organization (including ancestors and other agents), time and space are woven there into an inextricable meshwork, and the relationship to the land is performed on the canvas and bark. [30]

Reading maps as expressions of *relationships* renders a number of troubling issues obsolete.[31] It dissolves the disconcerting dichotomy of science versus indigenous knowledge or science versus art. It brings the author back into the picture. It could also open the legal floor for other forms of evidence than (western) maps to be accepted as evidence for depicting the relationships of indigenous peoples with the land in native title claims. It could also assist with the de-colonization of the map by simply re-conceptualizing it and opening up space for alternative visualizations;[32] it could indigenize mapping by re-framing it through the lens of indigenous values of relations/relationality. This re-conceptualization would call for the audience of maps to open up to new ways of mapping which move away from the Cartesian grid; in

---

30   I find the concept of "meshwork" introduced by Ingold, in which he integrates the "flesh" of phenomenology and the "web of life" of ecology (Ingold 2012: 437), very productive for all kinds of being and thinking in the world, e.g. Ingold 2012, 2011, 2007. I take it up again in my chapter in this volume.

31   Many of these troubling issues have been dealt with within the field of critical cartography, but I have not come across any ways of expressing them through the lens of a relational ontology.

32   In this way, maps might be models, as Eide (this volume) suggests. For understanding models, in his view, one needs to take the model makers and the model target (what is modelled) into account.

other words (as mentioned earlier) it would ask for a new cartographic literacy. This notwithstanding, reading maps as expressions of relationships still leaves space for multiple mapping and the combination of different ontologies in endeavors of visual representations, as promoted in many of the chapters in this volume.

In this way, the subtitle of this volume, *Cartographic Explorations with Indigenous Peoples in Africa*, can be read in two ways: it is an invitation to look at African indigenous being-in-the-world from a cartographic point of view. Meanwhile, it is also an invitation to look at cartography from the point of view of (African) indigenous people (and equipped with relational ontologies).[33]

As the Marauder's Map showed Harry Potter a set of passages he had never entered, I hope that this volume will show us a number of paths and perspectives to be further explored.

References

Abbot, Jo/Chambers, Robert/Dunn, Christine/Harris, Trevor/Merode, Emmanuel de (1998): "Participatory GIS: opportunity or oxymoron?" In: PLA Notes 33, pp. 7-34.

Adaptation Consortium (2015): Resource Atlas of Isiolo County, Kenya Community-based mapping of pastoralist resources and their attributes (http s://pubs.iied.org/pdfs/G03984.pdf, last accessed August 11, 2020).

Alcorn, Janis B. (2000): "Keys to unleash mapping's good magic." In: PLA Notes 39, pp. 10-13.

Alloa, Emmanuel (2016): "Iconic Turn: A Plea for Three Turns of the Screw." In: Culture, Theory and Critique 57/2, pp. 1-24. (DOI: 10.1080/14735784.2015.1068127).

Anoby, Erik/Murasugi, Kumiki/Dominguez, Martin (2018): "Mapping language and land with the Nunaliit Atlas Framework: Past, present and future." In: Sebastian Drude/Nicholas Ostler/Marielle Moser (eds.), Endangered languages and the land: Mapping landscapes of multilingualism, Proceedings of FEL XXII/2018 (Reykjavík, Iceland), London: FEL & EL Publishing, pp. 56-63.

---

33   The idea of seeing from another's point of view is also central in the chapter of Skaanes (this volume).

Appadurai, Arjun (1996): Modernity at large: cultural dimensions of globalization, Minneapolis: University of Minnesota Press.

Aporta, Claudio/Higgs, Eric (2005): "Satellite Culture Global Positioning Systems, Inuit Wayfinding, and the Need for a New Account of Technology." In: Current Anthropology 46/5, pp. 729-753 (DOI: 10.1086/432651).

Aporta, Claudio/Kritsch, Ingrid/Andre, Alestine/Benson, Kristi/Snowshoe, Sharon/Firth, William/Carry, Del (2014): "The Gwich'in Atlas." In: D. R. Fraser Taylor/Tracey P. Lauriault (eds.), Developments in the theory and practice of cybercartography. Applications and indigenous mapping, vol. 5, 2nd edition, Amsterdam: Elsevier, pp. 229-244.

Århem, Kaj/Sprenger, Guido, eds. (2016): Animism in Southeast Asia. London, New York: Routledge.

Astor-Aguilera, Miguel A./Harvey, Graham (2019): "Introduction: We have never been individuals." In: Miguel A. Astor-Aguilera/Graham Harvey (eds.), Rethinking relations and animism. Personhood and materiality, Abingdon Oxon, New York: Routledge, pp. 1-12.

Barad, Karen (2003): "Posthumanist Performativity: Toward an Understanding of How Matter Comes to Matter." In: Journal of Women in Culture and Society 28/3, pp. 801-831.

Barume, Albert K. (2010): Land Rights of Indigenous Peoples in Africa, Copenhagen: IWGIA.

Bird-David, Nurit (1999): "'Animism' Revisited. Personhood, Environment, and Relational Epistemology." In: Current Anthropology 40, Suppl., pp. S67-S79.

Bird-David, Nurit (2017): Us, relatives. Scaling and plural life in a forager world, Oakland, California: University of California Press.

Bird-David, Nurit (2018): "Size matters! The scalability of modern hunter-gatherer animism." In: Quaternary International 464, pp. 305-314 (DOI: 10.1016/j.quaint.2017.06.035).

Boden, Gertrud (2007): "Mapping culture, representing boundaries and politicising difference – reflections on two San cases in Namibia." In: Olaf Bubenzer/Andreas Bolten/Frank Darius (eds.), Atlas of Environmental Change and Human Adaptation in Arid Africa, Cologne: Heinrich-Barth-Institut, pp. 112-115.

Bodenhamer, David J./Harris, Trevor M./Corrigan, John (2013): "Deep Mapping and the Spatial Humanities." In: IJHAC 7/1-2, pp. 170-175 (DOI: 10.3366/ijhac.2013.0087).

Brightman, Marc/Grotti, Vanessa E./Ulturgasheva, Olga (2012): Animism in rainforest and tundra. Personhood, animals, plants and things in contemporary Amazonia and Siberia, New York: Berghahn Books.

Bryan, Joe (2011): "Walking the line: Participatory mapping, indigenous rights, and neoliberalism." In: Geoforum 42/1, pp. 40-50 (DOI: 10.1016/j.geoforum.2010.09.001).

Castree, Noel (2003): "Environmental issues: relational ontologies and hybrid politics." In: Progress in Human Geography 27/2, pp. 203-211 (DOI: 10.1191/0309132503ph422pr).

Chapin, Mac/Lamb, Zachary/Threlkeld, Bill (2005): "Mapping indigenous lands." In: Annual Review of Anthropology 34/1, pp. 619-638 (DOI: 10.1146/annurev.anthro.34.081804.120429).

Cook, Ian/Taylor, Ken (2013): A Contemporary Guide to Cultural Mapping: An ASEAN-Australia Perspective, Jakarta: ASEAN Secretariat.

Costa, Luiz/Fausto, Carlos (2010): "The Return of the Animists: Recent Studies of Amazonian Ontologies." In: Religion and Society 1/1, pp. 89-109 (DOI: 10.3167/arrs.2010.010107).

Course, Magnus (2010): "Of words and fog." In: Anthropological Theory 10/3, pp. 247-263 (DOI: 10.1177/1463499610372177).

Crampton, Jeremy W./Krygier, John (2005): "An Introduction to Critical Cartography." In: ACME: An International Journal for Critical Geographies 4/1, pp. 11-33 (https://www.acme-journal.org/index.php/acme/article/view/723/585, last accessed August 11, 2020).

Crawhall, Nigel (2009): The Role of participatory cultural mapping in promoting intercultural dialogue: We are not hyenas; a reflection paper, UNESCO (http://www.iapad.org/wp-content/uploads/2015/07/nigel.crawhall.190753e.pdf, last accessed August 11, 2020).

CTA (2010): Training kit on participatory spatial information management and communication. (http://pgis-tk-en.cta.int, last accessed on September 29, 2019).

Defo, Louis/Njounan Tegomo, Olivier (2008): "Rapport d'execution du projet: 'Indigenous people's participation in mapping of traditional forest resources for sustainable livelihoods and great ape conservation'". WWF; UNEP (http://www.iapad.org/wp-content/uploads/2015/07/WWF-CMR-report-IPs.pdf, last accessed August 11, 2020).

Del Casino Jr., Vincent J./Hanna, Stephen P. (2005): "Beyond The 'Binaries': A Methodological Intervention for Interrogating Maps as Representational Practices." In: ACME: An International Journal for Critical Geographies

4/1, pp. 34-56 (https://www.acme-journal.org/index.php/acme/article/vie w/727/589, last accessed August 11, 2020).

Descola, Philippe (2013): Beyond nature and culture, Chicago, London: The University of Chicago Press.

Descola, Philippe/Palsson, Gisli, eds. (1996): Nature and Society: Anthropological perspectives, London & New York: Routledge.

Dodge, Martin, ed. (2011): The map reader. Theories of mapping practice and cartographic representation, Chichester: Wiley-Blackwell.

Dodge, Martin/Perkins, Chris (2015): "Reflecting on J.B. Harley's Influence and What He Missed in 'Deconstructing the Map'." In: Cartographica: The International Journal for Geographic Information and Geovisualization 50/1, pp. 37-40 (DOI: 10.3138/carto.50.1.07).

Duxbury, Nancy/Garrett-Petts, W. F./Mac Lennan, David (2015): "Cultural Mapping as Cultural Inquiry: Introduction to an Emerging Field of Practice." In: Nancy Duxbury/W. F. Garrett-Petts/David MacLennan (eds.), Cultural mapping as cultural inquiry, 1st Edition, New York: Routledge, pp. 1-42.

Eide, Øyvind (2015): Media Boundaries and Conceptual Modelling. Between Texts and Maps, Basingstoke: Palgrave Macmillan.

Eide, Øyvind/McCarty, Willard (2018): "Editorial, Interdisciplinary Science Reviews." In: Interdisciplinary Science Reviews 43/3-4, pp. 209-212 (DOI: 10.1080/03080188.2018.1534714).

Fox, Jefferson/Suryanata, Krisnawati/Hershock, Peter D./Pramono, Albertus Hadi (2005): "Introduction Mapping Power: Ironic Effects of Spacial Information Technology." In: Jefferson Fox/Krisnawati Suryanata/Peter D. Hershock (eds.), Mapping communities. Ethics, values, practice, Honolulu, HI: East-West Center (Policy studies, 65), pp. 1-10.

Future Pasts (2015-2019): Cultural landscapes mapping | future-pasts. (http s://www.futurepasts.net/cultural-landscapes-mapping, last accessed August 11, 2020).

Geomatics and Cartographic Research Centre; University, Carleton (2011a): Inuti Siku Atlas. (https://sikuatlas.ca/index.html?module=module.sikuat las.cape_dorset.people#, last accessed August 11, 2020).

Geomatics and Cartographic Research Centre; University, Carleton (2011b): Kitikmeot Place Name Atlas. (https://atlas.kitikmeotheritage.ca/index.ht ml, last accessed August 11.2020).

Glasze, Georg (2009): "Kritische Kartographie." In: Geographische Zeitschrift 97/4, pp. 181-191 (https://www.researchgate.net/publication/259888705_K ritische_Kartographie, last accessed August 11, 2020).

Graeber, David (2015): "Radical alterity is just another way of saying 're-ality'". In: HAU: Journal of Ethnographic Theory 5/2, pp. 1-41 (DOI: 10.14318/hau5.2.003).

Guenther, Mathias (2015): "'Therefore their parts resemble humans, for they feel that they are people'." In: Hunter Gatherer Research 1/3, pp. 277-315 (DOI: 10.3828/hgr.2015.16).

Guenther, Mathias (2019a): Human-Animal Relationships in San and Hunter-Gatherer Cosmology, Volume I. Therianthropes and Transformation, Cham: Palgrave Macmillan.

Guenther, Mathias (2019b): Human-Animal Relationships in San and Hunter-Gatherer Cosmology, Volume II. Imagining and Experiencing Ontological Mutability, Cham: Palgrave Macmillan.

Halder, Severin/Heyer, Karl/Michel, Boris/Greth, Silke/Baumgarten, Nico/Boos, Philipp et al. (Kollektiv Orangotango), eds. (2018): This Is Not an Atlas. A global collection of counter-cartographies, Bielefeld: Transcript (DOI: 10.14361/9783839445198).

Halder, Severin/Michel, Boris (2018): "Editorial – This Is Not an Atlas." In: Severin Halder/Karl Heyer/Boris Michel/Silke Greth/Nico Baumgarten/Philipp Boos et al. (Kollektiv Orangotango) (eds.), This Is Not an Atlas. A global collection of counter-cartographies, Bielefeld: Transcript, pp. 12-21.

Hallowell, A. Irving (1960): "Ojibwa ontology, behavior and world view." In: S. Diamond (ed.), Culture in History: Essays in Honor of Paul Radin, New York: Columbia University Press, pp. 19-52.

Haraway, Donna J. (2015): "Anthropocene, Capitalocene, Plantationocene, Chthulucene: Making Kin." In: Environmental Humanities 6, pp. 159-165.

Harley, John B. (1989): "Deconstructing the Map." In: Cartographica: The International Journal for Geographic Information and Geovisualization 26/2, pp. 1-20.

Harris, Leila M. (2015): "Deconstructing the Map after 25 Years: Furthering Engagements with Social Theory." In: Cartographica: The International Journal for Geographic Information and Geovisualization 50/1, pp. 50-53 (DOI: 10.3138/carto.50.1.10).

Harris, Leila M./Hazen, Helen D. (2005): "Power of Maps: (Counter) Mapping for Conservation." In: ACME: An International Journal for Critical Geographies 4/1, pp. 99-130.

Harvey, Graham (2006): Animism: Respecting the Living World, New York: Columbia University Press.

Heywood, Paolo (2012): "Anthropology and What There Is: Reflections on 'Ontology'." In: The Cambridge Journal of Anthropology 30/1, pp. 143-151.

Heywood, Paolo (2017): "The Ontological Turn". (https://www.anthroencyclop edia.com/entry/ontological-turn, last accessed August 11, 2020).

Hirt, Irène (2012): "Mapping Dreams/Dreaming Maps: Bridging Indigenous and Western Geographical Knowledge." In: Cartographica: The International Journal for Geographic Information and Geovisualization 47/2, pp. 105-120 (DOI: 10.3138/carto.47.2.105).

Hodgson, Dorothy L./Schroeder, Richard A. (2002): "Dilemmas of Counter-Mapping Community Resources in Tanzania." In: Development & Change 33/1, pp. 79-100 (DOI: 10.1111/1467-7660.00241).

Holbraad, Martin/Pedersen, Morten Axel/Viveiros de Castro, Eduardo (2014): "The Politics of Ontology: Anthropological Positions – Cultural Anthropology." In: Cultural Anthropology Online January 13 (https://culanth.org/fi eldsights/462-the-politics-of-ontology-anthropological-positions, last accessed August 10, 2020).

Ingold, Tim (2007): Lines: A Brief History, London: Routledge.

Ingold, Tim (2011): Being Alive. Essays on Movement, Knowledge and Description, Oxon, New York: Routledge.

Ingold, Tim (2011 [2000]): The perception of the environment. Essays on livelihood, dwelling and skill, London, New York: Routledge Taylor & Francis Group.

Ingold, Tim (2012): "Toward an Ecology of Materials." In: Annual Review of Anthropology 41, pp. 427-442.

Ingold, Tim (2016): "A Naturalist Abroad in the Museum of Ontology: Philippe Descola's Beyond Nature and Culture." In: Anthropological Forum 26/3, pp. 301-320 (DOI: 10.1080/00664677.2015.1136591).

Ingold, Tim (2018a): Anthropology: why it matters, Cambridge: Polity Press.

Ingold, Tim (2018b): "From science to art and back again: the pendulum of an anthropologist." In: Interdisciplinary Science Reviews 43/3-4, pp. 213-227 (DOI: 10.1080/03080188.2018.1524234).

Kitchin, Rob/Gleeson, Justin/Dodge, Martin (2013): "Unfolding mapping practices: a new epistemology for cartography." In: Transactions of the Institute of British Geographers 38/3, pp. 480-496 (DOI: 10.1111/j.1475-5661.2012.00540.x).

Kohn, Eduardo (2013): How Forests Think: toward an Anthropology beyond the Human, Berkeley: University of California Press.

Kohn, Eduardo (2015): "Anthropology of Ontologies." In: Annual Review of Anthropology 44 /1, pp. 311-327 (DOI: 10.1146/annurev-anthro-102214-014127).

Laidlaw, James; Heywood, Paolo (2013): "One more turn and you're there." In: Anthropology of This Century 7, n.p. (http://aotcpress.com/articles/turn/ , last accessed August 12, 2020).

Lewis, Jerome (2012): "Technological leap-frogging in the Congo Basin, Pygmies and Global Positioning Systems in Central Africa: What has happened and where is it going?" In: African Study Monographs Suppl. 43, pp. 15-44.

Low, Chris (2007): "Khoisan wind: hunting and healing." In: Journal of the Royal Anthropological Institute 13 (s1), S71-S90 (DOI: 10.1111/j.1467-9655.2007.00402.x).

Low, Chris (2014): "Khoe-San ethnography, 'new animism' and the interpretation of Southern African Rock Art." In: The South African Archaeological Bulletin 69/200, pp. 164-172.

McLain, Rebecca/Poe, Melissa/Biedenweg, Kelly/Cerveny, Lee/Besser, Diane/Blahna, Dale (2013): "Making Sense of Human Ecology Mapping: An Overview of Approaches to Integrating Socio-Spatial Data into Environmental Planning." In: Human Ecology 41/5, pp. 651-665.

Law, John/Mol, Annemarie, eds. (2002): Complexities: Social studies of knowledge practices, Durham, NC: Duke University Press.

Monmonier, Mark (2018): How to Lie with Maps, 3rd Edition, Chicago: University of Chicago Press.

Muchemi, Julius/Kiteme, Boniface (2015): "Eastern and Southern Africa Partnership Programme: Highlights from 15 years of joint action for sustainable development." In: Albrecht Ehrensperger/Cordula, Ott/Urs Wiesmann (eds.), Eastern and Southern Africa Partnership Programme: Highlights from 15 Years of Joint Action for Sustainable Development, Bern, Switzerland: Centre for Development and Environment (CDE), pp. 51-54.

Nelson, John (2008): An Overview of Community Mapping with FPP in Cameroon. Forest Peoples Programme, Moreton-in-Marsh, UK: FPP (https://www.forestpeoples.org/sites/default/files/publication/2010/ 07/camerooncommunitymappingjuly07eng.pdf, last accessed August 12, 2020).

Nietschmann, Bernard (1994): "Defending the Miskito Reefs with Maps and GPS: Mapping with Sail, Scuba, and Satellite." In: Quarterly Survival 18/4, pp. 34-37 (https://www.culturalsurvival.org/publications/cultural-surviva l-quarterly/defending-miskito-reefs-maps-and-gps-mapping-sail-scuba , last accessed August 12.2020).

Niezen, Ronald (2003): The Origins of Indigenism, Berkeley, Los Angeles, London: University of California Press.

Njounan Tegomo, Oliver/Defo, Louis/Usongo, Leonard (2012): "Mapping of resource use area by the Baka pygmies inside and around Boumba-Bk National Park in southeast Cameroon with special reference to Baka's customary rights." In: African Study Monographs Suppl. 43, pp. 45-59.

Pearce, Margaret W./Louis, Renee (2008): "Mapping Indigenous Depth of Place." In: American Indian Culture and Research Journal 32/3, pp. 107-126 (DOI: 10.17953/aicr.32.3.n7g22w816486567j).

Pearce, Margaret W. (2014): "The Last Piece Is You." In: The Cartographic Journal 51/2, pp. 107-122 (DOI: 10.1179/1743277414Y.00000000789).

Pedersen, Morten Axel (2001): "Totemism, Animism and North Asian Indigenous Ontologies." In: Journal of the Royal Anthropological Institute 7/3, pp. 411-427.

Pedersen, Morten Axel (2012): "Common nonsense: a review of certain recent reviews of the 'ontological turn'." In: Anthropology of This Century 5, n.p. (http://aotcpress.com/articles/common_nonsense/, last accessed August 10, 2020).

Peluso, Nancy L. (1995): "Whose woods are these? Counter-mapping forest territories in Kalimantan, Indonesia." In: Antipode 274, pp. 383-406.

Perkins, Chris (2008): "Cultures of Map Use." In: The Cartographic Journal 45/2, pp. 150-158 (DOI: 10.1179/174327708X305076).

Peterson, Nicholas (2017): "Is There a Role for Anthropology in Cultural Reproduction? Maps, Mining, and the 'Cultural Future' in Central Australia." In: Sylvie Poirier/Françoise Dussart (eds.), Entangled territorialities. Negotiating indigenous lands in Australia and Canada, Toronto: University of Toronto Press, pp. 235-251.

Plumwood, Val (2002): Environmental Culture: The Ecological Crisis of Reason, London & New York: Routledge.

Poirier, Sylvie; Dussart, Françoise (2017): "Knowing and Managing the Land: The Conundrum of Coexistence and Entanglement." In: Sylvie Poirier/Françoise Dussart (eds.): Entangled territorialities. Negotiating indigenous lands in Australia and Canada, Toronto: University of Toronto Press, pp. 3-24.

Poole, Peter (2003): Cultural mapping and indigenous peoples. A report for UNESCO. UNESCO (https://www.creativecity.ca/database/files/library/unesco_cultural_mapping.pdf, last accessed 10 August 2020).

Povinelli, Elizabeth A. (1995): "Do Rocks Listen? The Cultural Politics of Apprehending Australian Aboriginal Labor." In: American Anthropologist 97/3, pp. 505-518.

Povinelli, Elizabeth. A. (2012): "The Will to be Otherwise / The Effort of Endurance." In: South Atlantic Quarterly 111/3, pp. 453-457.

Rainforest Foundation UK (2015a): The Mapping for Rights Methodology. A New Approach to Participatory Mapping in the Congo Basin, London: Rainforest Foundation UK (https://www.mappingforrights.org/wp-content/uploads/2020/04/RFUK-mapping-for-rights-methodology.pdf, last accessed 11 August 2020).

Rainforest Foundation UK (2015b): Tropical Forest Community Mapping Initiative Feasibility Study, London: Rainforest Foundation UK.

Rambaldi, Giacomo (2010): Participatory Three-Dimensional Modelling: Guiding Principles and Applications, 2010 Edition, Wageningen, The Netherlands: CTA.

Rambaldi, Giacomo/Muchemi, Julius/Crawhall, Nigel/Monaci, Laura (2007): "Through the Eyes of Hunter-Gatherers: participatory 3D modelling among Ogiek indigenous peoples in Kenya." In: Information Development 23/2-3, pp. 113-128 (DOI: 10.1177/0266666907078592).

Robbins, Paul (2003): "Beyond Ground Truth: GIS and the Environmental Knowledge of Herders, Professional Foresters, and Other Traditional Communities." In: Human Ecology 31/2, pp. 233-253.

Roberts, Les (2016): "Deep Mapping and Spatial Anthropology." In: Humanities 5/1, pp.1-7 (DOI: 10.3390/h5010005).

Rocheleau, Dianne (2005): "Maps as power tools: Locating communities in space or situating people and ecologies in place?" In: J. Peter Brosius/Anna L. Tsing/Charles Zerner (eds.), Communities and conservation. Histories and politics of community-based natural resource management, Walnut Creek, CA, Oxford: AltaMira Press, pp. 327-362.

Rocheleau, Dianne; Edmunds, David (1997): "Women, men and trees: Gender, power and property in forest and agrarian landscapes." In: World Development 25/8, pp. 1351-1371 (DOI: 10.1016/S0305-750X(97)00036-3).

Rose, Deborah Bird (2000): Dingo makes us human. Life and land in an Australian Aboriginal culture, Cambridge: Cambridge Univ. Press.

Rose, Deborah Bird (2015): "The Ecological Humanities." In: Katherine Gibson/Deborah B. Rose/Ruth Fincher (eds.), Manifesto for Living in the Anthropocene, Brooklyn, New York: Punctum Books, pp. 1-5.

Rose, Deborah Bird/van Dooren, Thom/Chrulew, Matthew/Cooke, Stuart/Kearnes, Matthew/O'Gorman, Emily (2012): "Thinking Through the Environment, Unsettling the Humanities." In: Environmental Humanities 1/1, pp. 1-5 (DOI: https://doi.org/10.1215/22011919-3609940).

Rose-Redwood, Reuben (2015): "Introduction: The Limits to Deconstructing the Map." In: Cartographica: The International Journal for Geographic Information and Geovisualization 50/1, pp. 1-8 (DOI: https://doi.org/10.3138/carto.50.1.01).

Roth, Robin (2009): "The Challenges of Mapping Complex Indigenous Spatiality: From Abstract Space to Dwelling Space." In: Cultural Geographies 16/2, pp. 207-27 (Doi: https://doi.org/10.1177/1474474008101517).

Rowling, J.K. (2011 [1999]): Harry Potter and the Prisoner of Azkaban, London: Bloomsbury.

Rundstrom, Robert (2009): "Counter-Mapping." In: Rob Kitchin/N. J. Thrift (eds.), International encyclopedia of human geography, place of publication not identified: Elsevier Science, pp. 314-318.

Scott, Colin (2006): "Spirit and practical knowledge in the person of the bear among Wemindji Cree hunters." In: Ethnos 71/1, pp. 51-66 (DOI: 10.1080/00141840600603178).

Skaanes, Thea (2015): "Notes on Hadza cosmology." In: Hunter Gatherer Research 1/2, pp. 247-267 (DOI: 10.3828/hgr.2015.13).

Skaanes, Thea (2017): Cosmology matters. Power objects, rituals, and meat-sharing among the Hadza of Tanzania, Aarhus: Aarhus University.

Sletto, Bjørn (2009): "'Indigenous people don't have boundaries': reborderings, fire management, and productions of authenticities in indigenous landscapes." In: Cultural Geographies 16/2, pp. 253-277 (DOI: 10.1177/1474474008101519).

Sullivan, Sian (2017): "What's ontology got to do with it? On nature and knowledge in a political ecology of the 'green economy'." In: JPE 24/1, p. 217 (DOI: 10.2458/v24i1.20802).

Sullivan, Sian/Hannis, Mike (2016): Relationality, reciprocity and flourishing in an African landscape: Perspectives on agency amongst ||Khao-a Dama, !Narenin and ||Ubun elders in west Namibia, Future Pasts Working Papers No. 2. Bath, UK: Future Pasts (DOI: 10.13140/RG.2.2.14662.47682).

Taylor, D. R. Fraser/Lauriault, Tracey P., eds. (2014): Developments in the theory and practice of cybercartography. Applications and indigenous mapping, Amsterdam: Elsevier.

Taylor, D. R. Fraser (2014): "Some Recent Developments in the Theory and Practice of Cybercartography." In: D. R. Fraser Taylor/Tracey P. Lauriault (eds.), Developments in the theory and practice of cybercartography. Applications and indigenous mapping, Amsterdam: Elsevier, pp. 1-15.

Taylor, Julie/Murphy, Carol (2006): "Land and natural resource mapping by San communities and NGOs: experiences from Namibia." In: Participatory Learning and Action 54, pp. 79-84 (http://www.iapad.org/wp-content/uploads/2015/07/PLA54_ch10_taylor_pp79-84.pdf, last accessed August 12, 2020).

Taylor, Julie J. (2008): "Naming the land: San countermapping in Namibia's West Caprivi." In: Geoforum 39/5, pp. 1766-1775 (DOI: 10.1016/j.geoforum.2008.04.001).

Taylor, Michael (2002): "'Mapping the land' in Gudigwa: a history of Bugakhwe territoriality." In: Pula: Botswana Journal of African Studies 16/2, pp. 98-109.

Thom, Brian (2009): "The paradox of boundaries in Coast Salish territories." In: Cultural Geographies 16/2, pp. 179-205 (DOI: 10.1177/1474474008101516).

Tobias, Terry N. (2000): Chief Kerry's Moose: a guidebook to land use and occupancy mapping, research design and data collection, Vancouver: Union of BC Indian Chiefs and Ecotrust Canada.

Vermeylen, Saskia/Davies, Gemma/van der Horst, Dan (2012): "Deconstructing the Conservancy Map: Hxaro, N!ore, and Rhizomes in the Kalahari." In: Cartographica: The International Journal for Geographic Information and Geovisualization 47/2, pp. 121-134 (DOI: 10.3138/carto.47.2.121).

Viveiros de Castro, Eduardo (1998): "Cosmological deixis and Amerindian perspectivism." In: Journal of the Royal Anthropological Institute 3, pp. 469-488.

Wainwright, Joel/Bryan, Joe (2009): "Cartography, territory, property: postcolonial reflections on indigenous counter-mapping in Nicaragua and Belize." In: Cultural Geographies 16/2, pp. 153-178 (DOI: 10.1177/1474474008101515).

Willerslev, Rane (2007): Soul Hunters: Hunting, Animism, and Personhood among the Siberian Yukaghirs, Berkeley, Los Angeles, London: University of California Press.

Willerslev, Rane (2013): "Taking Animism Seriously, but Perhaps Not Too Seriously?" In: Religion and Society 4/1 (DOI: 10.3167/arrs.2013.040103).

Wood, Denis (1992): The Power of Maps, New York: Guilford Press.

Wood, Denis/Fels, John/Krygier, John (2010): Rethinking the power of maps, New York: Guilford Press.

Xoms |Omis (2018): "Etosha Map - A different perspective of Etosha. Born in Etosha - keeping it alive" (https://www.xoms-omis.org/etosha-map, last accessed June 20, 2020).

Where is the map?

Øyvind Eide

Introduction

We find them everywhere. Visual representations that depict and denote spatial features and structures. Are they mapping the landscape, what happens there, or our conceptualizations thereof? That begs the question as to what the word "map" means. Is it the geometric image modelling the world, is it everything we use for geocommunication, or can it denote an even larger semantic area? Can this larger semantic area be mapped? What kind of a map would be the result of this mapping process? These are the questions discussed in this chapter. Several examples will show various senses of the word "map" and how they are used. The purposes served by maps will be analyzed in order to structure the area of tools and systems, physical as well as conceptual, used to depict and understand our environment.

Scratched on the walls of caves we find depictions of rivers and other landscape forms seen from a bird's eye view perspective, created by humans and possibly also by other hominidae. Between the stable land forms we see animals in a different perspective. Is the use of perspective clumsy and dysfunctional, or is it rather a complex use of perspective, to differentiate between the static land forms and the moving animals? Rock art, like all other art, is open to interpretation. Do we see a hunting scene? A super-natural scene? Is it depicting something that did happen, something that happens regularly, something that should happen, or is it about something quite different, such as a metaphysical understanding of the relationships between human, animal, and landscape? Is it all of the above?

We find humans and other animals depicted in rock art all over the world. In some periods (or whatever it is that creates stability and changes in forms of expression), humans have arms and legs, in other periods they are but lines

Figure 1: Rock art from Álttá/Alattio/Alta, Norway (Photo: Nina Tveter/NTNU)

on a boat form, sometimes both modes of depiction are used.[1] Some are men and women, others have no clear sex markers that can be understood by today's experts.[2] The environment is there, in the form of rivers and paths, huts and fireplaces. As a background? As a meaningful part of a communicative device? Often we do not know. The traces remain there on the rocks, in the form of recognizable pictures. There are parts of the world in which rock art is a living tradition,[3] accompanied by other cultural expressions such as stories. In other cases, the cultural context and the original stories might be lost in time.

Birch bark maps from North America (Woodward/Lewis 1998: 79-86); three dimensional maps, or geographical sculptures, from Greenland and the Pacific (ibid: 168-9; 481-4); drums with depictions of spiritual and physical objects and landscapes in the Nordic Arctic, used by Sami Noaides in shamanism (Manker 1950; Keski-Säntti et al. 2003); humans everywhere, across time and space, in cultures writing and non-writing alike, depict their environment. As documented by Harley et al. (1987–)[4], where many further examples can be found, many if not all human cultures create and use maps. Maps make

---

1   This development is clearly recognizable in Norwegian rock carvings.
2   This is claimed by some researchers to be the situation in rock paintings in Dâureb (Brandberg) in Namibia (see Lenssen-Erz 1998).
3   And indeed, is it possible to make a clear distinction between rock art and graffiti?
4   Volume 6 was published in 2015 but volume 5 is still forthcoming.

up a fundamental aspect of human culture, but should we count all these examples of depictions of environments as being maps?

There is something about these examples, true as they are as individual cases, that might be misleading. They make up a limited number of cases taken from large geographical areas over thousands of years. We might assume they are the tip of an iceberg of common practices of mapping happening anytime everywhere. But we cannot know. There is a risk of creating subconscious extensions of our own experience, of thinking anachronistically about the past.

The concept "map"

How is the word "map" defined by organizations of cartographic professionals? How is it used in the literature on the history of cartography? "Map" is often defined as a document depicting a landscape through a system of reference. Bagrow (1951: 13) simply stated: "The famous French cartographer J. L. Lagrange wrote in 1770: 'A geographical map is a plane figure representing the surface of the earth, or a part of it'; and this definition is perfectly adequate".[5] The International Cartographic Association (ICA) defines a map in the following way:

> A **map** is a symbolised representation of geographical reality, representing selected features or characteristics, resulting from the creative effort of its author's execution of choices, and is designed for use when spatial relationships are of primary relevance.[6]

Def of a map

While this definition does not state explicitly that maps are documents, the following definition of "cartography" on the same webpage goes far in assuming it: "**Cartography** is the discipline dealing with the art, science and technology of making and using maps."[7]

---

5   "Der berühmte Kartograph J. L. Lagrange (1770) sagte: 'Eine geographische Karte ist nichts anders als eine ebene Figur, die die Erdoberfläche oder einen Teil derselben darstellt', und diese Begriffsbestimmung ist vollkommend ausreichend."

6   This is the current definition, taken from the 2003–2011 strategic plan, see https://icaci. org/mission/ (last accessed August 4, 2020), original emphasis. The previous definition, from 1995, was identical apart from the word "image" instead of "representation" in the first clause, and two small grammatical alterations.

7   Ibid., original emphasis.

The multivolume historical cartography book project initiated in the 1980s, however, used what at the time were recent developments in geography to redefine maps in a less document-oriented direction. The definition in the first volume is: "Maps are graphic representations that facilitate a spatial understanding of things, concepts, conditions, processes, or events in the human world." (Harley/Woodward 1987: xvi)

Table 1: Key aspects of the three definitions of "map"

Definition	Representation method	Target of representation
Bagrow	plane figure	a landscape
ICA	symbolized	geographical reality
Harley et al.	graphic	things, concepts, conditions, processes, or events in the human world

Table 1 shows two important aspects of these three definitions and how they have many aspects in common, even if they are also different. The representational methods are quite similar but also include important nuances. At first sight Bagrow's definition seems to be a subset of ICA's, which again is a subset of Harley et al.'s. But there is actually no claim in the ICA definition that a map should be a figure or indeed graphic at all. A textual document or a song could be a map, according to this definition, as long as the expressions represent geographical reality. This is not the case for Harley et al., as they claim that the representational method should be graphic. Thus, it is clear that some rock art and some aspects of the other examples we saw above are maps according to all these definitions. Harley et al. would include most if not all of them, whereas Bagrow and ICA would not cover the representations of spiritual landscapes and the humans engaged in hunting (or whatever activity they are performing).

However, and beyond the definition printed in the first volume, Harley et al. actually go much further than any of the three definitions in their actual use of the concept of map and cartography. This is clearly pointed out in volume 2.3, where maps as parts of material culture are seen as less important than maps as cognitive systems and social constructions, made clear with concepts such as "performance cartography", which we will come back to below.

If we look at the use of the words "map" and "cartography" in scholarly and scientific publications, it becomes clear that maps as something also beyond graphical representations is the norm rather than an exception. We find it in literary studies, where for instance Bulson (2007) discusses literary cartography in a text about texts – it has little if anything to do with maps in the sense of documents with graphic representations but a lot to do with the spatial aspects of narrative.[8] The concept of cognitive maps extends the concept of the map from an external material document to something in the mind of humans and other animals, whereas the conceptual map is a map, external or internal, of objects and processes where geography or even spatiality is not necessarily privileged. Thus, the concepts in modern language are used for both document and non-documents, visual as well as textual representations, and for the representation of anything, whether it is a real landscape, a fictional landscape, or something else. Looking into the etymology of the words commonly used in European languages, focusing on forms of "map" and "chart"[9] we see that these are dated back to the 15th century only (Eide 2012: 29-30). There is a word used in medieval Latin usually connected to maps, *mappa mundi*, but this was also used to refer to textual documents (Schneider 2006: 26).

Is this merely playing with words? Is there no material basis for the concept of "map"? Must we choose between reductionist pragmatic prescriptive definitions, such as the one used in Eide (2015), or should we let the term loose entirely? I will defer the discussion about words here and instead focus on the essential aspects behind the words, on actual spatiality and actual mapping practices, as a basis for many of the discussions to follow in this book. Then I will come back to the word "map" towards the end to suggest how to cope with the problem of defining it.

Actual spatial thinking and land use practices based on physical landscapes can be grouped into four basic aspects:

---

8   As exemplified by the way the concept of the chronotope (Bakhtin 1981) has been and is understood in literary studies, the link between space and time, between landscape and event, is fundamental and intimate. Thus, the view of literary mapping as an only partially geographical endeavour, where the map as a graphical object is not really seen as an ideal or, in many cases, even a useful tool.

9   As this chapter is written in English and the discussion is about the English word "map", the focus here is on English and closely related languages. An extension to other languages, especially non-Indo-European, would be highly interesting but is beyond the scope of this chapter.

- **Landscape:** The physical landscape itself.
- **Landscape knowledge:** The animal (and human) internal representation or knowledge of the landscape.
- **Wayfinding tools:** The tools we use to find our way through the landscape.
- **Spatial media products:** Our communication about the landscape and the media products[10] we use in this communication.[11]

We have seen that at least the last three are commonly referred to with the word "map". Even the landscape itself, or at least the organization of space, can be seen as a map, as is commonly seen in architecture where the layout of a church, a Sami tent or a turf hut represents aspects of the spiritual world (Mathisen 1997: 124-125, 129); the layout of city parts can be seen as a map of historical periods such as modernism, or of ideological systems. In the following, I will focus our discussion about maps, and about the lack of maps, on these four aspects, denoted by the short forms used above. These short forms are not general terms, but rather short term references to the four aspects, which are intended to be easier to remember than numerical codes.

No maps

Wood/Fels/Krygier (2010) claim that there were no maps before 1500. Not meant to be taken literally, their argument is based on the fundamental change in the mapping situation in Europe at that time. When a map was made over an administrative area in the 14th century, for instance, when a monastery made a map of its areas, this mapping work would be done by one single monastery rather than developing into something that most or all of the monasteries in the area did. After approximately 1500, this changed. Over the next 200 years, all major and eventually also minor political powers in Europe initiated systematic mapping of the areas they control. This happened

---

10   "Media product" is here used as in intermediality studies, in order to denote mediated things used in communication, and can include everything from a book or a data file to a waving hand to order something or a humming sound intended to calm a child (Elleström 2010).

11   Spatiality is here meant to refer to the spatial reference system used by maps (MacEachren 2004), not to the general spatiality of two-dimensional objects – the latter is present for written and printed texts too. Thus, a printed textual landscape description is here seen as a non-spatial media product. See Eide (2015) for a more detailed discussion about the spatiality of text and map documents.

around the same time in Japan, but centuries earlier in China. These were spatial media products used to describe the landscape based on a certain landscape knowledge.

Smail (1999) describes extensive work on analyzing protocols from Notaricus Publicus in Marseille in late medieval to early modern times. In the many extant volumes he studied, which document a large number of legal land transactions, there is not one single map. All places were described in words only. The landscape knowledge is expressed through non-spatial media products.

In the seven protocols documenting the Danish crown's gathering of information in preparation for the border negotiations establishing major parts of the borders between today's Norway, Sweden and Finland in 1751,[12] no maps were included or even mentioned in the interviews with farmers or reindeer herders of Norwegian, Finnish and Sami background.[13] We also see an absence of maps in other documents with strong geographical aspects from that time. While the borders between parts of traditional farms became property borders in Norway as a consequence of the change from land leasing to free peasantry in the 17th century, with a resulting increase in land transactions (Holmsen 1966: 144-148), maps were not common in the documentation of these borders. There was an official call for maps in legal cases concerning ownership of land from 1719, but this was very rarely implemented in local courts, and only partially in higher courts (Kiil 1969: 84).[14] Again, we see that the expressions are mostly non-spatial. It is also interesting to see how all these examples involve finding places in relation to other places, even if they are not about navigation in the more direct sense of planning for actual travel from one place to another.

Many late 20th and early 21st century people are at first surprised by the limited use of maps we see in these examples when they are exposed to such source material. In order to understand why this is so, that is, to understand why the lack of map use looks so strange to many modern people even if it is common across many quite different historical and cultural periods, we will move back to the anachronistic thinking suggested above through an analogy with fiction:

---

12   The protocols are printed in Schnitler (1929; 1962; 1985).
13   At least one map was submitted by a priest, and Captain Peter Schnitler, who led the work, made some maps himself as parts of the protocol material.
14   See Brody and Vermeylen, this volume, on the use of maps in court cases.

> [T]he 'principle of minimal departure ... states that we reconstrue the world
> of a fiction and of a counterfactual as being the closest possible to the reality
> we know. This means that we will project upon the world of the statement
> everything we know about the real world, and that we will make only those
> adjustments which we cannot avoid (Ryan 1980: 406).

While this concept comes from the study of fictional works, it can also be helpful in understanding how historical evidence is interpreted. For people living
in a culture dominated by maps not only for navigation, but also for making sense of the spaces we live in and relate to, it is natural to assume that
similar map-based methods are used, and similar map-based sense-making
happens, in all cultures, even in different places and in different historical periods. Neither maps nor texts are incontestable true statements about reality
(Eide/Schubert 2021). Depictions and descriptions of landscapes have different levels of realism, both in terms of author/cartographer intention and of
the relationship between documents and what, in many cartographic traditions, including administrative maps in Europe, China, Japan, and other parts
of Asia, are seen as testable facts. Even in quite different traditions, such as
the one exemplified by the *Lienzo de Zacatepec*, which will be discussed later,
the existence of political units shown on the map were presumably testable
facts at the time of the creation of the map.

In an attempt to understand the history of cartography as a history of the
actual use of maps as spatial media products, the application of the principle
of minimal departure may be of some use. There are examples of the creation
and use of graphical representations of space from most, if not all, historical and many pre-historical periods, but there are also numerous examples
of extensive documentation of spatial information without the use of spatial
media products. Is what we see a wide-spread use of maps for a multitude
of purposes, of which only a few examples have survived until today, or is the
limited amount of extant documents due to the fact that only a very few were
made in the first place? Did people in many places and times simply not use
maps much, if at all? Are the examples of spatial media products that we find
in the documentation exceptions or are they rather examples of a widespread,
mostly lost, practice of mapping?

Or are these claims too unspecific to make any sense? At one level these
questions cannot be answered. As in all historical research we can know what
we have but we cannot know how much has been lost. We may assume that
many more spatial media products must have existed: ephemeral figures in

sand or snow, as well as more stable physical objects in wood, bark, parchment, stone, paper and other writeable surfaces which have disappeared over the centuries and millennia.[15] What remains clear is that most humans in most if not all cultures can quickly learn how to understand, use and create maps in the form of spatial media products when motivated to do so (Landau/Lakusta 2009), and that some have done so in a significant number of documented situations.

What remains unknown is how systematic, how widespread, this was in terms of actual activities, how much it was part of individual and societal normality. How often was the potential competence for map making put to practical use? The reality addressed by such questions depends on practicalities as well as on needs. How easy and practical was it to create, use, duplicate and transport objects carrying graphical representations? What was the cost of doing so, compared to the benefits? One usually does not need maps for navigation when living and moving in only a small area for the whole of one's life. However, even when maps are not needed for navigation they might still be useful, for instance for conceptualizing space.

The double enablers of need and ability apply to single individuals and small communities, as well as at a larger society level. The change in Europe around 1500 is related to the needs of the early modern state (Wood/Fels/Krygier 2010) but also to the increased possibilities for mass production of maps, first through woodcut printing, then through metal engravings. The development in Japan is concurrent with that in Europe, whereas in China it happened centuries earlier, which can again be explained by both the development of society-level spatial administrative management and by the availability of printing.

The purpose of maps as spatial media products

Imperial systems and national states give different impressions depending on their spatial coherence. Most modern states consist of one continuous land area, if broken by water only. The map shows *us* relative to *them*: here is the land of the Norwegians, there of the Swedes, there of the Finns, and there of the Russians. When one has no land, one has no place on the map. Or

---

15   See Vermeylen, this volume, for the use of contemporary bark paintings as a form of mapping in native title claims.

one can carve one's own place independently from the governmental maps, as the Sami artist Hans Ragnar Mathisen has done since the 1970s under the artist's name Keviselie.[16] Maps are used to express dominance and control, but also for counter-stories and to represent alternative visions of the world. Activist mapping is sometimes part of processes of striving for recognition by governments, with minority place names and landscape understanding becoming parts of official maps and stories. Land rights issues are intimately connected to mapping and map use (Tobias 2000), as will be discussed in detail later in this book.[17]

In the context of maps, knowing where one is is closely related to finding the way to somewhere else. Even if maps are made and used for many other purposes, wayfinding is there as a possibility.[18] The question "Where am I?" means "What is the location on this map representing the place in the land-scape at which I am standing?" This implies also the meaning of being "off the map", which means being in a place outside the area represented by the map, and being "lost." Being lost can be seen as the realization that one does not know which location on the map represents the place in the landscape where one is. Once one has gotten it right and one "knows where one is", one can find another place on the map where one wants to be and, given that the bearings are right, one can use the map to find the way there. The map is a generalized semiotic system with coherent reference functions to landscape types for the different symbols on the map; one can use the map to find the way through a previously unknown territory.

Thus, in addition to wayfinding as one of the four aspects of spatial think-ing, governmental control also has to be taken into consideration as a key el-ement in the creation and use of maps. The same can be said of various alter-native strategies, from stealing secret maps to counter-mapping. Control and navigation are indeed closely related, significant differences notwithstanding. In a Global Positioning System (GPS) based digital mapping system, the prob-lems of being lost or off the map do not usually occur. The dot on the map, based on satellite information, indicates the location ("I am here") and the map does not in principle have any border that can leave the map user "off the

---

16   Many of his maps can be found and bought at his webpage: http://www.keviselie-han sragnarmathisen.net/33514843 (last accessed February 14, 2020).

17   See e.g. Brody, Goldman, Vermeylen, this volume.

18   "Wayfinding" is here used without a clear distinction from "navigation." For a precise discussion of these and other concepts see Wood (1993) and Ingold (2000).

map". Exceptions do occur, often enough to make many people expect them and talk about them. Sometimes GPS signals are blocked by cliffs or houses, sometimes the addresses do not work, sometimes the map is just wrong. GPS based systems also rely on satellites, which are controlled by specific countries and strongly interconnected with military-industrial complexes. In addition to requiring the larger infrastructure to be working and available, the use of GPS also relies on the device one uses. It must have power and function correctly. However, this is the case for paper map navigation too – sometimes a map might dissolve due to rain or an unplanned fall into a river, sometimes the compass is broken.

A landscape is categorically different from landscape knowledge. The map is never the territory, and the relationship between claims on the map and the realities of the landscape people find themselves in can go in many directions.[19] Sometimes the map says something quite different from what one experiences on the ground.

> The DPR Korea is located in the middle of east of Asian Continent. It shares borders with China and Russia in the north with Rivers Amnok and Tuman in between. And it lies opposite Japan in the east with the East Sea of Korea in between. It lies in latitude 43°00'36"-33°06'43" and in longitude 124°10'47"-131°52'40". The Korean peninsula has an area of 223,370 sq.km. The northern half covers an area of 123,138 sq.km and the southern half 100,2321 sq.km.[20]

Political [handwritten margin note]

The implicit claim that there is no South Korea is supported by the map on the web page. The situation seen from the south is:

> In 1948, the two Koreas established their respective governments. Defined as two different countries under international law, they joined the United Nations simultaneously in September 1991. The Constitution of Republic of Korea, however, regards North Korea as part of the Republic of Korea.[21]

The same website shows maps where the whole of Korea is marked as one unit, with the border (or demarcation line) indicated as a thin red line. Thus, the maps and texts from both sides claim that Korea is one unit, showing

---

19   See Sullivan, Goldman, Vermeylen, this volume.
20   Official webpage of the DPR of Korea, see http://www.korea-dpr.com/location.html (last accessed February 14, 2020).
21   About Korea: http://www.korea.net/AboutKorea/Society/South-Korea-Summary (last accessed February 14, 2020).

awareness of the division, but not officially accepting it. Even when the text acknowledges the internationally recognized facts, such as the South Korean text giving the size of South Korea rather than that of the whole of Korea, the map sends different signals. Numerous other examples can be found from around the world, of maps that carefully (and sometimes less carefully) negotiate the relationship between international law, state level claims and the situation on the ground. The use of maps for governmental control was and still is a mixture of describing and creating spatial and political reality.

One of the most well-known extant Mixtec maps from what is now Mexico, *Lienzo de Zacatepec*,[22] shows the history and the boundaries of the Mixtec town of Zacatepec, with adjacent communities shown outside the area controlled by the town (Woodward/Lewis 1998: 202-3). Thus, the map shows not only the political situation and the physical space controlled by Zacatepec at a certain time in the 16th century, but also the history behind the then existing situation, with the genealogy of the rules shown as footpaths on the map, indicating time on the static map image. Another well-known example of the direct link between political power and maps is the painting of Queen Elizabeth I standing on a map.[23]

The rulers shown on maps do not have to be political leaders in a modern sense. The organization of the map can also be based on empires and powers different from the worldly ones. On several medieval maps the world is the body of Christ,[24] and Jerusalem, being seen as the centre of the earth, was commonly depicted in the middle of the map. The T-O map[25] from *Isidore von Sevillas Etymologiae* (early 7th century) identifies the three continents, Asia, Evropa and Africa, with the three sons of Noah: Sem, Iafeth, and Cham.[26]

When we look at extant decorated Sami ritual drums, traditionally used by Noaides in shamanistic rituals, there is a comparable mix of spiritual and

---

22 Instituto Nacional de Antropología e Historia (INAH), Mexico, see https://www.codice s.inah.gob.mx/pc/contenido.php?id=59 (last accessed February 14, 2020).

23 Marcus Gheeraerts, the Younger: *Queen Elizabeth I ('The Ditchley portrait')*. National Portrait Gallery, London, NPG 2561, see https://www.npg.org.uk/collections/search/portrai t/mw02079/ (last accessed February 14, 2020).

24 One example is the 13th century Ebstorf Map, see https://commons.wikimedia.org/wiki /File:Ebstorfer-stich2.jpg (last accessed February 14, 2020).

25 Named after the form of the map, a T inside an O.

26 Reproduction of this map based on a 15th century printed version, see https://com mons.wikimedia.org/wiki/File:T_and_O_map_Guntherus_Ziner_1472.jpg (last accessed February 14, 2020).

physical elements. The drums can include symbols representing deities of various sorts, but also physical locations, and can be used, for instance, in preparation for hunting. Indeed, according to Mathisen (1997), there are three representations of the Sami spiritual world: the "inner map" carried in the mind of people, the drum, and the layout of the dwelling mentioned above. These are three aspects of a moveable sacred space (Rydving 2010: 117-8). The map carried in the mind, used in the ritual, and reconstructed every time a tent is put up, also becomes a performance, in line with what Woodward and Lewis (1998: 4-5) described from several places around the world, including Australia, Meso-America, Colombia and Melanesia. It was suggested above that the landscape was not used as a map. And there is still a categorical difference between map and landscape. But when the maps grow, from a document in one's hand, via the document on the ground one gathers around and the map a queen stands on, into the layout of the tent one lives in, the distinction between landscape and map also starts to blur. The map gains aspects which belong to processes in addition to still being a document – performance cartography takes place. The processual view of maps will be a basis for the discussion about route directions in the next section and will be central in the final attempt to define "map" in the last section of this chapter.

Topology and topography: between spaces and lines

Maps of train systems, metros, bus and tram lines, and other public transport networks, make up a fundamental part of the daily life of many people, even if such maps are a fairly recent invention, with a history going back to Harry Beck's London Underground Tube map from 1933.[27] The structure of a network has its mathematical basis in graph theory, formalized by Leonhard Euler in the 18th century. Its use in the humanities and social sciences, of which we find some examples in the 19th century, became central in the 20th century (Eide 2020), and is also important at technological and societal levels through, for instance, computer networks and social networks.

Wayfinding is often a social, dialogical practice. In their studies of how people give each other route descriptions, Barbara Tversky and colleagues

---

27   See https://tfl.gov.uk/corporate/about-tfl/culture-and-heritage/art-and-design/harry-b ecks-tube-map (last accessed May 19, 2020).

have documented both textual and visual expressions over a series of experiments. The visual representations created by the participants in the experiments tend to be weak on what topographical maps are expected to convey precisely: correctly represented relative distances and geometrical relationships and forms. Roads and paths tend to be represented as straight lines even if curved, turns tend to be represented as close to 90° even if quite different from that in reality, and distances tend not to be relative.[28] These results are also consistent with how expressions are made and can be represented in different historical and cultural settings, as many of the maps in Harley et al. (1987–) show. It has been shown, and is consistent with this research, that the types of representations we find in the public transport networks mentioned above, which are called topological maps, as opposed to topographical maps, which are the scaled ones with representative distances, convey verbal route descriptions quite well (Eide 2015: 108-111).

When we look at the history of cartography, not least with a global perspective, and also when we look outside of cultures where writing was common, the division into topographical maps, topological maps, and written and oral texts is useful to understand how spatial information was mediated and, as is commonly claimed, also conceptualized.[29] This has been and still is extensively studied in the context of Mediterranean antiquity (Purves 2010; Palladino 2016). In this context, the network as representing a travel route, or as stars reflecting what one sees around oneself from a specific starting point (Evans/Jasnow 2014), is known as the hodological perspective, and is central to understanding antiquity as a period where the role of maps was quite different from what we see in many modern societies. The temporal dimension of the spatial, which comes not just from travel but also from the mixed spatial/temporal nature of many expressions about distance and/or travel time, is pinpointed by Herodotus, who expressed his mistrust in maps (Hdt. 5.49-50).[30] When he lays out a series of places visited they are differentiated in time as much as in space, making the spatial reference system less natural for the understanding of such relationships than what one often sees in modern

---

28   A number of publications show these results; see e.g. Tversky/Lee (1999) and Tversky (2019).

29   See Vermeylen, this volume.

30   The text of Herodotus' *Histories* is available from the Perseus archive, see http://data.pe rseus.org/citations/urn:cts:greekLit:tlg0016.tlg001.perseus-grc1:1.1.0 (last accessed May 19, 2020).

spatial thinking.[31] Not only due to Herodotus' critical remarks about maps, which can be read in various ways, but more based on what made sense as a scholarly method, the Hestia project, based on Herodotus' *Histories*, included lines expressing relationships as an important part of their map visualizations (Barker et al. 2016).

A graph is a non-spatial construction in the sense that it is mathematically defined as a set of nodes with edges connecting them. In a network visualization, the distance between nodes has no meaning and the physical appearance is often automatically created based on parameters for visual clarity. Concepts such as closeness do not refer to the length of single edges. Directions are also not relevant; the network can be turned around or turned upside down without changing as a graph structure. Therefore, topological maps as we know them from metro networks are not just graphs. They tend to have some orientation, usually with north on the top, even if it is not precise. A London underground map with Stratford on the left and Heathrow on the right would look peculiar to most users.

Many networks have a spatial meaning. The transport networks are prototypical, but networks of letter exchange also have nodes linked to places. Exactly how these links are understood might vary: the dwelling places of sender and receiver, the actual location the letter was sent from and addressed to, are two possible and often different choices. Other structures forming graph structures, such as kinship diagrams, taking into consideration that trees are graphs of a special type, can also be put on maps if some meaningful spatial aspects can be identified. The places where ancestors were born or dwelt can help us in making sense of or understanding other aspects connected to kinship structures. The result will not be the kind of ancestral map we saw in the Zacatepec example above, but it is related.[32]

A network can be visualized and interacted with as a network, with nodes having arbitrary locations. The same network can be put on a map, which fixes the location of each locatable node. Interactive studies of these different forms of visual representations are a research strategy with a significant potential, that computers in general, as well as specific tools for working with maps and networks, have made much easier over the last decades. Indeed, since 2010–2012 there has been a boost in the use of network-based methods

---

31   This is discussed in more detail in Eide (2016).
32   The question of kinship as related to spatial organization is also discussed by Dieck-
      mann, Sullivan and Skaanes, this volume.

across the digital humanities, also in various forms of spatial analysis, where network visualizations can be more or less connected to other spatial forms such as geographical maps. We see this, for instance, in historical disciplines as well as in the study of fiction (Eide 2020).

So what is a map, really?

Leaving the attempt to define the "map" concept aside, visual representations of landscapes expressed with different levels of concreteness have been discussed through examples spanning from Greek Antiquity to the current political situation on the Korean peninsula. In some cases we can and even must use terms that we do not define explicitly or precisely. Sometimes, encircling the concepts behind the term, as we did above, is all we can and should do. However, in closing this chapter a different strategy for getting closer to a definition of "map" will be attempted.

The relationship between a map and what is mapped is a special case of the relationship between a model and the system or object being modelled, that is, the target of the model (Eide 2015). Models cannot be defined by their material form; one must take the use of models in practice into consideration (Mahr 2009). What is a model for a new type of car for a car designer is a toy for her daughter. This understanding also highlights the need to take the person or group of persons doing the modelling into consideration, in what is called a pragmatic view of modelling (Gelfert 2016: 113). Many maps are explicitly created as representations of an external reality, and mapping practices in many cases are rule-based and scholarly reproducible. Measurements and projection methodologies are publicly accessible and the consequences of many of the methodological choices are available. However, the process can never be objective in a strict sense; there are always purposes behind the selection of features that the person or group of persons behind the map pursue, such as a governmental agency or a private company. This basic aspect of mapping is relevant to governmental and commercial actors at all levels: from the governments of large countries to indigenous political organizations, from Google to the Sami artist Hans Ragnar Mathisen mentioned above. It is a basic feature of mapping as a cultural production rather than being connected to who is behind the map, but the consequences vary from map to map. The level of truthfulness of maps can and must be discussed. The choices are always based on an agenda, which at best is open to public insight and critique, but in other cases is partly or fully one of propaganda.[33] This pragmatism fits well into an understanding of modelling as semiotic (Knuuttila 2010), especially where models are seen as icons (Kralemann/Lattmann 2013). Modelling in digital humanities is a practice-based methodology combining epistemological and ontological processes. The pragmatic and semiotic aspects of modelling are united in an understanding of modelling as an interplay between semiotic meaning making and the mediated ontological nature of models (Ciula/Eide 2017; Ciula/Marras 2018).

Models are media products insofar as they have a material form and express meaning in a communicative setting. Indeed, we find similar challenges in defining media products, where a functional definition also turns out to be necessary:

> Since being a media product should be understood as a function rather than an essential property, virtually any material existence can be used as one, including not only solid objects but all kinds of physical phenomena that can be perceived by the human senses (Elleström 2019: 11).

This leads to the suggestion that model, media product, and map can be understood in analogue ways, focusing more on the function than on essential ontological aspects.[34] A descriptive definition can never be all-encompassing. What is rather suggested is more in line with the wheel model of "text" in Sahle (2013), where different aspects of the concept must be understood, when studied empirically, as co-existing aspects of the phenomenon.

In the extended definition of "map" we find in Woodward and Lewis (1998), a map is what we use to understand a wide area of phenomena, expressing all sorts of landscape knowledge. In the narrower definition in Bagrow (1951), a map is a specific kind of a document, a spatial media product. The actual use of the word "map" must be understood in the span between the narrow and the wide sense of the word, without either of them completely taking over.[35] This, as we have seen, is not new and might very well be a key to understand

---

33   Discussions of such questions are found in, for instance, Monmonier (1996) and Wood et al. (2010).

34   See the Introduction to this volume, which stresses the importance of the *purpose* of the map.

35   This is also reflected in the various chapters in this volume. Some of the authors rather use a narrow definition of map, while others suggest embracing different sorts of landscape knowledge.

Figure 2: An English translation of Sahle's text wheel, showing how a definition of text covering the wide history of the concept must operate with a number of different understandings simultaneously.

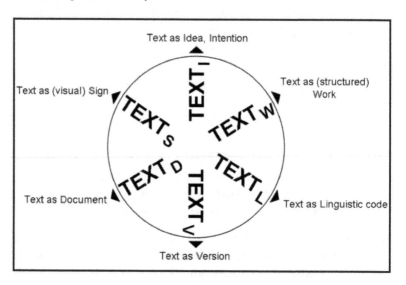

the meaning of all these representations of spatial thinking, concrete as well as metaphorical, across time and space. While it may be useful in many cases to limit the use of the word "map" to scaled spatial media products such as topographical maps, one must also remember that not only networks and conceptual maps, but also textual structures and cognitive processes are often referred to as maps, not only in general language use but also in science and research.

References

Bagrow, Leo (1951): Die Geschichte der Kartographie, Berlin: Safari-Verlag.

Bakhtin, Mikhail M. (1981): "Forms of Time and the Chronotope in the Novel. Notes toward a Historical Poetics." In: Michael Holquist (ed.), The dialogic imagination: four essays, Austin: University of Texas Press, pp. 84-258.

Banks, Andrew, ed., (1998): The Proceedings of the Khoisan Identities and Cultural Heritage Conference, Cape Town: Infosource.

Barker, Elton/Bouzarovski, Stefan/Pelling, Christopher/Isaksen, Leif, eds. (2016): New Worlds from Old Texts. Revisiting Ancient Space and Place, Oxford: Oxford University Press.

Bulson, Eric (2007): Novels, maps, modernity: the spatial imagination, 1850-2000, New York: Routledge.

Ciula, Arianna/Eide, Øyvind (2017): "Modelling in digital humanities: Signs in context." In: Digital Scholarship in the Humanities 32/suppl 1, pp. i33-i46.

Ciula, Arianna/Marras, Cristina (2018): "Exploring a semiotic conceptualisation of modelling in digital humanities practices." In: Alin Olteanu/Andrew Stables/Dumitru Borţun (eds.), Meanings & Co.: the Interdisciplinarity of Communication, Semiotics and Multimodality, Dordrecht: Springer, pp. 33-52.

Eide, Øyvind (2012): The area told as a story. An inquiry into the relationship between verbal and map-based expressions of geographical information, PhD Thesis, London: King's College London.

Eide, Øyvind (2015): Media Boundaries and Conceptual Modelling: Between Texts and Maps, Basingstoke: Palgrave Macmillan.

Eide, Øyvind (2016): "Verbal Expressions of Geographical Information." In: Elton Barker/Stefan Bouzarovski/Christopher Pelling/Leif Isaksen (eds.), New Worlds from Old Texts. Revisiting Ancient Space and Place, Oxford, Oxford University Press, pp. 301-318.

Eide, Øyvind (2020): "Modelling and networks in digital humanities." In: Stuart Dunn/Kristen Schuster (eds.), Routledge Handbook of Research Methods in Digital Humanities, Abingdon: Routledge, pp. 91-108.

Eide, Øyvind/Schubert, Zoe (2021): "Seeing the Landscape Through Textual and Graphical Media Products." In: Lars Elleström (ed.), Beyond Media Borders, Volume 2. Intermedial Relations among Multimodal Media, Basingstoke: Palgrave McMillan, pp. 175-209.

Elleström, Lars (2010): "The Modalities of Media: A Model for Understanding Intermedial Relations." In: Lars Elleström (ed.), Media borders, multimodality and intermediality, Palgrave McMillan, Basingstoke, pp. 11-48.

Elleström, Lars (2019): "Modelling human communication: Mediality and semiotics." In: Alin Olteanu/Andrew Stables/Dumitru Borţun (eds.), Meanings & Co.: the Interdisciplinarity of Communication, Semiotics and Multimodality, Dordrecht: Springer, pp. 7-32.

Evans, Courtney/Jasnow, Ben (2014): "Mapping Homer's Catalogue of Ships." In: Literary and Linguistic Computing 29/3, pp. 317-325.

Gelfert, Axel (2016): How to do science with models: a philosophical primer, Cham: Springer.

Harley, John B./Woodward, David (1987): Cartography in prehistoric, ancient, and medieval Europe and the Mediterranean, Chicago: University of Chicago Press, Volume 1 of The History of Cartography.

Harley, John B./Woodward, David/Lewis, G. Malcolm (1987–): The History of cartography, Chicago: University of Chicago Press.

Holmsen, Andreas (1966): "Gårdene' i den gamle matrikkel." In: Kåre Lunden (ed.), Gard, bygd, rike: festskrift i anledning Andreas Holmsens 60 årsdag 5. juni 1966, Oslo: Universitetsforlaget, pp. 134-160.

Ingold, Tim (2000): The Perception of the Environment. Essays in livelihood, dwelling and skill, Abingdon: Routledge.

Keski-Säntti, Jouko/Lehtonen, Ulla/Sivonen, Pauli/Vuolanto, Ville (2003): "The Drum as Map: Western Knowledge Systems and Northern Indigenous Map Making." In: Imago Mundi: The International Journal for the History of Cartography 55/1, pp. 120-125.

Kiil, Alf (1969): Arkivkunnskap: statsarkiva, Oslo: Universitetsforlaget.

Knuuttila, Tarja (2010): "Not Just Underlying Structures: Towards a Semiotic Approach to Scientific Representation and Modeling." In: Mats Bergman/Sami Paavola/Ahti-Veikko Pietarinen/Henrik Rydenfelt (eds.), Proceedings of the Applying Peirce Conference, Helsinki: Nordic Pragmatism Network, pp. 163-172.

Kralemann, Björn/Lattmann, Claas (2013): "Models as icons: modeling models in the semiotic framework of Peirce's theory of signs." In: Synthese 190/16, pp. 3397-3420.

Landau, Barbara/Lakusta, Laura (2009): "Spatial representation across species: geometry, language, and maps." In: Current Opinion in Neurobiology 19/1, pp. 12-19.

Lenssen-Erz, Tilman (1998): "The Third Gender: Human. Gender-related patterns of activity in the rock paintings of the Brandberg, Namibia." In: Andrew Banks (ed.), The Proceedings of the Khoisan Identities and Cultural Heritage Conference, Cape Town: Infosource, pp. 146-152.

MacEachren, A. M. (2004): How maps work: representation, visualization, and design, New York, Guilford Press.

Mahr, Bernd (2009): "Information science and the logic of models." In: Software & Systems Modeling 8/3, pp. 365-383.

Manker, Ernst (1950): Die lappische Zaubertrommel. Eine ethnologische Monographie. II. Die Trommel als Urkunde geistigen Lebens, Stockholm: Gebers.

Mathisen, Hans Ragnar (1997): "Tanker om kart." In: Anniken Greve/Sigmund Nesset (eds.), Filosofi i et nordlig landskap: Jakob Meløe 70 år, Tromsø: Universitetetsbiblioteket i Tromsø, pp. 120-133.

Monmonier, Mark (1996): How to lie with maps, Chicago: University of Chicago Press.

Palladino, Chiara (2016): "New approaches to ancient spatial models: Digital humanities and classical geography." In: Bulletin of the Institute of Classical Studies 59/2, pp. 56-70.

Purves, Alex C. (2010): Space and time in ancient Greek narrative, Cambridge: Cambridge University Press.

Ryan, Marie-Laure (1980): "Fiction, non-factuals, and the principle of minimal departure." In: Poetics 9, pp. 403-422.

Rydving, Håkan (2010): Tracing Sami traditions: In search of the indigenous religion among the Western Sami during the 17th and 18th centuries, Oslo: Novus.

Sahle, Patrick (2013): Digitale Editionsformen – Teil 3: Textbegriffe und Recodierung: Zum Umgang mit der Überlieferung unter den Bedingungen des Medienwandels, Norderstedt: Books on Demand.

Schneider, Ute (2006): Die Macht der Karten: eine Geschichte der Kartographie vom Mittelalter bis heute, Darmstadt: Primus. 1st edition: 2004.

Schnitler, Peter (1929): Major Peter Schnitlers grenseeksaminasjonsprotokoller 1742–1745. 2. Oslo: Norsk historisk kjeldeskrift-institutt.

Schnitler, Peter (1962): Major Peter Schnitlers grenseeksaminasjonsprotokoller 1742–1745. 1. Oslo: Norsk historisk kjeldeskrift-institutt.

Schnitler, Peter (1985): Major Peter Schnitlers grenseeksaminasjonsprotokoller 1742–1745. 3. Oslo: Norsk historisk kjeldeskrift-institutt.

Smail, Daniel Lord (1999): Imaginary cartographies: possession and identity in late medieval Marseille, Ithaca: Cornell University Press.

Tobias, Terry N. (2000): Chief Kerry's moose: a guidebook to land use and occupancy mapping, research design, and data collection, Vancouver: Union of BC Indian Chiefs and Ecotrust Canada.

Tversky, Barbara (2019): Mind in motion: how action shapes thought, New York: Basic Books.

Tversky, Barbara/Lee, Paul U. (1999): "Pictorial and Verbal Tools for Conveying Routes." In: Christian Freksa/David M. Mark (eds.), Spatial information theory: cognitive and computational foundations of geographical information science: International Conference COSIT '99, Stade, Germany, August 25-29, 1999: proceedings, Berlin: Springer-Verlag, pp. 51-64.

Wood, Denis (1993). "The fine line between mapping and mapmaking." In: Cartographica: The International Journal for Geographic Information and Geovisualization 30/4, pp. 50-60.

Wood, Denis/Fels, John/Krygier, John (2010): Rethinking the power of maps, New York: Guilford Press.

Woodward, David/Lewis, G. Malcolm (1998): Cartography in the traditional African, American, Arctic, Australian, and Pacific societies, Volume 2.3 of The History of Cartography, Chicago: University of Chicago Press.

What were we mapping? From the Inuit Land Use and Occupancy Project to the Southern Kalahari

Hugh Brody

Maps express the authority of those who make them, their claims to know and therefore own the world or the areas of the world that they thus declare to be theirs. Colonial and imperial expansion can be traced through a history of cartography. The names on British maps of Canada and much of southern Africa are evocative of their origins and purpose: members of the royal family, commanders of expeditions, explorers who represent the nation become headlands, islands, mountains and rivers. The challenge to these imperial claims, the assertion of prior or original entitlement to those lands, can also come in the form of maps. These set out different kinds of information about place, with names that belong much more deeply in the past and in the land. The authority behind these maps, and the needs that they meet, come from the peoples who have used and occupied the land 'since time immemorial'. The colonists' frontiers are thus revealed to be indigenous peoples' homelands.

The modern history of challenges to Canadian sovereignty, especially in the Arctic and British Columbia, is to be seen in a series of mapping projects. It was in these maps of indigenous life that representation of an altogether different way of knowing, using and laying claim to their lands, was pioneered. These rival maps, and the whole idea of cultural mapping, depended on a process and methodology that focused on achieving decolonization, originated in Canada and then spread across the social scientific and indigenous political world. I was fortunate to work on several of the Canadian projects, and also had the opportunity to help carry the methodology to the edge of the Kalahari Desert in South Africa. What follows here is a summary of this flow of mapping, a story about a set of stories each of which centers on a potential transformation of how the world should be seen and understood.

***

In Inuktitut, the Eskimo language of the Canadian central and eastern Arctic, *nuna* is the word for land. *Nanik nunaqarpit*, where do you have land? is to ask "where do you live," and can mean "where do you come from?" The Inuit called their new jurisdiction, created in 1999, *Nunavut*, our land; *Nunavik*, widely translated as "great land", is now the name for the large Inuit region of northern Quebec. Inuit jurisdiction in Labrador was given the name *Nunatsiavut*, our beautiful land. Before Europeans laid claim to the Arctic, Inuit named the details of their environment, and not the large areas themselves – it was in response to Canadian maps that Inuit coined their own names for these as well. But the new Inuit territories were established on the basis of extensive research into who and where Inuit in each region used and occupied their lands. And this underlying evidence for Inuit rights and title resulted from the earliest cultural mapping projects, first begun in the 1970s. Mapping what had so often seemed to be invisible to outsiders, and therefore had been so easy to disregard, was pioneered in the Canadian north.

The word Inuit use to refer to a map is *Nunannguaq*, and can be translated as "pretend land". The morpheme *nnguaq* or *nnuar* can be either an infix or affix, and carries a range of meanings, depending on linguistic context. "He/she plays" (i.e. a game, for fun) is *pi-nguar-tuq*[1]; "he/she pretends not to know" is *qaujimangi-nnguar-tuq*; and "he/she acts" (as in a drama performance) is *nnguar-nnguar-tuq*, meaning pretend to pretend. Simon Anaviapik, my wonderful guide and mentor in Pond Inlet, the Inuit community at the north tip of Baffin Island, would often refer to me as *Irninnguaq*, which I understood to mean "pretend", i.e. "adoptive son". So a map, *nuna-nnguaq*, is the land made unreal, in an imitative form: standing in for something else. Virtual land.

But *nuna* is not quite as easy to translate as these examples of its use may suggest. When speaking of *nunangat*, "their lands", the Inuit include everything that they use – land, lakes and rivers, of course, but also ice; and Inuit elders make the point that their land, *nuna*, is not separable from all the animals on it, just as it is not separable from the plants, mosses and other features of the environment that Inuit know and depend on.[2] So *nuna is often* used to refer to a totality of environment, and not just the earth or piece of

---

1   I insert hyphens to show the place of *nnguar*; these would not be used in usual roman orthography for Inuktitut.

2   In a recent filmed interview (January, 2020) George Qulaut, an Inuit elder from Igloolik, said that "land" without inclusion of all "the animals" did not make sense to Inuit.

territory that can be separated out as a distinctive party of geographical reality.

Consider the different connotations between European and North American uses of the word "land". When they speak of their land, Western Europeans, along with just about all societies that depend on agriculture, are likely to be referring to a piece of earth that is demarcated and privately owned, and will not thereby denote seashore or even the rights to fish in rivers running through their land. North Americans will be more likely to talk about "the land" as a whole, something stretching in all directions and comprising everything it contain – including waterways, forests, animals and fish etc.[3] Inuit use "land" far more in the North American than European way, implicitly disavowing, or at least not relying on, any notions of land as something inherently divided and owned. Thus, when Inuit speak of the value of the land to them, they are including everything that is in and on the land, animals, water, coastal sea ice – and a knowledge of all these in virtue of which a place, *nuna*, is theirs to use. This suggests that they are including their sense of occupancy at least as much as their use of the land. This is a crucial distinction that I will be returning to.

There is also the problematic of ownership itself. Inuit, like so many hunter-gatherer societies, do not speak of owning their land or the animals and plants they rely on. In a recent interview, an Inuit woman recalled how her father had laughed out loud at the idea of anyone 'owning' the land.[4] Each extended family of Inuit – often referred to in the anthropological literature as "miut groups" – had a set of seasonal camps and hunting or gathering areas that constituted their territory. When outsiders began to say that these territories, or the land as a whole, "belonged to the government" or was "Crown Land", Inuit were both bewildered and indignant.[5] It is not true that there is no way of speaking of ownership in the Inuktitut language – the term *nangminiga* translates as "it is mine", and is used to denote personal

---

3   The popular and populist North American song, for example, "This land is your land, this land is my land..." invites and relies on a meaning of 'land' that is totalizing - and striking for its place in democratic and anti-establishment discourse, seeking to oppose a dominant, European way of speaking of land in which private ownership and therefore inequity are embedded. Hence the resonances of the singing of the song by Pete Seeger and his followers in the 1960s.

4   Rhoda Inuksuk, personal communication, January 2020.

5   A powerful statement to this effect can be found in the film *The People's Land: Eskimos of Pond Inlet*, made in the Granada TV *Disappearing World* Series, 1975.

possessions. But the land is not a possession of this kind, and the idea of a "land claim" was puzzling to many Inuit until it was understood that this was an issue not so much of ownership but management and control. Imposition of southern Canadian hunting regulations or rules about uses of wildlife revealed the new colonial threats far more forcefully than the abstraction of governmental assertions of overall ownership. The land was the arena of Inuit independence as well as their zone of complex economic and cultural value.

***

The Canadian Inuit did not use writing of language until a syllabic script was introduced to the Arctic in the 1870s by missionaries and their first converts; the original purpose of this literacy centered on the Bible, or at least selected parts of it, as well as prayers and psalms. To receive and know the word of the Christian God, the Inuit were encouraged to be able to read some of the words for themselves. Before this intervention by outsiders, which transformed their spiritual lives, the Inuit – like most human beings in the long history of language – have learned, by listening as well as watching and doing. There was no such thing as a pencil or paper – the Inuktitut words for which vary from region to region. The Inuit used their flexible, agglutinative language to create multitudes of new words to name new pieces of material culture that came from the south.[6] Before Europeans provided writing materials, therefore, they did not make maps on paper. But I saw Inuit hunters sketch a travel map in the snow, and I am sure that this had in the past been a much-used way of sharing or talking about possible routes; so the facility for drawing maps predates any use of paper and pen.[7]

Inuit literacy consisted in a great facility to read the environment. The shape and orientation of ridges in snow can reveal the direction in which you are travelling in winter, even when all other indicators are invisible. The color and the patterns of meltwater on ice can show the safe routes to travel in

---

6   In the Ungava dialect, for example, the word for paper translates as 'resembles newly-formed (i.e. very thin) sea ice'. The word for writing has as its root a term referring to strangeness.

7   A fascinating exception might be the small wooden carvings made by Tunumiit hunters in east Greenland in the nineteenth century to reprise details of coastline and islands, see Harmsen (2018).

spring. Also, the landscape, and even the sea ice, is given meaning by multitudes of place names. There are many examples of this kind of literacy: through every working day, and perhaps in dreams as well, hunter-gatherers are reading, taking meaning from, their land. And sharing what they have 'read', passing on the meanings to others. To be able to make their own decisions, each hunter or gatherer depends on what others know and have learned; much time is given to hearing and reporting what has been experienced or remembered, contributing to an ever-expanding set of 'texts'. Much of this depends on great sophistication of both knowledge and perception, and remarkable feats of memory.[8] But none of this was recorded in any form of writing.

In 1822–23, at least fifty years before any Inuit had learned to read or write with syllabics, and some 100 years before missionaries first reached the Iglulingmiut, the people living at the very far north-west corner of Hudson Bay, two Inuit hunters were asked to draw maps. This request came from the captain of one of two ships that became trapped in the ice deep in Iglulingmiut lands. The ships were looking for the ever-elusive Northwest Passage, the imagined shipping route across the high Arctic from Europe to markets in Asia. Needing to work out this supposed route, and to understand where they were trapped, the captains of the ships, Parry and Lyon, both of whom had spent a great deal of time with the people they encountered, asked Inuit hunters to draw for them the shape and features of the coastline where they were trapped. This resulted in a set of three 'charts' that Parry in due course published as part of his report on the expedition (see Figure 1).[9]

The Inuit were able to draw for Parry and Lyon the coastline stretching far away from where the maps were made. One of the maps goes as far south as Southampton Island, a distance of 550 miles. Each of the maps shows both place names and information about the land and sea – places good for different kinds of hunting, productive fishing spots, qualities of tide and current, location of other Inuit groups etc. Parry reports that the Inuit who made the maps shaded the coastline with the pencil they were using. The detail and

---

8   See, for a very compelling example, John MacDonald (1998).

9   Parry was already among the most famous explorers in British naval history, having caused a popular sensation with his published report on his previous, 1818, expedition to the Arctic. He was quoted or cited, for example, by Byron, the Brontës and many other writers of the time, see MacDonald (2020). Both Lyon (1824) and Parry (1824) published detailed and illustrated journals.

precision are remarkable; even more so is the facility with what must have been a completely new tool and an unfamiliar kind of intellectual process. For the first hundred or so miles of coastline, the relative distances between places and features of geography shown on these maps are very accurate; further away, and as the maps show areas that are of less importance to the Inuit making them, relative distances are compressed. But this set of drawn coastlines shows an astonishing facility for drawing the outline features of the environment as seen from above. In the mind's eye of the hunter, the land can be envisaged as if spreading below them. Inuit shamans, with their claim to make spirit flights over the land, reinforce this facility. The 1822–23 maps from Iglulik reveal the cartographic skills of at least the Inuit hunters Parry and Lyon came to rely on. In the late 1880s, Franz Boas reports on his Inuit hosts on Baffin Island making more than forty maps for him.[10]

Early in the twentieth century the young Robert Flaherty, when travelling and living with Inuit in Arctic Quebec, 760 miles south of Igloolik, heard for the first time that a group of islands not far off the coast were large enough to be the lands of a distinctive Inuit community. At the time, in the early 1900s, these islands were marked on Admiralty Charts as little more than rocky outcrops, named the Belchers. But Flaherty's guide and travelling companion in 1910 was George Weetaltuk, who told Flaherty about his home out on the islands that white people did not believe existed. Intrigued and inclined to believe Weetaltuk more than the Admiralty Charts of the day, Flaherty asked Weetaltuk to draw a map of his homeland. With great care, he outlined a complex multitude of islands; and indicated that it would take three days by dog team to travel the full length of the longest of them. This meant that Weetaltuk's homeland was at least 90 miles long; his map further showed that this hypothetical dog team journey covered only a small proportion of the lands that were shown on the map. In due course, Flaherty would reach these islands and discover that Weetaltuk's map was astonishing for its accuracy of both intricate detail and internal relative distances (see Figure 2).[11]

---

10   For this and much other detail and critical discussion of Inuit map making see Woodward/Lewis (1998).

11   By the time Weetaltuk met Flaherty, the Inuit of Arctic Quebec and south Hudson Bay had long been in contact with southern institutions and Euro-Canadian material culture. Many Inuit in that region would have been familiar with writing and Euro-Canadian maps since the late 1700s. Weetaltuk's complex map of the Belchers – as opposed to maps of the Igloolik area elicited by Parry 1822–23 – may well reflect this. Weetaltuk's grand-daughter, Mini Aodla Freeman (2015: 66-70), recalls Weetaltuk and

Figure 1: Parry's Chart of 1822 based on the map done for him by an Igloolik hunter (Source: Parry 1824); Figure 2: Weetaltuk's map of the Belcher Islands, drawn for Robert Flaherty in 1910 (Source: Flaherty 1918)

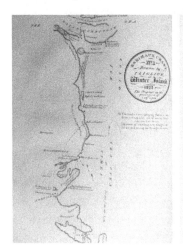 

***

In the late 1960s and though 1971 – the period during which a new oil and gas exploration frontier was opened up in extensive areas of the Mackenzie Delta – the need for coordinated resistance to large scale industrial development in the north was keenly felt across the communities of the western Arctic.[12] A new organization, the Committee of Original Peoples Entitlement (COPE), with headquarters in Inuvik, gave voice to local concerns. COPE represented all the regional groups that had strong cultural or economic interests in the region's land and wildlife – Inuvialuit, Dene, Métis and white trappers joined

---

his very remarkable life as community leader and boat-builder. The modern Inuktitut name for the Belcher islands is Sanikiluaq; for details of its fascinating topography see *Sanikiluaq Wikipedia 'images'*.

12   The new oil and gas frontier was not the first extensive intrusion into the Arctic of powerful outside interests. The Cold War, with USA fears of Soviet air invasion from the north, had led to the construction and maintenance from 1957 to 1988 of 63 Distant Early Warning stations, known as the DEW line. That was a set of military bases stretching the full width of the Northwest Territories (and beyond), some of them within easy distance of Inuit communities.

forces to protest, through COPE, against development activity that appeared to threaten their lands and livelihoods, and which seemed to be saying that the Mackenzie Valley was for the most part uninhabited 'wilderness'. COPE saw the apparent invisibility of local culture and economic activities as a central challenge. And from 1971, COPE was proposing that maps be made to show, as irrefutable defiance of the apparent blindness of developers and the government agencies that supported or licensed them, the nature and extent of hunting and trapping across the region. Nellie Cournyea, the first President of COPE, took a political lead in this initiative. Peter Usher, the Canadian geographer whose intensive and ground-breaking research into Inuvialuit economic life on Banks Island gave him a very sophisticated understanding of both local and national economic realities in the Mackenzie Delta, worked with COPE on the first conceptualization and design of this mapping.[13]

Alongside, and very much linked to this new phase of northern industrial development during the late 1960s and early 1970s, Canada's modern era of land claims began to take shape. At the same time as industrial development was coming to the north, the oil and gas frontier in the far north was opening up, and policies were being implemented aimed at establishing Canadian administration in even the remotest communities. A series of political-legal confrontations between hunters and trappers and developers or government (the two at times being inextricable entwined) shaped the national context. In 1967, an action was brought by the Nisga'a First Nation of northern British Columbia arguing that their Aboriginal Title to their lands and resources had never been extinguished. After losing in the lower courts of British Columbia, the Nisga'a case was taken to the Supreme Court of Canada. Its decision came down in 1973: The Court had split three to three on the central question of Aboriginal Title; and it was duly rejected on the deciding vote of the Court's senior judge. But this result was seen on all sides as a major victory for the Nisga'a, and a powerful blow to the government's view that all interests would be best served by further and final assimilation of indigenous peoples into Canadian society; Aboriginal Title could not be consigned to legal and political irrelevance.[14] At the same time, the James Bay hydro-electric project in northern

---

13   See Peter Usher's three volume report of his Banks Island work, where he gives detailed insight into how trapping and come to play a central role in western Arctic economic life and also documents the first incursion into the area of oil and gas interests (1971).

14   The assimilationist policy of the government of Pierre Trudeau was set out, famously, in the 1969 White Paper, which unleashed a furore of indignation and unrest in virtually

Quebec had triggered intense protest and opposition from both the Cree and Inuit whose lands and river systems were going to be drastically inundated or transformed. In 1971, this opposition secured an injunction, halting, albeit very briefly, all work on the project. This in due course led to the James Bay Agreement, negotiated through 1972–74 and signed into law in 1975. This Agreement recognized Cree and Inuit rights to their lands and resources, granted their entitlement to long-term compensation for damage being done to them, and established measures by which their way of life on the land be protected and developed in its own terms.[15]

These challenges to the assimilationist and development directions being taken by government were reinforced by intense concerns about Quebec separatism. In October 1970, activist members of the *Front de Libération du Québec* kidnapped the province's Deputy Premier and a British diplomat. Prime Minister Trudeau responded to this challenge by implementing The War Measures Act. In due course, the kidnappers released the diplomat, but murdered the Deputy Premier. For Canada, this was a crisis of sovereignty, and Trudeau's central concern a refusal to countenance forces that aimed at its fragmentation. Events in Quebec and calls for recognition of Aboriginal title were linked.[16] This buildup of pressures led the government of the day, still led by the charismatic Pierre Trudeau, to announce a remarkable political *volte face*. In 1969, his government had insisted that the entire apparatus of special interests of indigenous people in Canada and the special relationship that these had caused to develop within the Canadian body politic should all be dismantled. Then, Trudeau suddenly declared, in 1973, that the whole possibility of new arrangements and, in effect, modern treaties, should after all be "given a try". To this end the government set up funds and new administrative structures to deal with what came to be called "land claims".[17]

---

every Aboriginal community across the country. For a First Nations perspective and excellent summary, see "The White Paper 1969", https://indigenousfoundations.arts.ub c.ca/the_white_paper_1969/ (last accessed July 11, 2020).

15   For the text and implications of this Agreement, legally The James Bay and Northern Quebec Native Claims Settlement Act, see "Justice Laws Website, Canada", https://law s-lois.justice.gc.ca/eng/acts/ (last accessed July 11, 2020).

16   For details of the Quebec crisis, see http://faculty.marianopolis.edu/c.belanger/quebec history/chronos/october.htm(last accessed July 11, 2020).

17   The continuing and deeply complex arguments for Aboriginal Title, and related historical/legal issues, is elegantly explored in Culhane (1997).

Thus 70 percent of Canada's total land surface was thrown open to some form of negotiation that could result in a new Agreement on Treaty between 'Canada' and an indigenous people or First Nation.[18] With this policy u-turn, Canada appeared to establish itself as a global leader in a new kind of political morality, seemingly centered on respect and acknowledgment for indigenous peoples' rights to their lands and resources.

It is important to be cautious about these kinds of accolade or motivation: Canada was concerned to achieve non-conflictual development of its northern resources as well as to establish a new northern equity. The new land claims could be expected to create a stable, low-risk investment environment. Yet the discourse around the new policy, and the initiatives it launched, were striking for a lack of cynicism: Aboriginal people across Canada understood the Trudeau initiative as a recognition of their right to both lands and genuine self-government. Over the following decades, documentation of this right became a central challenge to many indigenous communities in northern and western Canada. Among the first to take on this challenge were the Inuit of what was then called The Northwest Territories; and the decision was made to make Inuit relationships to their lands visible on sets of maps.

A year before the policy change and its establishment of land claims as a feature of federal government policy and institutions, a newly formed organization, Inuit Tapirisat of Canada,[19] launched the first cultural mapping project. This came to be known as the Inuit Land Use and Occupancy Project (ILUOP). Its ambition was remarkable: at its center was the aim to make a map biography for every Inuit who had used and occupied the land, and that this should include details of every single form of resource harvesting and related land use. Further, the plan was that older Inuit would make separate complete maps for each of three possible phases of their lives – the time before there was a trading post in their territory, between the arrival of traders and the establishment of a day school in the settlement where they were now living, and the period since the arrival of the school. Younger hunters, trappers and gatherers would make just the one, post school map; but the expectation was

---

18   The link between Quebec separatism and Aboriginal land claims can be seen in the adoption of the word "Nation", to refer to Quebec and 'First Nations' to Canadian Aboriginal peoples, meeting a shared demand for recognition for their special statuses within Canada, i.e. the very identity that the 1969 White Paper had forcefully rejected.

19   *Tapirisat* translates as potential members of a team or brotherhood. It subsequently changed its name to *Inuit Tapiriit Kanatami* – "the Inuit teams/partnerships in Canada".

that each community, as a whole, would in this way be able to demonstrate not only the nature and extent of land use, but also the ways in which the pattern of use had changed in response to outside forces.

Further, the mapping also aimed to show the nature of Inuit intellectual and cultural relationship to their lands. To this end, separate maps were made to show place names, travel routes, locations of special importance (former living and camping sites, berry picking areas, graves, places of special non-economic importance, etc.); and maps were made to show Inuit understanding of biology – including, for example: caribou migration and calving areas, polar bear denning sites, relationships between killer whales, narwhal and spring ice conditions. The places Inuit had lived in previous generations were marked, as also the ancient, barely visible house sites of the peoples who were in their lands before the Inuit – the cultural ancestors of the Inuit, whom they often refer to as Tunit, and the culture that predated Inuit occupation of the Arctic by several thousand years, the so-called Dorset people. To amplify these bodies of knowledge, recordings were made of discussions with both Inuit elders and youth in which they shared memories, further details of their relationships to their land and their concerns or fears about the way Inuit life was changing or seemed to be under various kinds of threat. In combination, this constituted the first, and in many cases the only, detailed account of Inuit realities from an Inuit point of view.

This work revealed the way in which Inuit knowledge of the environment is built from multitudes of detail, with both place names and stories about specific places or areas creating a web of interconnected information. In her study of the Innuinait of the Canadian central Arctic, Beatrice Collignon (2006: 92-96) explains how this kind of knowledge, with routes that hunters travel creating sets of lines across the land combining with zones of use and stories in relation to both humans and animals, generates an intellectual "framework on which a mental image of the land can be anchored" (ibid: 96). This account of Inuinnait ways of understanding and knowing their environment echoes core findings of the Inuit Land Use and Occupancy work. In both cases, these are findings that reveal the extent to which a great deal of mobility can constitute mental structures that are well suited to the making of maps. The question has to be asked, however, about how two-dimensional maps can do justice to this multi-dimensional way of using and occupying the land. The multitude of data, background information and maps generated by the ILUOP speak to the great extent, depth and complexity of Inuit relationships to their lands.

The results of this vast, ambitious project were published in a three-volume report; and various essays have been written reflecting on the way the work was done and what it might have achieved.[20] The ILUOP was very soon followed by cultural mapping work, usually linked to pursuit of land claims or Aboriginal title, that adopted its basic methodology – the map biography and layering of 'occupancy' on or alongside 'use'. This series of projects meant that Inuit in Labrador (Nunatsiaq) and Arctic Quebec (Nunavik) set out their relationships to the North in areas not included in the Northwest Territories. These were followed by methodologically allied mapping projects carried out in Canada by Dene (the western subarctic), Ojibway (northwest Ontario), Danneza (northeast British Columbia); and, in due course by indigenous groups around the world. Some of these projects, including the ILUOP, led to land claims settlements (e.g. both the Inuvialuit Settlement Region in 1984 and the establishment in 1999 of Nunavut). All of the mapping projects also played important roles in building social and even psychological strength within communities and families; and in carrying the argument for recognition to centers of power. In each case, they were used to make visible that which had seemed to be, or was deemed to be, invisible.

The ILUOP relied on a small team of social scientists, each responsible for a region of the Northwest Territories. As a member of this team, I coordinated the work in the North Baffin and northern Foxe Basin area. In each community, the teams worked in a close partnership with elders and assistants. We spent many hours with Inuit as they set out on maps or in memories the multitude of places they had used and the ways they had used them, were impressed – and often deeply moved – by the excitement and joy that this work generated. I remember that in all the four communities where I either helped to create maps or had the job of going over composite maps to show combined areas of use and occupancy, the process had strong social and intergenerational dimensions. As an elder worked on the maps, both other elders who were visiting and members of the family in the house where the work was being done gathered round to watch – and, often, to share thoughts, ask questions, clarify details. Older men and women encouraged the young to be there, to hear the stories; while younger hunters and gatherers became ever more enthusiastic about making their maps.

---

20   The three volumes were published as: "The Inuit Land Use and Occupancy Project" (Freeman 1976); also Freeman (2011); Brody (2018).

This was a moment in northern history when relocation to new government-built settlements had just taken place. The Canadian government began its policy of creating relatively large, consolidated Inuit settlements in the 1950s. But in the central and eastern Arctic, this change did not take place until the 1960s, and was, in the remotest regions, still taking place in the early 1970s. Many individuals and families were experiencing new forms of stress as a result of the transition from a life centered on a set of hunting camps to life in a consolidated settlement. Some hunters struggled to get out onto the land as much as they would have liked, with concomitant feelings of despondency and some eruptive anger. Alcohol was beginning to arrive in large quantities, bringing unprecedented levels of stress and even violence. Older Inuit tended to be very critical of the young; and the young often spoke of their frustrations and disappointments. Schools were insisting on routines that did not fit well with previous established patterns of daily life and geographical mobility. Thus, the map making was for many people a chance to celebrate their way of using and knowing the land prior to the settlement era; and the project was also a chance to express deep anxiety about what people saw as new and powerful and, in their view, destructive social and economic forces. These considerations gave distinctive political and psychological energy to the mapping. The process as well as the results can be seen to have many kinds of value.

***

The importance and apparent success of the ILUOP and its intellectual progeny, however, should not leave some of its underlying conceptual and methodological tenets unchallenged. In fact, a first such critique came from another Canadian indigenous organization – the Gitksan and Wet'swet'en Tribal Council. In 1987, this alliance of neighboring, inter-related peoples in northwest British Columbia launched a legal action against the Provincial Government arguing that Aboriginal title to their lands had never been extinguished and that Gitksan-Wet'suwet'en jurisdiction and laws should prevail across the 45,000 square miles of their 'traditional territories'. From the start, this action decided to draw on the evidence of maps; a comprehensive and sophisticated cartographic project was set up in Hazelton, at the Tribal Council's administrative center in northern British Columbia. But this mapping work began with a challenge to the ILUOP and allied forms of land claims research.

The critique centered on the legal status of 'use and occupancy'. The Gitskan-Wet'suwet'en leadership and its legal team pointed out that use and occupation are not valid or appropriate criteria for jurisdiction and territorial ownership. They pointed out that no nation-state must demonstrate its actual use of lands to justify those lands being part of the national territory. Unoccupied off-shore islands are not excluded from a jurisdiction by virtue of not being used and inhabited. So why do indigenous peoples have to satisfy these criteria? Moreover, do these criteria mean that places from where an indigenous people has been driven out cease to be part of that people's land claim? For the Gitksan and Wet-suwet'en, whose lands had been taken over within the previous fifty to a hundred years by large numbers of southern, colonial settlers, this was a point of intense significance. Their mapping project reflected this conceptual challenge to the legal theory implicit in the ILUOP: rather than map places its people used and occupied, the Gitksan-Wet'suwe'ten Tribal Council prepared maps to show the outlines of the complex of family-based hereditary territories that, together, make up their two Nations. Alongside these maps they also set out the laws and traditions that ensured each such territory was named, managed and passed on from generation to generation. Thus, these maps did not concern themselves with hunting, fishing or gathering areas within each territory, and disregarded the presence of outsiders – be it their farms or towns. When working on a film related to the court case, I was fascinated and indeed very moved by the way in which one Wet'suwet'en elder stood below a mountain of great importance to his territory, giving its name and pointing out his inherited boundaries, disregarding the presence on his mountain of the Smithers ski slopes and, below the mountain, part of the town itself. The elder laid claim to his lands, just as any nation might assert its right to its territory, by virtue of long-established jurisdiction.

Use and Occupancy may have their place in other kinds of evidence of links to those lands, but on this view the underlying assertion of title depended on something else. Indigenous societies tend very much to understand their land and the animals living on it as existing in a web of interactive relationships, with each sector observing and responding to the other. Thus, there are links to animals in dreams, or responses of the land itself to human behavior, and a constant interplay between the success or failure of hunting and the observance of taboos or a careful respect towards all that humans depend on. In this complex way, the land, *nuna*, exists within the sphere of mutual responsiveness. The occupancy of the land, beyond and beneath use, depends on and

expresses this set of fundamental relationships. The management of these relationships speaks to how a territory is occupied and, of even greater potential
importance, how it is managed. This is a link to the nature and importance of
jurisdiction.

When the Delgamuukw Case – so-called because it was framed as a class
action through the name of one of the Gitksan senior hereditary chiefs – came
to trial, extensive oral history evidence was led by the chiefs.[21] The Gitksan-
Wet'suwet'en lawyers insisted that the basis for jurisdiction be established
through the maps of the family territories and the formal narratives, the
Adaox, that explain and affirm each territory. The Judge in the lower court
expressed great impatience with and grave misgivings about this form of testimony. He worried that it might all be subject to hear-say rules of evidence,
and would have to be struck out. In the event, he decided to allow the evidence
to be called and heard in full, reserving his right to rule on its validity later
(and he would indeed rule it to be "inadmissible").[22] This led to confrontations
between the judge and elderly witnesses, most striking when one of them sang
a song that was part of her Adaox – the moment in the trial when the judge
declared that she should not sing because he had "a tin ear" (see Brody 2000:
206-215). But the most intense examination of the First Nation evidence in
the course of the trial (which turned out to be the longest in Canadian legal
history) centered on the maps. Were the boundaries of each of the territories
to be trusted? Were there inconsistencies between different families' maps?
Was this system a reality of the past or a reconstruction to achieve a legal purpose? It was the maps that challenged the Euro-Canadian forms and ideals
of land ownership – they spoke to a very different and, in the context of the
case, a radical challenge to the colonial and settler achievements. Whatever
the fine judgment, however the dispute over jurisdiction might be resolved,
in effect the power of the maps was acknowledged on all sides.[23]

---

21   For the development and unfolding of the Gitksan-Wet'suwet'en claim, pursued in the
     Delgamuukw Case, see Culhane (1997); also see 'Blockade', the remarkable film explo-
     ration of this case, and issues to which it gave rise, made by Nettie Wild, 1994; https://
     vimeo.com/ondemand/thenettiewildcollection (last accessed July 10, 2020).
22   Though this ruling that it was inadmissible on the grounds of being 'hear-say', would
     in due course be overturned by the Supreme Court of Canada in its 1997 final judgment
     on the case.
23   The Supreme Court final ruling accepted that the Gitksan-Wet'suwet'en had unextin-
     guished Aboriginal Title to their lands; but did not specify what these lands encom-
     passed. So the principle but not the geography of the maps was endorsed. Hence

***

In 1996, I was asked to replicate the mapping work in northern Canada for a land claim being launched in South Africa by the ǂKhomani San of the southern Kalahari.[24] This claim was made possible by legislation that Nelson Mandela's African National Congress (ANC) government introduced soon after winning the 1994 election. The ANC had long said that once it secured power and the apartheid era was overthrown, it would ensure that those who had been dispossessed by racist laws would be able to claim that which they had lost – either with a view to its being returned to them or as a basis for compensation for their losses. Among its very first pieces of legislation, therefore, the new government created a Land Claims Office and put in place a process and legal mechanisms by which claims could be made by those who had been thus dispossessed since 1913. The significance of the date is twofold. First, it establishes that legal devices created in 1913 to take land away from black ownership and prevent black acquisition of land were going to be revoked and their consequences redressed. Second, these are claims originating in the legalities (and illegalities) of governance, not in anything like indigenous title. Nonetheless, the human rights lawyer Roger Chennells saw that the new ANC legislation meant that the San who had been evicted from their lands in the 1930s and 1970s by racial laws and racist administration could use the new land claims laws to file a claim. This led to the need to document relationships to those original lands. The ǂKhomani had been forced out of their homes and more or less disappeared from South African history; the challenge was to reverse this injustice and the consequent invisibility of the San; the decision was made to use maps to achieve this. Experience of the Inuit Land Use and Occupancy work was looked to for a possible template, giving a methodological starting point.

So, in 1996, I found myself sitting with a group of ǂKhomani in a small community center and extended family home at the edge of the Welkom township, a few miles from the gates to the Kalahari Gemsbok National Park, a

---

the 2019-2020 intense dispute in Wet'suwet'en territory in relation to a natural gas pipeline (see Boynton 2020).

24   ǂKhomani is a name that appears to have been given to the San of the Southern Kalahari by ethnographers in the 1930s. It does not appear to be a name they had been using to refer to themselves as a group as whole. The term that was most often used by elders when I was working with them was Nǂun/kwe, 'home people'. They are also identified as a group by virtue of their language, N/uu.

spectacular landscape of dunes and dry river beds where the borders of South Africa, Botswana and Namibia converge.[25] Leading members of the Kruiper and Malgas families, both of whom had lived within the park at least until the 1970s, began to draw on a set of topographical map sheets the places they had camped, hunted and travelled before their expulsion. And over the following two years, working in both Welkom and townships as much as 200 km from the Kalahari to which many San had gravitated in their dispossession, it was possible to document multiple and intricate relationships both to lands within the Park and to farms adjacent to it. But these relationships were not as anticipated. People told powerful stories about their lives, and spelled out the ways they had been driven off their lands and, in some narratives, hunted down and violently oppressed.

Figure 3: Oumas /Una and ╪Kabakas showing the area in the southern Kalahari where they had lived as children (Photo: Bill Kemp, 1998)

---

25   First created in the 1930s, the Kalahari Gemsbok National Park has been renamed the Kgalagadi Transfrontier Park. Our research revealed that two evictions had led to a final exclusion of San families from the Park; but also that many other related families, all coming from N/uu speaking heritage, and been dispossessed by Boer and Bastaar farmers from the late 19th through to the mid-20th century.

The focus of these narratives was loss, with memories that came from childhood and even, in some remarkable cases, from a time before the person was born – 'memories' that were spoken as recollection but which came from a passing on of events that was so vivid, or such special significance, or had such urgent reality, that what had happened to a parent became the lived experience of the child who had heard and internalized the story. And beneath or within this absorption of memory into experience there could have been a different concept of time. This sense of the past lived in the present informed much of the work - giving it intensity but also creating historical and conceptual puzzles. The narratives, spoken testimony coming from a profound tradition of oral culture, centered on lived experiences – for example, accounts of life as workers on farms adjacent to ancestral San lands, or being taken as part of the San dance troupe on show at the 1935 Johannesburg Empire Exhibition. But some of them also came from history they had heard. These recollections of history, however, were often told in the first person as if they were memory, or as memories within a San understanding of time, even though they pertained to events that we knew had taken place before the person was born – as, for example, description of the German army chasing down and shooting Nama speaking peoples fleeing the 1908 massacre.

The maps that were made to show these experiences and histories expressed this spread of time and geography, showing life as dispossession, with memories of use and occupancy or jurisdiction as the basis for a claim to an original home within the Park. Evidence on which to base this South African land claim was built with the narratives of diaspora, not accounts of 'traditional' hunting and gathering.[26] In this crucial regard, the southern Kalahari work was unlike both the Inuit and Gitksan-Wet'suwet'en projects. In fact, early in the process, when first sitting with San in front of maps of the lands from which they had been expelled, I realized that the ILUOP form of mapping had to be abandoned in all but a very small number of cases. The ǂKhomani testimony had to be built from narratives and experience of living away from places where they were born or which they looked to as ancestral homelands.

---

26   For extensive examples of these narratives and the background to the southern Kalahari mapping see the DVD: "Tracks Across Sand", directed by Hugh Brody, 2012 (https://store.der.org/tracks-across-sand-p342.aspx, last accessed July 12, 2020). For a summary of the ǂKhomani San land claim see Chennels 2002.

This meant that the people launching and then documenting the claim were drawn into questions about heritage and identity. In the case of both representatives of the South African National Parks view of them and anthropological critiques of San identity, their status as "Bushmen" or "hunter-gatherers" was contested. The "revisionist" strand within the so-called Kalahari Debate sought to deconstruct Kalahari hunter-gatherer self-definitions and putative heritage, urging the view that any such identity was either strategic fiction, self-deception under the influence of tourism and/or old-fashioned anthropologists, and a form of 'essentialism' on the part of either idealizing supporters or politically canny "Bushmen" themselves. The San who launched the southern Kalahari claim were all too aware of these challenges to their right to say they were Bushmen – dealings with officials of the Kalahari Gemsbok Park had included repeated expressions of hostile skepticism about their being anything other than "Coloured" or some sort of deracinated racial mix.[27] I heard aggressive examples of this when meeting with some of those officials in the course of the mapping work. In South Africa at that time, at the end of the Apartheid era, challenges on the basis of race were deeply discomfiting. And there was a troubling congruence between the positions taken by racist opponents of Bushman land claims and the discourse being promoted by anti-essentialist and post-modern strands in anthropology: they joined voices to achieve the dire aim of much colonialism – to drive the San out of their own history. But the narratives of dispossession, alongside linguistic evidence and many explanations of their history, showed that the southern Kalahari claimants were in no doubt themselves about their links to lands from which they had been driven, and a heritage that showed them to be a distinct group of San.

Yet the mapping of ǂKhomani experience and narratives was, in profound ways, unlike the land use and occupancy sets of maps. The extent and long history of dispossession meant that there was a more or less complete disappearance from the actual and metaphorical maps of South Africa; and, flowing from all this, an absence from history and an extensive repudiation of identity. Abandonment of language, along with much that was of distinct cultural importance, was part of almost every family's experience. In the course of the work, many elders spoke with great poignancy about this self-disappearance

---

27   For an anthropological expression of this skepticism see Steven Robins (2001); for a subsequent view of the complexities of the land claim for South African history see Frances/Francis/Akinola (2016).

phenomenon. In a remarkable interview, Ouma /Una Roi spoke of the way in which her people, under the violent pressure of the Boer, whom they worked for and came to depend on, had dug a grave for their language and buried it – anticipating that "when we have a place at the table" the language would be disinterred and given life again. Similarly, marriage between N/uu speakers and other peoples of the area, along with adoption of Khoekhoegowab, the language of the Nama herding peoples of the region, on the part of the families with the most recent links to their former homes and lands inside the National Park, meant that the ǂKhomani faced many complexities in documenting their claim. Mapping this degree and form of loss differs at its core from mapping a hunter-gatherer system that is extant, even if it also often turns to memory to find or set out its heartlands. To map that which is no longer actual, or to represent often uncertain and quite distant memory on maps, is a different kind of challenge.

***

Memory and stories, even at two or more generations remove, are vital parts of many peoples' sense of their heritage and their rights and title to lands and resources. Occupancy had to be mapped to show Inuit relationships to their land; it could be said that it is the combination, indeed, from the Inuit point of view, the inseparability, of occupancy and use that establishes the depth and meaning of those relationships. And the challenge of cultural mapping is, of course, to find ways to document 'culture' in map-like forms at least as much as the representation of the geography of hunting and gathering. Mapping projects need to find a way to include spirituality and myths. The more a society seeks to establish ancestral heritage, with a need to explain and show meaning and values as much as the nature of resources of an economic system, the more it is likely to move from the practicalities, with their routines of everyday practice, towards the representation of custom and ways of life in distinctive, metaphysical forms of narrative. These come with attempts to explain to an alien, skeptical and potentially hostile world things that can be bewildering to outsiders that have long seemed obvious to the people themselves. Methods have to be adjusted and processes adapted to meet the many kinds of experience and expression. This is far from straightforward. Many peoples are, or have become, wary of revealing and sharing their spiritual realities. The forms in which the spiritual is expressed are often centered on performance of ritual in songs, dance and myth narratives. These cannot, and,

[handwritten margin note: What should be made accessible to the public?]

from the point of view of many indigenous elders, should not be turned into public documents. There may be a boundary to map making. But a mapping project can and often should include acknowledgment and explanation of this other reality in the voices and images that a people themselves offer.

All the projects referred to here have one feature in common: in every case the need for maps arose from threats to vital heritage, be it tangible or intangible, lands or belief systems, rights to hunt or ways of speaking. To work with those who face these threats and have endured these kinds of loss is to be at the front line of indigenous peoples' struggles against colonial invasion and, for many of them, dismaying and threatening transformations. For these peoples, at these colonial encounters, to make a map is to give expression to various kinds of vulnerability – there can be deep anxiety about being misunderstood by those who have come to have great power over their lands or lives, or great fear about further losses. These projects have arisen from peoples' determination to mobilize knowledge as a means to resist and win rights to that which they have always supposed was theirs. In this intellectual and political arena, memory itself can enable and become a form of resistance. Those who work on cultural mapping will again and again find themselves at this poignant, vital place. This is work of paramount and enduring importance – for those whose way of life and rights to lands are being represented, but also to everyone. Without recognition of indigenous knowledge and rights to this knowledge, everyone is the poorer, and the land itself – the world – ever more at risk. Cultural mapping is continuing to play an important, perhaps essential, role in this affirmation of knowledge, experience and narratives that we may all depend on.

References

Aodla Freeman, Mini (2015): Life Among the Qadlunaat, University of Manitoba Press.

Boynton, Sean (2020): "Proposed agreement reached between Wet'suwet'en chiefs, gov't ministers after 3 days of talks." In: Global News, March 1, 2020 (https://globalnews.ca/news/6615733/wetsuweten-talks-agreement-reached/, last accessed 10 July, 2020).

Brody, Hugh (2000): The Other Side of Eden. Hunter-Gatherers, Farmers, and the Shaping of the World. London: Faber and Faber.

[handwritten margin note: importance of cultural mapping as tool of political resistance]

Brody, Hugh (2012): 'Tracks Across Sand', 16-segment DVD, (store.der.org › tracks-across-sand-p342).

Brody, Hugh (2018): "Making Arctic Maps" in Tim Dee (ed.), Ground Work: Writings on People and Places, London: Jonathan Cape, pp. 45-53.

Chennels, Roger (2002): "The Khomani San Land Claim." In: Cultural Survival Quarterly Magazine 26/1, March 2002 (https://www.culturalsurvival.or g/publications/cultural-survival-quarterly/khomani-san-land-claim, last accessed June 20, 2020).

Collignon, Beatrice (2006): Knowing Places: Inuinnait, Landscapes and the Environment. Edmonton: Canadian Circumpolar Institute.

Culhane, Dara (1997): The Pleasure of the Crown: Anthropology, Law and First Nations, Vancouver: Talon Books.

Dee, Tim, ed. (2018): Ground Work: Writings on People and Places. London: Jonathan Cape.

Flaherty, Robert J. (1918): "The Belcher Islands of Hudson Bay: Their discovery and exploration". In: The Geographical Review 5/6, p. 440.

Frances, Suzanne/Michael Francis/Adeoye Akinola (2016): "The edge of the periphery: Situating the ǂKhomani San of the Southern Kalahari in the political economy of Southern Africa". In: African Identities 14/4, pp. 370-383.

Freeman, Milton M.R. (2011): "Looking back – and looking ahead – 35 years after the Inuit land use and occupancy project". In: The Canadian Geographer, 55/1, pp. 20-31.

Freeman, Milton, M.R., ed. (1976): The Inuit Land Use and Occupancy Project, Ottawa: Minister of Supply and Services Canada.

Harley, John B./Woodward, David/Lewis, G. Malcolm (1987–): The History of cartography. Chicago: University of Chicago Press.

Harmsen, Hans: "Greenland's Hand-Sized Wooden Maps Were Used for Storytelling, Not Navigation". In: Atlas Obscura, May 2, 2018 (https://www. atlasobscura.com/articles/greenland-wooden-maps-ammassalik, last accessed June 19, 2020).

Lyon, George Francis (1824): The Private Journal. London: J. Murray.

MacDonald, John (1998): The Arctic Sky: Inuit Astronomy, Star Lore, and Legend. Royal Ontario Museum/Nunavut Research Institute.

MacDonald, John (2020): "Our Success has been Small – An Overview of Britain's Quest for a Northwest Passage." Unpublished MS.

Parry, William Edward (1824): Journal of a Second Voyage for the Discovery of a North-West Passage from the Atlantic to the Pacific. London: John Murray.

Robins, Steven (2001): "NGOs, 'Bushmen' and Double Vision: The ‡Khomani San Land Claim and the Cultural Politics of 'Community' and 'Development' in the Kalahari." In: Journal of Southern African Studies 27/4, pp. 833-853.

Usher, Peter (1971): The Bankslanders: Economy and Ecology off a Frontier Trapping Community, 3 Vols. Ottawa: Department of Indian and Northern Development.

Wild, Nettie (1994): "Blockade." (vimeo.com › Cinema Politica › Videos / Nettie Wild Collection).

Woodward, David/Lewis, G. Malcolm (1998): Cartography in the traditional African, American, Arctic, Australian, and Pacific societies, Volume 2.3 of The History of Cartography. Chicago: University of Chicago Press.

Haiǁom in Etosha: Cultural maps and being-in-relations[1]

Ute Dieckmann

Introduction

> Ute: When the people were at the *ǁgarudi* [seasonal water sources] in the winter time, did someone decide then, we have to go back to *tsaub* or *aus* [both permanent water sources] again or did they just see, ok, now the water in the *ǁgarudi* is finished, we will move now?
>
> Kadisen: Yeah.... there are men, who can walk around and look, how looks the world like. They look around, here are the tracks, how are the lion tracks, he looks. Then they [the people] are moving. First, it needs to be looked around.
>
> Willem: Yes, there are the tracks, how many animals were walking there...
>
> (Interview with Kadisen ǁKhumub and Willem Dauxab, 28.1.2001)

The interview excerpt above takes us directly into a cultural mapping project, carried out with the Haiǁom, a (former) hunter-gatherer group, in the Etosha

---

1   The research in Namibia was conducted within the framework of the Collaborative Research Centre 389 *Arid Climate, Adaptation and Cultural Innovation in Africa* funded by the German Research Foundation. Support to the project was also provided by Comic Relief and Open Channels, and to the chapter by the Collaborative Research Centre 806 *Our Way to Europe* and the DFG-AHRC project *Etosha-Kunene-Histories* (www.etosha-kunene-histories.net). Multiple people and organizations helped to make possible the research, among them the Ministry of Environment and Tourism, the National Archives of Namibia, WIMSA and the Legal Assistance Centre. My special thanks go to the people in the Etosha area, who shared their knowledge, wisdom and experience with me, above all Kadisen ǁKhomob, Hans Haneb, Jacob Uibeb, Willem Dauxab, Ticki !Noboses, Tobias Haneb, Axarob ǁOreseb and many others. I am also very grateful to Sian Sullivan, Hugh Brody, Saskia Vermeylen, and Margaret Wickens Pearce for their invaluable comments on earlier drafts of this chapter.

National Park in Namibia[2] around the turn of the millennium, in which I was involved. It serves as a case study in this chapter. The quote tells us that Hai‖om decisions on mobility were not (only) guided by the availability of water but that animal behavior played a major role. Significantly, and I will come back to this at the end of the chapter, reading tracks was of major importance.

I start with a short note on terminology. Maps – if understood as two- or three-dimensional representations of information related to space (with or without a standardized system of geographical reference) – are *per se* cultural, produced by specific humans embedded in specific environments (or 'cultures'); many examples in this volume document this (e.g. the contributions of Sullivan, Brody, Goldman, Pearce and Vermeylen, this volume). Any map whatsoever shows specific information only relevant in specific historical and political contexts. Therefore, it is misleading to only call the maps produced with and by indigenous peoples "cultural maps", as if indigenous maps are a deviation from the standard, implying that the standard is *not* cultural.[3] However, I stick to the term "cultural map" in this chapter for several reasons: first, the term was used in the mapping project which serves as the case study in this chapter; second, several authors in the book use the term too; and third, my critical enquiry starts exactly at this term and the ideas underlying it.

One can assess cultural maps from various perspectives, on different spatial scales and within various time frames. Many issues and side effects have been tackled to varying degrees with regard to specific mapping projects (see Rundstrom 1995; Wainwright and Bryan 2009; Sletto 2009; Roth 2009; Rocheleau 2005; Thom 2009).

My point of departure is inspired by the works of Tim Ingold,[4] Deborah Bird Rose,[5] Nurit Bird-David[6] and by many others who have published on spe-

(margin handwritten note: "politics of 'cultural map'")

---

2   For the sake of simplicity, I will mostly use Etosha when referring to the Etosha National Park or its predecessor, Game Reserve No 2, in this chapter.

3   At times though, the term "cultural maps" is used in a broader sense, referring also to maps depicting the cultural resources of various communities and sources (see e.g. contributions in Duxbury/Garrett-Petts/MacLennan 2015).

4   For example, Ingold 2011, 2011 [2000], 2012, 2016, 2018.

5   For example, Rose 1999, 2002, 2005, 2016, 2018.

6   For example, Bird-David 1999, 2017, 2018.

cific cases of hunter-gatherer ecologies, ontologies and animism;[7] influenced as well by the "ontological turn" and the concepts of "relational ontologies" and "new-animism", as well as by scholars from the fields of critical cartography[8] and the ecological (or environmental) humanities.[9]

I have revisited the outputs and the material gathered within the project and my experience with the Hai||om during the research more than a decade after the project took place.[10] Since many hunter-gatherer groups, including various San groups (cf. Guenther 2020a, 2020b), are described as being endowed with relational ontologies, it is appropriate to explore the Hai||om-Etosha ecology from a relational perspective.[11]

After describing the background of the project, I will critically assess the maps produced in the project. What information was provided and what images were created with these maps? I will then describe and analyze the various relationships of the Hai||om with their environment, with human and non-human entities therein, and explore what insights one might gain regarding their being-in-the-world, in the sense of experiencing, apprehending and acting in the world, as mentioned in the introduction.[12] Finally, I will present some preliminary ideas for mapping Hai||om being-in-relations. Therewith, the chapter aims to open possible paths for future cartographic endeavors.

---

7   For example, Descola 2013; Guenther 2015; Harvey 2015; Viveiros de Castro 2012; Willerslev 2013; Guenther 2020a, 2020b; Sullivan 2017; Sullivan and Hannis 2016; Århem and Sprenger 2016; Astor-Aguilera and Harvey 2019; Harvey 2015; Low 2012, 2007.

8   See, for example, Crampton and Krygier 2005; Crawhall 2009; Dodge 2011; Dodge and Perkins 2015; Glasze 2009; Halder et al. 2018; Rose-Redwood 2015.

9   See, for example, Haraway 2015; Plumwood 2002; Rose, 2013; 2015; Rose et al. 2012.

10   This reassessment was undertaken within the framework of the Collaborative Research Centre 806 at the University of Cologne, funded by the German Research Foundation.

11   It should be noted that a relational perspective is a methodological approach, which is not the same as a relational ontology (as a relational perspective doesn't make any presumptions of the primacy of relations versus the primacy of 'things'). However, a relational perspective might provide more insights into the existence of a relational ontology than an essentialist approach exploring the nature of 'things', as the latter tend to ignore relations.

12   In the Cartesian ontology, this might be described as 'culture', a term which I try to avoid nowadays, it being part of the nature/culture dichotomy.

The mapping project and the maps

Some contextualization

The Hai‖om are commonly referred to as one of the "Bushman" or San groups in Namibia (for a broader discussion on Hai‖om ethnicity in the Namibian context, see Dieckmann 2007) and are estimated to comprise between 7,000 and 18,000 of the 24,550 and 40,050 San inhabitants (Dieckmann et al. 2014: 23).

The Etosha National Park (22,935 km²) is Namibia's "flagship park" (Ministry of Environment and Tourism Namibia, n.d.), the premier tourist attraction and one of the world's largest national parks. Though Etosha is marketed as an African wilderness in the classical sense, the area south of Etosha Pan, where most of the tourist roads run, has long been the home of the Hai‖om, who lived across the whole region of northern-central Namibia in pre-colonial times and at the onset of the colonial period. The German Colonial Administration created the park in 1907 as "Game Reserve No 2". However, initially and for a long time afterwards, the Hai‖om were accepted as residents within the game reserve. With white settlers increasingly occupying the surrounding area, the game reserve became the last refuge where these people were still allowed to practice a hunting and gathering lifestyle. Up until the 1940s, the Hai‖om were regarded as "part and parcel" of the game reserve. All in all, between a few hundred and one thousand Hai‖om lived in the park until 1954, when all of the Hai‖om, with the exception of 12 families who were employed in the park, had to leave (Dieckmann 2001: 137).[13] The increasing interest in tourism was undoubtedly a major factor influencing this decision and the administration acknowledged the potential for nature conservation in this context. Although the game reserve still had a way to go in order to become the Etosha National Park (in 1968), by now, the "national park ideal" (Neumann 2002 [1998]) had emerged as the underlying concept for further development. 'Nature' and 'culture' had to be physically separated. The Hai‖om were not

---

13   During the late 1950s and 1960s, there was no lack of labor in Etosha and some Hai‖om could return to Etosha to work there. However, they had to stay in the staff quarters next to the police stations and tourist camps. Some (male) Hai‖om also lived alone 'in the bush', mostly off the radar of the park administration (see Dieckmann 2007: 199-203).

considered to be 'pure' enough (in the evolutionist paradigm) to count as 'nature', and therefore, 'nature' had to be cleansed of the Hai| |om.

Digging out meaning together: methodology of data gathering[14]

I went to Etosha for various research periods between 2000 and 2006 to explore the history of the Hai||om as part of my PhD research (Dieckmann 2007). In 2001, due to my ongoing research in Etosha, I became involved in a project which was aimed at the creation of cultural maps documenting the historical presence of Hai||om within the area, the representation of a "forgotten past", in order to deconstruct the image of Etosha as an untouched and timeless wilderness. To my knowledge, the project had been initiated by Hugh Brody, the main funding was provided by Comic Relief via Open Channels (both located in the United Kingdom) and the anthropologist James Suzman (Cambridge University) had started explorative field research. Strata 360, a small, independent organization set up in Montreal by Bill Kemp, who played a leading role in cultural mapping in Canada from 1973-2018, was contracted to develop and produce the maps.[15] The Working Group of Indigenous Minorities in Southern Africa (WIMSA), a non-governmental organization working with the San in Southern Africa, had taken an advisory role. During the course of the project, other researchers from various disciplines were temporarily part of the project over the years in manifold ways.[16]

The work, which had started rather informally, involving various individuals and organizations, needed to be formalized in a proper organization and the *Xoms |Omis* Project (Etosha Heritage Project), a community trust under

---

14   During presentations at the Etosha Ecological Institute in Okaukuejo and on other occasions, we introduced, amongst other things, the collected 'data'. Nowadays, I stumble over the term 'data' as it seems to compartmentalize entangled realities and experiences into a specific set of categories, which are supposed to be 'true'.

15   The donors of the Etosha mapping project (Open Channels and Comic Relief, UK) and the mapping company (Strata 360, Canada) had already started a similar mapping and documentation project in South Africa, with San who had lived dispersed and dispossessed for centuries and who had become known as ‡Khomani during court case preparations in the 1990s (see Brody, this volume). In the ‡Khomani project, mapping took place in and adjacent to the Kalahari Gemsbok Park (amalgamated with the Gemsbok National Park in Botswana in 2000 to become the Kgalagadi Transfrontier Park).

16   Harald Sterly, University of Cologne, geographer; Ralf Vogelsang, University of Cologne, archaeologist; Joris Peters, University of Munich, archaeo-zoologist; Barbara Eichhorn, University of Cologne, archaeo-botanist.

the guidance of the Legal Assistance Centre in Windhoek, was established. For various reasons, the main funding was stopped, donors and individuals withdrew and the Hai||om involved and I myself had to look for further small-scale funding opportunities. Over the years, the trust proved not to be sustainable and the main trustees, the Hai||om involved in the project, have passed away.[17]

During the research, we worked mainly with a group of elderly Hai||om men, and particularly with Kadisen ||Khumub (1940–2012), Willem Dauxab (1938–2008), Jacob Uibeb (1935-2006), Jan Tsumib (born in 1945), Hans Haneb (1929–2006), Tobias Haneb (1925–2005) and Axarob ||Oreseb (1940–2007). All of them were born in Etosha at various settlements in different areas and had worked in Etosha and on farms in the vicinity in the years after the eviction of the Hai||om. We got a research permit from the Ministry of Environment and Tourism to work in the Etosha National Park, which allowed us, under specific conditions, to leave the car and to walk around in the park.[18]

We regularly undertook journeys in the park, in order to visit old places of meaning for the Hai||om, to find places which had never been on or had disappeared from official maps and to hear their stories connected to the places. This on-site oral history as a means of "cultural landscape mapping" proved highly successful, as it revitalized knowledges, practices and experiences. The trips offered an opportunity for the Hai||om men to be-in-Etosha again, outside the rest camp (i.e. the staff location next to the rest camp) and outside of the formal working contexts (e.g. the construction and maintenance of roads, drilling and maintenance of boreholes, etc.). Furthermore, we worked

---

17   The project's developments and failures deserve a thorough analysis which goes beyond the scope of this paper. For this paper, it is enough to point out that I saw my role initially as an anthropologist working with the Hai||om and providing the documentation. I was not trained in development studies nor did I have thorough experience in the field of 'development' (i.e. in implementing sustainable livelihood projects or capacity building projects); furthermore, as a German student conducting fieldwork in Namibia, I had just started to build up relevant institutional networks in Namibia. I thought that WIMSA would take over that part of the project, i.e. use the documentation in order to develop projects with the Hai||om, but WIMSA faced serious organizational challenges and changes of staff membership and could not fulfil that role. The donor organization (Open Channels) applied for further funding from Comic Relief, but only got funding for other mapping projects.

18   In the following, I will either refer to them by their first name or by the term "Hai||om core team members", if the information evolved in discussions.

at the research camp at Okaukuejo in the Etosha National Park in order to deepen and revise the documented information. The work in this core team was complemented by interviews with other elderly Hai | | om in and outside of Etosha.

My own perspective on the landscape of the Etosha National Park changed considerably over the period of my fieldwork. Upon my arrival my perception was certainly not very different from common western views of African land-scapes in general and the Etosha area in particular. I saw an arid environment populated with an abundance of wild animals in an essentially bare and rather monotonous landscape, epitomized by the Etosha Pan, a huge salt-pan with-out any vegetation. However, due to my previous historical research in the Namibian National Archives on people categorized as "Bushmen" formerly liv-ing in Etosha, I was already aware that the Hai | | om must have lived rather comfortably within the Etosha area for – at least – some centuries. Driving through Etosha at first, it was hard to imagine how people survived in this landscape, which did not appear to be very hospitable. With the ongoing work and journeys with Hai | | om who remembered having been "part and parcel" of the Etosha landscape, my own perspective on the park changed consider-ably and the "hostile" turned into a more familiar and habitable environment.

However, I was deeply impaired by a rather Cartesian ontology, anthro-pocentric and anthropo-hubristic, embedded in a categorical thinking about objects, considering plant and animal species as 'resources' to be exploited by humans. I was not yet equipped with concepts of relational epistemolo-gies or ontologies, and lacked a fine grasp of persons-beyond-the-human, animism, human-animal transformations or integrated ecologies. The other researchers involved in the project must – by and large – have shared this 'cul-tural-intellectual' heritage; otherwise, *they* would have inquired more deeply into specific issues related to alternative ways of being-in-the-world. By way of excuse, most of the relevant academic discussions in these contexts took place later on.[19]

The shortcomings of the methodology of data collection and archiving were manifold, partly due to technical or logistic issues, partly due to our own (the researchers) thinking-*of*-the-world and acting-*upon*-the-world. Still, during the long period of our interaction and research with Hai||om who had other experiences of being-in-the-world, doors were slightly opened for a widened or alternative understanding, doors which were only fully

---

19   My idea of maps was also rooted in conventional western cartography.

opened when I began to become familiar with recent discussions within relational anthropology and related academic fields (see above), discussions which question our own scientific and philosophical heritage and aim at grasping the world from quite a different perspective.

The collected data

We roughly classified the material according to categories of places, bushfood documentation, social organization and way of life in former times, historical data, kinship data (family trees) and life lines. The information on places and plants was archived in Access Data Sets.

The information included in the Place Access Data Set (with around 180 entries) included original place names, meanings and GPS positions. Furthermore, we asked the core team if the place referred to was a water source (and which type), if it was a hunting or bushfood area, a permanent or temporary settlement (and the estimated number of people living there), or hunting or bushfood camp. The information also included the families (surnames) who lived in the area, the former headman, the bushfood common in the area, as well comments or stories connected to the place. For many of the places visited we also took photos and sometimes made video recordings.

With regard to plants in Etosha, we compiled an Access Data Set with more than 100 Hai||om plant names, the botanical names as far as possible (assisted by a archaeo-botanist and literature), photos, as far as possible (more than 500 digital photos), the uses of the plants (food, medicine, others), the parts that could be used (fruits, wood, bark, tuber and roots, etc.), their availability throughout the year and any further information.

Social organization referred to information regarding settlement patterns, territories, headmen, intra- and intergroup family relations, seasonal mobility in relation to animal movements and bushfood distribution, and access to resources in other areas. Since I came quickly to realize that kinship played a central role in the social organization of the Hai||om, I used the genealogy software *Family Tree Maker* to collect information on kinship and, although not all individuals were known, we ended up with more than 1000 related individuals in the file.

Historical material included archival documents about the history of the Etosha National Park, e.g. monthly and annual reports of the station commanders of Namutoni and Okaukuejo (1920s–1950s), reports of native commissioners, reports of magistrates, reports and correspondence in connection with park policy and Bushmen policy, and oral histories (Dieckmann 2001, 2003).

The cultural maps and other outputs

Within the project, we produced a place name map, a map on Hai||om traditional ways of hunting and distribution of resources, two hunting posters and two bushfood posters, two life line maps (drafts) and two community posters which were not published. After this, the main funding came to an end. Working with the core team, I wrote a tour guide book (Dieckmann 2009) and a children's book (Dieckmann 2012), and we produced some postcards and T-Shirts and a website[20] with other smaller funding from different donors,[21] in order to conserve and promote the 'cultural heritage' of the Hai||om and to raise some income for the project (see https://www.xoms-omis.org/, last accessed July 20, 2020)

It needs to be said that it was not clear how long the funding would last for the project, nor how many maps we could produce with the funding. Furthermore, the maps were *not* developed for the purpose of claiming land[22] but to document the inhabitancy and way of life of the Hai||om in the Etosha area. Therefore, we had more freedom than just documenting Hai||om presence on the Etosha maps. However, we started with products which followed rather general cartographic conventions.

A geographer from the University of Cologne and I worked with Strata 360 in Canada on the development of these maps. We went for a week to Montreal and later continued the work via e-mail correspondence, Skype sessions, etc. We then went back to Etosha to present, discuss and modify the draft maps.

I critically assess the two published maps to illustrate my argument; these were the place name map and the map illustrating hunting and distribution of resources.

---

20   See https://www.xoms-omis.org/ (last accessed June 14, 2020).

21   The German and Finnish Embassies in Namibia, the National Geographic Society, the German Research Foundation, the Legal Assistance Centre in Namibia, EED/Bread for the World and Gesellschaft für Internationale Zusammenarbeit (GIZ) in Germany.

22   Vermeylen and Brody's chapters (this volume) provide examples of cultural maps being used in indigenous land claims. In particular, Vermeylen invites critical reflection on the methodology of mapping and the formalization of maps when used in courts, and on the risk of enforcing a western way of thinking about land and ownership.

Map 1: Hai||om traditional place names of prominent landscape features in the Etosha National Park (Source: Xoms |Omis Project)

Map 1: Hai||om traditional place names of prominent landscape features in the Etosha National Park

The place name map was produced with the aim of revealing the strong connection of the Hai|||om to the land now included in the Etosha National Park.

The base map is a satellite image which presents processed and classified land cover information using a standardized classification system of GIS/ecological analysts, and not a classification system of land cover, based on local knowledge and classifications (see Robbins 2003).[23] It therefore pretends to represent 'nature', onto which 'culture' can be mapped. It is worth mentioning

---

23   Superimposing place names and other 'cultural' features on the satellite image implies the doctrine that satellite images present 'truth' according to a scientific understanding. It does not acknowledge that both scientific and indigenous knowledge systems are different but equal ways of apprehending the world but presupposes a hierarchy, namely that scientific knowledge is 'truer' than indigenous knowledge.

the fact that the satellite image could not have been taken around the first half of the 20th century, the period the maps aimed to refer to, but around 2000. The land cover must have changed tremendously during that period, due to the proclamation of Etosha as a National Park in the 1960s, the erection of game-proof fences around Etosha in 1973 (Berry 1997: 3) and the resulting increase in wildlife in the area.

On the left side of the map is a box with explanatory text on the history of Etosha and the Hai | | om. The text was supposed to provide a summary of the history of Etosha and the connection of the Hai | | om to Etosha. While there might be good reason to provide this kind of background to outsiders/map-viewers, it is worth mentioning that the text was not the (verbal) account of the Hai | | om themselves, but rather the 'official' history, mainly based on archival records, which is presented as 'the history' of Etosha.

The paragraph in the textbox on the place names serves as an explanation from outsiders for outsiders but is not the explanation given by Hai | | om about the significance of place names for them. "The names reveal the close connection of Hai | | om with their natural environment. They give identity to areas important for water, to landscape features such as hills or pans and to important areas of trees or bushes and even to individual trees. To Hai | | om the names brought meaning and order to the vast landscape of Etosha."

For the legend we used icons instead of symbols for the places, divided into the following categories: permanent water, bushes, hills, trees, other places, other (feature, i.e. area) names, and the boundary of the Etosha National Park. The categories were chosen by the researchers and not by the Hai | | om.

On the map itself are around one hundred original place names (some with the official names too) and around fifteen other (area) names. Seven photos of selected places (taken between 2000 and 2003) are also placed on the maps. These photos were chosen by the researchers in order to illustrate that different landscape features were of importance for the Hai | | om. Only for five places was the meaning of the name provided under the respective picture of the place, while in fact the meaning of place names testifies to the manifold connections of plants, people, animals, time, etc. to the land and at times to each other.

Also, we find mainly dots/symbols but no connectors on this map;[24] the only *lines* are either tourist roads or the border of the current national park.[25]

The photos and names of the main Hai||om team members (photos taken and chosen by researchers) are also placed on the maps in order to credit their knowledge and contributions. It might be self-evident that although most of the raw material was provided by these individuals (during interviews, journeys and informal conversations), the processing of the material (in the form of selection, interpretation and integration) was undertaken by the researchers. By silencing this fact on the maps, the maps pretend to be *their* maps and to represent *their* knowledge, whereas in fact, the maps were rather a product of cooperation and an attempt to translate parts of their knowledge for a (western) audience.

Map 2: Hai||om traditional ways of hunting and distribution of resources

This map was developed with the objective of elucidating the ecological system (including people, plants and animals), the impact of plants and animals on people and the human seasonal mobility patterns arising from it.

The use of the term "resources" in the title of the map already implies a certain way of thinking. The term denotes a one-directional relationship between the user (the subject, usually a human person or at least made up of human persons) and the item (object) itself, rather than a mutual relationship. In the present context, the term suggests a human or a community of humans exploiting 'nature'.

The background image chosen for this map presents vegetation zones, because the researchers considered vegetation zones as important for the distribution of resources. However, the classification of the zones follows the ideas of western scientists. It is hard to find relationships between the vegetation zones and the information on resources added on the map. The classification of zones also differs from the Hai||om's way of conceptualizing

---

24   This might also be related to the fact that the Hai||om had not been living in Etosha for some decades before the time of mapping, and (physical) connectors such as paths had disappeared or were not remembered anymore. Still, the detailed kinship knowledge woven into the landscape provides evidence that the interconnectedness between places, people, animals and other beings was still present.

25   Notably, the last change of boundaries took place in 1970 (Berry 1997: 4) and the park became much bigger during the time the map refers to, not only in the west (where the Hai||om had not lived) but in the south as well, an area inhabited by Hai||om and which was cut off from Etosha for white settlement in 1947 (Dieckmann 2007: 76).

Map 2: Hai||om traditional ways of hunting and distribution of resources (Source: Xoms |Omis Project)

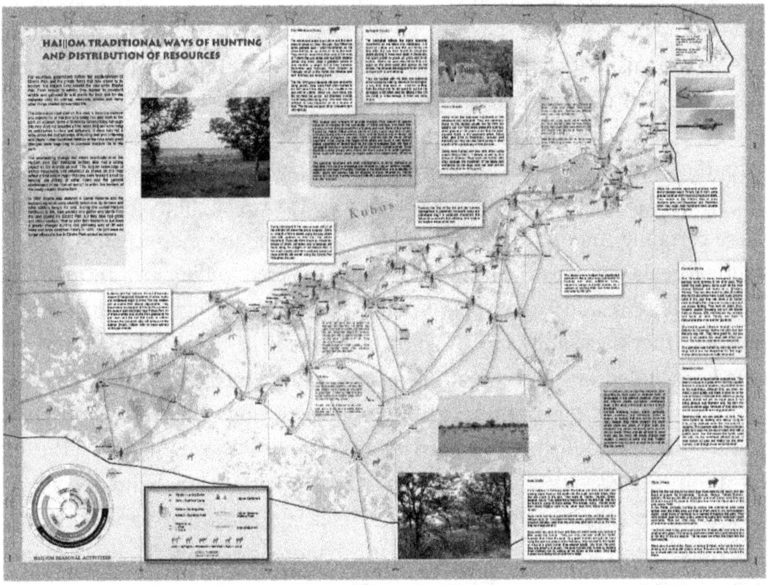

the landscape. The Hai||om would rather differentiate between various soil types (according to color and quality), landmarks (e.g. pans, dry river beds, hills) and dominant or specific vegetation (Widlok 2008: 364).

'Resources' depicted on the map are various prey animal species as well as certain plants, the prey animals being in the focus, with plants only being mentioned without further information, though it becomes clear through the icons for bushfood areas and camps, the graph on seasonal activities and some explanatory text on mobility that seasonal mobility was also influenced by the seasonal occurrence of vegetal resources. Surely, we - the map makers - had a clear bias towards hunting, while vegetable foods were in fact more important than meat in the subsistence of the Hai||om (Peters/Dieckmann/Vogelsang 2009: 157).

[handwritten margin note: trace implications on diet]

The legend explains the icons on the map: hunting and bushfood camps, hunting and bushfood areas, permanent waterholes (on this map differenti- ated between wells and open fountains), six prey animals (zebra, springbok, wildebeest, gemsbok, kudu and eland),[26] settlements, and arrows in different colors for animal migration and Hai||om seasonal walking trails (which do not indicate the actual trails but rather the connections on the map).

There is a box with explanatory text (by the researchers) on the left-hand side of the map. Another box provides information on the seasonal mobility of the animals (with information extracted from interviews with Hai||om, based on their observations, and not from biologists).

Separate boxes provide information about seven prey animals, their distribution, the (nutritional) value of the animal for the Hai||om and the hunting methods. The selection was suggested by the researchers. These animals were certainly important prey animals – among many more (Peters/Dieckmann/Vogelsang 2009) – but they were also selected to illustrate animals living in different landscape types and hunted with different methods. The text suggests that these animals were mostly objects to be exploited. No information is included on taboos or rituals, and no accounts are given about further meanings of the animals for Hai||om, implying other relations than a hunter-prey relationship (see more details below).

In three places, text is provided to illustrate seasonal mobility in connection to plants and animals. We used the names of months in the text. Although the Hai||om have names for months, much more important reference points are the rainy and dry seasons and temperatures (hot and cold).

The map conveys the message that mobility was guided only by the seasonal distribution of 'resources' and followed a rather strict annual pattern, whereas it was, in fact, very flexible, driven not only by subsistence aspects but also social aspects (see below), as well as job opportunities outside the park, etc.

Last remarks for both maps

Although both of these maps are about the Hai||om in Etosha, the Hai||om themselves are absent. Nor are there any depictions of non-Hai||om human beings, nor of non-human beings. Animals are depicted as 'resources', which assigns them 'object' status. These absences can be understood as symptomatic of our need for a conceptual nature-culture (and subject-object) divide, where humans (or beings?) are excluded from nature and are literally

---

26   We did not include an icon for the steenbok, because steenbok were found "everywhere".

above nature, looking down at the map. Furthermore, historical developments are only mentioned in the text, but not reflected in the maps.

Is it overstated to conclude that the maps represent an isolated Hai | | om community, as a group of people dependent only on 'natural resources' and frozen in the past?

Both maps followed the cartographic convention of placing north up and south down. It is noteworthy that the absolute (geocentric) frame of reference of the Hai | | om is based on the rise of the sun (east-west) and on a contingent landscape vocabulary (north-south), with the east-west axis being much stronger (Widlok 2008: 373-74). We did not ask the Hai | | om which way they would prefer.

Moreover, we forged a lateral mode of perception into a vertical mode of representation, a panoptic, global one (borrowing words from Ingold and Casey 1996: 30). The vertical mode presupposes a division between mind and body, while the lateral mode of perception, the organism, moves around from place to place and connects these places as nodes within a wider network of movement (Ingold 2011 [2000]: 227).[27]

Hai | | om being-in-relations

The lions and the Hai | | om, we are both the hunters. And here is no sign for the Hai | | om or the lions. We have to put it in, the lion and the Hai | | om. But the lions and the animals they stay in the bush. The lion knows exactly when the animals move. He is the man of the wind. The lion has to be in front and the Hai | | om behind... On the map we have to put all the hunting animals, like leopard, it has to be on the map. All the hunters. The jackal and the rooicat and the hyena, cheetah, all those who want to eat meat have to be on the map. And the vulture... Eagle. He catches meat as well. And the hare [?]. Those animals catch different animals. That eagle, he catches the hare. Duiker, steenbok, blue buck, Damara dik-dik, dassie, caracal, all those animals, we have to put on the map....and jackal... Perhaps we have to put the snake on the map as well, but the snake is the danger for the men who are hunting, for the lion, for everybody.

(Jan Tsumib, interview excerpt from a group discussion on the draft map *Hai | | om traditional way of hunting and distribution of resources*, 27.3.2003)

---

27   See also Vermeylen (this volume) on the different perspectives.

Evidently, Jan Tsumeb, an elderly Hai||om project participant, when presented with the draft of one particular map, though happy that there was a map, was not unambiguously enthusiastic about it, identifying mostly the omissions on the map.[28] It appears that he did not consider animals exclusively as 'resources' as he complained that only some important prey animals were depicted on the map. Furthermore, he considered it inadequate that the humans, the Hai||om, were not mapped, nor were their "colleagues" (as he called the lions in other contexts). He also remarked the relationships between lions and Hai||om, prey animals and prey, snake and hunters/lions. I would argue that he expresses an eco-zoological perspective in this comment, including both hunters, prey animals and others, and not an objectified resource perspective with resource 'users' excluded from the map.[29]

The omissions which Jan Tsumeb pointed out on one of the draft maps produced within the Etosha cultural mapping project are not at all exhaustive. There are many others, which I realized in retrospect and the following – in a self-reflexive manner – aims to point out the "silence on maps" (Harley and Laxton 2002: 67), to the shortcomings and distortions on the maps when looked at from a relational point of view. I don't think that this specific mapping project is exceptional in this regard, and many of the silences and distortions can be found in other African cultural mapping projects as well.

People-cum-land[30]

In a medium-scale (regional) context, the Hai||om used to group 'clusters' of people (Hai||om) according to the geographical areas they were living in. The people were named after physical characteristics of the land or the occurrence of specific plants important to them.[31] These 'clusters' of people were also

---

28   Admittedly, the final maps didn't include all the missing bits and pieces that Jan Tsumeb pointed out when looking at the draft maps.

29   Certainly, evaluating omissions can only be done with consideration of the purpose of the map and of the mapping project. In our mapping project, the overall objective was the production of cultural maps, to add the 'cultural' level to the Etosha National Park by mapping the cultural heritage of the Hai||om in the park.

30   I adapted this from Widlok who pointed out to a Hai||om "land-cum-people terminology" in which "landscapes and people are … regularly fused with one another" (2008: 366).

31   There were, amongst others, Xomkhoen (the people living south of the Etosha pan, xom.s referring to the Etosha pan), Sēkhoen (the people living south of the riverbed

referred to by missionaries (e.g. Pönninghaus 1926; Unterkötter n.d.), authors and ethnographers (cf. Friedrich 2009: 49; Widlok 1999: 82-85), though not all sources accounted for the same number of groups and exactly the same names. Still, this is an indication that there is continuity of the people-area associations. I don't have information about whether the same family groups were continuously associated with the same areas; Widlok noted that these names are to some degree independent of the demography and composition of the local groups (1999: 84).

People and land/places were connected to each other and personal identities belonged to the land. On a local level, specific family groups were linked to specific areas (as well as to specific other elements, e.g. animals, natural items such as salt or a poisonous plant used for hunting). The family groups living in specific areas (also called "territories")[32] were headed by family elders, who, as with many other hunter-gatherer groups, had to be respected men, sometimes women (called *gaikhoeb* or *gaikhoes*, big/senior man, big/senior woman or *gaob/gaos*, sometimes also called *danakhoeb/danakhoes*, literally head-man/head-woman) who could listen to the people, could mediate in cases of conflict and who were the ones overseeing the sustainable use of resources (in a western way of thinking). In my words, they were the ones who had responsibility (the decision-taking role) for caring for the people, the land and other elements of the ecology. Maybe one could also call them custodians or stewards of the land, a concept which was suggested for the Ju│'hoansi, another San group in Namibia (Low 2007: 80). These men (or women) could also be replaced, if it turned out that they were not fulfilling their duties. Usually a grandson or nephew was chosen by the *gaikhoeb* because of his personal qualities, was taught by him and would take over the role later in life. Furthermore, it was a nested system. For example, a certain man might have been considered the headman of a larger area comprising several settlements, but each settlement might have had a senior respected person as well. At times, the

---

called Omuramba Ovambo), Gogarakhoen, (people from the stony ground – between the Omuramba Ovambo and the town of Tsumeb), │Khomakhoen (the people of the mountains – between the towns of Otavi and Outjo), Khobakhoen (the people of the black ground, referring to parts of the southern Etosha area, e.g. waterholes *Tu!Aris* [Dunaries], │ │*Ai!Ab* [TkaiTkab]) and │Gomaikhoen (the people of the Mangetti trees, referring to the Mangetti area east of Etosha).

32   Just to give a rough idea about the size: Friedrich noted that these areas were more or less 20 km in radius (2009: 77). As can be seen on the map he compiled (Figure 3), there were huge differences in size (2009: 418-419).

headman of the bigger area would assign a certain place or area to another man, e.g. his nephew. At times, the Hai‖om core team members had to discuss who the headman of a specific area was; sometimes they also disagreed. Furthermore, the list of headmen which Friedrich compiled (2009: 420-426) shows differences from our own list of headmen at specific waterholes. This is a further indication that headmanship was a flexible institution, the important criteria being age and respect and that the elder *belonged* to the place, i.e. that he/she *related* to the land and was part of the family group connected to that specific patch of land.

The boundaries of specific areas were, at times, reportedly marked with beacons (e.g. rocks put in trees). They were well known to the Hai‖om in and around that specific area, and specific rules were reported to be in place if someone entered the territory of another group, in cases where specific kinship ties did not ensure immediate access (see next section).[33]

I argue that the existence of these outlined areas is not a proof of *ownership* in a western sense (as a very specific subject-object relationship, implying entitlements such as use, control and sale). It is rather an indication that family groups were tied to specific patches of land and had guardianship for that area, that places and people *belonged/related* to each other. Apart from the living elders, spirit beings and ancestors (‖*gamagu*) also cared for and looked after the land and took responsibility for human behavior towards it.

Putting the boundaries of these areas on a map, as Friedrich did (2009: 418-419, see Figure 3), can be understood as an acknowledgement of the fact that people were spatially organized. However, it is also misleading because it implies an idea of separate groups of people and land entities with fixed boundaries. In contrast, kinship *networks* played a major role in terms of the organization of land and people and of mobility (and crisscrossed these boundaries). People and places were connected with each other via footpaths that form a visible inscription of a network of social relations and of potential movement in the landscape. Moving from one place to another entails the enactment of family relations, which leads to the next section, on intra-Hai‖om relationships.

---

33   The information about these rules, their application and sanctions was at times incoherent, e.g. some Hai‖om claimed that the headman had to be asked permission when a hunter entered the area falling under his responsibility in order to hunt, while others claimed that a hunter killing in another area had to leave a piece of the meat or a poisoned arrowhead with that family elder.

Figure 3: "Gebietskarte" (Source: Friedrich 2009: 418-419)

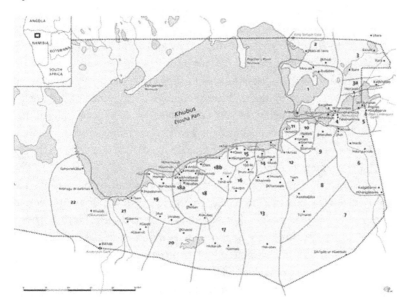

People-cum-people, intra-Hai||om relationships

Since surnames were often mentioned during conversations about/at places, when we worked more systematically on the place data set, we started to ask specifically for the *surnames* of the people who once lived at a specific place or in a specific area. We always got at least a handful of surnames for the places.

It is important to note in this context that in former times, the surname was passed on by cross-descent, from father to daughter and mother to son (this has changed with identification documents and official marriages, which confuses the system, because they were, at least in the past, not implemented consistently, and only gradually).[34] Surnames do play an important role for the social organization of Hai||om (see Widlok 1999: 194-197).

---

34   Jan Tsumeb, for instance, should – according to the traditional naming system – be Jan !Aib, because his mother was Christa !Ais. Public officers, not concerned with the traditional system, have transformed him to Jan Tsumeb. The same is true for Kadisen ||Khumub, who should actually be Kadisen |Nuaiseb, since his mother was |Nuaises.

categorical v. relational approaches

In retrospect, I think that we attempted to figure out the people/land units mentioned above. Trying to link surnames with specific areas/places followed a categorical conceptualization (sorting people and places together) rather than a relational approach. Not surprisingly, considering the naming system of the Hai||om, the same surnames were mentioned at various places and the surnames on their own did not provide sufficient and adequate information about socio-ecological organization. In order to reduce my own confusion, I fell back on the traditional ethnographic method of documenting kinship relations, using the software *Family Tree Maker*, as I realized that the Hai||om used to explain the *who-is-who* in terms of family relations. During this exercise the vastness of their kinship knowledge was revealed, not as much in generational depth but in width.[35]

Kinship plays a pivotal role in the social organization of the Hai||om (see also Widlok 1999: 179-193). The picture emerging throughout the whole period of research was that the vast kinship knowledge of the Hai||om is woven into the landscape; surnames do form a relevant and organizing part of this knowledge and they are, without doubt, connected to places but the kinship networks are also engrained in the landscape.[36] Both elements are crucial for an understanding not only of the social but also of the spatial organization of the Hai||om.

One example is used to illustrate this point. The numbers in brackets after the place names mentioned relate to the numbered areas on Friedrich's map (2009: 418-19, see Figure 3).

It refers to Willem Dauxab (in the Hai||om system, he should be Willem ||Gamgaebeb, because his mother was |Noagus||Gamgaebes). His father was Fritz Dauxab, who was from the *!Harib* area. Fritz had three different wives during his lifetime, originating from different areas: Aia ||Gamgaebes was born at *Tsînab* (18b), her sister |Noagus ||Gamgaebes was born at *!Gabi!Goab* (the old location at ‡*Huiob*, Okaukuejo) (22), and Anna ||Khumus was from ||*Nububes* (18). Fritz reportedly had at least nine children. Aia

---

and Fritz had six children born at *Tsînab* (18b), ||*Nububes* (18) and ‡*Huiob* (22). |Noagus and Fritz had one child, Willem, born at *Tsînab* (18b), who grew up with his stepfather Petrus !Khariseb, who was from the area of *Kevis* (most probably ‡*Kharikebes* (4) on Friedrich's map). Anna and Fritz had three children, born at ||*Nububes* (18) and ‡*Huiob* (22). Aia and |Noagus also had two brothers (or cross-cousins), with the surname !Noboseb (since their mother was a !Noboses). The brothers lived at ‡*Homob* (19). It is noteworthy that the father of |Noagus and Aia ||Gamgaebes also had three different wives during his lifetime and around ten children born in different areas.

An interview with Willem Dauxab recorded in Okaukuejo (September 20, 2001) is illuminating concerning the meaning of kinship with regard to mobility.

Willem was born at *Tsînab* (18b), where he stayed at times as a child with his mother |Noagus and stepfather Elias. I could not figure out whether he stayed there throughout most of the year during his childhood, but certainly, he considered it and the area around it as "our place". At times, they went to the area of *Namutoni* (4), where a sister of his stepfather Elias was staying and where Elias was from (it is close to *Kevis*, 4) and stayed there for a couple of months, at times during the rainy season, because there were a lot of ‡*huin* trees (*Berchemia discolour*) in that area (the berries of ‡*huin* could be collected and stored for a couple of months). *Tsînab* was also known for a lot of bushfood, both corms (e.g. *!handi*) and fruits and berries (e.g. *Grewia* sp.).

He said: "Every year, we went here and there, visit each other, there, ‡*Axab* (14), *!Nobib* (10), |*Ui!Goarebeb* (10), ||*Harubes* (9), *!Goas* (16), |*Uniams* (16), ‡*Uniseb* (10), *!Gûiseb* (4) , those were the places where we visited each other." I could not figure out the exact family relationships which he had to all these places.

He noted that ‡*Homob* (19) was also "their place", because the brother of his mother (Jan !Noboseb) and another brother (or cross-cousin) stayed there. He also explained the exact kin relations of Jan !Noboseb to another Hai||om woman I knew in Outjo, a town around 120 km south of Etosha.

Willem and his mother and stepfather from *Tsînab* (18b) used to stay at ‡*Homob* (19) at times as well, because Willem's mother's brother was living there. Note that his father Fritz also lived at ‡*Homob* (but in another settlement). Families with the surnames |Haudum and ‡Gaesen also lived in that area around ‡*Homob* (19), |*Aus* (19) and ‡*Gaseb* (21) and ‡*Huiob* (22) Apparently, the main settlement was at ⸰*Homob*, but "when they liked to, they went to

|Aus, when they liked to they went to ‡Gaseb. That is how they were moving around", and they also went to ‡Huiob.

Willem and his mother (||Gambaebes) only stayed with the mother's brother (!Noboseb) at ‡Homob, but did not move with the family group to the other places. Only one year, when there was a lot of rain (and mosquitoes), they also stayed around |Aus. Willem also related that there was a place of a man with the surname ||Gamgaebeb (implying "his" own family network), close to Otavi (a town east of the park nowadays, around 120 km away from ‡Homob), which he mentioned as another "place of ours", but he hadn't been there, "it was the place of the old people" (most probably referring to a time when mobility was less restricted, before the fencing of farms and the park).

In wintertime, the men living at Tsînab also went to |Goses (in the same area as Tsînab (18b), written as |Oses on the map) close to the pan, to hunt there and to make biltong. Willem mentioned many places close to the pan (e.g. |Ani Us, Gaikhoetsaub (both 18a), ‡Kharitsaub (18b)) where the men from Tsînab went hunting (while staying at |Goses), and several other places (wells, plains, etc., e.g. Bukas, Tsînab‡gas, not on map (18b)) where the hunters from Tsînab used to hunt during other seasons. The men also went hunting to places in other families' areas but had to ask permission from the elders living in these areas.

When they felt like getting uinan (Cyanella sp.), at the right time of the year, they went to the ||Nububes area (18), which included Kokobes, which was known as a good place for collecting uinan. Presumably they had to ask the elders there for permission as well.

Evidently, textual representation of these family relationships is highly inadequate for us to comprehend the network arising from kindship ties. However, the description above (in contrast to the map) is essential to illustrate how misleading "territorial" maps can be in the case of hunter-gatherers.

In sum, kinship ties imply spatial connections and guide movements. They literally do establish *common ground*. Obviously, areas from which parents (including stepparents) originated were regarded as "our" place, which meant that one could go and stay there for some time. One could stay at the places of one's parents' parallel siblings. In areas where close kinship of this kind could not be established as easily, one would need to show respect for the fact that one had entered someone else's land (e.g. in terms of asking permission or giving some of the game killed to the elders there), or, in other words, one first needed to establish a relationship to the inhabitants. The example also shows that the areas considered as "our place" could be located at some distance from each other, which meant that one needed to traverse other people's areas.

People and other humans, extra-Hai||om relationships[37]

The relationships of indigenous groups with 'outsiders'[38] are often silenced on indigenous maps; indeed, they are often the underlying reason for the mapping, e.g. when logging or mining companies enter the area, or protected areas are proclaimed (e.g. Brody 1981; Lewis 2012; Hodgson/Schroeder 2002), but these relationships are mostly excluded from maps.

In precolonial times, the Hai||om did not live in isolation but were in contact and sometimes in continuous relationships with other humans and other human communities. Some of the contacts were more restricted to a certain period, while others were maintained for a longer period of time. Some were more violent, while others were quite peaceful. A comprehensive overview is not within the scope of this chapter (some information can be found in Dieckmann 2007), but I will provide some examples of relationships related to places within Etosha.[39]

---

37 Noteworthy, some KhoeSan ethnonyms could be translated as people or real people (e.g. Khwe, Ju|'hoansi) but Hai||om means tree sleepers. However, the Hai||om team members also mentioned (with some amusement) that in the past, Ovambo, Damara or Herero were not considered as people, but rather as 'things' (see also Widlok 2017: 3).

38 My own observations and also Widlok's writings (e.g. 1999: 179-212) suggest that Hai||om's comprehension of kinship would allow 'outsiders' to be integrated in the kinship system, not only through marriage but also due to other relations with the individual. Unfortunately, I did not explore thoroughly the process of kin-making. Widlok wrote: "The practices of naming and social reference... suggest that Hai||om actively foster certain kin ties... In actual practice kinship and names are used in an open process that has several possible potentials which develop as the participants interact with each other." (1999: 212)

39 I include some historical information, which is not immediate part of the Hai||om knowledge (especially concerning dates or time periods), drawn from archival records, other publications, the 'official history', in order to provide a framework for 'outsiders' for the Hai||om accounts. The references for their historical understanding are not dates, and not exactly political periods (an exception is the time after Namibian's independence in 1990), like pre-colonial times, the German colonial period or the South African period, but rather generations (referring to grandparents' or parents' accounts).

ǂ*Khari Kevis* (Klein Okevi) was a Hai||om settlement within Etosha. The grave of Fritz !Naob, who died in 1945, is situated there (see also Friedrich 2009: 60-62). In archival documents of the 1930s, a man with the name Fritz Aribib was often mentioned as one of the Hai||om leaders. When asked about this man, the Hai||om core team members stated that Fritz Aribib must have been Fritz !Naob (named after his mother) who worked for the police at Tsumeb (a town east of Etosha) and who lived at ǂ*Khari Kevis* at the end of his life. He was a respected person, had some livestock and negotiated with the government. His father was "Captain Aribib" (as recorded in archival documents), a Hai||om man with whom the German colonial government concluded a so-called "protection treaty" (Gordon 1989: 145; Friedrich 2009: 53-62; Dieckmann 2007: 65-67). From a Hai||om perspective, certainly, Aribib could not have signed such a contract because it contravened the Hai||om social system, according to which respected elderly men or women only had responsibility in the small areas and in the family groups they were closely connected to, and a hierarchical leadership structure beyond this level was non-existent.

A place, or rather a tree, between *Bikab* and Okaukuejo testifies to the employment of Hai||om with the police and could be an anchor from which to relate stories on their relationships with white officers (as could many other places). *Augubdi/naras* (the "umbrella thorn of August") was explained to us in the following manner: It was the *Acacia tortilis* (|Naras: *Acacia tortilis subsp. Heteracantha*) of August ||Khumub, one husband of Magdalena ||Khumus, he was the father of Adam, and he worked for the police, he was riding a horse and used to rest in the shade of this tree. Many Hai||om men worked for a while as policemen for the Germans, as archival records testify (see Dieckmann 2007: 156, for more details).

Namutoni could also provide testimony to Hai||om-German relationships. Hans Haneb told us the following, when we had climbed Fort Namutoni, about the beginning of the German-Herero war in 1904, when Chief Nehale had sent his captain Shivute with 500 armed men to Namutoni and attacked the fortress. In an official version, seven Germans tried to defend the fortress but later fled to Tsumeb (Mossolow 1993). According to Hans Haneb, a Hai||om man (in Hans's version the brother of his grandfather), who was proficient in shooting, was issued with a rifle and ammunition and was defending the fortress with the Germans. Friedrich (2009: 191) was told the story slightly differently, by the son of the daughter of daughter's son of this person.

Several place names give hints at the relationship with other groups (e.g. Ovambo or Herero) or evoke memories about these relationships.

Hai||om in Etosha also engaged in relationships to tourists over a specific period of time (starting in the 1930s and gradually increasing until the 1950s). Kadisen ||Khumub, born at //Nasoneb, related that his family group usually stayed in the area during the winter months, as it was situated closer to the pan than //Nububes, the larger settlement in the territory of that particular family group. When asked why the Hai||om moved closer to the pan in the winter, Kadisen stressed that besides the fact that it was the best time to hunt at the pan, it was also the time when the tourists were coming to Etosha, i.e. to some of the waterholes close to the main Okaukuejo–Namutoni road.

People and beings-beyond-the human

A systematic study on Hai||om ontologies and Hai||om relations to beings-beyond-the-human is still outstanding. Low (e.g. Low 2012, 2007, 2009, 2015), who mainly worked on KhoeSan healing, and Guenther, who worked on San cosmologies (e.g. Guenther 1999, 2015, 2020a, 2020b), mention the Hai||om occasionally. Hints are also found in Widlok's publications (e.g. Widlok 1999, 2008, 2017). Evidently, Hai||om ontology (or ontologies?) shares some features with the ontologies of other KhoeSan in the region (for the latter, see e.g. Guenther 2020a, 2020b; Sullivan 2017). During the fieldwork for my PhD and the mapping project, my focus was different and I will merely provide some snapshots and fragments in this regard, which illustrate the particularity of western ontology (e.g. categories like humans, animals, natural and supernatural). Although there might be many other beings-beyond-the-human, I focus on only two here, namely animals and spirit beings (though the latter include various beings and are only lumped together as spirit beings for the lack of a better term/conceptualization).

People and Animals

The Hai||om distinguish between *xamanîn* and *am/naen*. *Xamanî* animals comprise most medium to large carnivore species; the term was explained as referring to animals who look evil and bite.[40] *Am/naen* refer to bigger non-carnivorous animals (such as eland, giraffe, gemsbok, greater kudu,

---

40   According to the Khoekhoegowab dictionary, it means "wild animals (esp. dangerous, including poisonous animals)" (Haacke/Eiseb 2002: 151).

blue wildebeest, hartebeest and Burchell's zebra)[41]. A specific ritual (/hâson) carried out when hunting am/naen is worth mentioning because it hints at the idea that animals are not mere resources. When the hunter(s) found the animal he had killed, he had to cut an incision into the animal's auricles at the base so that the ears could be folded downward to cover its eyes. Then the blood vessel beneath the eye would be slit to let out some blood, the upper tip of the bow was dipped into the blood and a vertical line drawn on the hunter's forehead. Then the lower tip of the bow had to be dipped into the blood as well, and used to draw a horizontal line across the chest and a vertical line on each of the lower legs (Peters/Dieckmann/Vogelsang 2009: 132-133). This ritual could be understood through various frameworks: in the context of animists' meat-eating dilemma (for a discussion see Guenther 2020b: 28-41) one could think that although the dilemma of eating other beings is not resolved, /hâson could be understood as an attempt to make the act of slaughtering and eating less cruel for the animal in preventing it from seeing it. Alternatively, one could explain it in view of the concept of "personhood": if seeing-each-other establishes "persons", the ritual terminated the other's personhood by preventing the two parties from seeing-each-other.

As for other San and African hunter-gatherer groups (e.g. Guenther 2020a; Skaanes 2017), the eland held a special position and the ritual to be carried out when an eland was killed was even more sophisticated than /hâson (see Peters/Dieckmann/Vogelsang 2009: 133).

Among the xamanîn, two "families" were distinguished, one comprising /noeb (cheetah), /noab (serval), ╪huinab (leopard), !nores (genet), /gîb (aardwolf), /hoab (African wildcat), //ab (bat-eared fox), //khom (pangoline), !hab (caracal), /noreaib (honey badger). These were usually hunted and eaten. The other "family" comprised the lion (xam), the spotted hyena (haibeb) and the brown hyena (//abub), who were considered khoe-xamanîn, human xamanîn. According to the Hai||om team members, the meat of hyenas was only consumed in times of food shortages.

The relationship with lions deserves special attention, as the above quote of Jan Tsumeb indicates. Lions were considered as colleagues and equals.

The Hai||om team members reported that Hai||om usually chased lions away with a piece of burning wood. However, when a lion was approaching (and no fire was around), they would shout at the lion: "//Gaisi ainâkarasa!",

---

41   It means in Hai||om "game (springbok and larger, excluding bird & fish)" (Haacke/Eiseb 2002: 9).

which they translated to us as: "You ugly face, go away!" Apparently, this did not always work and there are many stories about Hai||om-lion encounters, often (but not always) with a happy ending, i.e. that the Hai||om eventually managed to escape a lion's attack (see e.g. Dieckmann 2012: 44-47).

It is noteworthy that one of the spirit beings (||gamagu)[42] of the Hai||om (see more below) is a *xam||gamab* (a lion spirit), which can pass its spirit to specific people who can then become healers/shamans. The Hai||om team members explained the process in the following way: The lion spirit starts to like/love (or fall in love with) a person; they would be playing around in the bush and the lion would become a mate of the person, who would, caught by the spirit of the lion, disappear for several evenings in the bush. He would need the treatment of another *!gaiob* (healer/shaman), otherwise he would disappear altogether with the lion(s). With the treatment, he could become a healer himself. It was also said that the lion healer (*xam!gaiob*) received lion hair from the lion spirit.

Lion meat was usually not eaten at all. Only one family with the surname ||Oresen had the reputation of consuming lion meat (Peters/Dieckmann/Vogelsang 2009: 116, 118). One story recounts that a man with that surname had once killed a lion, prepared the meat and eaten some at the settlement next to the waterhole ||*Nububes*. What remained of the lion had to be buried, and all the people in the settlement were called by ||Oreseb to attend the burial, roaring like lions (Dieckmann 2009: 33). Evidently, the killed lion was treated like a fellow and the Hai||om performed a kind of mimicry, behaving like lions.

Other food taboos existed as well, e.g. concerning several birds, the secretary bird (*khoeseb*), the fork-tailed drongo (||*gauseb*), and rollers (*oo-oo||nâes*). The pied crow (*!kha-nub*) was a protected bird as well, because according to Hai||om tales, it brought back the rain after it was taken away from them by the animal "married to the rain", meaning the elephant (Dieckmann 2012: 12-13; Peters/Dieckmann/Vogelsang 2009: 118-119). The explanations regarding the food taboos indicate that these beings were not eaten, either because

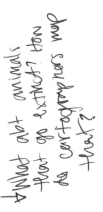

[handwritten margin note: What abt animals that go extinct? How do cartographers map that?]

---

42   I use the translation "spirit being" for ||*gamab*, due to the lack of a better translation. I don't want to use the word "supernatural being", as this would presuppose and reinforce a dichotomy of natural versus supernatural, a dichotomy which is – according to my understanding – non-existent in the Hai||om experience. For similar reasons, I try to avoid the term "mythical" (see also Bird-David 2017: 153, for the problem with terminology). However, "spirit being" also implies a division between the material and nonmaterial world and might therefore be inadequate too.

they were similar to humans (like the lion or the secretary bird), or because of what Rose calls "communicative benefits" (Rose 2005: 297), as in the case of the drongo and the roller, or other benefits, as with the crow. The latter case further indicates that there is no clear-cut distinction between the world of myth or legend and the 'natural' world. Compare it to the fox in Europe: many tales describe the fox as almost human, but this doesn't protect him from being hunted, whereas the crow, who brings back the rain, according to tales, is protected in the Hai||om environment.

Snakes, their meaning for and relations to humans would also deserve further exploration. I didn't collect enough material to be able to analyze their significance in the Hai||om environment, but snakes were mentioned in various contexts and at various places. It was reported that every big water had a water snake. Being alive, the snake would not trouble the people but when the snake died or was killed (as in the case of the waterhole *Bikab*), the water dried up. Furthermore, some stories related 'mythical' snakes; I term them 'mythical' because I could not imagine them, as there were reports about huge snakes, almost the width of a road. The existence of "Great Snakes" was reported for other KhoeSan groups as well, as was the occurrence of "water snakes" (e.g. Sullivan/Low 2014; Hoff 1997).

Furthermore, according to our team members, snake spirits are among the different *||gamagu*, the spirit beings which populate the world of the Hai||om and which can transfer their potency or spirit to healers/shamans.

Another aspect of human-animal relations is the potential of transformation, reported for other KhoeSan groups as well, where people have experienced changing into lions or leopards, jackals or little birds (Low 2007: 80). These transformations are linked to the possession of the "wind of an animal". Low explains: "The notion of possession and movement of form and qualities between organisms is an expression of how wind moves through and anchors within a body." (Low 2007: 80)

Although I did not explore the topic systematically, the possibility of transformation was mentioned when we passed a hill called */Khai/Khab* ("naked surface"). The hill was said to be haunted, and the Hai||om would avoid going there, because you could turn into a kudu at that place and when people came looking for you, they would just find a kudu.

And what about mapping? Some of the information provided above is clearly linked to places, e.g. the snake at the waterhole *Bikab*, the funeral of the lion, various lion encounters and the haunted hill. Other information could easily be connected to places (as it was often narrated at specific places), e.g. specific rituals or food taboos for the areas where the animals usually occur.

Importantly, some Hai||om families kept livestock within Etosha, mostly goats, but also cattle and donkeys (Dieckmann 2007: 154, 187; Peters/Dieckmann/Vogelsang 2009: 112). Their numbers were at times and at specific settlements considerable (e.g. in 1939, around 98 cattle, 4 donkeys and 204 goats were reported to have lived in the vicinity of Namutoni (Dieckmann 2007: 154). Dogs were also kept and used for hunting (Peters/Dieckmann/Vogelsang 2009: 162). None of these appeared on the maps.[43]

People and *||gamagu* (spirit beings, non-material beings, non-corporeal beings)[44]

I cannot provide a coherent picture of the relationships of humans to *||gamagu* (spirit beings), and maybe a coherent picture would in any case be but my own imagination. As I understand it, spirit beings seem to be (or were in the recent past) an integral part of the ecology, although it is said that they usually stay in *||gama||aes*, a place "up there".[45]

||Gamagu could do good but could also do harm, they could be moral guardians supervising the following of taboo rules (*sōxa*).

As mentioned beforehand, there are different *||gamagu*. The strongest one is the spirit of the rain (*/nanus*) (see also Sullivan/Low 2014: 232). Furthermore, there is a spirit of the lion (*xam||gamab*), the spirit of snakes (either *||gau!gub* "big snake" or *||gam/aob* "water snake") (see also Sullivan and Low 2014; Hoff 1997), and the spirit being of *Kaindaus* (see also Schatz 1993: 8; Wagner-Robertz

---

43   Widlok reports, from a free listing exercise with ‡Akhoe Hai||om east of Etosha, that livestock was generally not included in the *xamanin* category, which he translates as "animals" (Widlok 2017: 2). Still, whether or not they are regarded as "animals", they formed part and parcel of the Etosha ecology at that time.

44   Others report on only one *||gamab*, sometimes translating it as "god", (e.g. Wagner-Robertz 1977; Low 2012). However, our Hai||om core team members described several *||gamagu*. They have another single deity, which is called *Elof* or *!Khūb*. The Hai||om could directly address *||gamab* but not *Elof* or *!Khūb*. The relationships between *||gamagu* and *Elof* or *!Khūb* were not explained in detail. In general, adequate translations of a number of terms in this context are not possible due to the lack of comparable concepts. I am not content with the translation of "spirit being", but lack a better term.

45   The whirlwind is called *||gamasares* ("whirlwind of *||gamab*") because the *||gamab* is in the dust of this wind.

(margin note: lowk Slay)

1977: 7-8). The latter, termed a "ghost woman" by Low (2012: 84), was described to me as a malicious female being who would fall in love with and rape a man.

Besides these spirit beings, other-than-human beings, the spirits or souls of specific ancestors (also called //gamagu), are also around and stories about their misbehavior are abundant.[46]

Each //gamab has and provides different potency/spirit/wind (/gais) to a person. These can be transferred through (traumatic) events, where the person encounters the spirit being (or its agent). For example, a person can get the rain spirit from a lightning strike (see also Low 2007: 81), can get the spirit of the "ghost woman" Kaindaos by being raped by her (see also Wagner-Robertz 1977: 8), or the lion spirit from an encounter with a specific lion (or xam//gamab in the form of a lion).

Low captures /gais in the following way:

> The word /gais is used predominantly in north central Namibia but has deep roots in KhoeSan healing [...] The idea of having /gais overlaps with ideas of having spirits or winds. At a more everyday level it equates to having different talents or gifts to do or be something including, for example, an ability to dance or sing or an ability to heal using a particular animal's strengths. People know they have a particular /gais either because it is inherited, formally given to them by a healer, or it is divinely given through an event, such as being struck by lightning or a strange encounter with an animal which they recognise as meaningful at the time, or to which they later attribute changes they have noticed in themselves. People feel their /gais, or hear it or see it manifest in a particular skill they seem to have, such as hunting a particular animal. The idea of /gais sits within wider understandings of what constitutes a person. The meteorological conditions at a person's birth, for example, give people a relationship and a measure of influence on particular types of weather. (Low 2012: 78)

When a person gets the spirit/wind (/gais), he/she is reported to become crazy first, singing and running around in the bush, and would need to be treated by

---

46   Wagner-Robertz, whose description is based on the account of an elderly Hai//om healer, /Garagu //Khumob, reports only one //gamab, who lives in a settlement between the earth and the sky (presumably //gama //aes) with a snake, a leopard, Kaindaos, the souls of the dead, etc. (1977: 17-18). In both versions, i.e. one //gamab or several //gamagu, these beings (snake, ancestors, Kaindaos, etc.) are agents, carrying specific spirits/winds which can be transferred to human beings.

a *!gaiob* (healer/shaman) in order to become a *!gaiob* him/herself. *|Gais* enables the healer/shaman to communicate with the *||gamab*.

Depending on the specific *||gamab*, the *|gais* can be embodied in different forms, e.g. in the form of sticks, cochlea (rain) or lion hair (lion). These embodiments are put in a bag, which is essential during the healing ceremonies.[47] They can or are usually joined together with beads into kind of a necklace.

||Gamagu could also become or take the form of animals, which are usually hunted and consumed, e.g. iguana, but also antelopes, such as hartebeest, damara, dik diks or steenboks. If a hunted animal behaves in an unfamiliar or 'un-species-like' way, it might be a *||gamagu* and therefore should be avoided instead of being further processed and consumed (see also Peters/ Dieckmann/Vogelsang 2009: 132). However, *||gamagu* might not only take the form of animals; they could also ride animals (e.g. elephants, such as on the occasion of the spirit of a certain man with the surname Subeb, who had not behaved well while alive as human being, see Dieckmann 2012: 57).

Through their connection to *||gamab*, *!gaiogu* (shamans/healers) have a wide array of skills/tasks; they can, for instance, heal diseases, they treat bad luck in hunting, they help women during childbirth, and they bring rain (see also Wagner-Robertz 1977: 9-14).

During the healing/trance dance, the *!gaiob* (shaman/healer) can communicate and negotiate with the *||gamab*. Widlok has described the basic structure of these dance events in more detail (Widlok 1999: 240-41). In the present context, I only want to note that reportedly, during healing dances, the *!gaiob* takes or sucks the disease out of the patient, inspects it, shows it (a substance/object) to the other dance participants and puts it into his bag, inside which it will be destroyed (see also Widlok 1999: 241).

Relationships to spirit-beings might be the most difficult to map, at least from my current understanding, though some of the information has clear reference to space, because the information was extracted from narratives referring to particular events at specific places, e.g. being raped by Kaindaos, being stuck by lightning, or ancestors riding animals.

---

47   Low reported that *|gais* "are believed to live in particular key areas of the body, including the chest, solar plexus, and the temples and centre of the forehead" (2007: 81), but from the information I got, *|gais* are in the bag and can also get children into the bag. Kadisen ||Khumub, the son of a healer, also showed me the bag of his father. Wagner-Robertz also mentions containers ["Behälter"] for these embodiments (1977: 7).

As with the embodiments of the |gais (spirits/winds), my western back-ground did not immediately provide me with an adequate explanatory frame-work to understand what is going on. During my field research, I was al-ready struggling to make sense of more tangible issues, like historical devel-opments, bushfood, seasonal mobility, etc., and left aside those issues which westerners would easily classify as belonging to religion or the supernatural world. I mostly left them aside in academic publications too (and in the maps, see below), acknowledging that I lacked a proper understanding. However, equipped with ideas about relational ontologies, inspired by "new animism" etc., in the following, I do attempt to approach the material from a new angle; my view on the matter, however, is explorative and tentative.

Hai‖om being-in-the-world: A first attempt to understand

Although there are still many loose ends in my effort to figure out what it means for the Hai‖om to be-in-the-world,[48] I argue that the relational per-spective, as employed above, is a promising step to be further explored. I suggest that certain keys for understanding Hai‖om-being-in-the-world can be found in conceptualizations and experiences of relations and transforma-tions.

It is obvious from the above descriptions that Hai‖om in Etosha enter-tained a variety of relations with land, Hai‖om, other humans and beings-beyond-the-human and that these relations were constitutive of their being.

Land and kinship are intertwined and inseparable. Relationships to space established identities, as did relationships to people. Relationships to space and to other Hai‖om were important criteria for 'headmanship'. Relation-ships to animals revealed that animals were not merely seen as resources, as 'objects', but that they were or could be beings or persons (as indicated by cer-tain rituals) or that they could carry or *be* specific spirit beings. Relationships to spirit beings could transform a 'common' Hai‖om into a shaman/healer.[49]

---

48   I am aware of this generalization, but don't have a better solution for now.

49   Willerslev has noted: "[I]ndigenous peoples, like the Yukaghirs [a small community of indigenous hunters in the Siberian north], do not bequeath all things personhood all the time. If personhood is not an inherent property of people and things, but is rather constituted in and through the relationships into which they enter, then personhood is to be seen as a potentiality of their being-in-the-world, which might or might not be realized as a result of their position within a relational field of activity [...]. An animal, therefore, can be just that, or it can be a subject-person with a mind of its own. The re-

Furthermore, looking through the lens of a relational ontology, as a frame-work where relationships constitute beings, the phenomenon of transforma-tions turns from a troublesome (or 'irrational') brain-twister into a reasonable possibility: if relationships are the prime ontological principle (instead of the entities involved in relationships), then it makes perfect sense that beings could transform according to their mutual relationships.[50]

Evidently, Hai||om ontologies crisscross western conceptualizations. What we are trying to capture as winds/spirits can turn into 'material objects' (both called ǀgais) and vice versa; spirit beings can turn into animals and so can humans. The borders between the tangible or material world on the one hand and the intangible/invisible/non-material world is not as clear-cut as in western ontologies, and a "categorical ambivalence" (Sullivan and Low 2014: 226) is evident. Moreover, there is no strict boundary between the natural and the supernatural, the real and the mythical. Sullivan and Low noted for the KhoeSan that their understanding of "'ordinary' and 'supernatural'/mythical/entranced realms as in relationship with each other: as dynamically entwined and infused with potency" (ibid: 227). Further exploration is needed to establish whether the Hai||om have separate though connected concepts for the 'ordinary' and the 'supernatural' or if this division is only based on our conceptualization.[51]

But what constitutes a relationship? I argue in line with Bird-David's (1999) understanding of Nayaka, a group in South India, that *sharing* is a central con-cept/practice in this regard which, in my view, has not yet been given enough explicit attention in KhoeSan studies beyond the human-human sphere (for the latter see Widlok 2017). In the Hai||om case, sharing food (or tobacco) establishes or enforces relationships between humans (Widlok 1999: 140-43).

---

lational context in which it is placed and experienced determines its being." (Willerslev 2013: 49) This seems to be valid for the Hai||om as well.

50   It would be worthwhile but beyond the scope of this paper to look at these issues using the Agential Realism framework suggested by Karen Barad (e.g. 2003).

51   Likewise, Guenther (2015) speaks of a "First Order of existence", with ontological flu-idity/hybridity, and a "Second Order", the present one, which shows a lesser degree of ontological ambiguity, though both spheres can intersect. I have not found any indi-cation of this separation with the Hai||om (though this doesn't mean that it is doesn't exist; it would also be worthy of further exploration).

But sharing is not limited to human relationships.[52] As we have seen for the Hai||om, winds/spirits establish relationships, e.g. between //gamagu and humans who become healers/shamans (Low 2012); one could maybe say that sharing winds, spirits and substances establishes relationships. With regard to what I call sharing substances, Low describes KhoeSan healing practices, where potency is transferred through medical cutting: "Potency may be given to someone by rubbing the potent source into a small cut or series of cuts in the body." (Low 2007: 83) In my understanding, the potent source and the human share specific substances.

As brief as it is, this section can only suggest that further exploration of the topic is necessary, with fieldwork from another perspective, based on what Desmond calls "relational ethnography" (2014).

Looking through the lens of a relational ontology would also suggest that the structure of my analysis, namely the separation of relationships according to categories (people-people, people-beings beyond-the-humans, etc.) might be inadequate because it starts from a perspective which takes the constituents as the first structural principle and has difficulties in accounting for categorical ambivalence and fluidity and for the potential of transformations (e.g. animals and spirit beings). More work needs to be done.

However, for the sake of the argument proposed in this paper, in the context of cartography, it might suffice.

Conclusion: Mapping Hai||om-being-in-relations?

In the preceding paragraphs, I explained how the Hai||om are entangled in multiple relationships with other beings (including land and non-human actors). I also briefly explored how their being-in-the-world, like that of other San and hunter-gatherer groups, shares characteristics generally ascribed to relational ontologies.

---

52   Willerslev has noted for the Yukaghirs, "[s]haring is not limited to the human community, however. It also provides the moral framework for engagement with the nonhuman world of animal spirits follows the same principle of sharing." (2013: 53).

The *Xoms /Omis* maps described at the beginning might have fulfilled the purpose of acknowledging the cultural heritage of the Hai‖om in Etosha,[53] as other indigenous maps might have helped to secure land rights or land tenure systems. However, they are mostly silent on these manifold relations, which are an essential principle of their being-in-the-world. I used our own project to express my concerns, but they are relevant for many other indigenous mapping projects, in Africa and beyond.

I urge us, the researchers working with indigenous communities in mapping projects, to engage in continuous self-reflection, to develop our critical awareness of our own ontological bias as well as our own mapping traditions. Otherwise, we risk indigenous mapping (unintentionally) perpetuating colonial practices instead of assisting within the wider project of a decolonialization of maps by reinforcing the primacy of western ontology and thereby contributing to a further silencing of indigenous ontologies.

As outlined in the introduction to this volume, I would not throw out the baby with the bathwater and discard maps and atlases altogether, and I see lots of potential for cartography and cybercartography to communicate *alternative* ways of 'seeing' and experiencing the world and presenting a wider audience with examples of *being-with* (see Bird-David 2017).[54] Examples from other regions (see Introduction and Pearce, this volume) have demonstrated this potential.

How would I approach mapping Hai‖om-being-in-Etosha (i.e. Hai‖om being-in-relations), decades after the development of the *Xoms /Omis* maps? I am convinced that it would need another process and a new project, with a team of Hai‖om, anthropologists, cartographers etc. to jointly develop maps and related outputs. I just want to briefly outline some preliminary ideas to be further explored. While struggling with ideas about alternative ways of mapping, I turn to Ingold's suggestion of a "meshwork" as a way of apprehending the world, which I have already mentioned in the introduction. The "meshwork" is related to his reading of "animism" not as a way of "believing

---

53   They were launched officially by the Minister of Environment and Tourism in Windhoek in 2007 and were used as accompanying material in a Hai‖om land claim for Etosha.

54   In this regard, I belong to the revisionist and not to the rejectionist camp, as Caquard et al. call the different positions, the "revisionists" acknowledging the benefits of geospatial technologies but believing in the necessity of changing of thinking about cartography (Caquard et al. 2009: 84).

about the world," but as a "condition of being *in* it" (Ingold 2011: 67, original emphasis). He sees "animacy" as "the dynamic, transformative potential of the entire field of relations within which beings of all kinds, more or less person-like or thing-like, continually and reciprocally bring one another into existence" (Ingold 2011: 68). He stresses two points of an "animic perception of the world, [...] the relational constitution of being; [...and] the primacy of movement" (Ingold 2011: 69). The "meshwork" is the lifeworld constituted of organisms in a relational field, and organisms are trails of movement and growth and not entities set off against the environment. The environment, he envisages, is "a domain of entanglement":

> This tangle is the texture of the world. In the animic ontology, beings do not simply occupy the world, they *inhabit* it, and in so doing – in threading their own paths through the meshwork - they contribute to its ever-evolving weave. Thus we must cease regarding the world as inert substratum, over which living things propel themselves about like counters on a board or actors on a stage, where artefacts and the landscape take the place, respectively, of properties and scenery. By the same token, beings that inhabit the world (or that are truly indigenous in this sense) are not objects that move, undergoing displacement from point to point across the world's surface. Indeed the inhabited world, as such, has no surface [...], whatever surfaces one encounters, whether on the ground, water, vegetation or building, are *in* the world, not *of* it [...] and woven into their very texture are the lines of growth and movement, not as mobile, self-propelled entities, that beings are instantiated in the world. [...] The animic world is in perpetual flux, as the beings that participate in it go their various ways. (Ingold 2011: 71-72, original emphasis)

He goes on to provide examples of human groups where people, animals and celestial bodies are known for the characteristic trails they leave behind.

Capturing many aspects that I have encountered with the Hai||om, this "meshwork" seems to be a promising starting point to be further explored with regard to mapping Hai||om-being-in-Etosha/being-in-relations. For example, the Hai||om and other San are known as excellent trackers (see e.g. Liebenberg 1990) and the Hai||om do read their world at least partly through tracks, as the initial interview excerpt indicates. How about an atlas of maps with the tracks of individual beings of all sorts combined with narratives accompanying the maps? Maps could have different time scales and different spatial scales.

One could start with maps of Etosha depicting different kinds of tracks, human tracks, animal tracks, but also tracks of vegetal elements (seeds, corms and leaves can also be understood as traces/tracks), place names being parts of the map without dots (but rather as areas with an agglomeration of tracks, the tracks indicating, for example, the differences between waterholes and settlements, bushfood areas and hunting areas).

One could zoom in on specific areas and follow the tracks of a human person, e.g. a woman during the course of a day, going with other women in search of bushfood, together with children. Another map could depict her husband's day as he leaves the settlement, maybe with other hunters, following the tracks of specific animals or looking out for specific animal paths or waterholes. Hunting maps could tell the story about the hunt, of hunters following an animal, of how animal tracks might change, of when it is wounded, showing the place of butchering, the return to the settlement and the procurement of the meat. Other maps could include a focus on the police stations and rest camps, where Hai||om men were working occasionally or permanently. I imagine that "track maps" could also tell the story of how a person gets the spirit of a spirit being and later becomes a healer. Maps could also shift perspective and follow a lion, a snake, an ostrich or a springbok during a day, searching for water or food, encountering a human, or passing a settlement of humans.

Together with textual description and narratives, tracks on the maps could indicate the presence of various animals, the mutual reactions of different beings to each other (e.g. a hunter and a snake). Maps could depict the visits to other settlements and relatives and the contacts with other beings, cars or horses. And tracks are also able to depict transformations.

Following the cartographic endeavors of Pearce and Louis (2008; see also Pearce, this volume), one could also explore a shift of perspective from the orthogonal, aerial perspective to an oblique angle in order to enable a view situated in place. With this, other tracks and signs (e.g. in shrubs or trees), differences in light, daytime, weather and seasons could become visible. One could design maps for different seasons with the tracks according to season.

These multiple maps would have a temporal component. They would not perpetuate the supremacy of the human, or imply the presupposition of who is a being/person. They would not convey the picture of an isolated Hai||om community, living in harmony with nature; instead they would convey the message of the Hai||om being entangled in multiple relationships with many other beings, human and non-human.

In a way, this brings us back to the very start of this book, to the "marauder's map" of Harry Potter (in the introduction of the introduction to this volume), on which "thin ink lines began to spread like a *spider's web*", joining each other, crisscrossing and fanning "into every corner of the parchment" (J.K. Rowling 2011 [1999]: 143, emphasis added). Is it a coincidence, that Ingold chose the SPIDER ("skilled practice involves developmentally embodied responsiveness") as the epitome of his own position (meshwork vs. network) (2011: 65)?

As a final note, I think the Hai||om with whom I worked and other elderly Hai||om would be excited about such a project, not least because it would come closer to their way of 'reading' and apprehending the world. Mapping in this way would be a way of performing being-in-the-world again.[55] It could also contribute to a documentation of knowledge that would not 'squeeze' their knowledge into our conceptual framework but would get closer to merging different ontologies.

References

Århem, Kaj/Sprenger, Guido, eds. (2016): Animism in Southeast Asia, London, New York: Routledge.

Astor-Aguilera, Miguel Angel, and Graham Harvey (eds.) (2019): Rethinking Relations and Animism: Personhood and Materiality, Abingdon Oxon, New York: Routledge.

Barad, Karen (2003): "Posthumanist Performativity: Toward an Understanding of How Matter Comes to Matter." In: Journal of Women in Culture and Society 28/3, pp. 801-31.

Bird-David, Nurit (1999): "'Animism': Personhood, Environment, and Relational Epistemology." In: Current Anthropology 40, Suppl, pp. S67-S79.

Bird-David, Nurit (2017): Us, Relatives: Scaling and Plural Life in a Forager World. Ethnographic Studies in Subjectivity 12, Oakland, California: University of California Press.

Bird-David, Nurit (2018): "Size Matters! The Scalability of Modern Hunter-Gatherer Animism." In: Quaternary International 464, pp. 305-14 (DOI: https://doi.org/10.1016/j.quaint.2017.06.035).

---

55   See Vermeylen, this volume, for examples of mapping as performance.

Brody, Hugh (1981): Maps and Dreams: Indians and the British Columbia Frontier, London: Norman & Hobhouse.

Brosius, J. Peter/Tsing, Anna L./Zerner, Charles, eds., (2005): Communities and Conservation: Histories and Politics of Community-Based Natural Resource Management, Globalization and the Environment, Walnut Creek, CA, Oxford: AltaMira Press,

Caquard, Sébastien/Pyne, Stephanie/Igloliorte, Heather/Mierins, Krystina/Hayes, Amos/Fraser Taylor, D.R. (2009): "A 'Living' Atlas for Geospatial Storytelling: The Cybercartographic Atlas of Indigenous Perspectives and Knowledge of the Great Lakes Region." In: Cartographica: The International Journal for Geographic Information and Geovisualization 44/2, pp. 83-100 (DOI: https://doi.org/10.3138/carto.44.2 .83).

Casey, Edward S. (1996): "How to Get from Space to Place in a Fairly Short Stretch of Time: Phenomenological Prolegomena." In: Steven Feld/Keith H. Basso (eds.), Senses of Place, 1st edition, Santa Fe, New Mexico: School of American Research Press, pp. 13-52.

Crampton, Jeremy W./Krygier, John (2005) "An Introduction to Critical Cartography." In: ACME: An International Journal for Critical Geographies 4/1, pp. 11-33 (https://www.acme-journal.org/index.php/acme/article/vie w/723/585, last accessed March 16, 2018).

Crawhall, Nigel (2009): The Role of participatory cultural mapping in promoting intercultural dialogue: We are not hyenas; a reflection paper, UNESCO (http://www.iapad.org/wp-content/uploads/2015/07/nigel.crawhal l.190753e.pdf, last accessed August 11, 2020).

Descola, Philippe (2013): Beyond Nature and Culture, Chicago, London: The University of Chicago Press.

Desmond, Matthew (2014): "Relational Ethnography." In: Theory and Society 43, pp. 547-79.

Dieckmann, Ute (2001): "'The Vast White Place': A History of the Etosha National Park and the Hai||om." In: Nomadic People 5/2, pp. 125-53.

Dieckmann, Ute (2003): "The Impact of Nature Conservation on the San: A Case Study of Etosha National Park." In: Thekla Hohmann (ed.), San and the State: Contesting Land, Development, Identity and Representation, Cologne: Rüdiger Köppe Verlag, pp. 37-86.

Dieckmann, Ute (2007): Hai||om in the Etosha Region: A History of Colonial Settlement, Ethnicity and Nature Conservation, Basel: Basler Afrika Bibliographien.

Dieckmann, Ute (2009): Born in Etosha: Homage to the Cultural Heritage of the Hai||om, Windhoek: Legal Assistance Centre.

Dieckmann, Ute (2012): Born in Etosha: Living and Learning in the Wild, Windhoek: Legal Assistance Centre.

Dieckmann, Ute/Thiem, Maarit/Dirkx, Erik/Hays, Jennifer, eds. (2014): Scraping the Pot: San in Namibia Two Decades After Independence, Windhoek: Land Environment and Development Project of the Legal Assistance Centre and Desert Research Foundation of Namibia.

Dodge, Martin, ed. (2011): The Map Reader: Theories of Mapping Practice and Cartographic Representation, Chichester: Wiley-Blackwell.

Dodge, Martin/Perkins, Chris (2015): "Reflecting on J.B. Harley's Influence and What He Missed in 'Deconstructing the Map'." In: Cartographica: The International Journal for Geographic Information and Geovisualization 50/1, pp. 37-40 (DOI: https://doi.org/10.3138/carto.50.1.07).

Duxbury, Nancy/Garrett-Petts, W. F./MacLennan, David, eds. (2015). Cultural Mapping as Cultural Inquiry, 1st edition, New York: Routledge.

Friedrich, Reinhard (2009): Verjagt...Vergessen...Verweht... Die Hai||om und das Etoscha Gebiet, Windhoek: Macmillan Education Namibia.

Gibson, Katherine/Rose, Deborah B./Fincher, Ruth, eds. (2015): Manifesto for Living in the Anthropocene, Brooklyn, New York: Punctum Books.

Glasze, Georg (2009): "Kritische Kartographie." In: Geographische Zeitschrift 97/4, pp. 181-91 (https://www.researchgate.net/publication/259888705_Kritische_Kartographie, last accessed March 15, 2018).

Gordon, Robert (1989): "Can Namibian San Stop Dispossession of Their Land?" In: Edwin N. Willmsen (ed.), We Are Here: Politics of Aboriginal Land Tenure, Berkeley, Los Angeles: University of California Press, pp. 138-54.

Grupe, Gisela/McGlynn George/ Peters, Joris, eds., (2009): Tracking down the Past, Ethnohistory Meets Archaeozoology, Documenta Archaeobiologiae 7, Rahden, Westfalen: Leidorf.

Guenther, Mathias (1999): Tricksters and Trancers: Bushman Religion and Society, Bloomington and Indianapolis: Indiana University Press.

Guenther, Mathias (2015): "'Therefore Their Parts Resemble Humans, for They Feel That They Are People'." In: Hunter Gatherer Research 1/3, pp. 277-315 (DOI: https://doi.org/10.3828/hgr.2015.16).

Guenther, Mathias (2020a): Human-Animal Relationships in San and Hunter-Gatherer Cosmology, Volume I: Therianthropes and Transformation, Cham: Palgrave Macmillan.

Guenther, Mathias (2020b): Human-Animal Relationships in San and Hunter-Gatherer Cosmology, Volume II: Imagining and Experiencing Ontological Mutability, Cham: Palgrave Macmillan.

Haacke, Wilfrid H. G./Eliphas Eiseb (2002): A Khoekhoegowab Dictionary with an English-Khoekhoegowab Index, Windhoek, Namibia: Gamsberg Macmillan.

Halder, Severin/Heyer, Karl/Michel, Boris/Greth, Silke/Baumgarten, Nico/Boos, Philipp/Dobrusskin Janina/et al., eds. (2018): This Is Not an Atlas: A Global Collection of Counter-Cartographies, Bielefeld: Transcript.

Haraway, Donna J. (2015): "Anthropocene, Capitalocene, Plantationocene, Chthulucene: Making Kin." In: Environmental Humanities 6, pp 159-65.

Harley, John B./Laxton, Paul (2002): The New Nature of Maps: Essays in the History of Cartography, Baltimore, Mar.: Johns Hopkins University Press.

Harvey, Graham, ed. (2015): Handbook of Contemporary Animism, London: Routledge.

Hodgson, Dorothy L./Schroeder, Richard A. (2002): "Dilemmas of Counter-Mapping Community Resources in Tanzania." In: Development & Change 33/1, pp. 79-100 (DOI: https://doi.org/10.1111/1467-7660.00241).

Hoff, Ansie (1997): "The Water Snake of the Khoekhoen and /Xam." In: The South African Archaeological Bulletin, 52/165, pp. 21-37.

Ingold, Tim (2011): Being Alive: Essays on Movement, Knowledge and Description, Oxon, New York: Routledge.

Ingold, Tim (2011 [2000]): The Perception of the Environment: Essays on Livelihood, Dwelling and Skill, London, New York: Routledge Taylor & Francis Group.

Ingold, Tim (2012): "Toward an Ecology of Materials." In: Annual Review of Anthropology 41, pp. 427-42.

Ingold, Tim (2016) "A Naturalist Abroad in the Museum of Ontology: Philippe Descola's Beyond Nature and Culture." In: Anthropological Forum 26/3, pp. 301-20 (DOI: https://doi.org/10.1080/00664677.2015.1136591).

Ingold, Tim (2018): Anthropology: Why It Matters, Cambridge: Polity Press.

Lewis, Jerome (2012): "Technological Leap-Frogging in the Congo Basin, Pygmies and Global Positioning Systems in Central Africa: What Has Happened and Where Is It Going?" In: African Study Monographs Suppl. 43, pp. 15-44.

Liebenberg, Louis (1990): The Art of Tracking. The Origin of Science, Claremont, South Africa: David Philip Publishers.

Low, Chris (2007): "Khoisan Wind: Hunting and Healing." In: Journal of the Royal Anthropological Institute 13/1, pp. S71-S90. (DOI: https://doi.org/10.1111/j.1467-9655.2007.00402.x).

Low, Chris (2009): "Birds in the Life of KhoeSan; with Particular Reference to Healing and Ostriches." In: Alternation 16/2, pp. 64-90.

Low, Chris (2012): "KhoeSan Shamanistic Relationships with Snakes and Rain." In: Journal of Namibian Studies 12, pp. 71-96.

Low, Chris (2015): "The Role of the Body in Kalahari San Healing Dances." In: Hunter Gatherer Research 1/1, pp. 29-60 (DOI: https://doi.org/10.3828/hgr.2015.3).

Ministry of Environment and Tourism Namibia (n.d.): "Etosha National Park." (http://www.met.gov.na/national-parks/etosha-national-park/217/, last accessed April 10, 2019).

Mossolow, Nikolai (1993): Die Geschichte von Namutoni, Windhoek: John Meinert.

Neumann, Roderick P. (2002 [1998]): Imposing Wilderness: Struggles over Livelihood and Nature Preservation in Africa, Berkeley: University of California Press.

Pearce, Margaret W./Louis, Renee (2008): "Mapping Indigenous Depth of Place." In: American Indian Culture and Research Journal 32/3, pp. 107-26 (DOI: https://doi.org/10.17953/aicr.32.3.n7g22w816486567j).

Peters, Joris/Dieckmann, Ute/Vogelsang Ralf (2009): "Losing the Spoor: Hai||om Animal Exploitation in the Etosha Region." In: Gisela Grupe/George McGlynn/Joris Peters (eds.), Tracking down the Past, Ethnohistory Meets Archaeozoology, Documenta Archaeobiologiae 7, Rahden, Westfalen: Leidorf, pp.103-85.

Plumwood, Val (2002) Environmental Culture: The Ecological Crisis of Reason, London & New York: Routledge.

Pönninghaus, Fritz (1926): Die Buschmänner: Ergebnis Einer Vernehmung Von Buschmännern, Rheinische Missionsgesellschaft (RMG), file 2096.

Robbins, Paul (2003): "Beyond Ground Truth: GIS and the Environmental Knowledge of Herders, Professional Foresters, and Other Traditional Communities." In: Human Ecology 31/2, pp. 233-53.

Rocheleau, Dianne (2005): "Maps as Power Tools: Locating Communities in Space or Situating People and Ecologies in Place?" In: J. P. Brosius/Anna L. Tsing/Charles Zerner (eds.), Communities and Conservation: Histories and Politics of Community-Based Natural Resource Management, Globalization and the Environment, Walnut Creek, CA, Oxford: AltaMira Press, pp. 327-62.

Rose, Deborah Bird (2005): "An Indigenous Philosophical Ecology: Situating the Human." In: The Australian Journal of Anthropology 16/3, pp. 294-305 (DOI: https://doi.org/10.1111/j.1835-9310.2005.tb00312.x).

Rose, Deborah Bird (1999): "Indigenous Ecologies and an Ethic of Connection." In: Nicholas Low (ed.), Global Ethics and Environment, London & New York: Routledge Taylor & Francis Group, pp. 175-87.

Rose, Deborah Bird (2002): "Dialogue with Place: Toward an Ecological Body." In: Journal of Narrative Theory 32/3, pp. 311-25 (https://doi.org/10.1353/jnt .2011.0054).

Rose, Deborah Bird (2013): "Val Plumwood's Philosophical Animism: Attentive Interactions in the Sentient World." In: Environmental Humanities 3/1, pp. 93-109 (DOI: https://doi.org/10.1215/22011919-3611248).

Rose, Deborah Bird (2015): "The Ecological Humanities." In: Katherine Gibson/Deborah B. Rose/Ruth Fincher (eds.), Manifesto for Living in the Anthropocene, Brooklyn, New York: Punctum Books, pp. 1-5.

Rose, Deborah Bird/van Dooren, Thom/Chrulew, Matthew/Cooke, Stuart/Kearnes, Matthew/O'Gorman, Emily (2012): "Thinking Through the Environment, Unsettling the Humanities." In: Environmental Humanities 1/1, pp. 1-5 (DOI: https://doi.org/10.1215/22011919-3609940).

Rose-Redwood, Reuben (2015): "Introduction: The Limits to Deconstructing the Map." In: Cartographica: The International Journal for Geographic Information and Geovisualization 50/1, pp. 1-8 (DOI: https://doi.org/10.313 8/carto.50.1.01).

Roth, Robin (2009): "The Challenges of Mapping Complex Indigenous Spatiality: From Abstract Space to Dwelling Space." In: Cultural Geographies 16/2, pp. 207-27 (DOI: https://doi.org/10.1177/1474474008101517)

Rowling, J.K. (2011 [1999]): Harry Potter and the Prisoner of Azkaban, London: Bloomsbury.

Rundstrom, Robert A. (1995): "GIS, Indigenous Peoples, and Epistemological Diversity." In: Cartography and Geographic Information Systems 22/1, pp. 45-57.

Schatz, Ilse (1993): Unter Buschleuten Auf Der Farm Otjiguinas in Namibia. Tsumeb, Namibia: I. Schatz.

Skaanes, Thea (2017): Cosmology Matters: Power Objects, Rituals, and Meat-Sharing Among the Hadza of Tanzania, Aarhus: Aarhus University.

Sletto, Bjørn (2009): "Special Issue: Indigenous Cartographies." In: Cultural Geographies 16/2, pp. 147-52 (DOI: https://doi.org/10.1177/14744740081015 14).

Sullivan, Sian (2017): "What's Ontology Got to Do with It? On Nature and Knowledge in a Political Ecology of the 'Green Economy'." In: JPE 24/1, pp. 217-42 (DOI: https://doi.org/10.2458/v24i1.20802).

Sullivan, Sian/Hannis, Mike (2016): "Relationality, Reciprocity and Flourishing in an African Landscape: Perspectives on Agency Amongst ||Khao-a Dama, !Narenin and ||Ubun Elders in West Namibia: Future Pasts Working Papers No. 2." Future Pasts Working Paper Series. Unpublished manuscript, last modified September 24, 2018.

Sullivan, Sian/Low, Chris (2014): "Shades of the Rainbow Serpent? A KhoeSan Animal Between Myth and Landscape in Southern Africa – Ethnographic Contextualisations of Rock Art Representations." In: Arts 3/2, pp. 215-44. (DOI: https://doi.org/10.3390/arts3020215).

Thom, Brian (2009): "The Paradox of Boundaries in Coast Salish Territories." In: Cultural Geographies 16/2, pp. 179-205 (DOI: https://doi.org/10.1177/14 74474008101516).

Unterkötter, Alfred (n.d.): Die Buschmänner in SWA, Rheinische Missionsgesellschaft (RMG), file 2096, Rheinisches Missionsarchiv.

Viveiros de Castro, E. (2012): "Cosmological Perspectivism in Amazonia and Elsewhere - HAU Books." (https://haubooks.org/cosmological-perspectivism-in-amazonia/, last accessed June 18, 2018).

Wagner-Robertz, Dagmar (1977): Der Alte Hat Mir Erzählt: Schamanismus Bei Den Hain//om Von Südwestafrika. Eine Untersuchung Ihrer Geistigen Kultur, Swakopmund: Gesellschaft für Wissenschaftliche Entwicklung.

Wainwright, Joel/Bryan, Joe (2009): "Cartography, Territory, Property: Postcolonial Reflections on Indigenous Counter-Mapping in Nicaragua and Belize." In: Cultural Geographies 16/2, pp. 153-78 (DOI: https://doi.org/10.1177/1474474008101515).

Widlok, Thomas (1999): Living on Mangetti, Oxford: Oxford University Press.

Widlok, Thomas (2008): "Landscape Unbounded: Space, Place, and Orientation in ǂAkhoe Hai||om and Beyond." In: Language Sciences 30/2-3, pp. 362-80 (DOI: https://doi.org/10.1016/j.langsci.2006.12.002).

Widlok, Thomas (2017): "No Easy Talk About the Weather: Eliciting 'Cultural Models of Nature' Among Hai//om." In: World Cultures ejournal 22/2 (https://escholarship.org/uc/item/69n0s73f., last accessed February 16, 2019).

Willerslev, Rane (2013): "Taking Animism Seriously, but Perhaps Not Too Se-riously?" In: Religion and Society 4/1, pp. 41-57 (DOI: https://doi.org/10.31 67/arrs.2013.040103).

Densities of meaning in west Namibian landscapes: genealogies, ancestral agencies, and healing

Sian Sullivan and Welhemina Suro Ganuses

Introduction[1]

This chapter draws on an oral history and cultural mapping project in west Namibia that has documented remembered former dwelling places, particularly in today's Sesfontein and Purros communal-area Conservancies and the Palmwag Tourism Concession (see Figure 1). The research draws into focus past practices of dwelling, mobility, livelihood and environmental perception amongst Khoekhoegowab[2]-speaking peoples who refer to themselves

---

1   Contribution statement: Sian Sullivan has drafted the text of this chapter and carried out the literature review, with all field research and Khoekhoegowab-English translations and interpretations carried out with ‡Nūkhoe-Nama researcher Welhemina Suro Ganuses from Sesfontein / !Nani‖aus. We have worked together on and off since meeting in 1994.

2   Shortly after Namibia's independence in 1990, the glossonym (language name) and former endonym "Khoekhoegowab" was "officially reintroduced for the language that had become known as 'Nama' or 'Nama/Damara'": Khoekhoegowab "is the sole surviving language of the Khoekhoe branch of the Khoe family", "a dialect continuum with Nama as southernmost and Damara, Hai‖om and ‡Aakhoe as northernmost dialect clusters" (Haacke 2018: 133-134). Damara / ‡Nūkhoen (and small numbers of ‖Ubun) are a proportion of the 11.8 percent of Namibia's population (244,769 of 2,066,389) recorded in 2010 as speaking "Nama/Damara" (ibid: 141-142, after Namibia Household Income & Expenditure Survey 2009/2010). Haacke suggests that this figure for "Nama/Damara" speakers may be an underestimate for Khoekhoegowab "as most Hai‖om and ‡Aakhoe speakers presumably are included in the latter survey under the meaningless language category 'Khoisan'" (1.3 percent, 27,764 speakers) (ibid: 141-142).

as Damara / ǂNūkhoen and ||Ubun[3], who lived into at least the recent past as hunter-harvesters and small stock pastoralists throughout the wider west Namibian landscape.

A combination of historical factors cleared people from these lands, causing disruption to cultural, family and individual identities (see Sullivan/Ganuses 2020; Sullivan in press – we draw on both these texts in this chapter). Using a combination of methods – from recorded oral histories and musics associated with remembered sites, to logging mapped coordinates and associated information on google maps – this research aimed to (re)inscribe dimensions of cultural significance now occluded from maps of the area (see https://www.futurepasts.net/maps-1, last accessed August 10, 2020). The project has thereby made visible named places and other localities of significance not usually found on contemporary or historical maps, through working with people removed historically from large areas of land to which they formerly had access.

In this chapter we focus additionally on three dimensions that can be hard to make visible using conventional cartographic techniques:

1. the rhizomatically interwoven relationships between people, places and ancestors that on-site oral histories draw into focus as densely connected through past mobilities and genealogies;

2. the greeting practice *tsē-khom* that foregrounds the agentic presence of known ancestors and anonymous spirits of the dead associated with specific places and land areas;

and 3. the remembered significance of |gaidi praise songs and arudi healing dances linked with former living sites (sing. ||an-||huib).

Shorthanded as genealogies, ancestral agencies, and song-dances connected with varied registers of healing, our aim is to explore the unanticipated and sometimes surprising appearance of these dimensions of significance, as they arose in our mapping research. Their apparent significance contributes to

---

3   Many of the Khoekhoegowab words in this chapter include the symbols |, ||, ! and ǂ. These symbols indicate consonants that sound like clicks and which characterise the languages of Khoe and San peoples who live(d) throughout southern Africa. The sounds these symbols indicate are as follows: | = the 'tutting' sound made by bringing the tongue softly down from behind front teeth (dental click); || = the clucking sound familiar in urging on a horse (lateral click); ! = a popping sound like mimicking the pulling of a cork from a wine bottle (alveolar click); ǂ = a sharp, explosive click made as the tongue is flattened and then pulled back from the palate (palatal click).

Figure 1: Map showing the boundaries of current tourism concessions, surrounding communal area conservancies and state protected areas in southern Kunene Region, west Namibia (Source: Jeff Muntifering, October 2, 2019)

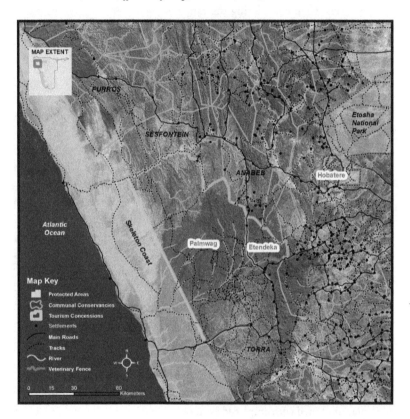

understanding of the detrimental cultural and livelihood effects of disrupting relationships people had with land areas from which they were removed (as also documented for Khoekhoegowab-speaking Hai||om by Dieckmann, this volume). We also share some of the attempted ways through which we have sought to convey the significance of these dimensions in representational terms.

Anthropologist Keith Basso writes in *Wisdom Sits in Places* (1996) that research that "maps from below" faces the challenge of how to represent layers of cultural significance entangled with land in a way that bridges gaps between oral and written dimensions of this knowledge and experience. He asserts further that as places and their histories come into focus, the landscape starts to take on a "density of meaning" (ibid: 28). As highlighted in the introduction to this volume, such representational challenges come into even sharper focus when considering the range of agency enacting entities that may be salient for specific cultural contexts but that are other to, and othered by, the parameters of modern cartographic techniques and categories.

Damara / ǂNūkhoen and ||Ubun, as well as those speaking Khoekhoegowab more generally (cf. Widlok (1999) and Dieckmann (2007) for Hai||om; Guenther (1999) for Naro), have framed, conceptualized and experienced land and the entities sustained thereby in terms and categories that sometimes exceed those tethered to conventional cartographic practices and their collusion with modern ideas of property and static representation (see e.g. Sullivan 1999, 2017a; Hannis/Sullivan 2018; Vermeylen, this volume). As theorized in the anthropology of landscapes more generally (Bender 1993; Tilley 1994; Ashmore/Knapp 1999; Ingold 2000; Bender/Winer 2001; Tilley/Cameroon-Daum 2017), these 'other' (and othered) understandings and experiences arguably emerge for onlookers only when culture and land are perceived as mutually constitutive domains, produced in relation to lived and remembered practices and experiences (Sullivan in press). Such analyses point towards both contrary and competing "regimes of visibility" at work in the deployment of cartographic techniques of representation (Tsing 2005: 44; see also Harley 1988, 1992 and as discussed by Goldman, this volume), and to the density of known, used and remembered places in the broader landscape that can remain diminished and displaced in postcolonial contexts. Recovering and historicizing elements of this "density of meaning" for elderly Khoekhoegowab-speaking inhabitants in the geographical context of southern Kunene Region, north-west Namibia, combined with emplaced exploration of the three dimensions noted above, is the focus of the remainder of this chapter. We argue that bringing these 'unmapped' culturally dense dimensions more systemically into present management and investment choices, might be a route towards amplifying equitability and recognition for diverse pasts linked with the present high-value biodiversity conservation areas of west Namibia. First, however, and given the focus of this volume, we consider the term "hunter-gatherer" and its relevance (or otherwise) for the Khoekhoegowab-speaking peoples of west Namibia, combined with a historicized 'positioning' of the peoples forming the focus of the mapping research discussed below. We elaborate the latter in some detail because of an ongoing context wherein the autonomous pre-colonial presence of Damara / ǂNūkhoen and ||Ubun is poorly recognized in archaeological, historical and anthropological discourse for Namibia.

Hunter-(herder-)harvesters of west Namibia?

We prefer the term "hunter-harvesters" instead of the more commonly used "hunter-gatherers" or "hunter-foragers", to emphasize that past peoples of west Namibia engage(d) in ways of living involving active tending and management of species from which food and other items were procured, as well as the strategic mobilization of considered technical knowledge in the accessing, harvesting, preparation and *storage* of these items (Sullivan 1999; also discussion in Budack 1983: 2). Such knowledge, access and management practices were/are consciously intended to ensure abundance into the future, as well as to enable the storage of suitable food items (Sullivan 1999), rather than deployed in a reactive mode based on a more-or-less opportunistic encountering of items of utility whilst moving 'in the field'. This perspective, then, is a departure from an "immediate returns" conception of a hunter-gatherer mode of subsistence (cf. Woodburn 1982) in favor of a mode of sustenance that acknowledges practices of care for both ancestral pasts and future socioecological abundance; combined with containment of the accumulative tendencies and inequalities fostered by 'delayed returns' economic practices and stockpiling (Skaanes, this volume, expresses similar concerns).

Although ecological circumstances were undoubtedly harsh and constrained at times, and as critiqued by anthropologists such as Sahlins (1972) and Clastres (2010 [1976]), it does not therefore follow that the hunter-herder-harvesters of west Namibia into the Namib desert sustained themselves through an 'economy of poverty' allowing them to barely assure society's subsistence. Instead, and mirroring circumstances elsewhere, we might imagine combinations of autonomy, autarky and affective/symbolic affluence to have infused the guiding values and principles of west Namibian 'social groups' (Sullivan 2006 [2001]), prior to historical encounters with cattle pastoralists and mercantile and capitalist economies in which accumulation (including of livestock) and a monetary profit motive were/are made possible through being relatively decoupled from egalitarian societal constraint (Polanyi 2001 [1944]; also discussed in Sullivan et al. 2021).

Archaeological research in west Namibia stretching towards the Namib suggests multiple and patchy in-migration events introducing livestock and associated symbolic and material culture (especially pottery) to the Namib (Sadr 2008), combined with indigenous dynamism and change incorporating new material and symbolic cultural elements (John Kinahan 2001[1991]). Material culture associated with the pastoral care of small stock from some 2,000BP[4] is seen in these landscapes to have become an integral and functional part of subsistence strategies in which gathered foods and hunted fauna were/are also central. Pottery conventionally associated with herders thus becomes an innovation in the collection, storage and preparation of the flesh and seeds of *!nara* melons (*Acanthosicyos horridus*) in coastal sites (connected through mobility with sites inland), as well as the seeds of grasses and *Monsonia* species acquired from harvester ant nests at sites inland (John Kinahan, 2001 [1991]: 116, 125; 1993: 381-382). Such combinations of hunting-herding-harvesting have continued in west Namibia into contemporary times (Sullivan 1998, 2005) and are deeply and repeatedly invoked in on-site oral histories with elderly people at places of past dwelling (Sullivan et al. 2019).

Historicizing the presence of Khoekhoegowab-speaking peoples of west Namibia

> The Berg-Damaras (also known as the Damaras or the Berg-Damas) are a people of mysterious origin, difficult to classify. Some say that they vie with the Bushmen for first claim to the country. (First 1968: 34)

> The Damaras in the area have all been – the word was in quotes – 'removed' and herded into a Reserve somewhere, the entire population. ... Damaras? – talking about Klip Kaffirs, in the stony hills around the dry [Khan] river bed.

---

4   Sheep remains found in Namib and pro-Namib sites have been dated to the first millennium, specifically 1550±50 BP at the Mirabib inselberg in the gravel plains of the Central Namib, where hair resembling that of fat-tailed sheep has been found (Sandelowsky 1977: 222, 255; Sandelowsky et al.1979: 50; for early evidence of small-stock in Erongo and Brandberg sites, also see Wadley 1979: 13-14; John Kinahan 2001 [1991]: 35-36; Smith et al. 1996: 38). More recent archaeological research pushes back the patchy presence of livestock in south-western Africa: Caprinae (sheep and goat) teeth found at Leopard Cave, Erongo, are dated to between 2312-2042BP and the associated faunal assemblage indicates 'that the inhabitants were hunting and consuming wild meat, such as birds, reptiles and antelopes [with]... limited exploitation of domesticate species, probably sheep' (Pleurdeau et al. 2012: n.p.; see also Sadr 2008).

We used to come upon them when we were youngsters out hunting buck, though how a buck or a man survives in a place like that is a mystery. They are there like the stones – no, were there like stones, apparently they aren't anymore. (Gordimer 1974: 113-114)

As noted above, this chapter focuses on Khoekhoegowab-speaking peoples who refer to themselves as Damara / ǂNūkhoen and ||Ubun. ǂNūkhoen means literally "black" or "real" people and establishes a distinction from *Nau khoen* or "other people". Historically, the ethnonym "Dama-ra" is based on an "exonym", i.e. an external name for a group of people, "Dama" being the name given by Nama pastoralists for darker-skinned people generally, with 'ra' "referring to either third person feminine or common gender plural" (Haacke 2018: 140). Since Nama(qua) pastoralists were often those whom early European colonial travelers first encountered in the western part of southern Africa, the latter took on this application of the term "Dama". This usage gave rise to a confusing situation in the historical literature whereby the term "Damara", as well as the central part of Namibia that in the 1800s was known as "Damaraland", tended to refer to cattle pastoralists described and racialized as dark-skinned and known as Herero (as, for example, in Alexander 2006 [1838]; Galton 1890 [1853]; Tindall 1959 [1839–55]). The terms "Hill Damaras" ("Berg-Dama" / "*!hom* Dama" / and the derogatory "Klip Kaffir"[5]), and "Plains Damaras" (or "Cattle Damara" / "*Gomadama*"), were used to distinguish contemporary Damara or ǂNūkhoen (i.e. "Khoekhoe-gowab-speaking black-skinned people") from speakers of the Bantu language Otjiherero.

Khoekhoegowab-speaking ||Ubun currently living in Sesfontein and environs are sometimes referred to locally as "Nama" and at other times as "Bushmen". A mythologized origin tale tells that they split from ǂAonin / "Topnaar Nama" at Utuseb in the !Khuiseb river valley (Figure 2 indicates the location of most of the places mentioned in this section), following a dispute in which a ǂAonin woman refused her sister the creamy milk (||*ham*) that the latter desired.[6] It seems possible that contemporary ||Ubun are descendants of a

---

5   After consideration we have elected to incorporate such terms that carry derogatory association *only* where their appearance in historical texts conveys information relevant for present understanding, for example, by clarifying the past presence of specific groups of people.

6   As related in multiple interviews and oral histories, for example, with Franz ||Hoëb (near ǂOs), April 6, 2014 and Emma Ganuses (!Nao-dâis), November 12, 2015.

"Topnaar group" called |Namixan, who in the 1800s under a "Chief ǂGasoab, lived in the !Khuiseb but came into conflict with ... returning [Topnaar groups] !Gomen and Mu-||in", causing the |Namixan to retreat northwards from the !Khuiseb (discussed in more detail below).

Figure 2: Map of places (purple markers) and rivers (blue markers) significant for Damara / ǂNūkhoen and ||Ubun histories in west Namibia

Map ✓
much in
English... &

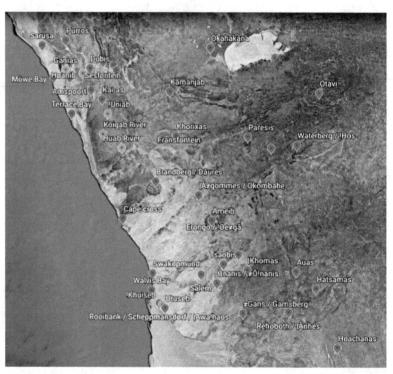

It is impossible to know exactly the ethnicity or language of those whose activities in the drylands of west Namibia left the material remains surveyed and analyzed by archaeologists today. This situation is also amplified by the often simplifying maps of language and ethnic groups created for the territory under the various (neo)colonial regimes of the past 140 years. As the quotes opening this section suggest, the identity and presence of "Damara" in west Namibia is additionally cast by onlookers in mystery. What is known, however, is that written records by varied predominantly male European interlocutors of the south-western areas of Africa tell of a diversity of encountered peoples speaking languages characterized by click consonants. From the 1600s, a series of ship's logs thus describe meetings with peoples along the coast whose sustenance was procured through combinations of fishing, !nara preparation, storage and consumption, and the herding of small and large stock connected with pastures inland (John Kinahan 2001 [1991]; Jill Kinahan 1990, 2000). Late 1700s texts also tell of encounters with peoples described as 'dark-skinned' who, with Nama, Oorlam Nama[7] and Hai||om, spoke Khoekhoegowab and were similarly observed as engaging in a diversity of livelihood-procuring practices. In the remainder of this section we trace in some detail historical references to the ancestors of those who prefer to refer to themselves as ‡Nūkhoen specifically. Whilst this history of past presence is important in terms of contextualizing our mapping research below we acknowledge that it is also quite dense especially for readers not familiar with Khoekhoegowab terms, who may wish to skip this detail and proceed straight to page 152.

***

The earliest written mention of those apparently later known as "Berg-Damara" / ‡Nūkhoen appears to be in the 1778–79 journal of Hendrik Jacob Wikar, a Gothenberg-born Swede who travelled along the Orange River after deserting from the Dutch East India Company operating from Cape Town, before being pardoned in 1779 (Mossop 1935: 3-4). Wikar learned of different "Dama" groups interacting with Nama, described as "of a darker complexion than the Namacquas". They lived near the coast and in mountainous areas near the Kai||khaun ("Keykoa") / Rooinasie / "Red Nation" Nama settlements and grazing grounds, which stretched at least from Hoachanas in the east to Hatsamas, south-east of present-day Windhoek in what was then known as "Great Namaqualand". These "Dama" made and traded copper and iron beads and other products for "she-goats" on apparently favorable terms, acted as "middlemen" in cattle trade between the eastern "Bechuana" and the

---

7   Oorlam Nama are described as '[b]eing of mixed Khoesan and slave descent, acculturated to the Dutch settler way of life, and having horses, guns, and the Bible' (Jill Kinahan 2017: 303 after Penn 2005: 200, 217; also see especially Lau 1987a). From the mid- to late 1700s, and as the frontier of the Cape Colony expanded northwards, they increasingly moved north across the Orange River (!Garieb) to become established and entangled with Nama lineages in 'Great Namaqualand'.

Kai||khaun, were apparently feared magicians, and resisted allegiance to the chief of the Kai||khaun (Wikar in Mossop 1935: 29, 75-81).

In 1836–37, travelling north from Nanebis in the south of present-day Namibia to the !Khuiseb river, the British Captain James Edward Alexander encountered so-called "Hill Damara", stating that they "are a numerous nation, extending [southwards] from the heights south of the Swakop to the Little Koanquip [Konkiep] river ... in small communities under head men" (2006 [1838]: 135-136). At "Tans mountain" (‡Gans, now called "Gamsberg", located in the upper !Khuiseb), he wrote of "Hill Damara" living apparently autonomously in the foothills (see Figure 3). They carried bows, spears and the spoils of hunting, their dwellings contained conical clay pots "in every hut", and Alexander noted their dances and healing practices, observing that the men dance "with springbok horns bound on their foreheads" (ibid: 135-138). It is tempting to consider that the peoples Alexander encountered were associated with Headman (*Gaob*) Abraham ||Guruseb ('Seibeb' in Hinz/Gairiseb 2013: 186) (preceded by Kai Gaob !Gausib ||Guruseb), understood to have been head of a community at ‡Gans from *ca*. 1812–65, before moving to |Â‡gommes (Okombahe) (Haacke 2010: 23).

Figure 3a: "Hill Damara" village in foothills of the table-topped "Tans [‡Gans] Mountain", as sketched for the 1830s narrative by British Captain James Edward Alexander; Figure 3b: The commercial, freehold Gamsberg farming area as it is today (Photo: Sian Sullivan, March 8, 2014)

A "Bergdama" is amongst those baptized by Missionary Scheppman at Rooibank (Scheppmannsdorf / |Awa-!haos) on the !Khuiseb in 1846 (Köhler 1969: 107), and around this time British mercantile explorer Captain William Messem encounters "a tribe of Berg Damaras" at a "high mountain" inland from Cape Cross, with "water, and plenty of goats, but no cattle" (1855: 211).

Travelling inland from Walvis Bay in 1850, Francis Galton (British) and Charles John Andersson (Anglo-Swede) observe apparently permanent "Hill Damara" settlements in the Swakop River catchment such as at Onanis (ǂŌ!nanis – Lau 1987b: 18) and Tsaobis (Andersson 1861: 89), where in the 1890s German Schutztruppe officer Hugo von François (1896) photographs a "Bergdamara" village and hut (Figures 4a and b), as well as a Schutztruppe target practice (Figure 4c). Galton (1890 [1853]: 30) describes Berg Damara living in mountainous localities such as Erongo (!Oeǂgā), Brandberg (Dâures), Auas, |Khomas, Parēsis and Otavi ("cattle Damara", i.e. Herero, having taken space on the plains). Guided by Berg Damara in his party, he visits their relatives at Erongo (their "remarkable stronghold"), finding them to have "plenty of sheep and goats", although also to be "always fighting" with Damara of the plains, i.e. Herero (ibid: 59, 63).

Figure 4: Plates of Tsaobis under German colonial occupation: a. 'Bergdamara village'; b. 'Bergdama hut'; c. Schuztruppe military exercise (Source: Von François 1896: 293, 299, 133, out of copyright originals held at British Library and available on Wikimedia)

An 1864 Rhenish Mission Society Chronicle of Otjimbingwe records that "Bergdama" and "Bushmen" were living in the Sesfontein area when the |Uixamab !Gomen ("Topnaar") and later Swartbooi Oorlam Nama lineages consolidated there from around the 1860s, in part to escape escalating Herero–Nama conflict in central parts of the territory (Köhler 1969: 111).[8]

---

8   Swartbooi Nama were defeated in these struggles and forced to leave |Ânhes / Re-
     hoboth (previously settled by "Berg Damara") from where they trekked "along the
     Kuiseb River, and thence to the Swakop River in order to find new dwelling places in
     Hereroland"; only to be pursued by the expansionary Oorlam Nama leader Jan Jonker
     Afrikaner who overtook them and set fire to their wagons in retaliation for Swart-
     booi support for the Herero leader Kamaherero. This experience sped up their retreat
     along the !Khuiseb, from where they settled at Salem on the Swakop River; then mov-

The American trader Gerald McKiernan met "Berg-Damara" living at the Waterberg (!Hob, Omuvereoom) in 1875 (Serton 1954: 67), and Missionary Büttner in 1879 observes that "a few Dama chiefs are living north of the Waterberg plateau who have apparent authority over several 1 000s of people" (Büttner 1879: 286). In 1918, Damara Chief Judas Goresib (||Guruseb?) of Okombahe confirms that "[our] Chief's [Nawabib's] village used, many years ago, to be at the place now known as Okanjande near the Waterberg. It was known to us by the name of Kanubis [⸗Khanubis] ..." (Union of South Africa 1918: 104). In 1896, Captain Peter Möller, a Swedish traveller who journeyed from Mossamedes southwards through "Owampoland" and "Damaraland" to Walvis Bay, photographs "Bergdamara" west of Etosha pan in the area of Okahakana (Rudner/Rudner 1974 [1899]) (see Figure 5a). To the right of Figure 5a can be seen oblong wooden bowls used especially for making and sharing *sâu* beer[9], as recently demonstrated to us by Jacobus ||Hoëb of the Hoanib Cultural Group, Sesfontein[10]. These bowls appear identical to a bowl found in the area of Onanis (⸗O!nanis) in the Swakop river catchment (see Figure 5b) where "Hill Dama" had been settled at the time of Galton and Andersson's visit in 1850.

From 1866, under the Chieftainship of Abraham Goresib (?, ||Guruseb – see above), many "Berg-Damara" became consolidated at Okombahe / |Â⸗gommes. Okombahe Damara are described in 1877 by the British Cape Colony magistrate, W.C. Palgrave, as making "gardens in which they grow mealies, pumpkins and tobacco", with "a mile of the river-bed under cultivation" from which "300 muids"[11] of wheat were harvested, "the greater part of which was sold for more than 40 shillings a muid, being also a provident

---

ing towards Fransfontein and Sesfontein where they settled, via Ameib in the Erongo mountains, finding !Oe‡gā "Bergdama" there, some of whom also subsequently moved north, both with the Swartbooi and independently (see Lau 1987b: 100, 104; Wallace 2011: 61). These treks to the north-west by !Oe‡gā Dama have also been reconstructed through multiple interviews with Elizabet Ge !Nabasen Tauros and her daughter Julia Tauros of the 'Purros Dama' family now living in Sesfontein. !Oe‡gā is the Damara / ‡Nūkhoe name for the Erongo mountains.

9   Made from *Stipagrostis* spp. grass seeds (*sâun*) collected from harvester ants nests and honey (*danib*) (described fully in Sullivan 1999).

10   At a performance by Sesfontein's Hoanib Cultural Group, Kai-as, May 23, 2019.

11   A *muid* consisted of around three bushels, see https://dsae.co.za/entry/muid/e05002 (last accessed June 6, 2020).

Figure 5a: "Bergdama" group encountered in 1896 at Okahakana, west of Etosha pan. To the right of the image are two distinctive oblong wooden bowls used for making and sharing beer (!khari) made from Stipagrostis spp. grass seeds (sâun) and honey (danib) (Source: scan from Rudner and Rudner [Möller] 1974 [1899], opp. p. 147); Figure 5b: Wooden bowl bearing close resemblance to those to the right of Fig. 5a, found cached in a rock crevice in the vicinity of Onanis / ǂŌ!nanis (Photo: Sian Sullivan, April 3, 2018)

people ... fast becoming rich in cattle and goats" (Palgrave 1877 quoted in Union of South Africa 1918: 105-106).

In seeking deposits of guano in association with lucrative British trading interests in this fertilizer, George Elers in 1906 builds a road so as to travel northwards towards Sesfontein, accomplished with "a large number of Berg-Damaras who live in this [sic] Velds. I may say that these natives gave me every assistance and made nearly 100 miles of new road taking in new water places, as so many of the known ones were dry" (quoted in Jacobson/Noli 1987: 173). On the coast near the Hoanib mouth Elers encountered "[a]n old sea Bushman [who] remembered the birds [white breasted cormorants] nesting there as he used to kill them for food and take the eggs" (ibid.). Between the Hoanib and Hoarusib he found "some Berg-Damaras and Bushman who live close to the sea ... constantly walking up and down the coast in search for whales that come ashore [with] their Kraals all the way to Khumib" (ibid.). In 1910, a geologist for the Kaoko Land und Minengesellschaft notes "Bergdamara" at places along the !Uniab river called "Gamgamas" and "Swartmodder", and also meets "Bergdamara" (possibly or also ||Ubun) returning from "Uniab-Mund".[12] In 1917, the First Resident Commissioner for Ovamboland, Major Charles N. Manning, encountered people he refers to as "Klip Kaffirs" at Kowareb, Sesfontein and north-west of Sesfontein along the Hoanib and Hoarusib rivers.[13] In 1946, a settler farmer, David Levin, looking for grazing in the area of Twyfelfontein / |Ui-||aes, found a Damara / ≠Nūkhoen family living there who regularly moved for grazing between "Gwarab" (Kowareb, south-east of Sesfontein), Grootberg and |Ui-||aes (Levin/Goldbeck 2013: 17).

Of note in these historical texts are the diverse combinations of livelihood practices observed to be enacted by "Berg Damara" whose "mode of production" incorporated "elaborate hunting methods involving large-scale cooperation and extensive areas" (RMS Berichte 1849, quoted in Lau 1979: 31-32), as well as keeping goats and sheep (Andersson 1861: 300) and sometimes cattle (Lau 1979: 31). Regarding cooperative hunting linked historically with Berg Damara, a report of 1852 "states that the enclosures made from thorn tree branches are 4-6 feet wide, sometimes 'several hours long' and become lower in height towards the apex. Along these were posted watchmen who chased the game along" (Lau 1979: 50, 211, Appendix 3; also Gürich 1891: 138). Most communities also "grew tobacco, processed it, and traded it with Nama, Herero and Ovambo" (Lau 1979: 13), copper smelting was undertaken in central and southern Namibia (Kinahan 1980), a wide variety of plants and invertebrates were sources of food and medicines (Sullivan 1998 and references therein), and wooden bowls and ceramic containers were made for storing and cooking foods (Du Pisani/Jacobson 1985).[14]

***

Historical encounters and mentions such as those described above are mapped in more detail online at https://www.futurepasts.net/historical-refe

---

12   NAN.A.327 Krause and Kuntz, Kuntz 25/8/1910, report to the Kaoko Land und Minen-gesellschaft.

13   Manning Report, ADM 156 W 32 National Archives of Namibia, 1917, p. 6 and *Traveller's Map of Kaokoveld*. Manning did not travel south of Sesfontein so his report is unable to provide information about this more southerly area.

14   The making and use of black clay pots called *!nomsus* have been recalled in several oral histories. Michael |Amigu Ganaseb (Purros), 13 April 2015, described cooking mussels in black pots in his early life in the northern Namib, and a ||Ubu man Franz |Haen ||Hoëb (Sesfontein), 4 April 2019, demonstrated to us how such pots were made in the past.

rences-dama-namibia, last accessed August 1, 2020 (see screenshot at Figure 6).

Figure 6: Screenshot of online map for historical references to the presence of Damara / ‡Nūkhoen in Namibia. Source: see links https://www.futurepasts.net/historical-refer ences-dama-namibia (last accessed August 1, 2020)

Figure 6 thus provides an indication of pre- and colonial dwelling locali- ties of Damara / ‡Nūkhoen. Compiled through spatialising references in his- torical texts from the late 1700s on, each placemark on the map represents written mentions of people encountered for which the name and context clar- ifies them as Damara / ‡Nūkhoen. Clearly the map is limited by the extent of travel by the writers – for example the area north of the Brandberg / Dâures remains more-or-less a blank in terms of historical record until the late 1800s – as well as the biases the writers bring to their encounters and observations. Nonetheless, the map provides some idea of the localities of past presence of those identified as Damara / ǂNūkhoen.

Displacement

Damara / ǂNūkhoen and ‖Ubun now have access to only a small part of these formerly occupied land areas. Displaced in the 1800s as Oorlam Nama from the Cape Colony and Herero pastoralists from the north competed for pastures and trade routes in the central and north-west parts of the territory, and later as British and German colonial interests increasingly appropriated land in the southern and central parts of the country, Damara / ǂNūkhoen were squeezed into a handful of 'native reserve' areas: mainly around Sesfontein and Fransfontein in the north, and Okombahe and Windhoek in the south (for detail on the multiple historical displacements affecting Damara / ǂNūkhoen and ‖Ubun, see Sullivan 1996; Sullivan/Ganuses 2020). Sesfontein and environs, positioned north of the veterinary cordon or "Red Line" that once marked the extent of colonial control, escaped the fenced alienation of land into surveyed and settled farms (see Figure 1 for the current position of the vet fence), permitting to a greater extent the dynamic sustenance of socialized land relationships and mobility practices into recent decades and remembered pasts. Nonetheless, these and other areas of the north-west forming the focus of this chapter have also been impacted by several layers of land reorganization. Clarification of these experiences can make more visible some of the 'gaps' – or perhaps more correctly 'aporia' or 'blindspots' – in many normalized narratives and cartographic representations regarding Namibia's north-west (cf. Harley 1992, drawing on concepts developed by Jacques Derrida).

In early decades of the twentieth century, for example, a livestock-free zone north of the "Red Line" veterinary cordon dissecting Namibia from east to west was coercively cleared of people living there so as to control the movement of animals from communal areas in the north to settler commercial farming areas in the south (Miescher 2012)[15]. Africans including

---

15   As also occurred in other parts of the country. In the 1930s, for example, West Caprivi in the north-east of the country was similarly designated a livestock free zone, resulting

"Berg Damara" were repeatedly and forcibly moved out of the western areas between the Hoanib and Ugab Rivers, although inability to police this remote area meant that people tended to move back as soon as the police presence had left (ibid: 154; SWAA 1930: 14). Some years later, an Agricultural Officer Inspection report for the Kaokoveld recommended that the then derelict gardens at Warmquelle, at the time under small-scale agriculture by several families, be used "... to provide grazing and gardening ground for the Damaras who moved to Sesfontein from the Southern Kaokoveld".[16] Moments of this clearance process are vividly remembered by elderly informants in the present. At the waterhole of ǂKhabaka in the present-day Palmwag Tourism Concession (see Figure 1), Ruben Sanib thus recalled his experience of being evicted from the formerly large settlement of Gomagorra in Aogubus (see Figure 7), now also in the Palmwag Concession. This eviction was an event that occurred prior to the memorable death of Husa, then Nama captain of Sesfontein / !Nani|aus, who in 1941 was mauled by a lion at the place known as ǂAo-daos (see below):

> The government said this is now the wildlife area and you cannot move in here. We had to move to the other side of the mountains - to Tsabididi [the area also known today as Mbakondja]. Ok, now government police from Kamanjab and Fransfontein told the people to move from here. And the people moved some of the cattle already to Sesfontein area, but they left some of the cattle [for the people still in Hurubes and Aogubus, see below] to drink the milk. Those are the cattle the government came and shot to make the people move. [Some of these cattle belonged to a grandfather of Ruben's called Sabuemib] And Sabuemib took one of the bulls into a cave at |Gui-gomabi-!gaus and he shot it there with a bow and arrow [so that they would at least be able to eat biltong from the meat and prevent the animal being killed by the authorities]. Other cattle were collected together with those of Hereros [also herding in the area] and were shot by the government people at Gomagorras [named after the word *goman* for cattle and located in the hills south of Tsabididi]. Some of Sabuemib's cattle were killed in this way.[17]

in relocation outwards of Bantu language-speaking agropastoralists living in the area at the time (Paksi 2020: 24 after Boden 2014).

16   Inspection report, Kaokoveld. Principal Agricultural Officer to Assistant Chief Commissioner Windhoek, 06/02/52, SWAA.2515.A.552/13 Kaokoveld - Agriculture.

17   Ruben Sauneib Sanib (ǂKhabaka), November 20, 2014. This process and experience of eviction is similar to the evictions of Khoekhoegowab-speaking Hai||om and their

In the 1950s, relief grazing and farm tenancies were made available in this north-western area to Afrikaans livestock farmers under Namibia's South African administration (Kambatuku 1996), who were thereby able to gain from the prior clearances of local peoples. These newly surveyed farms later comprised relief grazing areas for settler farmers, and overlapped with former Damara / ǂNūkhoen living places (sing. ||an||huib). The settlement of Soaub, for example, formerly under the leadership of a man called !Abudoeb and the place where the ||Khao-a Dama man Aukhoeb |Awiseb (maternal grand-father of Ruben Sanib mentioned above) is buried (see Figure 7 and genealogy in Figure 13 below), is located in what became Farm Rooiplaat 710 (ibid: v).

Figure 7: Ruben Sauneib Sanib sits at Aukhoeb's grave at the former living place of Soaub (Photo: Sian Sullivan, May 15, 2019)

From 1950 onwards, several diamond mines were established in the north-ern Namib, at Möwe Bay, Terrace Bay, Toscanini and Sarusa (Mansfield 2006), making this territory a "restricted access area". This is a remembered process

livestock from the then Game Reserve No. 2 (now Etosha National Park) in 1954, car-ried out by the Native Commissioner of Ovamboland (Mr Eedes) under the direction of P.A. Schoeman, the Chief Native Commissioner based in Windhoek (as documented in Dieckmann 2007: 191).

that displaced especially ||Ubun living and moving in this far-westerly area, as well as offering new employment opportunities in the mines thereby established. In 1958, and following the westward and northward shift in 1955 of the so-called Police Zone boundary and the opening up of farms for white settlers in this area, the boundary of the former "Game Reserve No. 2", now Etosha National Park (ENP), was extended westwards to the coast following the Hoanib River in the north and the Ugab River in the south (Tinley 1971) (see Figure 8), briefly conjuring the landscapes between the Hoanib and Ugab rivers as a formally protected conservation area.

In sum, these overlapping processes particularly affected the land areas (*!hūs*) known as ǂKhari Hurubes, !Nau Hurubes,[18] Aogubus, and Namib (see below), where a number of Damara / ǂNūkhoe and ||Ubu families recall living in the past at specific places where their family members are buried. ||Khao-a Dama of ǂKhari Hurubes and Aogubu Dama of Aogubus mostly became consolidated in the northern settlements of Sesfontein / !Nani|aus, Anabeb, Warmquelle and Kowareb. Dâure-Dama of the more southerly !Nau Hurubes mostly became concentrated in the vicinity of the Ugab River and the associated former Okombahe Reserve. The broader geographical area that experienced these historical shifts is the focus of research drawn on in the remainder of this chapter, set in an understanding that the close relationships with places and broader landscapes recounted below are likely to have once been relevant for the much wider area of Damara / ǂNūkhoen historical habitation indicated above and in Figure 6.

'Unmappable' dimensions of Damara / ǂNūkhoe and ||Ubu relationships with land in west Namibia

The contexts and observations outlined above complexify the category 'hunter-gatherer', whilst also affirming the past significance of both 'hunting' and 'gathering' as Damara / ǂNūkhoen and ||Ubun food-acquiring practices, together with the conceptual and symbolic registers with which these practices might be accompanied and informed. The historical background is also suggestive of past circumstances of relative autonomy that have become progressively constrained and disrupted in the years since. Historical forces

---

18   Also '||Hurubes' (Hinz/Gairiseb 2013: 186).

Figure 8: The shifting boundaries of Game Reserve No. 2 / ENP, 1907–1970 (Source: Dieckmann 2007: 76, reproduced with permission)

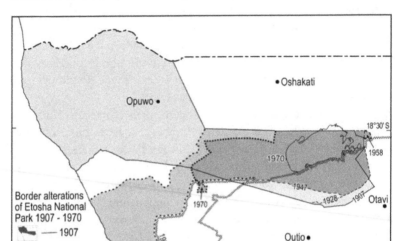

and events privileging epistemologies and ontologies of representation associated with colonial and apartheid statecraft have thus conspired to make certain presences and relationships more-or-less 'unmappable' in the present (as considered in more detail in Sullivan/Ganuses 2020; Sullivan in press). What is able to be mapped today are the traces remaining in a history severely constrained by land appropriations serviced and supported by cartographic land-claiming techniques, combined with normalized categories of mapping in the present that are exceeded by many dimensions of experience, meaning and value (see also Pearce, this volume). How, then, might the 'unmappable' be mapped in this context? We respond to this question with reference to three interconnected and variously emplaced dimensions: genealogies, ancestral agencies, and song-dances associated with varied registers of healing.

For all these dimensions, their significance has in fact emerged through research practices associated with mapping. Specifically, multiple recorded oral accounts have been gathered during a series of multi-day journeys with elderly Damara / ǂNūkhoen and ||Ubun individuals currently living in the settlements of Sesfontein / !Nani|aus and Kowareb, see Table 1. These journeys, undertaken in 2014, 2015 and 2019, constituted a process of (re)finding, and recording coordinates and information for, places mentioned in prior interviews as where an array of now elderly people used to live. For the reasons mentioned above, they have focused particularly (but not exclusively) on the area now designated as the Palmwag Tourism Concession (see Figure 1). This method of 'on-site oral history' led by research participants constitutes what anthropologist Anna Tsing (2014: 13) describes as 'historical retracing': 'walking the tracks of the past even in the present' to draw out 'the erasure of earlier histories in assessments of the present [thus] infilling the present with the traces of earlier interactions and events' (also Sullivan 2017a, in press). Such documentation can draw into the open occluded and alternative knowledges, practices and experiences that continue to 'haunt' the present despite their diminution through various historical processes (Bird Rose 1991; Bell 1993[1983]; Basso 1996; Tsing 2005: 81; De Certeau 2010: 24).

Table 1: Journeys forming the basis for on-site oral histories in the broader landscape with elderly Khoekhoegowab-speaking inhabitants of Sesfontein and Anabeb Conservancies.

Date	Name	Ethnonym	Focal Places
27-281014 & 20-231114	Ruben Sauneib Sanib, Sophia Opi ǀAwises	ǁKhao-a Dama, ǁUbun	Kowareb, Mbakondja, Top Barab, Kai-as
17-190215	Ruben Sauneib Sanib	ǁKhao-a Dama	Kowareb, Kai-as, Hunkab, Sesfontein
21-220215	Ruben Sauneib Sanib	ǁKhao-a Dama	West of Tsabididi, ǂKhari Soso, Aoguǁgams, Bukuba-ǂnoahes, ǁHuom
07-100315	Ruben Sauneib Sanib	ǁKhao-a Dama	Sixori, Oruvao/ǁGuru-Tsaub, Sanibe-ǁgams
07-091115	Ruben Sauneib Sanib, Sophia Opi ǀAwises	ǁKhao-a Dama, ǁUbun	Kowareb, ǁKhao-as, Soaub (Desert Rhino Camp area)
13-141115	Christophine Daumû Tauros, Michael ǀAmigu Ganaseb	!Narenin Hoanidaman / ǁUbun	Sesfontein, Purros, Hoanib
20-261115	Franz ǁHoëb, Noag Ganaseb	ǁUbun	Sesfontein, Hoanib, coast, Kai-as
05-090519	Franz ǁHoëb	ǁUbun	Sesfontein, !Uniab mouth, Hûnkab, Mudorib, ǁOeb, Hoanib
12-150519	Ruben Sauneib Sanib	ǁKhao-a Dama	Sesfontein, Gomagorras, ǀNobarab, ǁKhao-as, Soaub
17-200519	Julia Tauros	Purros Dama	Sesfontein - Purros
22-240519	Hoanib Cultural Group, Sesfontein (n = 18, + 7 facilitators)	Multiple	Kai-as

The iteratively updated mapped dataset of named springs, former dwelling places, graves and landscape features recorded through this research, combined with stories, memories, genealogies and images is located online at https://www.futurepasts.net/cultural-landscapes-mapping (last accessed August 5, 2020) (see Figure 9). In this dataset, detailed descriptive place names (toponyms) speak of acute observation of biophysical characteristics of the landscape (cf. Basso 1984, 1996). Identification of people and events with particular places, tells of the remembered emplacement of defining moments in local history. Memories of places that have been home, communicate the loss of both pasts and futures that comes from being unexpectedly displaced through historical forces not of one's choosing (Jedlowski 2001; see also Albrecht 2007). This 'counter-mapping' research has formed the basis for reporting to the Namidaman Traditional Authority (TA) (Sullivan et al. 2019) and has been submitted as part of this TA's submission to the Ancestral Land Commission established by the Namibian government in 2019 (Tjitemisa 2019). As reported elsewhere in this volume (for example, in the chapters by Brody, Dieckmann, Vermeylen) there is thus the possibility for legal agency to be performed through such 'counter-mapping' practices, although the full possible scope of such agency has yet to be seen in this case.

These journeys with now elderly people to find remembered places were themselves partly a response to learning (in the 1990s) of a series of named places that tend not to appear on mapped representations of the area. This iterative mapping process has itself generated new understanding regarding a different set of concerns, as we now outline.

1.   Genealogies, identity and belonging

Field research in the Sesfontein area of north-west Namibia beyond the "Red Line", where Damara / ǂNūkhoen and ǁUbun have retained some continuity of habitation for at least several generations, has helped clarify relationships of belonging linking familial groups (!haoti) with named areas of land (!hūs) – termed "local-incorporative units" by anthropologist Alan Barnard (1992: 203). We elaborate this first 'dimension' of experience at some length to illustrate both the different conceptions of land and identity at play here, and the intimate realities of past lived experiences of these areas shared by our interlocutors and their families (see also Sullivan/Ganuses 2020; Sullivan in press).

Some time ago, the late headman of Kowareb, Andreas !Kharuxab, explained to us that a !hūs is a named area of the !garob or "veld":

> From the !Uniab River to this side it's called Aogubus. And the Hoanib River is the reason why this area is called Hoanib. And from the !Uniab to the other

side (south) is called Hurubes. That is Hurubes. From the !Uniab to that big mountain (Dâures) is called Hurubes. If you come to the ||Huab River – from the ||Huab to the other side (south) is called ||Oba (now Morewag Farm). Khorixas area is called |Huib. And from there if you pass through and come to the !U‡gab River we refer to that area as |Awan !Huba, i.e. "Red Ground". *Every area has got its names.*[19]

Oral testimonies affirm Damara / ‡Nūkhoen identification with reference to the *!hūs* that they or their ancestors hail from, at least in recent generations, for example:

... the people get their names according to where they were living. ... My mother's parents were both Damara and my father's parents were both Damara. I am a Damara child; I am part of the Damara 'nation' (*!hao*). I am a Damara (*Damara ta ge*). We are Damara but we are also Dâure Dama. We are part of the Dâure Dama "nation" (*!hao*). We are Dâure Dama. (*Dâure Dama da ge*).[20]

My father was really from this place [Sesfontein/!Nani|aus], and my mother was from Hurubes. Really she's from Hurubes. She's ||Khao-a Damara.[21]

!Narenin were living in the western areas of Hoanib and Hoarusib. Where we were just now [i.e. Hûnkab area] was ||Ubun land. ||Ubu people were living in the places close to the ocean like Hûnkab, !Uniab, |Garis, Xûxûes. Those are the areas of *Huri-daman ||Ubun di !huba* [lit. the 'Sea-Dama (referring to !Narenin, see below) and ||Ubun land'].[22]

Dynamic relationship with a lineage-associated land areas (sing. *!hūs*) is further reflected in the location and orientation of families in larger settlements, and the directions in which people travel when venturing into the *!garob* to herd livestock, gather foods and other items, and previously to hunt. Figure 10 shows named land areas (sing. *!hūs*) for a series of *!haoti* in north-west Namibia who have been associated with these areas for at least several generations such that, despite recent restrictions on access, some claims for con-

---

19   Andreas !Kharuxab (Kowareb), May 13, 1999, see also Sullivan 2003, in press.

20   Andreas !Kharuxab (Kowareb), May 13, 1999. (Nb. 'Dâures' is the Khoekhoegowab name for the Brandberg massif).

21   Philippine |Hairo ||Nowaxas (Sesfontein), April 15, 1999.

22   Ruben Sauneib Sanib (|Awagu-dao-am), April 19, 2015.

Figure 9: Screenshot of online map indicated former ||an-||huib (living places) and other sites (such as springs, graves, Haiseb cairns and topographic features) in the broader landscape of the Sesfontein, Anabeb and Purros conservancies (Source: on-site oral history research, 2014–2019, building on oral history documentation in the late 1990s)

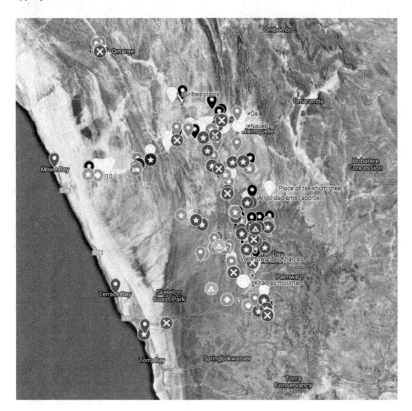

tinuous habitation can be made. Oral histories clarify these *!haos / !hūs* relationships and interactions over the last few generations, as outlined below for !Narenin, ||Ubun and ||Khao-a Dama. In southern Kunene, these different groupings are now categorized under the broader linguistic, lineage, and land-based grouping of *Namidaman* and represented by the Namidaman Traditional Authority (TA).

Figure 10: Named land areas (sing. !hūs) as dynamically known in recent generations by Damara / ‡Nūkhoen and ||Ubun inhabitants of present-day conservancies in southern Kunene (shaded) (Source: fieldnotes and on-site oral histories)

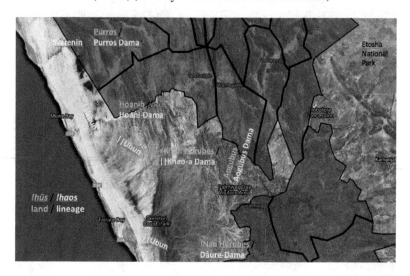

!Narenin are Damara / ‡Nūkhoen associated with the western reaches of the northerly Hoanib and Hoarusib rivers, who for as long into the past as people can remember relied significantly on the flesh and seeds of *!nara*, hence their ethnonym (Sullivan et al. 2021). They harvested *!nara* from the Hoarusib River and from near Dumita (towards the mouth of the Hoarusib), Ganias and Sarusa springs[23]:

> ... my great, great-grandfathers and mothers were there at Sarusa, and I was born here [in Hoanib] at ‡Hoadi||gams.[24]

> ... my family are the people who are/were living in the *!nara* area, and they collect the *!naras* – that's where the name [!Narenin] is coming from.[25]

---

23   Reportedly the ‡Aonin of the !Khuiseb River have also at times been given the alternative name of !Narenin or !Naranin, derived from the word "*!nara*" and inflected with a derogatory connotation when used by other Nama people (Budack 1977: 2).

24   Christophine Daumû Tauros (Purros), November 13, 2015.

25   Hildegaart |Nuas (Sesfontein), April 6, 2014.

... they would move in between the Hoarusib and Hoanib. In Hoanib in the rain time they came here to collect food, especially ≠ares[26] and ≠namib[27] – the latter is not found in Hoarusib. At this time they wore leather skirts from springbok leather. They would collect *lots* and take back bag by bag to the Hoarusib. The *!naras* grow ripe in the Hoarusib at this time and were harvested by *!narab* Dama [i.e. !Narenin].[28]

The !Narenin people were the people living next to the ocean [i.e. "Huridama", see above]. And when the *!naras* is ripe then they go to the ocean side of the *!naras* and then they stay there, and when they are finished with the *!naras* it's now the *xori*-time, and the *xoris*[29] is now ripe and so they came to the Hoanib [to harvest *xoris*] and they stay there. So, they are not the people who are staying in one place – they are moving from place to place.[30]

In recent generations at least, !Narenin and ||Ubun would interact and intermarry in these northern Namib areas:

The !Narenin people were living in Purros and the ocean side is where the *!naras* are living, and the ||Ubun were at !Ui||gams / Auses in the Hoanib. Now when they are looking for the food they meet and it's where the !Narenin men take the ||Ubun women and the ||Ubun women take the !Narenib,[31] like that. So they were moving from place to place because of the *sâu* and *bosû*[32] – when it's now the time of the *sâu* and *bosû* they came to ||Gams [Amspoort], and Dubis and |Aub [all are places along the Hoanib

---

26   i.e. Grass seeds from *Setaria verticillata* collected from underneath especially *Acacia tortilis* trees. Nb. Manning reports so-called "Klip Kaffirs", i.e. "Berg Damara" harvesting these seeds in the Hoarusib river on his *Traveller's Map of Kaokoveld* compiled from journeys in 1917 and 1919 (National Archives of Namibia).

27   Grass seeds of *Danthoniopsis dinteri* that appear white when 'cleaned'.

28   Eva |Habuhe Ganuses, *née* ≠Gawuses (Sesfontein), 1995.

29   Fruits of *Salvadora persica*.

30   Christophine Daumû Tauros and Michael |Amigu Ganaseb (Purros), November 13, 2015.

31   Khoekhoegowab is a gendered language in which nouns and names ending in 'b' are denoted as masculine whilst those ending in 's' are feminine, thus '!Narenib' here means a !Narenin man.

32   Seeds of *Monsonia* spp. (usually *M. umbellata*) collected from harvester ants' nests (see Sullivan 1999).

River] – those are the places where they stayed because of *sâu* and *bosû*. So at the *!nara* time then they go back to !Ui||gams.[33]

As noted above, *||Ubun* are a Khoekhoegowab-speaking people sometimes referred to locally as "Nama" and at other times as "Bushmen", who "a long time ago" split from peoples living along the !Khuiseb. They are likely to be amongst those coastal peoples associated with the term "Strandloper" in historical texts. As noted above, it seems probable that contemporary ||Ubun are descendants of a "Topnaar group" called |Namixan, who in the 1800s under their "Chief ǂGasoab, lived in the !Khuiseb", coming into conflict with "Topnaar" groups called !Gomen and Mu-||in, a conflict that continued "between ǂGasoab's successor, *Chief ǂHieb*, and Chief Khaxab of the Mu-||in" (Vigne 1994: 8, emphasis added[34]). The |Namixan reportedly withdrew "to the sea-coast" from where "Chief ǂHieb and two companions travelled secretly to Rooibank [in the lower !Khuiseb] to look for any of his people left there"; being "surprised at a Mu-||in werf [settlement] by a commando which attacked from the dunes rather than approaching them along the river, killing Chief

---

33   Christophine Daumû Tauros and Michael |Amigu Ganaseb (Purros), November 13, 2015.

34   Drawing on an archived late 1800s statement by Piet !Haibeb, son of Mu-||in "Topnaar" leader Frederick Khaxab, to an agent of German colonial settler Adolf Lüderitz. Further indicating the fluidity and dynamism of pre-colonial circumstances, the "Topnaar" captain Khaxab is described as having migrated from Kaokoveld around 1820-30 (or perhaps several decades earlier, according to Köhler 1969: 106) via the Swakop mouth, and then to the place "ǂKisa-||guwus commonly known as Kuwis or Sandfontein, located about three miles from the coast and settled south of what is now Walvis Bay" (Köhler 1969: 106). In the 1840s, Khaxab enters into an alliance with the Oorlam Nama captain Jonker Afrikaner "who became overlord of the Topnaar and appointed them his agents to sell cattle for arms", placing Jonker in control of the trade route between Walvis Bay and Lake Ngami in present-day Botswana, from which Oorlam Nama levy heavy tolls over the next 30 years (Jill Kinahan 2017: 303 after Vigne 1994: 7). When Missionary Scheppmann arrived at Rooibank on the !Khuiseb in December 1845, "Captain Frederik Khaxab was Oherhaupt of Topnaar. He lived in ǂKisa-||guwus, also called Sandfontein or Sand Fountain, where a spring was present" (Köhler 1969: 108). In 1850, Fredrick Khaxab is again mentioned in accounts by Galton (British) and Andersson (Anglo-Swede) as they prepared for their journey inland from Walvis Bay. He and his small community at ǂKisa-||guwus occasionally brought them "some milk and a few goats, as a supply for the larder, in exchange for which they received old soldiers' coats (worth sixpence a-piece), handkerchiefs, hats, tobacco, and a variety of other trifling articles" (Andersson 1861: 21-23).

‡Hieb and his companions" (Vigne 1994: 8). The |Namixan were again led away from the !Khuiseb *under Chief ‡Hieb's son"* (ibid., emphasis added).

Given known naming practices in which sons of especially lineage leaders may be named after their fathers, the possibility exists that "Chief ‡Hieb's son" here is the maternal grand-father ‡Gîeb remembered and described to us by the elderly ||Ubu man Franz ||Hoëb. Franz was born at the *!nara* fields near Auses / !Ui||gams waterhole in the lower Hoanib river and now lives in Sesfontein / !Nani|aus. ‡Gîeb was his maternal grandfather, alive at a time when Franz's family were harvesting *!nara* in the lower Hoanib and moving between *!nara* fields in the !Uniab and Hoanib via Kai-as (see below). ‡Gîeb's grave is next to a former dwelling site called Daniro on the banks of the !Uniab, where ‡Gîeb and others first encountered German men, described to Franz as being the first occasion when these ||Ubun had seen white men and encountered food in tins. This encounter was perhaps with the 1896 journey by Ludwig von Estorff which finds "deserted, circular reed huts at the Uniab River mouth" and on return a month later encounters here, "a band of 30 'Bushmen' who had just arrived from the Hoanib River. They were living off narra for the most part [using] a narra knife made from elephant rib at the Hoarusib River" (Jacobson/Noli 1987: 174).

In May 2019, Franz led us to the grave of his grand-father ‡Gîeb in the lower !Uniab river, located exactly as he had described in numerous prior interactions, in the present-day Skeleton Coast National Park (see Figure 11).

The story goes that when those who became known as ||Ubun travelled north to the !Uniab river a *!nara* plant was found by their dog and when they saw the dog eating the *!nara* without being harmed they also started eating the *!naras* (Sullivan et al. 2020).[35] ||Ubun would move between *!nara* fields in the !Uniab and Hoanib river mouths via Kai-as and Hûnkab springs, now in the Palmwag Tourism Concession.[36] ||Ubun also stayed at Dumita where there is a fountain,[37] and are considered to be:

---

35   Hildegaart |Nuas (Sesfontein), April 6, 2014; Franz ||Hoëb (near ‡Ōs), April 6, 2014.
      This story itself iterates a trope in which dogs are a 'companion species' (Haraway 2008)
      considered closely linked with human being, perception and sociality, an attribute also
      conferred to lions (Hannis/Sullivan 2018: 287; discussed too in Guenther 2020; and for
      jaguar in Kohn 2013).

36   Documented through journeys with Franz ||Hoëb and Noag Ganaseb, November 20-
      26, 2015, and Franz ||Hoëb, May 5-9, 2019.

37   Hildegaart |Nuas (Sesfontein), April 6, 2014.

... the people who built the houses at Terrace Bay and Möwe Bay and were living there. Those circle houses with the rocks at !Uniab are also the houses of the ||Ubun – my great grandparents were coming from those rock houses.[38]

... when other people saw them in the Namib with their houses built very close together (i.e. '||ubero') they exclaimed over the way the houses were being made – hence the name ||Ubun'.[39]

||Ubun presence in the northern Namib appears to be confirmed at least as far back as 1893 by the name "Hubun" in the lower reaches of the Hoarusib and Hoanib rivers on the *Deutscher Kolonial Atlas* of this year (see Sullivan/Ganuses 2020: 301).

Figure 11: Franz |Haen ||Hoëb stands at the grave of his grandfather ‡Gîeb in the lower !Uniab river, near to the former dwelling place known as Daniro (Photo: Sian Sullivan, May 7, 2019)

||Khao-a Dama are associated with the land area known as Hurubes and are a lineage that in times past was linked with ||Khao-as mountain, a large mountain at the confluence of the ‡Gâob (Aub) and !Uniab rivers in

38   Franz ||Hoëb (‡Os), April 6, 2014.
39   Emma Ganuses (!Nao-dâis), November 12, 2015.

the present-day Palmwag Tourism Concession (see below). A known ancestor of the |Awise ||Khao-a Dama family is buried at the former settlement of Kai-as, and a more recent ancestor (Aukhoeb |Awise), alive at least until the ca. 1930s, is buried at Soaub in !Nau ("fat") Hurubes (see Figure 7), having also previously herded livestock at Sixori south-west of Sesfontein in ǂKhari Hurubes (see below).[40] Three ||Khao-Dama brothers from the |Awise family of several generations back are buried on the edge of the settlement of Sesfontein.

Drawing out the interwoven relationships between places, people, ancestors, and varied beyond-human natures clarifies that none of these are distinct and atomized, but rather are rhizomatically associated and generatively connected. In this dimension then, a rather conventional mapping process consisting of finding and recording coordinates and other information for remembered named and significant places, has itself generated unanticipated complex and multilayered information by allowing dynamic genealogical connections with sites to be specified (cf. Bank 2006; Bollig 2009). By way of further illustration, we invoke below a short series of four sought-out places (see Figure 12) that turned out to be densely connected through past mobilities and genealogies, often in spite of the imposed governmentalities constraining access possibilities over the last few decades (as elaborated in the section above on 'Displacement').

Sixori

A high point of our on-site oral history documentation was finding Sixori, the birth-place of Suro's grandmother |Hairo. This ||gâumais (stock-post) effectively kickstarted our mapping research when |Hairo began the first oral history interview we recorded in 1999 with the words "I was born at Sixori in Hurubes." Neither of these names appear(ed) on maps of the area. After several failed attempts to (re)locate this ||gâumais, eventually we made it to the spring Sixori that in 1999 started this thread of enquiry. Sixori is named after the *xoris* (*Salvadora persica*) bushes that grow around a permanent spring of clear, sweet water and whose fruit provide a filling dry season food. The spring is located in the deeply incised landscape to the south-west of Sesfontein. Finding it on a brutally hot day in March 2015 required triangulating the orientation skills of the elderly ||Khao-a Dama man Ruben !Nagu Sauneib Sanib – a locally renowned hunter who remembered Sixori from past visits

---

40   Multiple oral histories with especially Ruben Sauneib Sanib and Sophia Opi |Awises.

Figure 12: Localities of four remembered places – Sixori, ‡Au-daos, Soaub and Kai-as

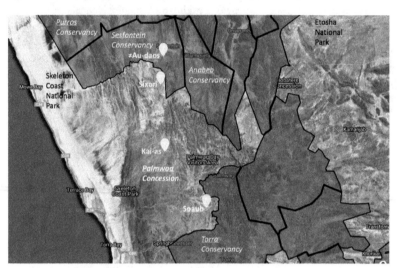

– and Filemon |Nuab – a younger man and well-known rhino tracker, who knew from present patrols in the area the location of the spring, but had not previously known its name of 'Sixori'.

As we sat in the shade of a rocky overhang close to the spring Ruben Sanib recalled harvesting honey (*danib*) from a hive in the vicinity of Sixori when he was a much younger man. He was with three older men: Aukhoeb |Awiseb (also called ||Oesîb after his daughter ||Oemî[41]), Seibetomab and Am-!nasib (also known as Kano). Aukhoeb was the brother of |Hairo's mother (Juligen ||Hūri |Awises). He was living and herding livestock at Sixori, a stock-post (*||gâumais*) linked with Sesfontein / !Nani|aus. ||Hūri was visiting him when she gave birth to |Hairo, Suro's grandmother, the year of which we think is *ca.* 1910 (see genealogy in Figure 13). The honey cave was west of Sixori. Sanib and companions travelled there to *sam* (to pull) the honey out from this cave, coming to Sixori afterwards to make *sâu* beer with that honey. From Sixori they walked back to Sesfontein through the pass that is called ‡Au-daos (see below). At that time, they did not have a donkey so they carried the honey in

---

41   As Hoernlé (1985 [1925]) documents for Khoekhoegowab-speaking Nama, parents may be referred to by the name of their children.

big tins on their shoulders. Aukhoeb was later buried at Soaub (see Figure 7 and detail below), illustrating past connections and mobilities between fairly distant springs and living places in the now cleared tourism concession of Palmwag.

Figure 13: Emplaced genealogy for the ||Khao-a Dama |Awise lineage now residents of Sesfontein (Source: fieldnotes and on-site oral histories)

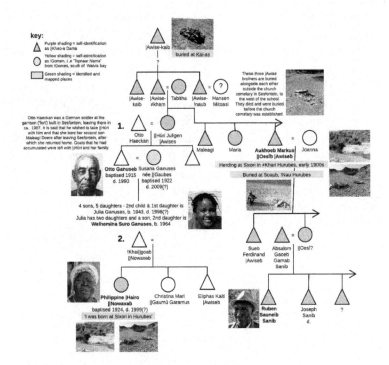

‡Au-daos

⸭Au-daos means "the road between two mountains" – "*dao*" is a mountain pass, and '⸭Ao' is the name of the white-flowered plant *Salsola* sp. which grows here and from which soap can be made.[42] This plant was reportedly gathered

---

42   Philippine |Hairo ||Nowaxas (Sesfontein), April 15, 1999.

in the past by Damara / ǂNūkhoen who had been recruited from their dwelling places in the wider !garob to work for an emerging Nama élite as this became consolidated in Sesfontein / !Nani|aus from the late 1800s. They would make soap from the ashes of the plant, combined with animal fat[43]. ǂAu-daos (Figure 14) is a potent place, having been the site where the then Nama headman of Sesfontein – Nathaniel Husa |Uixamab – died after being mauled by a lion here in 1941 (also see Van Warmelo 1962 [1951]: 37, 43-44). As related by Ruben Sanib, the story goes that cattle belonging to a Herero herder were bitten by a lion here and Husa, accompanied by his paternal cousin Theophilous ||Hawaxab (and later captain in Sesfontein), Namasamuel and a ǂNūkhoe man GamāGâub, came to shoot that lion. The lion was lying there in a cave nearby and when Husa shot the lion the lion came to Husa and grabbed him, dragging Husa to a |narab (Acacia tortilis) tree, and attacking Husa after he had shot the lion. As the lion was pinning Husa down, Theophilous ||Hawaxab grabbed hold of its ears to try and pull him off. Meanwhile, GamāGâub shot the lion from far away (even though the others told him to get closer) and, although he managed to hit the lion, he also accidentally shot Husa in the side, which killed him. When GamāGâub shot Husa, Namasamuel came and took the gun and shot the lion in the ear. When Husa was shot he called for his wife De-i, and when she came he talked to her and then he passed away. They then brought Husa over to a big |narab tree where, it is said, they made the |araxab [stretcher] on which they carried him back to Sesfontein.

---

43   Interview Ruben Sauneib Sanib (Kowareb), March 9, 2015. Soap-making in this way is described by James Edward Alexander (2006 [1838], vol. 1: 83), at the Nama-influenced reed mat hut of field-cornet Agganbag in the northern Cape, where he finds the "three fresh and strapping daughters [of the field-cornet] boiling soap, prepared with fat and the branches of the soap-bush". A fictionalized account of such soap-making is also conveyed in the Northern Cape novel *Praying Mantis* by the late André Brink (2006). At ǂAu-daos reportedly so much of the soap-plant was collected that there is little left here now, although the plant grows extensively further downstream in the Hoanib River.

Figure 14a: view north towards ⸗Au-daos (Photo: Sian Sullivan, March 9, 2015)

Figure 14b: ⸗Au-daos at location where in 1941 the Nama captain of Sesfontein, Husa |Uixamab, was attacked by a lion (Photo: Sian Sullivan, March 9, 2015)

Soaub

On a later journey we relocated the grave of Aukhoeb, |Hairo's uncle who had been herding livestock of the Ganuses family at Sixori (see Figure 7). Aukhoeb died and was buried at the *||an-||huib* – the living place – of Soaub. Today Soaub is located in the private Wilderness Safaris tourism concession associated with Desert Rhino Camp in the Palmwag Tourism Concession, these new names telling of the emphasis on tourism and wildlife conservation saturating the area in recent decades. Clearly a formerly large settlement with multiple dwellings in the past, whose headman was called !Abudoeb when Sanib knew the settlement, Soaub was later linked with allocations of reserve grazing to Afrikaans settler farmers, especially in the 1950s (Kambatuku 1996). Aukhoeb's grave is unmarked but located exactly where Sanib remembered: he led us with little hesitation to this grave. Its location had clearly lived on in his memory of past dwelling places, recalled in the present through the possibility and experience of return.

Kai-as

Kai-as, the fourth and final place described here, was once an important focus of past settlement for ||Khao-a Dama and ||Ubun at the site of a large permanent freshwater spring which used to feed a garden (Figure 15). People would congregate at Kai-as after the rains had started, and it was also considered an important place on routes between locations of key resources. ||Ubun, for example, would move between !nara (*Acanthosicyos horridus*) patches in the !Uniab and Hoanib river mouths via Kai-as and Hûnkab springs to the north-west of Kai-as. Ruben Sanib and Sophia Obi |Awises recalled how people from different areas (*!hūs*) used to gather at this place to play their healing dances called *arudi* and praise songs called *|gaidi*. These were times when young men and women would meet each other. Times when different foods gathered in different areas were shared between people, and when much honey beer (*!khari*), made from the potent foods of *sâui* and *danib*, was consumed (see Sullivan 1999). Being able to be present at these times in such places also enabled ongoing connection with ancestors associated with these places, the significance of which is described next.

2.   Ancestral agencies

> The relationship between the living and the dead, is no more than the projection, on the screen of religious thought, of real relations between the living. (Levi-Strauss 1987: 199 quoted in Wilcken 2010: 192)

For especially elderly ǂNūkhoen and ||Ubun people who have long associations with the west Namibian landscape, moving through the landscape requires greeting and offering practices that connect people alive today with people now physically dead, who were previously associated in some way

Figure 15: Kai-as detail (Source: Sullivan et al. 2019: 10)

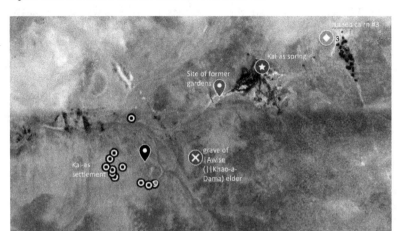

with these landscapes. Although attenuated through displacement, acculturation and the variously disruptive effects of modernity, such practices remain current and significant. Ancestors are communicated with through a practice called *tsē-khom*, understood as "speaking with the ancestors in the daytime"[44] (and thus distinguished from a different practice of communicating with one's ancestors during night-time healing events in order to understand the causes of sickness).

Tsē-khom usually involves offering and smoking tobacco, through which ancestors or *kai khoen* (literally big or old people) in the realm of the spirits of the dead are also able to enjoy this smoking. Through *tsē-khom*, ancestral agencies are requested to act in the present to open the road so that travelers can see the best way to go. They are asked for guidance regarding the most appropriate ways of doing things, and their support is evidenced through the intuitions people receive in response to queries that may arise as they are travelling. They are also asked to mediate the activities of potentially dangerous animals such as lions, who are understood very much as other ensouled beings who assert their own agencies and intentionality (Sullivan 2016; Hannis/Sullivan 2018). Ancestors thus greeted include recent family members

---

44   Translated literally as *tsē* = "to separate" and *khom* = "to keep holy" (Krönlein 1889: 325, quoted in Schmidt 2014a: 144).

whose graves are located in places travelled to and through; unidentified dead (or what Schmidt refers to as "'the invisible representations of anonymous dead") (Schmidt 2014a: 135); and sometimes a more broadly referenced ancestor-trickster-hero known as Haiseb. The latter is considered to have been a real person who lived in the distant past, did wonderful and clever things, and with whom large cairns found throughout the dryland environment from the Cape to the Kunene River are associated (see also Schmidt 2011, 2014a and b).

Ontologically, the ancestors are spirits or souls (i.e. *gagas* – see Inskeep 2003: 329) that have left humans whose bodies have died. As these spirit beings they have ontological reality in the present: they are not simply people who lived in the past, nor are they entities that require worship. They are understood more as specific types of entities that through pragmatic relationship practices are called upon to intervene – to assert agency – in the present, so as to influence outcomes (Sullivan 2017a). Sometimes this includes intervention in the agency of other non-human agents, such as lions, a species with which humans in west Namibia continue to live in close contact, as they have done throughout the remembered past. Other nonhuman agency-enacting entities in this context include animals as ensouled beings that both see us and act in relation to this seeing (cf. Kohn 2013), and the personified, supernatural force behind the phenomenon of rain – known as |*nanus* – that asserts agency in selecting those humans who become healers (Low 2008; Hannis/Sullivan 2018).

Indeed, the affirmation of agency and intentionality in multiple entities and selves beyond-the-human might be considered as key to 'KhoeSan' and other 'animist' perspectives on 'reality', through which agency, shaped by the diverse form, materiality and perceptual capacities of actors, is considered to be present everywhere, requiring constant attention and attunement in choices by humans (Harvey 2005; Sullivan 2010, 2013, 2019; Brightman et al. 2013; Descola 2013; Kohn 2013; Sullivan/Low 2014; Guenther 2020). Animist perspectives emphasize the ethical values and practices that may arise when people live and act as if diverse other kinds of being can see and in some way represent 'us' (Kohn 2013: 1). In structuring understandings of the nature of being, this worldview assumes that all activity by agents who can be animals, components of weather, plants, spirit-beings, ancestors and so on, is simultaneously imbued with a moral, if relative and frequently ambiguous, dimension (Ingold 2000), requiring ongoing awareness, participation and adjustment in relation to the actions of all these acting others (Deleuze/Guattari 1988 [1980]: 258, 266-267). Given, however, that ancestors are linked closely with places or areas (often those where they are buried), displacement from these areas makes it hard for people to maintain these ancestral connections, and thus to sustain the values associated with and encouraged by the *kai khoen*.

Ruben Sanib reminds us of the simultaneously pragmatic, spiritual and forceful dimensions of *tsē-khom* in this translation:

> You [= |Gabikhoeb[45]] who are sitting in the cave where you were eaten by a lion,
> when I am coming from the other side I greet you from afar.
> Let the dangerous animals go so that they can't frighten me.
> Let me sleep.
> Let me see Sixori tomorrow morning, so that I can come easily to Sixori.
> When I come to Orubao[46] I come because of you.
> I greet you my brother, lying in the cave.
> My goat was missing because of you [refers to a past event].
> Yes, you agree, yes you agree, yes you agree, yes mmm, yes mmm.[47]

3.   Song-dances, place and healing

In April 2014, we drove from |Giribes plains north-west of Sesfontein (see Figure 1), southwards towards the Hoanib River, with Christophine Daumû Tauros and Michael |Amigu Ganaseb who now live in Sesfontein. As we were approaching Borro – a tight rocky 'gateway' between the mountains – Christophine began singing a |gais song. The song told of how |Amigu's father's brother Bitirijan had once chased a young male oryx down towards Borro. He wanted to kill that oryx for food, but the oryx was running away, and Bitirijan made a song about that oryx running. As Christophine sang this song, a young lone male oryx ran past us, as we drove slowly down towards

---

45 |Gabikhoeb is a ‡Nūkhoe man who was a friend of Ruben Sanib's and who was killed by a lion in a cave near Sixori when he was out collecting honey. For details see Sullivan 2016.

46   Orubao (also called ||Guru-tsaub) is the name of a distinctive tall mountain to the east of Sixori.

47   Ruben Sanib, *tsē-khom* before trying to find Sixori, 7 March 2015. A recording of this *tsē-khom* greeting from the evening prior to our final attempt to relocate Sixori (see above) can be heard at https://soundcloud.com/futurepasts/ss-tse-khom-by-sanib-before (last accessed August 8, 2020).

Borro. It was as if the song had brought an event from the past into the present as we moved through the place in which the song had arisen.

Table 2: |Gais song sung by Christophine Daumû Tauros as we approached Borro, leading into the Obias River, April 6, 2014.

Khoekhoegowab	English
Borro di dai ||gôako |gaero mai aise	I am going to Borro and if I go to Borro I am thinking about the oryx
Borro da koro ‡âib ge |gaero mau aise	If you think about the oryx then you have to think about Borros
‡Habe di ‡âiko ||gûdi ôaba aise	Bitirijan was chasing a young oryx (to hunt it) and the oryx ran away and came through Borros
Borro di ||gôako ||gôa da re aise	And he sings about the oryx who ran through Borros

The act of singing praise songs (*|gaidi*) and healing songs (*arudi*) is indeed described as re-living and re-seeing the events, people, places and entities of which the song is about. In this way, songs and their performance reaffirm identities, values and histories about people and places, thereby constituting a form of 'indigenous mapping'.

Experiences of singing and dancing engender enjoyment, affective intensities and experiences of connection. *|Gaidi* are specifically described as sung "for happiness and the heart". Elderly people in Sesfontein remember a long list of *|gaines* – celebrated leaders of *|gaidi* played in celebratory dances that lasted through the night. Accompanied by complex clapped rhythms and collective polyphonic vocal arrangements, the songs allow(ed) participants to recursively and affectively (re)experience places, events and values expressed in the songs. With regard to *arudi* specifically, their performance also supports the skills of healers – those who have the rain-spirit and can see and attend to sicknesses in the people.

Place, storytelling, cultural identity: all these elements are poetically entangled and expressed through songs and dances. For elderly people returning to places they remember but are now unable to inhabit, it is often the loss of playing their *|gaidi* and *arudi* in these places that is recalled most vividly. On returning to Kai-as in November 2014, for example, Ruben Sanib and Sophia

|Awises recalled how when their families congregated here they would dance their |gaidi songs of celebration and their arudi healing songs. "Our hearts were happy here" (sida ǂgaogu ge ra !gaia neba), they said[48]. These recollections prompted through journeying to Kai-as led in May 2019 to an initiative to support a two-day filmed 'festival' there of |gaidi praise songs and arudi healing song-dances by the Hoanib Cultural Group from Sesfontein (see The Music Returns to Kai-as at https://vimeo.com/486865709, last accessed February 01, 2021).

As described above, sometimes the very act of revisiting a place prompted recall of a song connected with that place, pointing towards the importance for what is often labelled "cultural heritage" of being able to access places with which heritage practices may be entangled (Impey 2018). Sophia |Awises thus burst spontaneously into an arus song as we approached ||Khao-as mountain, from where the ||Khao-a Dama !haos is said to have acquired its name (as outlined above). We happened to have the voice-recorder on at the time and the moment of Sophia singing forth this place-linked arus can be heard online here: https://soundcloud.com/futurepasts/arus-about-khao-asmountain-081 115, last accessed August 08, 2020).

Figure 16 is one of a series of images (including the image used for the cover of this book) in which we tried to convey this multifaceted intimacy with which people know and experience places in west Namibia, in combination with the stark, 'wild' beauty of these same landscapes as captured in high resolution aerial photographs. It shows Ruben Sanib and Sophia |Awises standing in front of ||Khao-as mountain on their first visit there for perhaps some decades. This photograph was made during the journey in which Sophia sang the arus mentioned above that told of the merged relationship between ||Khao-a Dama people and ||Khao-as mountain, which is also shown from above. The series of composite images of which Figure 16 is one, were inspired by this simultaneous character of intimacy and wildness shaping how west Namibian landscapes are known, and the loss described as 'heartbreak' caused as people became disconnected from the possibility of experiencing this intimacy[49].

---

48   Ruben Sauneib Sanib, Sophia Opi |Awises (Kai-as), November 22, 2014. See also Sullivan 2017b.

49   This series of images can be viewed in the online exhibition Future Pasts: Landscape, Memory and Music in West Namibia, see especially https://www.futurepasts.net/memory (last accessed August 8, 2020).

Figure 16: Ruben Sauneib Sanib and Sophia Opi |Awises with ||Khao-as mountain behind and to the side of them. (Original photo by Sian Sullivan, November 2015. Composite image by Sian Sullivan and Mike Hannis, incorporating aerial images supplied by the Directorate of Survey and Mapping, Windhoek)

Conclusion

> ... there can be no possibility of an equitable future without due recognition and understanding of the past. (Bird-Rose 1991: xxiii)

The French philosopher George Bachelard (1994 [1964]: 6) writes in *The Poetics of Space* that "[i]t is because our memories of former dwelling-places are relived as daydreams that these dwelling-places of the past remain in us for all time".

We have been able to variously 'map' the above places and their multiplicitous meanings in the present because memories of them have lived on in the day-dreams of people who once lived there. It follows that if people can no longer go to the places of their memories, there is a limit to how long these places can live on as day-dreams. The contemporary moment is infused with structural processes that can seem to enforce forgetting, leading to erasure of the density of cultural meaning with which the landscapes of west Namibia have been known. Nonetheless, the place-entangled histories, values and practices related above continue to haunt the present, conferring complexity, friction and sadness.

The Namibian constitution of 1995 is often celebrated for its clear statement regarding environmental care and protection, with Article 95(l) affirming that,

> [t]he State shall actively promote and maintain the welfare of the people by adopting, inter alia, policies aimed at … maintenance of ecosystems, essential ecological processes and biological diversity of Namibia and utilization of living natural resources on a sustainable basis for the benefit of all Namibians, both present and future. (GRN 2014 [1990])

At the same time, the constitution also includes the right to culture (cf. Paksi 2020). Article 19 states that "[e]very person shall be entitled to enjoy, practise, profess, maintain and promote any culture, language, tradition or religion", although adding that this is "subject to the terms of this Constitution and further subject to the condition that the rights protected by this Article do not impinge upon the rights of others or the national interest" (GRN 2014 [1990]). When the ability to enact and sustain cultural knowledges and practices is linked with access to the places and 'resources' with which cultural expression is entangled, there can clearly be tensions between these two dimensions of the constitution.

These tensions arise in particular when a *decoupling* of indigenous and local cultures from nature has been part and parcel of the historical creation of 'wild' African landscapes associated with biodiversity conservation and with both tourism and trophy-hunting income (Adams/McShane 1996; Dieckmann 2007). Thus, although great effort has gone into establishing locally-run "conservancies" from which members can benefit from wildlife-related incomes, cultural and historical dimensions of land-use and value remain relatively weakly entangled with conservation concerns. The "densities of meaning" "mapped" in this chapter arguably open up different realms of value in relation to the conservation landscapes of west Namibia. They beg questions of whether and how "cultural heritage" and an appreciation of peoples' pasts might be connected more strongly, and with mutual benefit, to conservation activities in the area.

Acknowledgements

Multiple people and organisations in Namibia helped to make the research possible on which this chapter is based, not least the individuals and families who shared their stories and views with us and to whom we are indebted. Trudi Stohls (Sam Cohen Library, Swakopmund), Werner Hillebrecht (National Archives of Namibia, Windhoek), Namibian botanist Pat Craven, and Michael Bollig (University of Köln) assisted with finding and sharing archival documents referenced herein. Kapoi Kasaona at Palmwag Lodge, Chairman of Sesfontein Conservancy Usiel |Nuab, Emsie Verwey at Hoanib Camp, friends at Save the Rhino Trust – Jeff Muntifering, Simson !Uri-ǂKhob, Sebulon ||Hoëb, Andrew Malherbe and Alta van Schalwyk – and Fredrick ||Hawaxab of the Namidaman Traditional Authority, all helped in different ways to make it possible for the on-site oral history mapping work to take place. The field research and documentation could not have happened without the guidance of Sesfontein resident and Rhino Ranger Filemon |Nuab. Mrs Esther Moombolah-|Goagoses and Mrs Emma |Uiras at the National Museum of Namibia supported Sian's research affiliation with this organisation, as have Gillian Maggs-Kölling and Eugène Marais at Gobabeb Namib Research Institute. Chris Baas at Donkerhuk West kindly shared the wooden bowl pictured in Figure 5b. I am especially grateful to Ute Dieckmann, Thea Skaanes and Saskia Vermeylen for their astute comments on earlier drafts of the chapter. Last, but in no way least, we are grateful to the UK's Arts and Humanities Research Council (AHRC) for grants that have supported this research (AH/K005871/2 www.futurepasts.net, AH/N504579/1 https://dsrupdhist.hypotheses.org/ and AH/T013230/1 www.etosha-kunene-histories.net, last accessed August 2, 2020).

References

Adams, Jonathan S./McShane, Thomas O. (1996): The Myth of Wild Africa: Conservation Without Illusion, Los Angeles: California University Press.

Albrecht, Glenn (2007): "Solastalgia: The Distress Caused by Environmental Change." In: Australasian Psychiatry 15, pp. 95-98.

Alexander, James E. (2006 [1838]): An Expedition of Discovery into the Interior of Africa: Through the Hitherto Undescribed Countries of the Great Namaquas, Boschmans, and Hill Damaras, Vols. 1 and 2, London: Elibron Classics Series, orig. published by Henry Colburn.

Andersson, Charles J. (1861): Lake Ngami or Explorations and Discovery During Four Years of Wanderings in the Wilds of Southwestern Africa, New York: Harper & Brothers.

Ashmore, Wendy/Knapp, Arthur B., eds. (1999): Archaeologies of Landscape: Contemporary Perspectives, Oxford: Blackwell Publishers.

Bachelard, Gaston, (1994 [1964]): The Poetics of Space, Boston: Beacon Press.

Bank, Andrew (2006): Bushmen in a Victorian World: The Remarkable Story of the Bleek-Lloyd Collection of Bushman Folklore, Cape Town: Double Storey Books.

Barnard, Alan (1992): Hunters and Herders of Southern Africa: A Comparative Ethnography of Khoisan Peoples, Cambridge: Cambridge University Press.

Basso, Keith H. (1996): Wisdom Sits in Places: Landscape and Language Among the Western Apache, Albuquerque: University of New Mexico Press.

Basso, Keith H. (1984): "'Stalking with Stories': Names, Places, and Moral Narratives Among the Western Apache." In: Bruner, Edward (ed.), Text, Play and Story: The Construction and Reconstruction of Sect and Society, Illinois: Waveland Press Inc., pp. 19-53.

Bell, Diane (1993 [1983]): Daughters of the Dreaming, St Leonard's: Allen and Unwin.

Bender, Barbara, ed. (1993): Landscape: Politics and Perspectives, Oxford: Berg Publishers.

Bender, Barbara/Winer, Michael. eds. (2001): Contested Landscapes: Movement, Exile and Place, Oxford: Berg.

Bird-Rose, Deborah (1991): Hidden Histories: Black Stories From Victoria River downs, Humbert River and Wave Hill Stations, Canberra: Aboriginal Studies Press.

Boden, Gertrud (2014): 'Elephant is My Chief and My Councillors Are Kudus, We Don't Talk and I Will Not Get Development' - Status of Crop Cultivation Projects and Other Livelihood Options in Bwabwata National Park, Unpublished research report.

Bollig, Michael (2009): "Kinship, Ritual, and Landscape Amongst the Himba of Northwest Namibia." In: Michael Bollig/Olaf Bubenzer (eds.), African Landscapes: Interdisciplinary Approaches, New York: Springer, pp. 327-351.

Brightman, Marc/Grotti, Vanessa Elisa/Ulturgasheva, Olga, eds. (2013): Animism in Rainforest and Tundra: Personhood, Animals, Plants and Things in Contemporary Amazonia and Siberia, Oxford: Berghahn Books.

Brink, André (2006): Praying Mantis, London: Vintage.

Budack, Kuno F.R. (1977): "The ǂAonin or Topnaar of the Lower !Kuiseb Valley, and the Sea." In: Anthony Traill (ed.), Khoisan Linguistic Studies 3, A.S.I. Communication no. 6, Johannesburg: University of the Witswatersrand, pp. 1-42.

Budack, Kuno F.R. (1983): "A Harvesting People on the South Atlantic Coast." In: South African Journal of Ethnology 6, pp. 1-7.

Büttner, Carl G. (1879): "The Berg-Damara." In: Cape Monthly33 Magazine 18, pp. 285-294.

Clastres, Pierre (2010 [1976]): Archeology of Violence, trans. by Jeanine Herman and Ashley Lebner, Cambridge, Massachusetts: Massachusetts Institute of Technology Press.

De Certeau, Michel (2010) Heterologies: Discourse on the Other, trans. by B. Massumi, Minneapolis: University of Minnesota Press.

Deleuze, Gilles/Guattari, Félix (1988 [1980]) A Thousand Plateaus: Capitalism and Schizophrenia, vol. 2., trans. by Brian Massumi, London: The Athlone Press.

Descola, Philippe (2013): Beyond Nature and Culture, Chicago, Illinois: University of Chicago Press.

Dieckmann, Ute (2007): Hai||om in the Etosha Region: A History of Colonial Settlement, Ethnicity and Nature Conservation, Basel: Basler Afrika Bibliographien.

Du Pisani, E./Jacobson, Leon (1985): "Dama Clay Vessel from Gomatsarab, Damaraland, and its Relevance for Dama Ceramic Studies." In: The South African Archaeological Bulletin 40/142, pp. 109-111.

First, Ruth (1968): South West Africa, Harmondsworth: Penguin.

Galton, Francis (1890 [1853]): Narrative of an Explorer in Tropical South Africa, London: Ward, Lock and Co.

Gordimer, Nadine (1974): The Conservationist, London: Bloomsbury.

GRN (2014 [1990]): The Constitution, Windhoek: Government of the Republic of Namibia.

Guenther, Mathias (1999): Tricksters and Trancers: Bushman Religion and Society, Bloomington: Indiana University Press.

Guenther, Mathias (2020): Human-Animal Relationships in San and Hunter-Gatherer Cosmology, Volume II Imagining and Experiencing Ontological Mutability, Basingstoke: Palgrave Macmillan.

Gürich, Georg (1891): "Deutsch Südwest-Afrika: Reisebilder und Skizzen aus den lahren 1888 und 1889 mit einer Original Routenkarte." In: Mitteilungen der Geographischen Gesellschaft in Hamburg 1, pp. 1-216.

Haacke, Wilfred (2010): "The Hunt for the Damara |Haihāb in 1903: Contemporary Oral Testimony." In: Journal of Namibian Studies 8, pp. 7-25.

Haacke, Wilfred (2018): "Khoekhoegowab (Nama/Damara)." In: Tomasz Kamusella/Finex Ndhlovu (eds.), The Social and Political History of Southern Africa's Languages, London: Palgrave Macmillan, pp. 133-158.

Hannis, Mike/Sullivan, Sian (2018): "Relationality, Reciprocity and Flourishing in an African Landscape." In: Laura M. Hartman (ed.), That All May Flourish: Comparative Religious Environmental Ethics, New York: Oxford University Press, pp. 279-296.

Haraway, Donna (2008): When Species Meet, Minneapolis: University of Minnesota Press.

Harley, John B. (1988): "Maps, Knowledge, and Power." In: David Cosgrove, David/Stephen Daniels (eds.), The Iconography of Landscape, Cambridge: Cambridge University Press, pp. 277-312.

Harley, John B. (1992): "Deconstructing the Map." In: Trevor J. Barnes/James S. Duncan (eds.), Writing World: Discourse, Text and Metaphor in the Representation of Landscape, London: Routledge, pp. 231-247.

Harvey, Graham (2005): Animism: Respecting the Living World, London: Hurst and Co.

Hinz, Manfred O./Gairiseb, Alexander, eds. (2013): Customary Law Ascertained, Volume 2: The Customary Law of the Bakgalagari, Batswana and Damara Communities of Namibia, Windhoek: University of Namibia Press.

Hoernlé, Winifred Agnes (1985 [1925]) "The Social Organisation of the Nama Hottentots of Southwest Africa." In: Carstens, Peter (ed.), The Social Or-

ganisation of the Nama and Other Essays by Winifred Hoernlé, Johannesburg: Witswatersrand University Press, pp. 39-56.

Impey, Angela (2018): Song Walking: Women, Music, and Environmental Justice in an African Borderland, Chicago: Chicago University Press.

Ingold, Tim (2000): The Perception of the Environment: Essays in Livelihood,
Dwelling and Skill, London: Routledge.

Inskeep, Adi (2003). Heinrich Vedder's 'The Bergdama': An Annotated Translation of the German Original with Additional Ethnographic Material, Köln:
Rüdiger Köppe Verlag.

Jacobson, Leon/Noli, D. (1987): "An Eye Witness Account of Coastal Settlement
and Subsistence Along the Northern Namibian Coast." In: South African
Archaeological Bulletin 42, pp. 173-174.

Jedlowski, Paolo (2001): "Memory and Sociology: Themes and Issues." In: Time
& Society 10/1, pp. 29-44.

Kambatuku, Jack R. (1996): Historical Profiles of Farms in Former Damaraland: Notes From the Archival Files, DRFN Occasional Paper No. 4, Windhoek: Desert Research Foundation of Namibia.

Kinahan, Jill (1990): "The Impenetrable Shield: HMS Nautilus and the Namib
Coast in the Late Eighteenth Century." In: Cimbebasia 12, pp. 23-61.

Kinahan, Jill (2000): Cattle for Beads: The Archaeology of Historical Contact
and Trade on the Namib Coast, Uppsala, Dept. of Archaeology and Ancient
History: Studies in African Archaeology 17.

Kinahan, Jill (2017): "'No Need to Hear Your Voice, When I Can Talk About You
Better Than You Can Speak About Yourself...' Discourses on Knowledge
and Power in the !Khuiseb Delta on the Namib Coast, 1780-2016 CE." In:
International Journal of Historical Archaeology 21/2, pp. 295-320.

Kinahan, John (1980): "Eighteenth Century Coppersmiths in Central Namibia:
Comments on Some Sources and Syntheses." In: Namibiana 2/2, pp. 17-22.

Kinahan, John (1993): "The Rise and Fall of Nomadic Pastoralism in the Central Namib Desert", In: Thurstan Shaw/Paul Sinclair/Bassey Andah/Alex
Okpoko (eds.), The Archaeology of Africa: Foods, Metals and Towns, London: Routledge, pp. 372-385.

Kinahan, John (2001 [1991]): Pastoral Nomads of the Namib Desert: The People
History Forgot, Windhoek: Capital Press.

Köhler, Oswin (1969): "Die Topnaar Hottentotten am Unteren Kuiseb", In: The
Ethnological Section (ed.), Ethnological and Linguistic Studies in Honour
of Nicolaas Jacobus Van Warmelo, Ethnological Publications 52, Pretoria:
Dept. of Bantu Administration and Development, pp. 99-122.

Kohn, Eduardo (2013): How Forests Think: Towards an Anthropology of Nature beyond the Human, Berkeley: University of California Press.

Krönlein, Johann G. (1889): Wortschatz der Khoi-khoin (Namaqua-Hottentotten), Berlin: Deutsche Kolonialgesellschaft.

Lau, Brigitte (1979): A Critique of the Historical Sources and Historiography Relating to the "Damaras" in Pre-colonial Namibia, BA Dissertation, Cape Town: University of Cape Town.

Lau, Brigitte (1987a): Namibia in Jonker Afrikaner's Time, Archeia 8, Windhoek:, National Archives of Namibia.

Lau, Brigitte, ed. (1987b): The Matchless Copper Mine in 1857: Correspondence, Charles John Andersson Papers Vol. 1, Archeia 7, Windhoek: National Archives.

Levin, Michiel/Goldbeck, Mannfred (2013): Goldbeck, David Levin of Twyfelfontein: The Unknown Story, Windhoek: Gondwana Collection.

Levi-Strauss, Claude (1987): Anthropology and Myth: Lectures, 1951-82, Oxford: Wiley-Blackwell.

Low, Chris (2008): Khoisan Medicine in History and Practice, Köln: Rüdiger Köppe Verlag.

Mansfield, Christina (2006): Environmental Impacts of Prospecting and Mining in Namibian National Parks: Implications for Legislative Compliance, Stellenbosch: Unpublished Masters Dissertation, Univ. Stellenbosch.

Messem, William (1855): "The Exploration of Western Africa." In: Nautical Magazine April, pp. 210-215.

Miescher, Giorgio (2012): Namibia's Red Line: The History of a Veterinary and Settlement Border, Basingstoke: Palgrave Macmillan.

Mossop, E.E. (ed.) (1935): The Journals of Wikar, Coetsé and Van Reenen, Cape Town: The Van Riebeeck Society.

Paksi, Attila (2020): Surviving 'Development': Rural Development Interventions, Protected Area Management and Formal Education With the Khwe San in Bwabwata National Park, Namibia, Unpublished PhD Thesis Presubmission, University of Helsinki.

Penn, Nigel (2005): The Forgotten Frontier: Colonist and Khoisan on the Cape's Northern Frontier in the Eighteenth Century, Athens: Ohio University Press.

Pleurdeau, David/Imalwa, Emma/Détroit, Floren/Lesur, Josephine/Veldman, Anzel/Bahain, Jean-Jack/Marais, Eugene (2012): "Of Sheep and Men: Earliest Direct Evidence of Caprine Domestication in Southern Africa at Leopard Cave (Erongo, Namibia)." In: PLoS ONE 7(7): e40340 (DOI: https://doi .org/10.1371/journal.pone.0040340).

Polanyi, Karl (2001 [1944]): The Great Transformation: The Political and Economic Origins of Our Time, Boston: Beacon Press.

Rudner, Ione/Rudner, Jalmer (1974 [1899]) Journey in Africa Through Angola, Ovampoland and Damaraland 1895-1896 by Peter Möller, Cape Town: C. Struik.

Sadr, Karim (2008): "Invisible Herders? The Archaeology of Khoekhoe Pastoralists." In: Southern African Humanities 20, pp. 179-203.

Sahlins, Marshall (1972): Stone Age Economics, New Jersey: Aldine Transaction.

Sandelowsky, Beatrice (1977): "Mirabib – An Archaeological Study in the Namib." In: Madoqua 10/4, pp. 221-284.

Sandelowsky, Beatrice/Van Rooyen, J.H./Vogel, J.C. (1979): "Early Evidence for Herders in the Namib." In: South African Archaeological Bulletin 34, pp. 50-51.

Schmidt, Sigrid (ed.) (2011): Hai||om and !Xû Stories from North Namibia: Collected and Translated by Terttu Heikkinen (1934-1988), Köln: Rüdiger Köppe Verlag.

Schmidt, Sigrid (2014a): "Spirits: Some Thoughts on Ancient Damara Folk Belief." In: Journal of the Namibian Scientific Society 62, pp. 133-160.

Schmidt, Sigrid (2014b): "Some Notes on the So-called Heitsi-Eibeb Graves in Namibia: Ancient Heaps of Stones at the Roadside." (https://baslerafrik a.ch/wp-content/uploads/2017/04/WP-2014-3-Schmidt.pdf, last accessed August 08, 2020)

Serton, Petrus, ed. (1954): The Narrative and Journal of Gerald McKiernan in South West Africa: 1874–1879, Cape Town: Van Riebeeck Society Journal 35.

Smith, Andrew B./Yates, Royden/Jacobson, Leon (1996): "Geduld Contra Kinahan." In: South African Archaeological Bulletin 51, pp. 36-39.

Sullivan, Sian (1996): The 'Communalization' of Former Commercial Farmland: Perspectives from Damaraland and Implications for Land Reform, Windhoek: Social Sciences Division of the Multidisciplinary Research Centre, University of Namibia, Research Report 25.

Sullivan, Sian (1998): People, Plants and Practice in Drylands: Sociopolitical and Ecological Dynamics of Resource Use by Damara Farmers in Arid North-west Namibia, including Annex of Damara Ethnobotany, London: PhD Anthropology, University College London.

Sullivan, Sian (1999): "Folk and Formal, Local and National: Damara Cultural Knowledge and Community-based Conservation in Southern Kunene, Namibia." In: Cimbebasia 15, pp. 1-28.

Sullivan, Sian (2003): "Protest, Conflict and Litigation: Dissent or Libel in Resistance to a Conservancy in North-west Namibia." In: Eeva Berglund/David G. Anderson (eds.), Ethnographies of Conservation: Environmentalism and the Distribution of Privilege, Oxford: Berghahn Press, pp. 69-86.

Sullivan, Sian (2005): "Detail and Dogma, Data and Discourse: Food-gathering by Damara Herders and Conservation in Arid North-west Namibia." In: Katherine Homewood (ed.), Rural Resources and Local Livelihoods in Sub-Saharan Africa, Oxford: James Currey and University of Wisconsin Press, pp. 63-99.

Sullivan, Sian (2006 [2001]) "On Dance and Difference: Bodies, Movement and Experience in Khoesān Trance-dancing." In: William Haviland/Robert Gordon/Luis Vivanco (eds.), Talking About People: Readings in Contemporary Cultural Anthropology, 4th Edition. New York: McGraw-Hill, pp. 234-241.

Sullivan, Sian (2010): "'Ecosystem Service Commodities' – A New Imperial Ecology? Implications for Animist Immanent Ecologies, With Deleuze and Guattari." In: New Formations: A Journal of Culture/Theory/Politics 69, pp. 111-128.

Sullivan, Sian (2013): "Nature on the Move III: (Re)countenancing an Animate Nature." In: New Proposals: Journal of Marxism and Interdisciplinary Enquiry 6/1-2, pp. 50-71.

Sullivan, Sian (2016): "Why Are Pastoralists Poisoning Lions in West Namibia?" (https://www.futurepasts.net/single-post/2017/02/16/Why-are-pastoralists-poisoning-lions-in-west-Namibia, last accessed August 8, 2020).

Sullivan, Sian (2017a): "What's Ontology Got to Do With it? On Nature and Knowledge in a Political Ecology of 'the Green Economy'." In: Journal of Political Ecology 24, pp. 217-242.

Sullivan, Sian (2017b): "'Our Hearts Were Happy Here' – Recollecting Acts of Dwelling and Acts of Clearance Through Oral Histories in West Namibia.", (http://dsrupdhist.hypotheses.org/227, last accessed August 8, 2020).

Sullivan, Sian (2019): "Towards a Metaphysics of the Soul and a Participatory Aesthetics of Life: Mobilising Foucault, Affect and Animism for Caring

Practices of Existence." In: New Formations: A Journal of Culture, Theory & Politics 95/3, pp. 5-21.

Sullivan, Sian (in press): "Maps and Memory, Rights and Relationships: Articulations of Global Modernity and Local Dwelling in Delineating Land for a Communal-area Conservancy in North-west Namibia." In: Sian Sullivan/Michèle Baussant/Lindsey Dodd/Olivette Otele/Irène Dos Santos (eds), Conserveries Mémorielles: Revue Transdisciplinaire, Special Issue on 'Disrupted Histories, Recovered Pasts | Histoires Perturbées, Passés Retrouvés'.

Sullivan, Sian/Ganuses Welhemina Suro (2020): "Understanding Damara / ǂNūkhoen and ||Ubun Indigeneity and Marginalisation in Namibia." In: Willem Odendaal/Wolfgang Werner (eds.), 'Neither Here Nor There': Indigeneity, Marginalisation and Land Rights in Post-independence Namibia. Windhoek: Land, Environment and Development Project, Legal Assistance Centre, pp. 283-324.

Sullivan, Sian/Ganuses, Welhemina Suro/|Nuab, Filemon and senior members of Sesfontein and Anabeb Conservancies (2019): Dama / ǂNūkhoen and ||Ubun Cultural Landscapes Mapping, West Namibia, unpublished in progress report to Namidaman Traditional Authority, Sesfontein. Bath: Future Pasts.

Sullivan, Sian/Ganuses, Welhemina Suro, with ||Hoëb, Franz/Ganaseb, Noag/Tauros, Christophine/Ganaseb, Michaal/Sanib, Ruben/|Awises, Sophia/|Nuas, Hildegaart/|Nuab, Filemon (2021): !Nara Harvesters of the Northern Namib: Retrieving Disrupted Socio-ecological Pasts Through On-site Oral Histories. Future Pasts Working Paper Series 9 (https://www.futurepasts.net/fpwp9-sullivan-ganuses-et-al-2021last accessed February 02, 2021).

Sullivan, Sian/Low, Chris (2014): "Shades of the Rainbow Serpent? A KhoeSān Animal Between Myth and Landscape in Southern Africa – Ethnographic Contextualisations of Rock Art Representations." In: The Arts 3/2, pp. 215-244.

SWAA (1930): Territory of South-West Africa, Report of the Administrator for the Year 1930. Windhoek: South West Africa Administration.

Tilley, Chris, (1994): A Phenomenology of Landscape: Places, Paths and Monuments, Oxford: Berg.

Tilley, Chris/Cameron-Daum, Kate (2017): The Anthropology of Landscape, London: UCL Press.

Tindall, Benjamin A. (1959): The Journal of Joseph Tindall: Missionary in South West Africa 1839-55, Cape Town: The Van Riebeeck Society.

Tinley, Ken L. (1971): "Etosha and the Kaokoveld." In: Supplement to African Wild Life 25/1, pp. 3-16.

Tjitemisa, Kuzeeko (2019): "President appoints ancestral land commission." In: New Era, February 22, 2019.

Tsing, Anna L. (2005): Friction: An Ethnography of Global Connection, Oxford: Princeton University Press.

Tsing, Anna L. (2014): "Wreckage and recovery: four papers exploring the nature of nature", In: AURA Working Papers 2 (Arhus University), pp. 2-15.

Union of South Africa (1918): Report on the Natives of South-West Africa and Their Treatment by Germany, Windhoek: Administrator's Office.

Van Warmelo, Nicolaas Jacobus (1962 [1951]): Notes on the Kaokoveld (South West Africa) and its People, Pretoria: Dept. of Bantu Administration, Ethnological Publications 26.

Vigne, Randolph (1994): "'The First, the Highest', Identifying Topnaar of Walvisbay and the Lower !Khuiseb River." Paper Presented at Symposium on Writing History, Identity, Society, University of Hannover.

Von François, Hugo (1896): Nama und Damara. Deutsch-Süd-West-Afrika, Magdeburg: Baensch.

Wadley, Lynn (1979): "Big Elephant Shelter and its Role in the Holocene Prehistory of South West Africa." In: Cimbebasia B 3/1, pp. 1-76.

Wallace, Marion (2011): A History of Namibia: From the Beginning to 1990, London: Hurst & Co.

Widlok, Thomas (1999): Living on Mangetti: "Bushmen" Autonomy and Namibian Independence, Oxford: Oxford University Press.

Wilcken, Patrick (2010): Claude Lévi-Strauss: The Poet in the Laboratory, London: Bloomsbury.

Woodburn, James (1982) "Egalitarian Societies." In: Man 17/3, pp. 431-451.

Mapping multiple in Maasailand: Ontological openings for knowing and managing nature otherwise

Mara Jill Goldman

Mapping with Maasai

It was a nice overcast morning as we set out on foot to ground truth the maps that I was trying to make of the two villages I was conducting research in. I had my hand-held Geographic Positioning System (GPS) unit with me and three interlocutors: my regular field assistant, Landis K; another man of the Landis-age-set, Landis M, who had been helping out with the wildlife transects and had additional knowledge of the local landscape; and Naibor, an extremely knowledgeable Makaa junior elder who had agreed to lead the expedition.[1] While they were all men, our goal was to capture GPS points for place names that had been delineated through "mapping" exercises with separate groups of men and women. While that exercise had proven quite problematic at first, it eventually led to some great hand drawn maps of different places, named and used by Maasai women and men in the area.

I put mapping in quotation marks because Maasai do not draw maps, nor do they have an equivalent word in Maa for map, or mapping. It was not until I asked them to make maps for me that I realized the problematic nature of my request. I had become frustrated with my inability to talk to Maasai about where they took their livestock, or where they saw wildlife, without knowing

---

1   Maasai society is organized along age-set and clan lines. For men, the age-sets have names beginning with the period when they are *ilmurran* (*olmurrani*, sg., translated into English as warriors), junior, senior, and retired elders. Women are often referred to only by their age-grade/place within the society – young uncircumcised girl (*endito*), new wife (*esiangiki*), mother (*yeiyo*), grandmother (*koko*). While I use pseudonyms, I use the name of the age-set/age-grade to provide guidelines for power and age dynamics.

how they saw and spoke about the landscape. When I realized how heavily Maasai relied on their own place names, I became determined to create 'Maasai maps' of the study area that reflected these names. To do so, I called different groups of individuals (men, women, *ilmurran*) for participatory mapping exercises (on paper or on the ground, whichever they were more comfortable with). I asked them to think about what they were going to do on any series of days and draw a "map" (Swahili: *ramani*) of the areas that came to mind. I realized how flawed my approach was when I noticed that the Swahili word for map, *ramani*, was not being translated into Maa. I then began to notice that the word was actually used by Maasai, even when speaking amongst themselves in Maa, to refer to official state delineated boundaries, the marker of the "map" between two separate state recognized entities (e.g., villages, districts). When I first asked a group of elders to draw a *ramani* I was told, "But we, we Maasai, we do not have maps." Another elder remarked, "I don't have anything to really say, but it's very good if you could explain to us more about the map. There is no map at all in all of Maasailand, but there's a map between Babati and Monduli [districts]."

Once I realized my mistake, I clumsily tried to remedy it by asking them to instead draw a picture, as in a mental map. I soon realized that this too reflected my own ontological bias associated with mental mapping processes, assuming that maps exist as preconceived mental orderings or static pictures in our own heads of our reality, rather than an active performance (Crampton 2009, Turnbull 2000).[2] My notion of mental mapping also assumed the existence of places separated out in space, which is not necessarily the way in which Maasai know/enact their landscapes.[3] I finally settled on rather lengthy explanations that seemed to reflect what I had observed and was different for the different groups. For the elders it went something like this: "when you wake up in the morning you have an idea of where you want the cattle to go that day, and you need to explain it to the *ilmurran*, right? How do you do that? What are the various places you can think about and could you draw

---

2   Crampton (2009: 846), cites Kitchin and Dodge (2007) in their use of mapping as ontogenetic as in always becoming, rather than with a sense of ontological security. Turnbull (2000) similarly critiques the notion of mental mapping as a universal way of bringing order to the world that all humans practice in a particular way (2000).

3   As Ingold explains, "[m]any geographers and psychologists have argued that we are all surveyors in our everyday lives, and that we use our bodies, as the surveyor uses his instruments, to obtain data from which it assembles a comprehensive representation of the world – the so-called cognitive map" (2007: 88).

them for me (on paper or on the ground)?" Realizing this too was limiting, I asked them to include all the places they thought of as important. I did the same with a separate group of *ilmurran* (but rather places where they would go, places they think about/picture/know), and the same for the women. This seemed to work reasonably well and resulted in unique drawings/maps from each group, reflecting their own areas of expertise and interest.

I was quite pleased with the final results and now wanted to make official looking maps with Geographic Information Systems (GIS) software. I originally thought this would be difficult and would somehow betray Maasai spatial ontologies of place names by forcing them into standard cartographic classifications. But to my surprise, all the mapping exercises resulted in the drawing of discrete shapes that could quite easily be turned into polygons in a GIS map.[4] So that is how I ended up on this refreshingly overcast day walking with three Maasai men to collect GPS points of place names on the ground. And here, once again what seemed like it should be a simple and straight forward exercise, proved far from. We started off with Naibor in the lead, instructing me when to take a GPS mark –which we did at the beginning, middle and end of a particular place; more if the place was particularly large. At one point he told me we had reached the end of a place (*Lera Olkunda*, see Figure 1), for me to 'mark' it with the GPS. I did so and we continued walking.

> Naibor, as we are walking, he looks over at me and with a forward gesture of his arm he says: "And up there ahead is Lera Lendim."
>
> Mara, stopping where I am standing, and taking out the GPS: "So we are in that place now?"
>
> Naibor: "No. It's just up there." Keeps walking
>
> Mara, catching up to him, but then stopping again: "So then we are still in Lera Olkunda?"
>
> Naibor, confused, he looks at me and back in the direction we came from: "No, we have already left Lera Ollkunda, didn't you mark it?"
>
> Mara: "I did mark it. But then if we have left Lera Olkunda but we are not yet in Lera Lendim where are we?"
>
> Naibor: "We are in between!"
>
> Mara: "So there are in-between places that are not a part of one place or the other?"

---

4   The challenges of this process and what potentially gets lost in translation are discussed more below.

Naibor, stops walking to gaze at me with an exasperated look on his face, leaning with an authoritative pose on his walking stick (engudi): "Yes, we are in between. In America, one person's house and land goes all the way up to the boundary of another persons' land? There is no space in between?"

At this I just stopped and laughed. Laughed at my own inability to imagine "spaces in between" and at Naibor's inability to imagine a place without them. Now I can see that while we were standing in the same place and walking the same path through the landscape, we were experiencing the place and the walk quite differently. We were, in Ingold's words, practicing two very different "modalities of travel, namely wayfaring and transport" (2007: 81). According to Ingold, the path of the wayfarer (in this case Naibor),

wends hither and thither, and may even pause here and there before moving on. It has no beginning or end. While on the trail the wayfarer is always somewhere, yet every 'somewhere' is on the way to somewhere else. The inhabited world is a reticulate meshwork of such trails, which is continually being woven as life goes on along them. Transport, by contrast, is tied to specific locations. Every move serves the purpose of relocating persons and their effects and is oriented to a specific destination. The traveler who departs from one location and arrives at another is, in between, nowhere at all. Taken all together, the lines of transport form a network of point-to-point connections. (Ingold 2007: 81-84).

So, while Naibor was the one who insisted that we were "in between" two named places, this was naturally a part of the well-trodden path. For me, I was mapping places as discrete entities, and my path was just connecting these entities or points, which themselves were being created by the connection of points (with the GPS unit). Our way of moving through the landscape, and thus our way of knowing it were fundamentally different.[5]

Introduction

Maps have power. Power to create and reinforce certain spatial relationships at the expense of others. Power to lay claim to resources – by placing and

---

5   These differences are clear as well in the existence of a village called *Katikati*, Swahili for "in the middle," most likely an outcome of early mapping attempts when Maasai were asked by the surveyor where they were.

Figure 1: Maasai Place Names in Study Area (Source: Goldman 2020; map: Sam Smith)

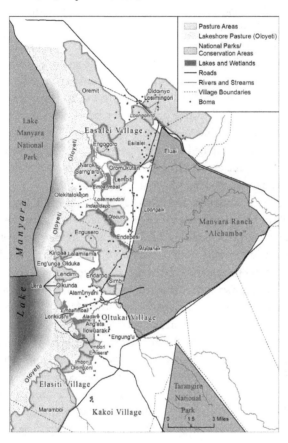

naming them on an official document. And as official documents, or as digital data stored in a computer, maps have power as objects – ones that travel well in scientific and public circles as legitimate expressions of knowledge, seen as a source of "objective" information (Lovell 2017). As objects, maps not only reflect (and reinforce) particular versions of reality, they simultaneously create them – through the process of mapping certain spatial knowledge and not others, and then managing the space (including resources and people) accordingly. As such, map making has long been recognized as political, and thereby always a contested process.[6] The short vignette above describes a moment of ontological conflict when I tried to align Maasai place-making practices with those by which I know and live, those of western cartography – first in having Maasai map their landscapes and then to put Maasai place names into a GIS map. I resolved the conflicts, at least in part, by more carefully choosing my words, and then by stretching the methods of the GIS software to accommodate Maasai spatial framings – by leaving visible spaces in between on the map that I created of their place names, or at least trying to (see Figure 1). But I want to suggest, and will argue in this chapter, that this is far from where my work should end. The ontological conflict provided an opening to explore techniques to bring Maasai ways of knowing and being into a format visible to the western trained eye, and thereby useable for local conservation planners, state agencies and employees of non-governmental organizations (NGOs), without jeopardizing what made them Maasai.[7]

But can we (as academics and activists working with indigenous communities) really use standard western cartographic techniques to make maps *with* and *for* indigenous communities that remain true to their ways of knowing and being with and *relating* to landscapes? Or to use Ingold's words, can we reconcile wayfarer (inhabitant) and transport (occupier) modes of being – one that exists, lives, knows and makes the world by traveling through it, with one that plans from above and travels over a landscape, from point to point, often with the goal to occupy, partition, and enclose (2007)? I think that the answer is yes, *but* cautiously and critically; all the while recognizing without fetishizing differences (ontological and epistemological) and working in alliance with the people and communities involved. I stand in agreement here with the call made over ten years ago by Bjørn Sletto (2009: 445), for "ethnographers and cartographers engaged with participatory mapping" to "move beyond cultural relativism and facilitate an emancipatory politics," by exposing and addressing "tensions, negotiations, and contestations," involved in the map-mapping process. This also reflects the warnings previously voiced by Rocheleau (2005: 339) that maps, "may be mobilized in both creative or destructive acts of transformation," and her subsequent call to map carefully and differently from the

---

6   See introduction to this volume for a thorough overview of the literature on this.

7   See Bryan (2009, 2011) for the politics involved in producing 'indigenous' maps. See Simpson (2017) for the complex ways that mapping can still be used in this way by Indigenous elders.

standard methods often employed, especially when for, with and by communities.

My initial goal in doing this mapping work, was far more than academic, but rather grew out of mounting frustration with mapping projects that were already underway in the area at the time (2002-4). Conservation agencies and Maasai NGOs alike were working with various Maasai communities in the area on "participatory land-use maps (PLUMS)". Despite being called participatory, these projects often involved only a handful of powerful village men, and always began with western informed boundaries for seasons and places. Maasai participants were then just asked to fill in the appropriate spaces (i.e. wet season grazing area) on the map, or to show places on the ground (i.e. ground truth GIS classifications) while sitting comfortably in a Landcruiser.[8] This process and others like it, silence the multiple Maasai ways of being in and knowing landscapes spatially and temporally. One can argue with such projects, participation becomes more a harm then a good (more destructive and less creative), by simultaneously concealing and reinforcing existing power dynamics and continuing colonial practices of land and knowledge extractions (Goldman 2003, Hayward/Simpson/Wood 2004). I began my own mapping projects with the hope that in reconciling western mapping techniques with Maasai place-making practices, I could provide a template for mapping and planning otherwise. My goal was to move beyond standard participation techniques towards decolonizing the methodologies, theories, and practices of mapping.

In this paper, I talk about the process I used and how much remains to be done (with proper collaboration with a cartographer), to not only decolonize or indigenize the map making process, but to *map multiple*. By this I do not mean making multiple maps, but rather producing maps that are "more than one but less than many," through a deep engagement with and bringing together (but not merging) different ways of knowing, being in, and managing the landscape. My argument expands on Dianne Rocheleau's call to map differently through "multimaps, alternative maps, and alternatives to maps" (2005: 344), while drawing from the theoretical contributions of Anne-Marie Mol and John Law on complexity, multiplicity, and ontological politics. In the next section, I briefly explain this framing and how it can work to reconcile what Ingold refers to as different ways of traveling and producing knowledge of the land, without subsuming one into the other, or mistranslating across

---

8   On the problems of this process in Tanzania, see Hodgson and Schroeder (2002).

ontologies. I then introduce the specific social history of the case study before going into the particular ways of 'mapping multiple' in Maasai landscapes that are also heavily used by wildlife and thereby coveted by conservation agencies and state actors.

Mapping multiple: More than one but less than many

> [T]he discovery of multiplicity suggests that we are no longer living in the modern world, located within a single *epistème*. Instead, we discover that we are living in different worlds. These are not worlds – that great trope of modernity – that belong on the one hand to the past and on the other to the present. Instead, we discover that we are living in two or more neighboring worlds, worlds that overlap and coexist." (Law/Mol 2002: 8).

By using the term "mapping multiple" I am suggesting producing maps that expose the type of overlapping multiple worlds that Law and Mol refer to above. I am drawing from the title of Mol's 2002 book, *The Body Multiple*, which is about the ways in which medicine deals with the human body and its diseases. In following various actors working with lower limb atherosclerosis in a Dutch hospital (doctors, patients, lab technicians, etc.), Mol found that they were enacting different versions of the disease that nonetheless were made to fit together. *"The body multiple,"* she contends, "is not fragmented. Even if it is multiple, it also hangs together. The question to be asked, then, is how is this achieved" (Mol 2002: 55, original emphasis). Together with Law, she explains further that "we are not dealing with a single body, but neither are there many different and unrelated bodies; for the various modes of ordering, logics, styles, practices, and the realities they perform do not exist in isolation from one another" (Law/Mol 2002: 10). They are related, overlap, sometimes interfere and at other times partially connect. There are of course different ways that power can and often is used to enforce one version of a reality over another, to attempt to produce a singularity, which leads to what Mol calls ontological politics.

So, what does all this have to do with mapping? John Law builds on Mol's work to explore the ramifications for doing social science (and I would say mapping) differently (Law 2007 [2004]). He suggests that we need a range of metaphors to begin thinking in this way – where the world is composed of "fractional objects" – bodies, machines, organizations which are "more than one and less than many. Somewhere in between" (Law 2007 [2004]: 62). And furthermore, that we need social science methods dedicated to exposing/revealing multiplicity in ways that don't attempt to either smooth it into singularity and 'other' all that does not fit; or to leave it as a relativistic complex incomprehensible mess. This is extremely useful for thinking critically about mapping differently. For it enables a move beyond what Rocheleau refers to as "the duel between maps and counter-maps and on to the use of mutually intelligible maps" (2005: 357). Rocheleau too has argued for "multimapping" to map the various ways of knowing, being with, managing and accessing land and resources in different places. She suggests that "a well-designed GIS can enable multimapping yet retain the ability to represent the various standpoints in a standard, and thus comparable, format" (2005: 357). With GIS, one can produce multiple overlays of various maps into one map – which I suggest can be seen as a map that is more than one but less than many.

The advantages of this approach are many. Perhaps first and foremost is that it neither dismisses indigenous knowledge and ways of being in the landscape as 'other', to be preserved in cultural maps only; nor does it extract indigenous knowledge to be translated into standard cartesian metrics and subsumed into traditional maps. I suggest that it also helps in two other substantial ways. First, this approach exposes the multiplicity inherent in categories that are assumed to be singular – and usually 'othered' or assimilated – such as community, indigenous, or Maasai. For various political reasons, Maasai (as with many indigenous peoples) need to present a unified version of the 'Maasai way', which of course *includes* multiple ways of being in/with, knowing, and accessing land and resources along lines of gender, location, age, class, clan and other access of difference. Secondly, I argue that there is a need to actually make different ways of being and knowing the land "hang together" in a non-hierarchical fashion. To refer back to Ingold's (2007) description of practices of wayfaring and habitation as in opposition to the surveying mode of occupation; mapping multiple could map these as separate layers that form one map. For many indigenous communities, Maasai included, use both modalities (and the resulting sets of boundaries) in their political and daily lives. It would therefore be useful for them to have both sets on a map.

To conclude, by mapping multiple I mean 1) paying close attention to multiple ways of knowing, being with, relating to and using land/environment *within* communities along various overlapping axes of difference (i.e. gender, age, clan); and 2) recognizing the multiple ways of place-making and resulting sets of boundaries used by many indigenous communities today on a daily basis – including those they did not draw but must contend with (i.e. administrative and conservation boundaries).

Providing some context: Maasai and conservation in East Africa

Maasai are a group of people that occupy the semi-arid rangelands of Tanzania and Kenya adjacent to some of the world's most famous national parks. They historically practiced a predominantly pastoralist semi-nomadic lifestyle. This meant that vast areas of land left 'open' for grazing by livestock, were also used by wildlife. For the most part, Maasai did not hunt,[9] nor did they historically cultivate on a large scale, relying on regular trade with agriculturalist neighbors. As a result, "Maasailand has retained one of the world's largest concentrations of wild animal population[s]" (Parkipuny 1979: 137).[10] Rather than benefiting from this situation, Maasai have been disproportionately impacted by land loss through the creation of national parks in Tanzania and Kenya, starting during the colonial regimes in both countries (Germany and Britain in Tanzania, Britain in Kenya), and continuing today.[11] Many of the areas where Maasai live continue to support relatively large wildlife populations, and are thus subject to some form of conservation status, with subsequent limitations on resource use. Yet Maasai are rarely recognized by conservation professionals as knowledgeable actors regarding the land they live on and the wildlife they often share it with. They are not asked to contribute their way of knowing and being with wildlife to conservation planning, which may very well challenge the boundaries (material and ideological) drawn and relied on by conservation science and practice.[12] They

---

9   Maasai historically viewed wildlife as "second cattle" (Western 1997) hunting only in times of extreme need, otherwise shunning it as something only the poor (*ildorobo*), without cattle do. Today, many Maasai eat game meat when given the opportunity, but hunting for meat is still culturally unacceptable, though this varies by sections (see Roque de Pinho 2009 for Matapato).

10   For more on this historic co-habitation see Deihl 1985; Collet 1987; Parkipuny/Berger, 1993.

11   Including Amboseli, Tsavo, and Nairobi National Parks and Maasai Mara Game Reserve in Kenya; Serengeti, Manyara, and Tarangire National Parks, Ngorongoro Conservation Area, and Mkomazi Game Reserve in Tanzania.

12   Exceptions may include the research by Homewood and Rodgers (1991) in Tanzania, which was nonetheless not followed by the Ngorongoro Conservation Area authority

are, however, often asked to fill in maps by wildlife researchers in the area – to explain where wildlife are, and to provide the foundation for community-based land use planning (Hodgson/Schroeder 2002).

For me, to even define the study area for this research itself requires multimapping to include the various practices of line/boundary drawing in this area over time – that overlap, interact, sometimes relate and sometimes conflict. These various sets of lines include the national boundary between Tanzania and Kenya (which cuts through Maasai occupied lands), Tanzanian administrative boundaries (village, ward, division, district, region), conservation boundaries (National Parks, Manyara Ranch, and Wildlife Management Areas), and Maasai cultural/territorial boundaries of section (*olosho* sg., *iloshon* pl.), and sub-section (*enkutoto* sg., *inkutot* pl.). The mapping work that I discuss in this paper occurred in two Maasai villages in Tanzania that are situated in between two national parks (Tarangire and Lake Manyara) and adjoined by a relatively new (since 2002) conservation area or "conservancy", the Manyara Ranch. According to Maasai customary cultural/territorial distinctions, the area is part of the *Ilkisongo* Maasai section (*olosho*), and the *Emanyara* sub-section (*enkutoto*). Maasai in the study site use all sets of boundaries on a nearly daily basis to negotiate land use and make management decisions, as well as plan cultural events and livelihood practices. For this reason, it is necessary to take all sets of boundaries seriously, along with other forms of place-making that do not include boundary making practices – such as place names. In the following section, I outline my interpretation of Maasai spatial-temporal enactments through place names, before moving into how these can be mapped as a layer in a mapping multiple approach.

Maasai spatial enactments: Place names

We experience the contours of the landscape by moving through it, so that it enters ... into our 'muscular consciousness.' ... In their journeys along paths and tracks, however, people also move from place to place. To reach a place, you need cross no boundary, but you must follow some kind of path. Thus there can be no places without paths, along which people arrive and depart;

---

or the IUCN, or the early work by David Western (Western 1989; Western/Gichohi 1993), which similarly was not followed by the Kenyan Wildlife Service.

and no paths without places, that constitute their destinations and points of departure. (Ingold 2000: 204)

In discussing wildlife and livestock movements, or giving directions, Maasai will often suggest the movement pattern with the use of their arms, the roll of their eyes, or the shift of their head. These bodily gestures are accompanied with the names of the various places along the pathway of movement. Places are known through movement and stories of ecological, physical, and social histories that are visible to the trained eye and shift over time. Sometimes these features result in discrete boundaries, such as the closed shapes that participants drew during mapping exercises and as seen on the landscape where the tall grass ends, and trees grow. Sometimes they reflect well known social histories such as former settlements or farms. Terms for cardinal directions are not often used for explaining space.[13] In fact, in the study area there was only one word for north and south (kopikopi), meaning the place where the sun neither rises nor sets.[14] Cardinal directions do impact Maasai spatial thinking, in the ways they build their homesteads (gates must face kopikopi-either north or south), and during particular ritual events where one must face east or west. Cardinal directions are not however used to talk about and navigate space, place names are.

Place names reflect differences in vegetation composition and structure, water sources, animal presence, social history, soil type, elevation, and more. Place names are used in conversations between Maasai men and women, adults and children. When I asked elders to tell me about their grazing patterns, they were often at a loss for what to say until I informed them that I knew their place names. This inspired an almost universal sigh of relief and

---

13   For this reason, it is my experience, that Maasai are notoriously bad at giving directions when traveling in a car. When reaching a break in the path, they direct with their arms (often behind your head), saying merely "that way", "this way", but rarely if ever, right or left, east or west.

14   In Kenya kopikop very specifically means north, referring to a rift in the north of Kenya near Kerio, the place of origin for Maasai. It is possible that Maasai in Tanzania, being far from these mountains, have lost the significance of the term, for in everyday conversations kopikopi can mean either north or south. However, there is an understanding of its original meaning, as one elder woman explained (May 29, 2003): "Kopikop is the place where neither the sun nor the moon come from or go to [i.e. both north and south]. But it is really the place to the right of god, and god is in the east [where the sun comes from]. It is the place of Yemate, the rift towards Kerio, where Maasai come from."

then they would begin talking... "Today they went to *Lorkiushi* for water and then to *Eng'unga Olduka* for grass..."[15] Place names help Maasai navigate their use of the land. They are used to direct young men, *ilmurran* (often translated "warriors" in English) where to go to capture seasonal change and resources for livestock and to talk about rainfall patterns, and animal movements (livestock and wildlife). They are used by women to talk about where to collect grass, medicinals, and water, where to avoid wildlife, and where to graze small stock.

Places are named at various overlapping scales, some places nested inside other places. A small water inundated area may exist inside a larger grassland, and the use of names within names, reflects these nested relationships. For example, there is a large grazing area called *Lera*, plural for *Oleria* – Maa for Yellow Fever Tree (*Acacia xanthophloea*), that is further divided into different areas, all with names. On the south side there is *Lera Shingo*, and *Lera Olkunda*, which both refer to the names of Maasai *inkang'itie* (Maa for homesteads, pl., singular *enkang'*) that used to be located here. Today, the area is not dominated by *ilera* trees nor are there any *inkang'itie* located in this area. Conversations about the names reveal that the area used to be dense with *ilera* trees but they have thinned out due to the combined effects of flooding of the saline lake during El Niño, a particular disease that affects this tree, and cutting of the tree by villagers (for building thorn fences for their *enkang* and cattle enclosures). *Inkang'itie* (homesteads) that used to be located in this area relocated up to the higher ground as access to fresh water became a problem and people began farming, since the soils in *Lera* are not good for farming and the water table had begun to dry up. Two additional names divide *Lera* by vegetation density. *Lera Lentim* – in the bush/forest – is the area, which at least in the near past, was heavily forested with *Lera* trees. Today, a walk through the area reveals that while it is no longer a forest, the dense stands of yellow fever trees are returning, creating a dense thicket. *Lalamilama* to the northeast is the area where the trees are not dense but are separated out at a distance apart. And this is in fact what the area looks like – a much less dense wooded area then *Lentim* (see Map 1 and Figure 1). *Enkungu Olduka* to the north is the uplifted area with *Oldukai* trees, that is a place within *Lera* where the palm trees mix with the Acacia trees.[16] Here the name reflects both

15   Interview, Makaa Elder, Oltukai November 2003.
16   *Enkungu* also means knee in Maa. Mol (1996: 214) defines *enkungu* only as knee and the masculine version, *Olkungu*, as rounded small hills, "rounded like knees." Kisongo

a change in vegetation composition as well as a change in elevation. A place where water passes through is denoted as *Naikurkur* – the sound that the water makes as it roars its way past the tall grass towards the lake. Places exist inside of other places and places exist as parts of larger places, all named and co-existing.

Figure 2: Maasai cattle in Lera (Photo: Mara Jill Goldman)

A place may have several names – one referring to the type of water present, the other to the type of soil, and yet a third to the species of grass. All refer to the same place, the name used depends on the context and scale of concern, as well as the person using the name. In other words, place names are relational – reflecting relations to these places by different people (and sometimes animals) at different times, on particular paths, for particular reasons.[17] Names are either clear or complex, but the unraveling of them is

---

Maasai in my study area used both the masculine and the feminine version to refer to slightly elevated areas, the former being a larger area then the latter.

17   For instance, the lake shore of Lake Manyara in Oltukai and Esilalei villages is referred to as *E-Makat* (the saltwater lake) if you are talking about the lake, or the whole general area, surrounding the lake. It is referred to as *Emborianda* (the hard crusted soil) if you are trying to distinguish that part of the lake shore that is in fact *emborianda* as op-

always informative of the contemporary or historical ecological structure of the area and/or social history. For names often stay the same, as the ecology of an area changes, and thus the name itself is historical data, in a non-literary society. Names can also change, however, with a different generation of men taking over the leadership and decision-making capacity in an area, and reflecting the changes in ecology. When the ecology changes so much that the name is no longer appropriate, or a new phenomenon demands attention, a change can also take place. But the old name is not lost, merely referred to as the old name. We are all familiar with such occurrences in our own lives, as roads are named after former presidents or deceased heroes, and we need to refer to both the new and the old name to find our way.

Maasai name all landscape variations – small and large, including changes in elevation and soil structure. And here, language subtleties are important, with the feminine preface *en-* donating small, such as the small uplifted area of *Enkunga* (also Maa for knee), versus the masculine preface *ol-*, such as the large uplifted area *Olkunga*.[18] Place names combine the general and specific to reflect differences in vegetation composition and elevation (*Lera* low laying grasslands with yellow fever acacia trees versus *Enkunga Olduka* for small up-lifted area with date palm trees); vegetation structure (*Lera Lentim* - the densely wooded acacia grassland, versus *Lera Lalamilama* - the sparsely wooded acacia grassland), water sources (as natural depressions, man-made wells, small creeks); animal presence (where the wildebeest stay, the field of the lion, the hiding place of the lion), and historical social ecology (the names of former resident locations).

Similar types of places can have the same general names, with qualifiers added when needed. For instance, there are many places throughout Oltukai referred to as *alamunyani*, which refers both to a soil type – mixed sand and clay with a high saline content that is seasonally flooded – and the type of

---

posed to still grassy; and it is referred to as *Oloyeti* (the dominant grass species) if you are talking about grazing. Yet a fourth name – *Naong* (the sounds of the wildebeest) reflects the relationship of wildebeest to this area and is used when discussing wildlife use of the area. All the names however, could be used inter-changeably to refer to the entire area.

18   Masculine and feminine versions of the same word can also refer to known versus un-known entities. *Entim*, for instance refers to forested, bushed areas which are often large in size. Here the feminine prefix refers to the unknown qualities of this 'wild' place. The masculine version of the word, *oltim*, refers to a specific large branch (a known piece of the bush) that is used to close a Maasai homestead at night.

vegetation it supports: annual grasses, what Maasai referred to as *nyepesi* in Swahili,[19] meaning "light, quick grasses", and dicots/forbs/scrub that Maasai call *embenik* in Maa. One can speak of *Alamunyani o Lera*, suggesting the one near *Lera*. Both villages consist of areas referred to as *Engesero* (low-laying seasonally water inundated short grass plains which are great for grazing) and *En-kunga*, or *Ol-kungu* – small or large (respectively) raised areas which are good for farming. These names and many others can be found throughout Maasailand to note similar types of vegetation, soil types and elevation; they often co-exist with other names that refer to specific local social histories. And again, the subtleties matter. An area called *Endepesi* is bound to have *Acacia tortilis*, but also be smaller in size then an area called *Oldepesi*. The names are not only used locally but can help visiting Maasai navigate their way to sites for grazing, fuelwood, shelter, and so on.

Mapping multiple I: Speaking differently with names[20]

> What we call the landscape is generally considered to be something "out there," But, while some aspects of the landscape are clearly external to both our bodies and our minds, what each of us actually experiences is selected, shaped, and colored by what we know.
> (Barrie Greenbie, *Spaces: Dimensions of the Human Landscape*, cited in Basso 1996: 71)

In the above section, I presented Maasai place names as if they were universally 'Maasai', but this is not exactly true. Nor is it false. There are names that are used throughout Maasailand that mean the same thing, but there are also differences by section (*olosho*) and sub-section (*enkututo*) as well as by villages – based on different localized ecologies, social histories, and regional dialects. For instance, the term *alamunyani* seems particular to the area in Tanzania where I worked, near to Lake Manyara, with no usage found in other parts of Maasailand.[21] Yet this distinction of an area as *alamunyani* matters regionally for recognizing a very specific soil-mineral-water make up that

---

19   This is a generalized term for annual grasses. Individual grass species have names in Maa.

20   I am drawing on the title of Chapter 3, *Speaking with names* in Keith Basso's *Wisdom Sits in Places* (1996).

21   I asked various people about this all over Kenyan and Tanzanian Maasailand.

limits grass growth. While visiting conservation practitioners would often refer to these areas as overgrazed, Maasai would shake their head and say, no,
it's just *alamunyani*. So regional differences matter. But there are other areas of difference. Maasai are internally differentiated along lines of location
(*olosho/enkutoto*) clan, age, class, and gender. These differences matter. They
create and mold different sets of knowledge and experiences. But this does
not mean that they are not all also Maasai.

I tried to capture this internal multiplicity in the mapping exercises with
Maasai, by working with different social groups – elder men, younger men,
and women. This enabled more space for certain individuals to speak without
the constraints of respect associated with age and masculinity that often in-
hibit speaking in front of others with certain sets of relations (Goldman 2020).
It also produced very different maps. Whereas the elders began their drawing
far from the village, at the place where the main water source comes from up-
stream, the *ilmurran* began with the dirt road that passes through the center
of the village. And the women mapped locations of water in far greater detail than either of the groups of men. They also mapped stories about wildlife
encounters such as places where the lions hide, or the elephants go, that are
often thought of as the knowledge purview of men.

Yet in the end I made one map of place names for the area. How did I do this
and in doing it did I erase the multiplicity of Maasai ways of knowing and
experiencing the landscape? First, I took all the various drawings and created
a list of place names to be mapped. I then went out into the landscape with
three Maasai men – an elder and two senior *ilmurran* – to locate the place
names on the ground with a GPS unit so that they could be put into a GIS map.
In hindsight, I was wrong to not include any women in this process, though
I did make sure that their places were on the list.[22] I then sat with one man,
a senior *ilmurran* at the time who was also my most trusted interlocutor, at a
computer screen in a GIS lab at first in Tarangire National Park and then at the
International Livestock Research Institute (ILRI) in Nairobi, to match up the

---

22   I fell into the trap that many do and that I myself critique (Goldman and Jagadeesh
      forthcoming) which is to take the easy way out by not taking the extra effort to find
      woman who could participate given their often-busier schedules, many being con-
      strained by their husbands, many not feeling they are knowledgeable, and others not
      able to participate with certain men because of social norms of respect. It would have
      been doable, and I did begin shortly after to include women in the wildlife transect
      work when possible.

GPS points with the drawings and a remotely sense image of the area. Since many of the place names refer to soil or vegetation characteristics, they were clearly visible on the false color composite remotely sensed image. Together we traced the contours of reflection, for instance of black cotton soil areas (*Engusero*), the salt encrusted lake sure (*Emakat* and *Emborianda*), raised and forested areas. Finally, I presented draft versions of the maps in village wide meetings and to small groups of individuals to get feedback and make any necessary changes.

In this particular case, the different sketch maps made by the different groups were *different but compatible* and could be brought together into one map that presented a combination of inputs for place names. If I had been mapping resource use and access, there may have been more difference and potential conflict, but even then, as Rocheleau (2005) illustrates, it is possible to create one map with different knowledge, access rights and responsibilities listed in symbols. The final map was more than one but less than many: a Maasai relational landscape for this region, that included various Maasai input. With place names, there is not often disagreement about the placement of names, but there can be different foci on what is important to be mapped, or what name should be used, and the stories that are told to explain a name. A better map would include these levels of complexity. Unfortunately, as mentioned above, most maps made with Maasai in the area by visiting scientists and local NGOs alike, start and end with the exclusive input of male leaders, excluding the knowledge of women. As a result, important water sources, clean and accessible for human consumption, are often missing from local planning maps, with clearly important implications for regional planning. But the divisions of knowledge are not always as clear as many would expect – in our mapping exercises, women often mapped in great detail particular hiding places of wildlife that the men did not. They also mapped their farm spaces. These differences matter when mapping for wildlife conservation planning. Recognizing knowledge differences across and within groups is important and demands that mapping practices are always multiple. This is not the same as being inclusive. Mapping multiple means mapping in groups so people can tell different stories with their maps; maps which may or may not fit together smoothly. GIS can be used to fit different layers on top of each other, to leave spaces in between, to show overlap and scale, and even to tell different stories. Narratives are missing from the maps that I created, as they distill place names into shapes on a GIS map. But this can be done differently, to include narratives in the map (see Pearce, this volume; Pearce 2008). In this section, I argued how the places and the narratives need to always be seen as multiple, while still being 'Maasai.' I now turn to why putting the place names on the map, where they cross and connect with other sets of lines, matter.

Mapping multiple II: Across epistemological and ontological realms

> From time to time in the course of history ... imperial powers have sought to occupy the inhabited world, throwing a network of connections across what appears, in their eyes to be not a tissue of trails but a blank surface. These connections are lines of occupation. ... Unlike the paths formed through the practices of wayfaring, such lines are surveyed and built in advance of the traffic that comes to pass up and down them. ...Drawn cross-country, they are inclined to ride roughshod over the lines of habitation that are woven into it. (Ingold 2007: 81)

As mentioned above, Maasai "do not have maps" in the sense of having boundaries. Yet boundaries were introduced across Maasai inhabited lands by colonial administrators, conservation agencies, and later representatives of the independent Tanzanian state. In the process, some of the long-distance social and spatial relations and categories that Maasai customary land use relied on were manipulated, stretched, but also disrupted and severed. Boundary drawing practices by the independent Tanzanian state built on pre-existing Maasai cultural-political boundaries (i.e., *inkutot*) to enact official administrative categories of governance (i.e. wards, districts) that did not always match Maasai customary management processes (Goldman 2020).

Maasai have adopted some of these new boundaries, with customary leaders strategically utilizing Tanzanian decentralized governance categories (i.e. district, village) to multiply their numbers and strengthen their own legitimacy (Goldman, in prep.). Village boundaries are also used to manage grazing access by Maasai from outside villages, sometimes following and sometimes contradicting Maasai boundaries of *enkutoto/olosho* and clan. Maasai elected leaders have also started participating in the boundary-making processes, by seeking official government titles for village lands and dividing villages to create new ones so as to better regulate resources and access state and NGO support. Legally recognized boundaries, they are told, will protect their land from theft for conservation and other land uses. The land titling process demands land use planning maps, which requires zoning village land for wet and dry season grazing areas, reserve grazing areas, farming, housing, etc. Sometimes this is done in a way that recognizes cross-village land use practices, for instance by placing grazing pastures adjacent to each other across village boundaries.[23] Most often, though, Maasai place making practices are ignored and new place making practices enacted through the map making process.

What if these land use maps were *also* populated with Maasai place names (beyond those already turned into official village and sub-village names)? What if they *also* reflected Maasai seasonal distinctions, which breaks resource (pasture and water) availably into five seasons rather than just two? Doing so entails the second key aspect of *mapping multiple*, by placing Maasai spatial and temporal categories *together* with (alongside of, on top of, across) those of western cartography and scientifically recognized seasons. This is not the same as translating indigenous knowledge *into* western categories. It is rather placing the different categories as different *layers* in a map, not to produce a singular complete map, but rather a map that is *more than one but less than many*. These different layers could include multiple categories of spatial organization such as: Maasai place names, Maasai cultural-territorial boundaries, land use categories, village boundaries and conservation units.

Maasai navigate their place names alongside of, together with, and sometimes in spite of state and conservation-based boundaries. This matters. When Maasai cross village boundaries to graze they do so with implicit or explicit permission, and in accordance with their own territorial demarcations of *enkutoto* and *olosho*. When they cross the boundary of a conservation area to graze their cattle illegally inside, it is not because they do not know or care that the administrative boundary is there. Nor is it because the boundary does not matter. The movement occurs *across* the boundary. Sometimes on purpose and with intent to claim the land and show a disregard for the rules in place. Sometimes at night to be discrete and hide the transgression, sometimes with cash in hand to bribe authorities, and sometimes as a group to

---

23   This is the case with the work of the organization, Ujamaa Community Resource Trust (UCRT), which is working to help Maasai and other indigenous communities in Tanzania secure legal tenure rights through Certificates of Customary Rights of Occupancy (CCROs). While they recognize that Maasai grazing practices cross village lands, they are compelled to map at the village level to ensure rights to communities within the legal framework of the Tanzanian state (pers. communication with the Director; see also http://www.ujamaa-crt.org/, last accessed July 17, 2020).

show solidarity in claiming this right, while also hiding individual blame. In other words, the boundaries matter and are crossed, challenged, or used, and called on for various resource management and political purposes. Rather than obscuring or ignoring imposed boundaries, mapping multiple would place them all on the map where they can be seen in relation to the place names and social boundaries that Maasai also use, which could help explain how introduced boundaries are put to use, challenged or manipulated, as well as how they may be misplaced ecologically and socially.

I use an example to highlight how overlapping boundaries can help explain resource conflicts. According to Maasai customary norms, movement to access pasture and water resources usually occur freely within *olosho* and *enkutoto* boundaries. In times of acute need, such as droughts, customs of reciprocity declare that no hungry herder can be denied pasture. During the drought in 2009, Maasai moved in large numbers throughout Tanzania and from Kenya into Tanzania. Many Maasai from the study area moved to access pastures in villages in Simanjiro district. To do so, they negotiated across *enkutoto* lines and village boundaries. With some villages receiving large influxes of herders from across Tanzania, they began to turn people away based on rainfall patterns in a different *inkutot* (pl for *enkutoto*) and along village lines. For instance, as *Emanyara* received rainfall, many Simanjiro village leaders sent herders from *Emanyara* home. As the drought dragged on, villages throughout Tanzanian Maasailand came up with their own rules for allowing visitors in – either along set boundaries in particular places, or by attaching themselves to existing *inkang'itie* (homesteads). Place names, Maasai customary boundaries and village political boundaries all worked together and overlapped in managing resource access.

In the study villages, there was an additional boundary that became very important – the conservation boundary of Manyara Ranch. The abundance of grass available in the conservation area became known across Maasailand, along with various misconceptions related to Maasai access to it (as a community-based conservation area that included Maasai on the steering committee, see Goldman 2011). As such, Maasai from all over Tanzania and Kenya came to the villages surrounding Manyara Ranch with hopes of accessing grazing within the ranch. What many did not know was that access to Manyara Ranch was limited to surrounding villagers and regulated through official requests. In the end, village residents and visitors alike entered the conservation area together, illegally, to access the abundant pastures inside. Conservation authorities saw these as politically motivated violations of the law. They demanded local Maasai keep "outsider" Maasai out of the Ranch, and threatened failure to do so with livestock confiscation and fines. What these state and NGO workers failed to see, and what was not visible on *any* map, was that for local Maasai these were not outsiders, but insiders to certain Maasai recognized boundaries – those of *Olosho* (some were *Kisongo* Maasai and thus with explicit rights to the area for Maasai), and others were just from within the larger boundary of Maasailand (see Figure 3). Neither of these boundaries are easy to draw, though anthropologists have tried to outline them over the years, as have I (see Figure 4). They remain fuzzy, but important. Mapping multiple would mean putting these boundaries, however fuzzy, on the maps so they become visible when planning at village levels, for recognizing social norms or reciprocity, and for negotiating larger scale land use systems for grazing and wildlife conservation.

Ingold suggests that different modalities of travel are not necessarily commensurable. He states that "place-names that index specific landmarks are told in sequence to form stories or 'verbal maps' describing lines of travel for people to follow" (Ingold 2007: 89). He suggests as such that place names are relational, attached to movement and storytelling and that drawing them onto official cartesian maps solidifies the fluid continuous movement trails of habitation or narrative lines of place names with rigid lines of occupation and enclosure. While this may very well be true, many have argued that it is possible to map otherwise, in ways that maintain continuity, movement and even narratives (Pearce this volume). When I first mapped Maasai place names, I presented them as a verbal tour, and used an arrow on the map for the reader to follow the verbal description that I put into words in the text (Figure 4; see also Goldman 2020). Even taking away the line (Figure 1), the spaces in between named places remain visible and there is an attempt to blur the lines of the boundaries. Earlier versions also contained a detailed index with the meanings of the names included. Since Maasai place names do not exist in isolation from the lines of occupation and enclosure drawn on maps, I argue that it is better to find ways to put them on the maps as well – not by changing their ontological ordering, nor to map them inside of other existing boundaries – but to map them as best as we can as part of the landscape along with other boundaries. In this way, we can map multiple in a way that produces maps that are mutually intelligible to Maasai, conservation and development NGOs, and state agencies, without epistemological or ontological hierarchy.

When I mapped Maasai place names for the study area, I mapped all places named by participants even when they crossed village boundary lines.

Figure 3: Research Areas (Source: Goldman 2020; map: Sam Smith)

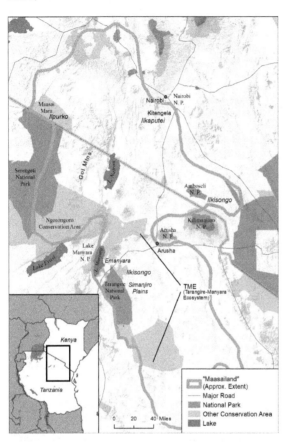

The two specific focus villages were previously one village and there was not yet an official boundary between the two, coupled with an on-going boundary negotiation.[24] For this reason, and to avoid conflict and distraction from the

---

24   This was common in areas, like this one, where original villages were split into two or three. The new boundaries were drawn on maps at both the district level and the national level with very little communication on the ground. These were different from the new official boundaries being drawn by villages themselves for village land titles, or Certificates of Customary Rights of Occupancy (CCROs), because they were demar-

Figure 4: Walking Tour Place Names (Source: Goldman 2020; map: Joel Przbylowski)

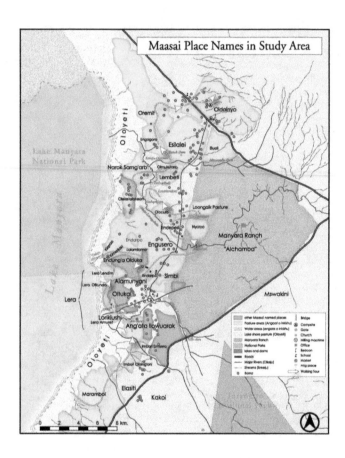

goal of the map, I did not include a boundary between the two villages, though other administrative boundaries were included. I did not include Maasai *enku-toto* or *olosho* boundaries for scale reasons – all mapped places were inside

cated at the district level not locally). At the point of writing, village boundaries have been determined with the help of UCRT for both villages.

the *Emanyara enkutoto*. Yet in producing the larger map for my book (Goldman 2020), I put in only the *olosho* and *enkutoto* distinctions that were vital to my story. I did include the larger Maasailand boundary, national boundaries (Tanzania and Kenya), regional administrative boundaries and conservation boundaries (Figure 2). There are no limits to what a mapping multiple perspective can do, the challenge is to make sure the map is not too complex to read. For instance, I managed to map ecological wildlife data, Maasai wildlife knowledge (listed as opportunistic on the map), administrative and conservation boundaries, and Maasai place names into one map (see Figure 5). The map is however missing distinctions of areas important for grazing by Maasai during different seasons.

Conclusion

Despite the fact that Maasai occupy much of the land now targeted for wildlife conservation in East Africa, Maasai place making practices are rarely acknowledged or taken seriously by conservation agencies and land use planners – even when 'participatory' land use planning is pursued. Why not use Maasai place names to talk about wildlife presence on Maasai lands? Why not use Maasai socio-spatial management frames for land use planning? Doing so would require taking multiple Maasai time-space relationality with the land seriously (by internal differences of gender, age, etc.), alongside conservation and state boundaries.

On the contrary, international and even local NGOs, state agencies, and conservation organizations continue with their own map making practices, with Maasai asked to fill in the gaps while following standard cartographic and scientific breakdowns for time and space. Part of this is due to the hegemony of western mapping technologies (Lovell 2017), and assumptions of epistemological hierarchy. Maasai ways of knowing and being in the world are simultaneously not taken seriously and thought to not easily match up to western cadastral traditions and seasonal land use maps. This is particularly true for wildlife management, which has historically been dominated by western ontologies and epistemologies. Yet, I have argued here that in order to move beyond the rhetoric of participatory processes – as related to mapping, conservation, and land use planning – we need to change the language, context, and ways in which we bring different participants to the table. We cannot give up on mapping, but rather need to bend the map to do

Figure 5: Wildlife sightings by transect and by Maasai,
April-May 2003 (Source: Goldman 2020; map: Sam Smith)

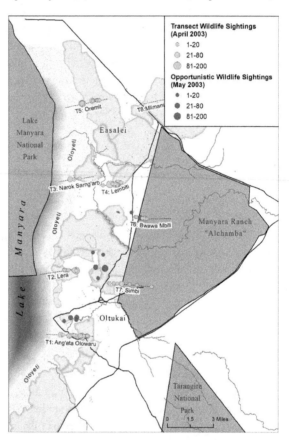

more than it is often expected to do in specific legal/scientific settings. We need to map multiple.

Mapping multiple can mean different things, and I have just begun to explore the possibilities here. It can mean mapping Maasai place names together with village boundaries, conservation boundaries, and Maasai cultural-political *enkutot* and *olosho* boundaries. It could mean mapping across scales – including the over-arching Maasailand boundary along with ecological boundaries such as the Tarangire-Manyara boundary, despite the ambiguity of both. It means recognizing that while there are great hopes in theory and practice about decolonizing conservation, the academy, and cartography – today many indigenous peoples, including Maasai – regularly use multiple sets of boundaries in their daily lives, and in their political fights for rights to their land (Simpson 2017). Mapping the different sets of place-making and boundary drawing together does not legitimize one over the other but recognizes their use in practice. Cartographic skill can be used to emphasize and de-emphasize, but all the competing, sometimes co-used boundaries are in view to be discussed, understood and respected as existing.

References

Basso, Keith H. (1996): Wisdom Sits in Places: Landscape and Language Among the Western Apache, Albuquerque: University of New Mexico Press.

Bryan, Joe (2009) "Where would we be without them? Knowledge, space and power in indigenous politics." In: Futures 41/1, pp. 24-32.

Bryan, Joe (2011): "Walking the line: Participatory mapping, indigenous rights, and neoliberalism." In: Geoforum 42/1, pp. 40-50.

Crampton, Jeremy W. (2009): "Progress in human geography." In: Cartography: performative, participatory, political. 33/6), pp. 840-848.

Collet, David (1987): "Pastoralists and Wildlife: Image and Reality in Kenya Maasialand." In: David Anderson/Richard Grove (eds), Conservation in Africa: people, policies, and practice, Cambridge, UK: Cambridge University Press, pp.129-148.

Deihl, Colin (1985): "Wildlife and the Maasai: The Story of East African Parks." In: Cultural Survival Quarterly 9/1, pp. 37-40.

Goldman, Mara J. (2003): "Partitioned nature, privileged knowledge: Community based conservation in Tanzania." In: Development and Change 34/5, pp. 833-862.

Goldman, Mara J. (2011): "Strangers in their own land: Maasai and wildlife conservation in Northern Tanzania." In: Conservation and Society 9, pp. 65-79.

Goldman, Mara J. (2020): Narrating Nature: Wildlife Conservation and Maasai Ways of Knowing, Critical Green Engagements: Investigating the Green Economy and Its Alternatives, Tuscon: University of Arizona Press.

Goldman, Mara J. (in prep): The Problem with tradition is that it keeps on changing: Making sense of Maasai 'traditional' leadership in the twenty-first century.

Goldman, Mara J./Jagadeesh, Shruthi (forthcoming): Intersectionality and Triage: Accountability in accounting for difference in conservation research and action with communities, a look at work from South India.

Homewood, Katherine/Rodgers, Alan (1991): Maasailand Ecology: Pastoralist development and wildlife conservation in Ngorongoro, Tanzania, New York: Cambridge University Press.

Hayward, Chris/Simpson, Lyn/Wood, Leanne (2004): "Still left out in the cold: Problematising participatory research and development." In: Sociologia Ruralis 44/1, pp. 95-108.

Hodgson, Dorothy L./Richard A. Schroeder (2002): "Dilemmas of counter-mapping community resources in Tanzania." In: Development and Change 33/1, pp. 79-100 (DOI: 10.1111/1467-7660.00241).

Ingold, Tim (2000): The Perception of the Environment: Essays in Livelihood, dwelling and skill, New York: Routledge.

Ingold, Tim (2007): Lines: A Brief History, London Routledge.

Kitchin, Rob/Dodge, Martin (2007): "Rethinking maps." In: Progress in Human Geography 31/3, pp. 331-344.

Law, John/Mol, Annemarie, eds. (2002): Complexities: social studies of knowledge practices, Durham, North Carolina: Duke University Press.

Law, John (2007 [2004]): After Method: Mess in social science research, International Library of Sociology, New York: Routledge.

Lovell, Eric J. (2017): "Roads, Lines, and Boundary Objects: A Critical Cartographic Look at the Development of the Serengeti Highway." In: Cartographica: The International Journal for Geographic Information and Geovisualization, 52/4, pp. 310-321.

Mol, Annemarie (2002): The Body Multiple: Ontology in Medical Practice, Durham, North Carolina: Duke University Press.

Mol, Frans (1996): Maasai: Language and Culture, Narok, Kenya: Mill Hill Missionary.

Parkipuny, M.L. Ole. 1979. "Some Crucial Aspects of the Maasai Predicament." In: Coulson, Andrew (ed.), African Socialism in Practice: the Tanzanian Experience, Nottingham: Spokesman, pp. 136-57.

Parkipuny, M.L. Ole/Dhyani J. Berger (1993): "Maasai Rangelands: Links between Social Justice and Wildlife Conservation." In: Dale Lewis/Carter,

Nick (eds.), Voices from Africa: local perspectives on conservation, Washington, District of Columbia: World Wildlife Fund, pp. 113-131.

Pearce, Margaret W. (2008): "Framing the Days: Place and Narrative in Cartography." In: Cartography and Geographic Information Science 35/1, pp. 17-32.

Rocheleau, Dianne E. (2005): "Maps as Power Tools: Locating Communities in Space or Situating People and Ecologies in Place?" In: Brosius, Peter/Tsing, Anna/Zerner, Charles (eds), Communities and Conservation, Oxford: Altamira Press, pp. 327-362.

Roque de Pinho, Joana (2009): Staying Together: People-Wildlife Relationships in a Pastoral Society in Transition, Amboseli Ecosystem, Southern Kenya. PhD, Colorado State University.

Simpson, Leanne Betasamosake (2017): As we have always done: Indigenous freedom through radical resistance, Minneapolis; London: University of Minnesota Press.

Turnbull, David (2000): Masons, tricksters and cartographers: comparative studies in the sociology of scientific and indigenous knowledge, Amsterdam: Harwood Academic.

Western, David/Gichohi, Helen (1993): "Segregation effects and the impoverishment of savanna parks: the case of ecosystem viability analysis." In: African Journal of Ecology 31/4, pp. 269-281.

Western, David (1989): "Conservation without Parks: Wildlife in the Rural Landscape." In: Western, David/Pearl, Mary (eds), Conservation for the Twenty-first Century, New York: Oxford University Press, pp. 158-165.

Western, David (1997): In the Dust of Kilimanjaro, Washington, District of Columbia: Island Press.

Mapping materiality – social relations with objects and landscapes

Thea Skaanes

Figure 1: The scenic view over the Yaeda valley, Tanzania (Photo: Thea Skaanes)

Let us, dear reader, find a vantage point from which to overlook the land-scape. A suitable place is to climb the mountain and find a good spot (see Figure 1). From here we will try to perceive and interpret the Hadza land-scape before us. In his fascinating account on speaking with names, Keith Basso noted that landscapes do not interpret their own significance (Basso

1988: 100). Interpretations and ascriptions of meaning require people, they require relationality. So, have a look and take in this scenic view. Sitting on a mountain top, overlooking the valley far below and the mountain rim at the other end of the valley, we may notice the landscape's strong combination of presence and distance, of grandeur and of the miniscule; we are there on the cliff feeling the silencing awe of it all.

On the day the picture was taken, we had set out from the Hadza camp in the morning and had both found honey and eaten copious amounts of tubers; we were filled to satiety and the sun heated warmth of the rock radiated from under us as the afternoon heat began to wane. The breeze was turning soft and kind, changing from the mid-day hot and tiringly hostile winds. We pointed to places we had been recently, to the pack of zebras and three impalas grazing under the trees far below, and made a few remarks, but the dialogues ebbed away and silence flooded in as we eventually sat down and looked, not at each other, but at this landscape before us, in an atmosphere of reflective contemplation.

The words could be many more,[1] but the landscape itself speaks by other means than words. As she beholds the landscape, the emic 'reader' (Scott 1998) of the landscape with the trained eye could be in a vivid dialogue with a myriad of words, a dialogue full of specificities and significance; propelled by points, traces, memories, narratives and relationships. But for the novice, for the unfamiliar, untrained, not-so-well-acquainted eye, the landscape dialogue is more sparse; it does not provide you with strings of specific words connecting into a story of significance. Keith Basso describes unfamiliarity with this extreme tangibility in this way:

> Emphatically 'there' but conspicuously lacking in accustomed forms of order and arrangement, landscape and discourse confound the stranger's efforts to invest them with significance, and this uncommon predicament, which produces nothing if not uncertainty, can be keenly disconcerting. (Basso 1988: 99)

---

1   I would like to thank Ute Dieckmann for a wonderful collaboration and for being an exemplary editor and reviewer. I would also like to thank Sian Sullivan and Mara Jill Goldmann for their careful reading and for giving invaluable comments and feedback in their reviews of this chapter. And how uplifted I was and utterly grateful for the inspirational discussions and lectures that formed part of the *Mapping the unmappable*-workshop in December 2019 in Cologne that preceded this publication. Thank you for inviting me to partake in this inspirational process.

In order to access the landscape, to learn its distinctiveness, and to be able to invest it with significance, 'we' need to mediate and conceptualize it in order to attach meaning to it. 'We', here, refers to us as field-working, visiting researchers, i.e. those of us who are not indigenous to the area we work in. The translation challenge is key in this point, as we are novices looking at and trying to learn about and appreciate a new landscape. We devise our own cartography as we seek to identify significant entities, sections, types and kinds that we connect and relate to other kinds in grids, schemes and maps. We make drawings, take photographs, note GPS coordinates; we keep memorabilia and souvenirs in the hope that they might be a key that will open the door to a place of knowing for us. And as we include parts in the picture, even tiny bricks in a seemingly giant multidimensional puzzle, of layers of experience, emotions, discourse, we weave systems of meaning around us, as a means of learning, of translation, or, as Donna Haraway says, *ways* of seeing:

> [A]ll eyes, including our own organic ones, are active perceptual systems, building in translations and specific *ways* of seeing, that is, ways of life. ... there are only highly specific visual possibilities, each with a wonderfully detailed, active, partial way of organizing worlds. All these pictures of the world should not be allegories of infinite mobility and interchangeability, but of elaborate specificity and difference and the loving care people might take to learn to see faithfully from another's point of view... (Haraway 1991: 190, original emphasis)

Ever so individually fashioned, translation processes like those described by Haraway here would provide comfort and lessen the feeling of being alien. However, as Donna Haraway puts it, these "partial ways of organizing worlds", the systems we fashion, should not only be "allegories of infinite mobility and interchangeability", but rather a process of "elaborate specificity and difference and the loving care people might take to learn to see faithfully from another's point of view". In this way, Haraway warmly encourages us to transgress the boundaries of the systems we have set in place for ourselves, i.e. the systems that Basso called "accustomed forms of order and arrangement". With eloquence and humor, she calls on us to try faithfully to learn about and gradually to better appreciate the systems that we have not fashioned ourselves. If we strive to learn about the landscape and how it is conceptualized by the people who are so familiar with it, in this case the Hadza of Tanzania, a rather fundamental rearrangement will be needed. Again, I use the words of Keith Basso:

> In other words, one [as an ethnographer] must acknowledge that local understandings of external realities are ineluctably fashioned from local cultural materials, and that, knowing little or nothing of the latter, one's ability to make appropriate sense of 'what is' and 'what occurs' in one's environment is bound to be deficient. (Basso 1988: 100)

In the editor's invitation to contribute a chapter to the present volume, I found a call for this deeper search or rearrangement (see Introduction, this volume). It aired a critical query regarding the ways cartographic theories and methods have been applied to African environments, the multispecies ecologies carved by alternative ontologies, and how the two theories, or world views, as systems of ideas, have resulted in a fundamental mismatch of ontological and epistemological incongruities in many cases. How may we proceed adequately? Echoing Keith Basso, the question remains: How can we make appropriate sense of "what is" and "what occurs" in the ontological schemes of African hunter-gatherers? Furthermore, how may we as researchers communicate our findings? Can maps be a viable way?

With Haraway's firm and feminist critique of objectivizing narratives, Basso's call for absolving the subjective understanding, and being informed of the vivid debate in anthropology called "the ontological turn", which questions our very application of concepts (see Henare et al. 2007), the task ahead seems almost impossible. How will we be able to know what the women and children on the mountain top saw that afternoon as they contemplated the landscape before them?[2] Questions of cultural translation led to decades of numbing self-reflection in academia, facing the demons of privilege, and silencing claims based on epistemological or ontological translation by the nightmarish questioning of the very legitimacy of the academic practices of border-crossing scholarly work. This critique was due and, like a grindstone, it sharpened our scholarly diligence and ethical attention. But how do we turn that sharp-

---

2   Many scholars have argued that contemplating the landscape is a specific and western construct (see Ingold 1993) relating to the rise of romanticism (see Hirsch/O'Hanlon 1995). I acknowledge the perceptive analyses in these contributions; however, I am describing the empirical situation of us sitting on the mountain top, as speech ebbed away, and quietly looking – not closing the eyes – at the scenery before us. Therefore, let us not rid the Hadza of this experience either, but keep an open mind as to what they saw, what it meant, and with which conceptual schema or sensorial faculties this experience would match for them.

ened blade away from ourselves and into constructive use, i.e. how do we reengage? How may we draw maps of that which, it seems, is unmappable?

I am neither a trained cartographer, nor have I worked in the role of a cartographer. But what I notice is that we[3] all draw maps; and we all maneuver within ideational frames. Such frames that we navigate are both frames that we set ourselves and frames that were set by others before us. Annette Markham, talking about visual methods, argues:

> Frames function like maps. They shape how we move, how we think and how we put boundaries around things. And they shape our behavior and it's not unless something jars us loose of a conceptualization like this that we notice that there was a frame operating at all. That could be questioned. It is a fantastic corrective map of the world that really does transform how we think of it. (Markham 2012, personal communication)[4]

In this way, frames function like maps, and maps function like frames. We set frames and navigate both visible and invisible maps. These might be maps of places, routes and sites, but also of logistics systems, kinship relations, social dynamics, economic exchanges, strings of currencies in transvalue systems, cosmologies, and all kinds of resources, to mention but a few examples. As researchers, we draw correlations and identify kinds. We set the frames for our research in a myriad of ways in order to define the areas for our work, or, with other spatial terms, the *spheres* (Bohannan 1959), *fields* (Bourdieu 1984), or *scapes* (Appadurai 1996). This is what we do, both as researchers and as humans in general.

Let me take us to the opposite end of the area before us, or rather, let me shift metaphors here, to the other side of the matter at hand. My own background as a social anthropologist and curator at a cultural history museum steered me in my own research into asking questions around "local understandings of external realities fashioned from local cultural materials" (see Basso above) in order to ever so tentatively start learning about "what is" and "what occurs" (see Skaanes 2017a). The question that motivated me was whether new information could be gleaned from the examination of selected objects in connection with practices, ideas and phenomena such as sharing,

---

3   We, here again, is the scholarly 'we'. In the spirit of full transparency, I am a trained social anthropologist and museum curator.

4   Lecture held during the course *Cultural Methods, Methods of Culture*, at Aarhus University, Fall 2012.

ritual and symbolism that carry both material and immaterial constituents. Could following this path help us understand the structures of social relations among the Hadza – and would cosmology really matter (Skaanes 2017a)?

Moving on in this chapter I will digress from maps and landscapes in order to bring you to the world of things, a field closer to my own scholarly attention than cartography. I will trace how applying novel frames to material objects provides new insights, and I suggest a similar change as one method among many others that will allow us to jerk loose from the naturalized theory-bound conceptualization of land and environments. To give you, dear reader, peace of mind, as we move along, I argue for considering social relations in spheres beyond the human. In order to be able to make this leap from objects to landscapes, I identify connecting concepts in the potency of special objects with that of special places. This way, I will eventually address questions of "social relationships, non-human agents and [briefly and more implicitly, though] the dimension of time" (as outlined in the introduction to this volume) when trying to reengage with landscapes and mapping informed by these findings. But before we proceed, let me briefly introduce the Hadza and the empirical case for this chapter.

Introducing the Hadza hunter-gatherers of Tanzania and their environment

From the famous work of James Woodburn, the Hadza are well-known among hunter-gatherer researchers working in Africa. In terms of terminology,[5] they are small-scale, semi-nomadic, immediate-return hunter-gatherers living in the south-eastern areas around Lake Eyasi in northern Tanzania. The fieldwork informing this chapter was conducted in a camp, 'Ika 'e 'a-dzua,[6] just at the foot of the Kideru mountains.[7] The ecology of the area reflects the semi-

---

5   The way we introduce an area, a field, and a group of hunter-gatherers seems to me to be fixed in a genre, a certain style, that assumes correctness and objectivity, but that to some degree carries objectifying measures and troublesome applications of the Cartesian theory-bound assumptions, that we seek to critically undo here.

6   Anonymity is ensured by different kinds of cloaking tactics. Altered names, altered places, altered kin relations or altered descriptions. However, I pay attention to keeping the resource of the empirical data intact.

7   The Kideru Mountains are part of the southern bifurcation of the eastern branch of the East African Rift of the Great Rift valley system.

arid conditions. You find heavy rainfall in the rainy season, with rain water pouring down the surrounding mountains. The water turns into roaring rivers where there used to be roads and creates dangerous erosion around constructions (bridges, the odd bricked house, or cemented construction around water supplies, such as wells, pumps, etc.). As it reaches the lowlands it floods large areas in the valley, from the swamp – which is further downhill from the camp – upwards. In the rainy season, the need for shelter might be beyond the capacity of the thatched huts, so people seek shelter in rocky caves in the mountains. The dry season's dusty and windy heat, conversely, carries all humidity away, and with the sun's rays reflected by the grains of sand and minerals in the soil, the environment turns into a sun-oven, with unbearable heat. Housing and shelter in the dry season involve high demands for shadow, breezy areas for the morning and late afternoon, and insulation from the midday heat inside the cool thatched hut. The dry season is animated by wind, the swirling dust-devils and tumbleweed that create movement and catch the eye in the otherwise stillness of the sizzling landscape. Such are the extremes of the surrounding environment. Yet it is also fertile, green, vibrant and accommodating in between these extremes. This is why we also find encroachment in the area, both by agricultural farmers (mostly Iraqw and Isansu) clearing land and sowing corn, wheat or watermelon fields, and by increasing numbers of cattle and goats, causing ecological deterioration as they are brought into the area by Iraqw and Datoga pastoral families. At the same time, families from neighboring ethnic groups are hesitant to move here, despite the escalating national crisis of land shortage, due to their fear of the feral factors in the area, especially the dreaded tsetse fly, the man-eating large cats, the huge elephants, packs of hyenas and venomous snakes.[8] Dehumanizing stereotypical views of the Hadza also contribute to the overall image of the

---

8   Living here you share physical space with and partake in an ecology made up of animals such as the ones mentioned here, but also large mammals such as eland, hippopotamus and buffalo and the numerically rich herds of zebras, Thomson's gazelles, and the small dik-diks. The prevalence of animals relates to the many game reserves in the area. To the north-west we find the Maswa Game Reserve, which further up extends into the Serengeti National Park. Ngorongoro is to the north, to the north-east we have the Lake Manyara National Park, and south of that, we find the Tarangire National Park. It is an area with a relatively high number of game animals, but it is not a residence area as such. There are both lions and leopards in the area. Due to the shallow burial practices of the Hadza, these have sometimes scavenged and eaten human flesh, which adds to people's fear of the cats as having crossed over into being man-

area as ferocious and dangerous.[9] Another factor is that the infrastructure is scarce and poorly maintained. At the time of my fieldwork, there were no operating water lines, no electricity apart from the odd solar panel left behind by a researcher,[10] the few roads were poorly maintained, and the mobile phone coverage was highly limited and untrustworthy. So, in most regards, what the Hadza consider their homeland is conceived of as a peripheral and inhospitable area by most others.

The Hadza are excellent bow-and-arrow[11] hunters and powerful digging-stick[12] gatherers. They live in band-sized camps (20-50 inhabitants, mostly related by kin), characterized by a high degree of flexibility of composition (i.e. people frequently and easily move in and out of camp) and with a rather limited amount of possessions. According to a recent census conducted by the anthropologist Brian Wood in 2012, the total population is around 1200 Hadza (Pontzer et al. 2015; Wood, personal communication, 2012), whereof an estimated 400 remain primarily hunter-gatherers (Marlowe 2010:38; Woodburn 1968a).

To categorize a society as hunting and gathering requires attention to the formal definitions of the term.[13] An unequivocal, yet restricted, definition was provided by Murdock, who states that to qualify as hunting and gathering, a society should base less than 5 percent of its subsistence on other strategies than hunting and gathering, e.g. farming and herding (1981: 92,

---

eaters. Whether this is a huge problem or not, stories among the Hadza flourish about a leopard that has tried its luck.

9   Even just spending the night in the valley was considered dangerous by neighbors living as close as on the mountain rim, and spending multiple nights was seen as risking your life, whereas for the Hadza these nights formed a large part of creating a sense of togetherness in camp, of performing rituals, of storytelling and poetics (Skaanes 2017b, 2017a).

10   The sheer amount of equipment that researchers came to the area with (water tanks, food, boots, sunglasses, nets, hats, hats with nets, backpacks, locks, solar panels, computers and other electronic equipment) and arriving not only in one but often two 4x4s, taking great care to follow safety protocols, only reaffirmed the assumption that this was a dangerous area.

11   In ordinary Hadza hunting, there is no use of firearms, traps or fishing, but only the use of bows and arrows, occasionally with the addition of a very potent plant-based poison to the iron-headed barbed arrows (/ /' ana or / /' anako, see Woodburn 1970) to kill large prey.

12   The digging stick is also referred to as the woman's bow.

13   See Sullivan (this volume).

106). However, as described by Lee (2005) and Widlok/Tadesse (2005), recent developments in hunting and gathering societies reveal that hunter-gatherer economics and sharing practices often coexist with commoditization. A more complex definition of hunter-gatherers was provided by Nurit Bird-David; it pointed to characteristics independent of subsistence-strategies, bringing attention to "a distinctive mode of sociality" (Bird-David 1999: 235). She mentions the band-based society with its valuation of individual autonomy and social relatedness, resource-sharing, and universal kinship as characteristics (ibid.). She states that the ethnic groups categorized as hunter-gatherers do not seem to categorically distinguish between 'nature' and 'culture' or between the human and the non-human worlds (ibid.). Furthermore, as a critique relating to Murdock's definition, she points to remarkably flexible adoption of "additional subsistence pursuits" that seems to be done with ease, and that these adopted ways are just as easily abandoned again, leaving no disturbing trace on the societal structures. The Hadza that I worked with were hunter-gatherers by all of these definitions.[14]

Despite the relatively small population, most Hadza in the Yaeda Chini valley display linguistic resilience, as they speak Hadzane[15] in daily conversation; however, as quite a few especially elderly Hadza disapprovingly told me, the obligatory schooling in distant boarding schools is increasingly depriving the youth of valuable knowledge about living in the bush and is creolizing young people's language, turning it into a mixture of Swahili and Hadzane (for further information, see Skaanes 2017a).

Anthropologists and scholars of evolutionary theory display a special interest in Hadza research, which is revealed through the cornucopia of published papers dealing with Hadza conditions. Taking their small population into consideration, the Hadza have provided empirical material for an impressive quantity of studies and their case elicits claims of remarkable scale in academia. Professor Emeritus, James Woodburn, as the most respected and esteemed Hadza researcher of more than six decades, used the long awaited *Tenth International Conference on Hunting and Gathering Societies* (CHAGS10) in 2013 as an opportunity to encourage researchers to begin to look elsewhere, implying that not much is left to be said about this overly-studied people. I

---

14   The identification of these areas as being of significance is something that I recognize and find to be key in the Hadza case as well.

15   Hadzane is a click language and might be a linguistic isolate (Sands 1998).

think he might have been right in terms of the operating frames that are predominant in these prior studies, but changing the prevalent discourses would indeed bring new insights to academia.[16]

Shifting the operating frames

During the symposium *Man the Hunter* at the University of Chicago in April 1966, discussions were lively, and we are fortunate that they were transcribed and published along with the presented papers (Lee/Devore 1968). Following Marshall Sahlins' contribution (1968) a discussion on hunting and happiness came up. In it, two main themes emerged in relation to the Hadza: the absence of concern for the morrow and the relative lack of binding social relations expressed through commitment and obligation. Addressing the latter, James Woodburn stated the following:

> It may be worth mentioning a lack of commitment different from the lack of commitment to the morrow and yet, perhaps, related to it. The Hadza are strikingly uncommitted to each other; what happens to other individual Hadza, even close relatives, does not really matter very much. ... With a few exceptions, a Hadza does not depend on specific individuals standing in particular relationships to him for access to property or to adult status, or for assistance in cooperative activities. (Woodburn 1968b: 91)

Woodburn restated this a decade later (Woodburn 1979: 257). Family ties, responsibilities and sense of obligation along kin lines were at that time and have since been manifestly downplayed when discussing the Hadza case. According the existing studies, the Hadza seem to live the simplest[17] version of

---

16   Furthermore, gender also matters. The group in the Hadza society that are subjected to the most restrictions to knowledge, i.e. the group that people withhold most information from based on social conventions, are non-initiated men. Simply being a woman would allow more information to be passed on to me than if I had been a man. So, both gender and framing, along with methodology, are factors that carry high significance for what is rendered visible – and conversely, invisible – in academic accounts.

17   The Hadza and the Mbuti are singled out as scoring zero as regards the degree of societal complexity (Marlowe 2010: 70); the remaining hunting and gathering societies are all placed at the low end of the scale. Scores rank from 0 to 40, and the average score for hunting and gathering societies, or, as Marlowe terms them, "foraging societies", was 6. Frank Marlowe sums this up: "It does not surprise me that the Hadza ranked at

society that we know of; they are strikingly tied to the present, and their weak family relationships do not carry burdensome dependency.

Turning to religion, the Hadza case is used as an inverse position to religious beliefs or symbolic constructs, or, as James Woodburn denotes them, "ideological elaborations" (1982a; Barnard/Woodburn 1988). Woodburn (1982a) compared mortuary rites and beliefs in four hunting and gathering societies (!Kung, Baka, Mbuti and Hadza) and in conclusion he stated:

> All these themes that might provide a starting-point for elaboration into a set of systematic beliefs about fertility and regeneration in death but the evidence does not, I think, support the idea that such a set of systematic beliefs has already developed in any of these four societies. (Woodburn 1982a: 204)

With an assessment that the Hadza were a society without systematic beliefs (see Marlowe 2010: 60) or that was minimally religious (Apicella 2018) being broadly accepted in academia, there has been very little subsequent research on Hadza rituals and cosmology (although see Purzycki et al. 2017; Apicella 2018; Power 2015; 2017; and Power/Watts 1997 for notable exceptions).

During my doctoral work, I worked with a small selection of power objects that I had read about in James Woodburn's British Museum publication (Woodburn 1970), which is physically modest but magnificent in its contribution. In it, he provides in-depth descriptions of each object in the British Museum's Hadza collection: a collection that Woodburn had collected years before and then divided into collections for the British Museum and the Horniman Museum. He described three objects that were part of the ritual called the *epeme* night dance: namely, a stick (*naricanda*), a calabash (*a'untenakwiko*) and a doll (*han!anakwete*).

Relating to these objects,[18] Woodburn, as the ground-breaking author, was the one to point to their exceptionality. He did so by altering the description from the otherwise prevalent technical, political or practical-economic descriptions to use a discourse of ceremony, ritual and efficacy. He notably did so by describing these special objects as "children" (Woodburn 1970: 57). This is a strong way of diverging from the practical-economic discourse. In his description of objects that relate to the ritual *epeme* night dance, he wrote:

---

the bottom of the complexity scale; we would be hard-pressed to find a less complex society." (Marlowe 2010: 70)

18   The following section also appears in different sections of Skaanes (2017a).

> He [the male solo dancer, the *epeme*] dances first in his own name and later
> in the names of his children and he may also dance for three types of ob-
> ject which he refers to as his children, the *a'untenakwete*, which are engraved
> gourds used to hold clarified animal fat, secondly the *han!anakwete*, stone
> or mud dolls which may be decorated with beads, and thirdly the *naricanda*
> which are incised sticks made by men for female initiates to use during the
> ceremonies associated with female circumcision. At these ceremonies the
> initiates use the sticks to beat and stab any man who does not run away as
> they approach. Each individual *a'untenakwete* gourd, *han!anakwete* doll and
> *naricanda* stick belongs to a woman and may be named by her. (Woodburn
> 1970: 57, original emphasis)

How does this statement correspond with a society scoring zero on a complexity scale (Marlowe 2010)? Or with living firmly in the present with no care
for the morrow (Lee/Devore 1968)? And, maybe most strikingly, with family
relations not being of significance? I noticed that this description indicated
a crack in an otherwise tightly fashioned narrative about the Hadza as en-
tertaining only a few rituals and having a rather fragmented cosmological
narrative (see Woodburn 1982a; Marlowe 2010: 60).

Indeed, in my doctoral work, as I tracked and researched the significance,
symbolism and application of these objects, new perspectives came to light.
The stick, the gourd and the doll, and the way Hadza relate to them, are not
representative of the way Hadza relate to things or possessions in general.
These are ritual objects and they stand out as functioning objects of power
for the Hadza. Power object is not an emic term. I apply it as an analytical concept that, I suggest, could gain the status of a cover term for artefacts such as charms and exemplars that carry spirit, are magical, mystical or
particularly ritualistic. This term may save analysts from the discomfort, or
even embarrassment, of resorting to the related concept 'fetish' (see Pietz 1985;
Guardiola-Rivera 2007; 2009).[19] In a likened process of terminating a concept,

---

19   A caption at the British Museum's Africa exhibition in front of a large display case with
     anthropomorphic and non-anthropomorphic sculptures, mostly of wood, refers to this
     concept and defines it in the following way: "Objects of power Wooden sculpture com-
     monly offers a way of fixing and controlling powers that are of natural or supernatural
     origin or can even be part of an individual's own body" (British Museum, transcript from
     exhibition text in Africa exhibition, December 2013). In the Hadza context, objects of
     power are not only wooden or sculptures, but they are specifically related to powers
     and they are indeed part of the women's bodies. Other terms that are in use would be

of putting it to rest, most famously done by Claude Lévi-Strauss for the concept of totemism (1962), Pietz, with his articles (most prominently 1985), also effectively terminated the application of the concept of the fetish. This has created a void for an agreed-upon cover term in academia. My suggestion is that we identify such a term, e.g. power object, in order to ensure academic dialogue.

I argue that the objects singled out here are materializations of social relations and of time. The present self (*a'untenakwiko*) indicates the specific person and her being's present and corporeal potency; the past (*naricanda*) connects the woman to her forebears, living or dead; and, thirdly, the woman extends into the future through her children (*olanakwete*) (see Skaanes 2015; 2017a for elaboration).[20] As such, the woman extends beyond the boundary of her skin; in her material forms, i.e. her body and her material names, she materializes relationships both to different times and to family within her

---

object-beings (Grimes 1990) and biographical objects (Hoskins 1998). However, power object as a term seems to be broad enough to encompass both object-beings (ontological aspect) and symbolic or connecting objects (epistemological aspect) and allows us to address objects that are, in both understandings (epistemologically and ontologically), more than objects. I am grateful for the inspiring discussions during the international conference *The Power of Objects. Materiality, Forms, Ritual Action*, in Toulouse, May 2013.

20 The observant reader will notice that I have substituted Woodburn's *han!anakwete*-doll with this *olanakwete*. When I inquired about the *han!anakwete*, *epeme* men told me that they did not know about such a doll. However, they did know about another doll that had the same use, i.e. a name called in the *epeme* night dance ritual, and one that, in my subsequent analysis, proved to be a tangible ecology of social relations (Skaanes 2018; 2017a). I am, however, aware now that there is a very secretive doll, which is indeed called the *han!anakwete*. James Woodburn, when collecting the *han!anakwete* for his material collection, noted a clear hesitation to disclose it and became acutely aware of the secretive nature of the doll (Woodburn 2013, personal communication). However, contrary to Woodburn (1970) and Kohl-Larsen (1959), it seemed to me that this was not an object that was open to the *epeme* men nor related to the *epeme* rituals and hence it had a different function from that of the two other tangible names, the *naricanda* and the *a'untenakwete*. I should add that both the *a'untenakwete* and the *olanakwete* are gendered, and that this is reflected in the word for them. A female gourd is *a'untenakwiko* and the female doll is an *olanakwiko*. Even though there are slight differences in the gourd's applicability relating to gender (Skaanes 2017a), in order not to write both genders when I address them, I have chosen the female gourd and the male doll as the standard representation here.

encompassing self – including here the external objects that are considered '(of) her'.

The objects that form the case for this chapter are objects that, based on the findings in my research, are intimately viewed as (related with/to) persons. Before we take the objects in hand and examine them, let us consider what others have said in the literature about the Hadza and objects, property or possessions. Frank Marlowe wrote a chapter on Hadza material culture, and in it he remarks:

> With the exception of having the bow and poisoned arrow (and perhaps the ax), Hadza technology is about as simple as that of any society ethnographically described and probably as simple as that of most foragers before agriculture first appeared. (Marlowe 2010: 70)

In his chapter on material culture, Marlowe stresses that he only considers the material culture, and: "…let the reader decide how simple or complex the nonmaterial culture is" (ibid.). James Woodburn takes a more holistic view, tying material and immaterial culture to a systematic and logical principle. As he proposes, specific key factors in Hadza social dynamics are instrumental in producing a specific relationship to property:

> [...] we have here the application of a rigorously systematic principle: in these societies the ability of individuals to attach and to detach themselves at will from groupings and from relationships, to resist imposition of authority by force, to use resources freely without reference to other people, to share as equals in game meat brought into camp, to obtain personal possessions without entering into dependent relationships – all these bring about one central aspect of this specific form of egalitarianism. *What it above all does is to disengage people from property, from the potentiality in property rights for creating dependency.* (Woodburn 1998: 445, original emphasis)

This quote shows how material culture and the way people engage or disengage with it are valid and important sources for learning about systematic principles operating in society. As Woodburn focuses on egalitarianism (above, see Woodburn 1982b), he emphasizes that properties, belongings and possessions carry the characteristic ability to be potential generators of inequality.

This link to material culture has also been carefully examined in a remarkable variety of perspectives by Widlok and Tadasse (2005). They presented us with a rich range of contributions on hunter-gatherer correlations between property and equality and pointed to rich aspects of this multifaceted field (ibid.). Being of importance and influence, these perspectives have informed the general focus in literature on property as related to dependency, power structures and as practical-economic resources (ibid.; Marlowe 2010; Widlok 2017).

The view on belongings in most studies in the Hadza context confine objects to being mundane, having a resource value that when transacted has a transposing effect on the distribution of resources, hence implicitly assuming the practical-economic instrumental rationale of the actors administering these things (see Apicella et al. 2012; Marlowe 2010; Hawkes et al. 1997). The widespread use of resource discourse, i.e. a discourse related to the property-qualities of materials and objects, is also prevalent in descriptions of hunter-gatherer environments and cartography,[21] and I find this a common premise for engaging with both objects and land relations. Instead, I propose that a change in framing in relation to objects and the insights that such a change enables might provide a model for how to see both land and cartography differently.

The objects that are singled out for this study, however, do not share these practical-economic characteristics in society: in contrast to material practices in general among the Hadza, they may be inherited,[22] they are ceremonial, serve ritual functions, they are personal, stored, kept, cherished, and not circulated. This attests to their special status, and that they are not merely objects, but something else as well. Leaving aside Marlowe's point about the simplicity of Hadza material culture, I proceed with a new point of view on material culture as focusing and expressing *social relations*:

> *From another point of view material culture may be regarded as part of social relations*, for material objects are chains along which social relationships run, and the more simple is a material culture the more numerous are the relationships expressed through it. ... A single small artifact may be a nexus between persons, e.g. a spear which passes from father to son by gift or inheritance *is a symbol of their relationship and one of the bonds by which it is main-*

---

21   See Introduction and Dieckmann, this volume.

22   Inheritance practices are interesting among the Hadza. A person's possessions at the time of death are distributed based on consideration of practicality and needs. However, certain objects, like the objects discussed here, are dealt with in accordance with customary considerations. It is significant who inherited the objects and from whom they came and what it entails to receive such an object.

tained. Thus people not only create their material culture and attach themselves to it, but also build up their relationships through it and see them in terms of it. As Nuer have very few kinds of material objects and very few specimens of each kind, their social value is increased by their having to serve as the *media of many relationships* and they are, in consequence, often invested with ritual functions. (Evans-Pritchard 1940: 89, emphasis added)[23]

What I found was that Evans-Pritchard's descriptions, although describing processes in a pastoral system, shared traits with the system operating through these three objects among the Hadza. The three objects were not well described through the discourse of property, but rather, as suggested by Evans-Pritchard, as social relations, as connectors of people, and as having a ritual function rather than an economic one. As power objects, the objects are efficacious objects, linked to the very spirit of women and giving tangible form to a string of social relationships. They specifically materialize spirit and kin relations across generations, and producing such objects was an act of tangible co-creation of time.

---

23   Evans-Pritchard's argument is strongly contested by Alan Barnard and James Woodburn, however. They write: "Evans-Pritchard's characterization is right for the Nuer and is right, too, for delayed-return hunter-gatherers including the Australian Aborigines. People build elaborate relationships with each other through symbolic elaboration of ties with and through 'things', especially, in the hunter-gatherer cases, with and through artefacts and land. These ties include various forms of identification, but property rights, with their rules of inclusion and exclusion, are of central importance. But Evans-Pritchard was wrong, quite wrong, if he thought that symbolic elaboration is something to do with having a simple material culture. People in immediate-return systems, users of an even simpler material culture than the Nuer one, do not symbolically elaborate the relations between people and things, to any great extent except in a few restricted contexts usually linked with marriage and more generally with relations between the sexes." (Barnard/Woodburn 1988: 30-31, emphasis added) Barnard and Woodburn do not dismiss that such relations could exist in immediate-return societies like the Hadza, but they argue that they do so in "a few restricted contexts" generally relating to "relations between the sexes". Barnard and Woodburn emphasize the mundane relation between people and things, while I would argue that a significant part of the material system operating among the Hadza includes these objects as part of social relations (see Skaanes 2017a). Putting their disagreement aside, what both Evans-Pritchard and Barnard and Woodburn seem to agree on is that such descriptions are powerful and must be undertaken with caution in order to carefully capture the fine webs of significance that lie between humans and their objects.

In our collaboration during this research, the people living in the camp 'Ika 'e 'a-dzua and I needed another frame to be set around these objects – a frame that allowed for connections, for stories of social relations, kinship, time, cosmology and ritual – in order to make space for how these objects reflect on world views and the way they give shape and tangibility to systems of ideas.[24] The people living in 'Ika 'e 'a-dzua and I changed the framing and discourse from one of property to one of social relations as a way to work with the local materials that these objects were. And as materials of social relations, a rich story came to life about names, kinship, cosmology, ritual and time.

Objects: material name-cases

A particular example could be instructive in communicating the argument of this chapter. I describe a material case involving the three power-objects: the *naricanda* stick, the *a'untenakwiko* gourd and the *olanakwete* doll (Skaanes 2015; 2017a; and see Figures 2-4).[25] These objects are to be understood as names, i.e. tangible names in themselves, as well as being names of the woman they

---

24   The methods of my research were primarily ethnographic. Doing ethnography includes, for me, being present and staying for relatively long periods of time in the community, allowing me to take part in life lived in the camp, e.g. digging for tubers not as a method, but as a way of sustaining myself, writing fieldnotes every evening in the red light from my head-lamp in my tiny one-man tent, and conducting different kinds of interview (some were instigated by myself while others were not, some followed a route, an inquiry, that I had intended, while others did not; some brought insights regarding the interlocutor(s)'s perspective, some served to triangulate information, some interviews taught me about connections, others again provided long story-lines; all in their own way taught me about the nature of humans and non-humans). These were all part of this research. The collaborative aspect gained further prominence when I was advised to work with someone who was kin to the majority of the people in the camp I worked in, and I followed this advice. Then we started working together. The material collection that we made for the museum was made collaboratively. Especially when it comes to the power objects, these objects were given to me out of a recognized necessity for keeping and storing cultural materials for future generations. Being tasked by the Hadza to make such a cultural heritage material collection and to document and safe-guard their intangible heritage turned the work into a collective endeavor with a shared objective.

25   A fuller description of the three objects is to be found in my PhD dissertation "Cosmology Matters" (2017a), see also Skaanes 2015.

belong to.[26] What, then, is in a name? As is well-known from a wide range of ethnographic accounts from all over the world, the event of a birth, also in the Hadza understanding of events, is not the time of creation of the social person. A child who is born does not have spirit until it is named. It is mere biology, a mere body. A child becomes someone when he or she is named. So names, including these tangible, material objects, hold transformative powers that can transform more or less irrelevant biology into deeply emotionally connected and relevant kin.

What happens when a Hadza is named? Along with the name, spirit enters the body. Not just any spirit, but the spirit of the one in the family whose name is now given. Thus, naming, besides providing a nominal identifier, is an act of rebirth along kin-lines (Skaanes 2017a).

Figures 2-4: The three power-objects are the naricanda *stick, the* a'untenakwiko *gourd and the* olanakwete *doll (Photos: Thea Skaanes)*

Let me give you an example (see Figure 5). During my doctoral fieldwork, I was adopted, named and thus given a position in the kinship system.[27] I was named after my maternal grandmother by my mother, Pa'akokwa. Receiving her name provided me with two positions in the kinship diagram, both my

26   All women will have a *naricanda* stick, since they are given a stick when they are named. The doll is related to coming of age, in preparation for maternity, and the gourd is mostly given to even older women. I was given both a stick and a doll, but not a gourd yet.

27   The kin terms, e.g. mother and brother, thus relate to the relations in the Hadza kinship system, that I became part of. This integration posed a significant change in a general acceptance of me as a relevant and more whole social person. A major reason for this change was that with this integration, I too became an embodiment of kin relations.

Figure 5: Kinship diagram. The horizontal lines are generations – moving downwards indicates a forward move in time. Red markings are my ego-positions. The yellow marking is the namesake of the doll.

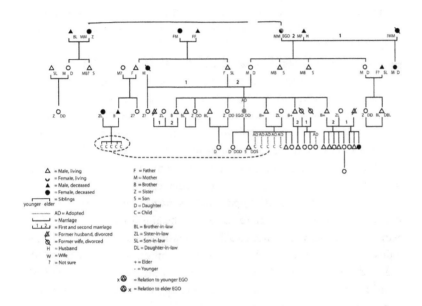

own and that of my maternal grandmother's (red markings); I remember how my brother looked at me with deep, warm affection as he would reminisce our past together, i.e. how as a child he adored spending time with me, his grandmother. During fieldwork, I was also given a clay doll, one of the other power-objects, a tangible name, and she was named Masako after my older mother (yellow marking). Pa'akokwa's father had had another wife before he met Pa'akokwa's mother (me). They had a girl, who died when still a child. It was her name that was given to the doll, Masako.[28]

---

28   The Hadza kinship system bears similar traits to the classificatory model identified by Morgan in 1871 as the Hawaiian kin structure. However, exceptions to this type are instructive, as I have affirmed elsewhere: "Terms of kinship differ according to the relation to kin, e.g. the word for 'mother' differs according to whom we are talking about:

The doll was indeed considered my *child* (Woodburn 1970), my daughter, and, positioning myself as my alter-position (older), Masako (the human) would also be my daughter. At the same time, however, she would also be my own mother, since to my (younger) position Masako (MFD, yellow) would be my older mother. We were both mothers and daughters to each other at the same time: a fractal and inverse replication of our relationship. In this way, I found that naming and kin is an embodied, endemic relation even within a person.

Hadza consider other Hadza to be relatively close kin. But *how* you are related, i.e. whether it is through paternal or maternal family lines, you may not know. And sorting out these relationships is essential, since it determines not only who the people you meet are, but also *who you are*. This need to get the relationships sorted out stems from the naming practices: parents give their new-born child two names when they name him or her: one from the father's family and one from the mother's family, reflecting the system of double descent. Each name comes with a spirit, a social ego; in this way, within your body you have two spirits anchored in the two names, and they are two different social persons. Furthermore, as seen in the kinship diagram above, each name also carries a reference to older generations. Observe that in the kinship diagram above, I have only indicated relationships from one name. This means that before you and your interlocutor can engage in a meaningful relationship, you need to establish what kin relationships you have to each other. That is, until you know who you are for your interlocutor, and vice versa, you do not know how to socially anchor the relationship you are about to engage in.

---

it indicates whether the mother mentioned is my mother, your mother or their mother (Miller 2016: 323). [Three] other exceptions distinguish the Hadza kinship system from the Hawaiian type of kinship that it resembles the most: '(1) there are three sets of terms for the same classificatory relationships, for example aya-ko 'mother/aunt', pa'a-ko '(your) mother/aunt', and asu-ko '(their) mother/aunt'; (2) men and women use different roots for brother/parallel sibling, hedl'a'ali and murunae, but both sexes use murunae for sister/cross-sibling; and (3) cross-uncles are classificatory akaye 'grandfathers' rather than bawa 'father/uncles', without a corresponding distinction among aunts or cousins.' (Miller 2016: 323; orthography normalized to this thesis) From these linguistic precisions, we may infer that both generation, gender and most of all, specific relation, are of importance as a structuring principle to order social maps from." (Skaanes 2017a: 105)

Giving a child (or an adult in my case) a name serves to link the child to the family and the spirit powers. As we see with the doll as well, this adds a manifestly diachronic dimension to the named. Whereas the doll pushes spirit into the future, the stick manifests a relationship to someone in your family's older generation – living or dead. This is what the *naricanda* stick emphasizes the most. The specific stick belongs to a specific woman – it emphasizes her kinship and deep relations to the past. With this relationship, it also connects her to specific forebears residing in the abode of the spirits, a god mountain. We will come back to that below.

The stick, however, even though it is so endemically (of) a woman, i.e. it is her very name, is in itself a male object. It is tightly connected to the menarche rites of passage called *maitoko*.[29] The *maito* and *maitoko* are rituals for men and women, respectively, to embrace the other, to shift status, and to assume the other's point of view (see Power/Watts 1997). The stick also attests to this. The rites of passage involve an inversion of roles, where ritually women hunt, and men turn into prey. By definition, women are not hunters (Skaanes 2017a). A man undergoing a *maito* will, during the time of the ritual experience, be danced for, mediated by 'the *naricanda* of the *maito*' – such mediated dances are ordinarily only done for women.[30] *Maito/maitoko* is thus a process that involves the intimate embracing of and shifting into the significant other (see Skaanes 2019; Power 2017). To move beyond who you are is a central part of the ritual, to become a new person with new insights and new experiences after the ritual.

We have touched upon the stick and the doll, but what about the last object, the calabash gourd? It is called *a'untenakwete* (m) or *a'untenakwiko* (f) and it may be both male or female, i.e. oblong calabashes are male, and rounded ones are female. Both gourd genders may be women's names, as we have also

---

29   It is also tied to the male counterpart, the initiation rite of passage *maito*, as the *epeme* collective will choose a stick to be the neophyte's friend and companion, because when entering the ritual, he is separated from his friends and cohort, and would otherwise be alone when he goes through the initiation ritual.

30   A good example of the way these objects are names is their role in the *epeme* night dance ritual. When a dancer dances in men's names, he will do so directly, simply communicating (in whistled language) that he is about to dance for/as this person. Then that person's spirit will enter the dancer. When he dances in women's names, he will say that he dances in, e.g. the *naricanda* of Thea. That would be the call for me, for my name, and for my Thea-spirit to go to – and enter – the dancer, as he called my name. In the case of the *maito*, he will also be danced for through "the *naricanda* of the *maito*".

seen from the gendered dolls and the male stick. Above, we left the idea of rebirth somewhat unexplained: would giving you your grandmother's name turn you into your grandmother? This seemed to be the case with the brother's reminiscence. However, to help untangle these very intangible relationships, the gourd is an indicator. But first of all, a principle needs to be explained. We are talking about a spirit that is passed on through naming, which, analytically, uses the language of material transactions: something is passed on to someone. But unlike finite material or physically limited substances, I found that a human spirit is able to be in more bodies at once: it is both transferred and kept at the same time. It is called *polysômie* in French, here meaning "to evoke the fragmentation of a single divine into multiple bodies" (Malamoud 1989, referenced by Guillaume-Pey 2018). It is the idea that a single spirit may reside in multiple bodies simultaneously, a non-finite substance, so to speak. It is the ability of a spirit to be able to move without leaving.

We find this polysômic principle to be operating in the Hadza naming process. A name is not only passed on from deceased family members; the originator from the older generation might still be alive when her name is passed on to a neonate. This does not leave the originator dispossessed of her spirit, even though she, i.e. her spirit, is already been reborn. Another example is the *epeme* night dance, this ritual dance performed monthly, where the *epeme* men, the collective of men initiated through *maito*, will dance in the name of family members (see Skaanes 2017b). Calling somebody's name during this ritual will allow his or her spirit to enter into the *epeme's* body during the dance, and the dancer will become a hybrid being, carrying forward the spirit of the one whose name has been called in his body. When an *epeme* dances in the name of his son, the son's spirit will enter the *epeme*. But the son will still be himself while the dancer dances. Likewise, an *epeme* will also dance in the names of female family members, but that would necessarily have to be through one of these three tangible names – the doll, the stick or the gourd. Doing this would allow the spirit of the woman to enter into the dancer while he dances, but the one danced for is still spiritually intact. Thus, we find a capacity for polysômic fragmentation of a spirit into multiple bodies.

The gourd manifests an idea of the self, that you are relevant in your form, in this flesh, as this person.[31] Thus, even though we find ideas of the self as

---

31   In accounts from all over the world, we find multiple containers, like gourds, pots, chalices, and the like to have a special relation to women, to their reproductive capacity, and to their selves. But what is it that this container contains? The *a'untenakwiko* is used

being extended onto objects, into other persons, to other times, this gourd – the last name-object – firmly asserts the self, your being as in your body and in the here and now. Thus, the someone that the neonate girl becomes is a composite being, not simply a rebirthed person, but also someone in her own right (see Skaanes 2017a). This aspect is also manifested in the event of a woman's death, where her *a'untenakwiko* will be broken on her grave (Woodburn 1982a). This is a stark way to materially demonstrate: She is no more, her being has ended.

The three objects both connect and form social relations, both across times and across genders (see Skaanes 2018). They show us how the Hadza conceive of notions of person, body, spirit and materiality in a way full of relational significance, of kinship ties, of cosmological reference and ritual efficacy.

Land-scapes: social relations

What may we glean from the case presented above? How might it convey insights to the query we have at hand? Let me start by pointing to the conceptual intersections between *objects* and notions of environments and *land*. Both form material, physical entities that humans interact with. Both have been given prominence as an essence, a relevant element, in differentiating between human cultures. This is why these aspects are used as qualifiers in order to classify and describe African hunter-gatherers, e.g. when we say that we work with "forest hunter-gatherers" (indication of environmental context), "bow-and-arrow hunters" (material-technical indication), and the like.

Which role has the concept of land played in the general academic discussion around African hunter-gatherers? Land is framed, generally speaking,[32] in a politico-legal and technical-economic fashion, which, I acknowledge, is highly important. Arguments along these lines have been instrumen-

---

for animal fat. Fat is a power-substance that adds efficacy to the gourd and enables its ritual power (see Skaanes 2017a; Mguni 2006; Sullivan/Low 2014). Examining this further brought me to investigate inter-species relationships of potency, which opens up another chapter that I will not explore here in this nascent story of Hadza ritual and cosmology (see Skaanes 2017a). Here we have only followed one thread deriving from tangible names in the vast fabric of Hadza cosmology.

32   For notable exceptions, see Sullivan/Ganuses (this volume), who consider the landscape as saturated with memory-based relations and personal history. Vermeylen (this volume) poses an example of advocacy in land right disputes, but proposes a radically

tal in generating impact and in speaking with authority in cases of advocacy; this discourse is particularly well-suited to pointing to important aspects of encapsulation, inequality, discrimination, exploitation, etc.[33]

When we consider the academic conceptual intersections between notions of objects and notions of land, we find an array of points that align (see Figure 6). Firstly, as mentioned above with the 'bow-and-arrow' and 'forest' typologies, both concepts of technology (objects) and of physical environment are used in societal classification. Secondly, both land and material objects are viewed in terms of property. This means that they are material entities that form part of the estate, the things and land that you might consider to be at your disposal. This links closely to the third idea: that these matters, i.e. land and objects, these properties, are talked about in terms of ownership: to whom do they belong? Are they your possessions or someone else's? Fourthly, the idea of ownership is again tightly linked to viewing both land and objects as resources. They represent economic value, a resource that, fifth, might be transacted, inherited, shared or stolen. Both land and objects form part of economic systems of transaction, and being viewed as resources, as value, sixth, and lastly, they have the capacity and potential to be generators of inequality and dependency.

Figure 6: Conceptual intersections between land and objects

- Societal classification
- Property
- Ownership
- Resources
- Transmission and economic transactions
- Generators of dependency and inequality

However, even though these efforts and views deserve our closest scholarly attention, this is not the only discourse available to shed light on objects, nor

---

alternative standard for court recognition. Another example of breaking away from the general idea of landscape as resource is to be found in Du Plessis (2018).

33   I fully acknowledge the importance of this work. In the Hadza case, they gained collective land-ownership in 2011 through a certificate of Customary Rights of Occupancy, which was fought for and brought to fruition as a major accomplishment of the NGO URCT (http://www.ujamaa-crt.org, last accessed July 08, 2020). This was a huge achievement with important ramifications and one that I fully applaud.

on land. During fieldwork, as the people in the camp and I set new frames, changing the premises and the questions, I found that this set of special objects were knots of social relations. What would happen if we allowed for a similar change of framing, or discourse (Basso 1988), around land as well? Arjun Appadurai used the word 'landscape' to coin his analytical five concepts of 'scapes': mediascapes, technoscapes, ethnoscapes, financescapes and ideoscapes (1996). In relation to land, we might look at different scapes, too, whereof the economic is only one: consider for instance findings elicited from comprehending land as cosmoscapes, as transactionscapes and as time- or kinscapes?[34]

Figure 7: Suggestions for land-scapes (alone or in combination, eg. cosmo/gender-scapes)

- Cosmoscape
- Ritualscape
- Genderscape
- Speciesscape
- Transactionscape
- Timescape
- Kinscape

The way land is looked upon – by researchers from different disciplines, visitors from various backgrounds and by those who are intimately familiar with the ecology – comes in a plethora of ways that cover these 'scapes' and many others. However, this has rarely found its way into ways of mapping or into cartography (several exceptions are to be found, e.g. in this volume). What if we considered paths and special places of efficacy, ritual or kinship as the significant elements to be mapped? How would that reshuffle the figure/ground hierarchies in terms of mapping processes, meanings and units in the environment marked on the map?

My findings suggest that special places, like the special objects discussed above, are carriers of social relations in the Hadza landscapes; I find social

---

34   Appadurai's theoretical work is ingenious, rich and complex. The point, I am making, though, is a cartographic point, i.e. how we choose to frame what we analyze is generative of our findings: when we search the landscape for traces of gender- or species-differentiation, or indicate where rituals are performed, correlations become visible, discernable, and relevant.

relations that are manifested in specifically gendered spaces, in segregating and efficacious ritual sites, in the territories that are homes for gods, forebears and multispecies cohabitation.[35] This carries new implications for how to allow for and process an idea of landscape that embodies time, connects kinds such as humans and non-humans, deceased and alive, and the ways that different genders, materials and forms combine (see Sullivan/Ganuses; Dieckmann, this volume).

Let us take mountains that the Hadza consider special as an example. First of all, what is most salient when looking at the Hadza landscapes are the mountains. Framing them through gender-, ritual- and cosmoscapes, we find that certain mountains house forebears and spirit-sharing specific animals, and that they form designated places for rituals. Just as we observed with the power objects, these mountains are special, they are gendered places of efficacy, and they stand out from other mountains in the area as such. These mountains, Sanzako, Dundubi'i and Anao/Anahu are more than physical places, they are gods (see Figure 8). The mountain Sanzako is feminine (observe the suffix -ko) and the mountain Dundubi'i (suffix -bii) is masculine. Their names relate to space and directionality as they are named by/naming the corners of the world. This is also reflected in their location in the environment, i.e. Sanzako is in the north, Anao in the south, and Dundubi'i to the west of the Hadza homeland. It is unclear whether people relate to directionality through reference to the gods or whether the names of the gods reflect the directionality of their situatedness. However, in any case, the gods are hyper-spatial, prominent in their visual and material presence, and tied to pointers in navigating space.

Figure 8: Mountain gods
- Sanzako: literally means north. This mountain is the most powerful god.
- Anao/Anahu: literally means south. This mountain is a sacrificial site.
- Dundubi'i: literally means west. This mountain is a god who provides; visits include sounding lithophones.

---

35   I have not had the opportunity to systematically conduct fieldwork inquiring along these lines, but observations in this field can be found in my field notes. Therefore, this suggestion is put forward as a thought experiment rather than elaborated with interview excerpts and published findings in this contribution.

The mountains are also sites for rites, such as sacrifice and communication with forebears. We also find a strong presence of the gods in mortuary rites: those left behind place the body of the deceased with the head towards the relevant forebears' homestead. This is not always straight-forward, since, because of the semi-nomadic lifeways, the naming practices and the double-descent system, there might be divergent views as to where – i.e. to which mountain – a person would belong. Families orient towards different mountains, so the necessity of making only one choice in death may cause controversy.

The gods themselves are agents that take action, perform and engage in rituals, and that are bound by similar conventions like the Hadza. The gods may engage in communication and exchange when called to do so. Being named is also to be given a person whom you would address when talking to the mountain gods. You belong to the community and have access to the god through the namesake, as illustrated in the following exchange with a middle-aged *epeme* man.

> "T: And this your own spirit, is it very old?
>
> P: Yes!
>
> T: It is very old.
>
> P: Yes, yes! It comes from my grandparents inside of my family. Yes!
>
> T: It comes from your name.
>
> P: Yes. Like I am my name. My name is from my grandfather. Now my grandfather's spirit is watching me closely. And it is inside [my body]. And another one of his spirits is there at Dundubi'i. And it is watching me as well. But my spirit is inside [of me]. And this is why when I go to Dundubi'i, I have to address this old man [my grandfather]. Are you paying attention? Uhmm? [Laughs]. (Interview transcript, my translation)

Descendants may come to the god-mountain to discuss matters or communicate with forebears – some matters are explicitly targeted to the specific forebear (e.g. asking a recently deceased person if he or she arrived safely after their death?), some address the forebears with issues meant for the god to take action on (the common practice of indirect communication by proxy), and some address the god directly (which is highly demanding and requires ritual, spiritual stamina and power). The gods are even approached with demand-sharing and are thus, like other Hadza, compelled to share. The god may also conduct rituals and, when doing so, the god may blow *kelaguko*, an active plant-based agent (water-plant root) used in many Hadza rituals. The distinctive traces in the air of the odor of *kelaguko* cover large areas when the god blows this ritual agent.

The gods are not confined to their physical stasis. The personal name-spirits, the forebears that reside in the mountains, may be sent out by the mountain god to the Hadza bush areas to guard and protect all beings. For instance, when a hyena tracks down the prey left by a hunter as he goes to camp to call for help to carry the load, the god gives the prey away to help the hyena. I suggest that communication by proxy, as well as this way of extending action through mobile spirits, might reflect an understanding of the mountain god as the exemplar of all Hadza spirits. In Evans-Pritchard's famous work on the Nuer, he described how lesser spirits were the hypostatization of the higher god's "modes and attributes" (1956: 9), i.e. that they were forwarded refractions of the god: "the diverse spiritual figures of Nuer thought are to be regarded as social refractions of God" (1953: 203). Diverse kinds of spirit are named by Evans-Pritchard, e.g. "totemic spirits", the "spirit of the flesh" and the "nameless spirits" (ibid: 208), but in their diversity, they are all "of the same exemplar", i.e. "God is both the one and the many – one in his nature and many in his diverse social representations." (ibid.) This corresponds well with the refractions of spirit that we found in the principle of polysômie described earlier (Guillaume-Pey 2018). And then we find the gods to be both embedded in the landscape and social agents on the landscape; they are related to as kin, and their hypostatization through personal name-spirits (from the god, through forebears, to living name-sakes) will – to some extent – also integrate an element of mountain-godliness as an intimate part of living life as a Hadza.

This case of the mountains is just one among many others to be unfolded (see Figure 9). Looking at landscapes as scapes and realms of social relations, we find a wide array of salient features to be explored. Meat-sharing and other transaction practices and how they are distributed in space come into prominence. After a successful hunt, some of the cuts of meat will be carried home to the camp for equal distribution, but specific cuts are categorically consumed away from camp by the exclusive group of initiated men, the *epeme* collective (see Skaanes 2017a, chapter 5); in the same manner, some ritual interactions with spirits take place in camp, while others categorically do not. Marshall Sahlins' famous model of "Reciprocity and Kinship Residential Sectors" indicates the inclination towards gaining increasing yields of the transactions (from generalized, over balanced, to negative reciprocity) as sectoral distance increases away from the house (home, family) (Sahlins 1972: 198-199).

These transaction forms, he argues, are dominant in and correspond to types of social relations. Thus, social relations produce certain transaction forms. However, the cause and effect are also reversible: by transacting through certain kinds of reciprocities, we create social relations accordingly: "If friends make gifts, gifts make friends" (Sahlins 1972: 186). In this way, he points to the correlation between space, i.e. the sectors, and social relations, i.e. systems of reciprocity. Using his analytics, we might similarly ask, what kind of social relations are created by the actions taking place at these places, and vice versa?

Figure 9: Findings on landscape as scapes and social relations
- Kinship relations are manifested spatially in relation to mountain gods and directionality.
- Mountain gods: Active gods that are also counterparts in ritual performance, communication and exchange.
- The mountain gods are places: Inside, they are spaces where forebears' and animal spirits cohabit. On their surface, they are sites for ritual practices.
- Sharing practices: sharing takes place in different places. Some sharing occurs in and some out of camp (Sahlins). The distinction carries significance.[36]

Conclusion

What were they seeing, the Hadza, sitting on the mountain top that afternoon? Along what lines did their thoughts wander? I do not know. However, I argue that these tangible names and divine mountains, all these efficacious materials discussed in this chapter, point to the basic need for us – as humans - to engage socially and symbolically in meaningful relationships; to

---

36   It is interesting that quite a lot of sharing practices are regulated by space and sectoral distance or proximity (Sahlins 1972). Some meat-sharing takes place in the center of the camp, while other kinds of ritual meat-sharing need to be done secretly and away from camp. In another ritual, the *epeme* night dance ritual, the efficacy is brought into the heart of camp. When these rituals take place, young uninitiated men have to flee into the bush to escape the dangers of being exposed to the efficacy of the transformative ritual (see Skaanes 2017a; 2019).

ascribe meaning to our actions, breathing notions of soul or spirit into animals, objects and landscapes, and thereby turning them into power objects and totems.

Tim Ingold, much like Keith Basso (1988), once wrote that landscape is "the world as it is known [to/in those] who dwell therein, who inhabit its places and journey along the paths connecting them" (Ingold 1993: 156). David Turnbull (2007), like Ingold, speaks of studying paths and trails, i.e. hodology.[37] Both Ingold and Turnbull bring matters and bodies to the core of the hodological perspective, e.g. by arguing that material environments such as places, paths and artefacts are relevant factors in the social processes of producing the meanings, specific understandings and knowledge that reflect our worlds (Ingold 1993; Turnbull 2007: 142). Yet this is to stay within the boundaries of a system; a key focus in this chapter is the question of how to translate,[38] communicate or represent such knowledge.

What would a cartography of this landscape look like? I encourage us as researchers to consider social relations in other spheres than the human, i.e. in relation to objects but also in relation to landscapes. I would like to support the cartographers who boldly work in this field and I hope to encourage all of us to radically consider emic understandings, materials, forms, scapes and operating frames with regard to the environment when drawing maps, even though this might entail, for the cartographer, positioning oneself in the

---

37   Hodology is the study of paths or trails (see Eide, this volume, for the hodological perspective). The hodological perspective as I see it is an immersed perspective; it is situation-specific, it is embodied, particular, personal, a prerequisite for establishing trustworthy social relations in fieldwork situations. Hodology as a mapping regime does not assume the all-encompassing gaze; rather, it is the path followed, the trail trodden, one among so many others. In this way hodology allows for caution against indiscriminately disclosing all aspects and spreading them out on a map for all eyes to see. Not taking such things into consideration in map-making might tamper with delicate and important structures of esotericism (Skaanes 2017a).

38   Globally, we currently (spring/summer 2020) find new social movements fueled by decades of structural injustice based on ethnic and gender identity. The movements question the legitimacy of hierarchies of power, entitlement and cultural appropriation. This poses the question of cross-cultural advocacy, i.e. the legitimacy of cultural translation. Ethical challenges remain unresolved in this respect and the time is ripe for addressing inequalities, asymmetrical power structures and recognition. I hope that we will learn to create better structures across cultural divides but not that we will stop communicating, being inspired, and learning from each other. The suggestions in this chapter are based on the premises that we address communication across borders.

disconcerting situation of not-knowing the landscapes and accepting the confounding lack of ability to readily see or read landscapes (Basso 1988). Indeed, this would entail a bold scholarly movement that reverses the familiarity, the relevant language and the power balance between those whose ecologies are represented on the maps and those habitually operating the scholarly conventions of mapping (see Vermeylen, this volume).

This latter part anticipates the question: why map environments as social relations? The historical legacy attests to a need for turning the tables and approximating a more diverse power structure in cartographic practice (see Brody, this volume). Two additional reasons stand out. One is that ethnographic accounts should be reliable, accurate, rigorous and detailed. Ethnography matters – both because of our commitment to the people whose life worlds we, as researchers, as outsiders, are allowed to take a glance into, and also in order to provide qualitatively good data (not in the positivistic sense, but rather as ethically balanced and diligent descriptions, faithful renditions of perspectives, patterns, relations and world-views) to academia. With Basso and Haraway, I think that an ideal would be if we all, with each our phenomenological perceptual systems, strove to learn about "what is" and "what occurs", considering the local materials, in a quest to learn how to lovingly appreciate other people's ways of seeing. Secondly, this is 'us' learning. Analytical reasoning needs to be multiple. When we apply our analytical apparatus, we *make* worlds. And time has demonstrated to us that we cannot create or find a singular, all-encompassing, totalizing view by means of our analytics.[39] But by applying new analytics, we discover new worlds, new possibilities, new correlations, that we might immerse ourselves in analytically in order to get a glimpse of new landscapes that are "emphatically there but conspicuously lacking in accustomed forms of order and arrangement" (Basso 1988: 99), i.e. to learn to see novel spaces, the beings that inhabit these spaces and, indeed, their social relations.

What not to map? In this chapter, I have argued for an understanding of materiality, such as objects and landscape, as forming part of social relations. When we work with social relations, ethical considerations are indispensable. Besides doing and getting it right and paying attention to details, ethics might also take the form of cloaking tactics, i.e. of not rendering visible, not exposing, and not shedding light on all parts. The maps we create should be sensitive to and accommodate intended invisibilities, i.e. that which should not be

---

39   See Goldman, this volume.

exposed, those interrelations that are not for all to see, that which prevents a totalizing view. If we look at physical, rounded objects,[40] much like analytical apparatuses, they cannot be fully grasped from one angle in a totalizing encompassing gaze. As objects they stand out visually to the beholder, but at the same time you cannot have a totalizing view of them: you only have one perspective and you rely on letting that one perspective go while embracing another to get a fuller visual impression of the object.[41] As we observe with the three power-objects presented in this chapter, we find the power of objects to be the ability to be inherently multiple, flexible and shadowy; they connect, anchor and communicate relations through their very material presence: relations to land, relations to spirit, relations to kin, and relations to time. Could this ability form part of a new mapping regime?

Social relations, certainly among the Hadza, are powered by ambiguity, by flexibility, by shadows and by the creative multitude of perspectives available around a single phenomenon (Skaanes 2017a; see Parkington 2003; Guenther 1999; 2020 for similar findings in other cases). Thus, allowing for a rematerialization of maps at the expense of the indiscriminate ability to decode the

---

40   Looking at museum collections, we find materialized maps in the shape of a range of different canvases, figures and power-objects. Texture, color, pattern and material seem to be key in the maps we find in the form of artistic canvases (see Vermeylen, this volume), north American buck skin maps, and esoteric patterned maps painted on the belly skin of clan members in Northeast Arnhem Land. Tangibility and touchable physicality are key in the wooden *Ammassalik* maps, whereas the curved sticks and shells of the Marshallese stick charts teach the seafarer about the sea voyage's envisioned dynamics. The nomadic Mongol felt tents, *gers*, are spacious and sheltering cosmological and social maps. The *ger's* organization and multi-form montage creates material structures of the universe that you immerse yourself and your family in (Skaanes/Lehrmann 2018). Finally, the *lukasa* boards made by the Luba of the Democratic Republic of the Congo are good examples of esoteric power-objects that are materialized maps that hold rich stories of memories, diachrony, knowledge, cultural heritage and the mapping out of places. This multitude of stories told by material maps seems to be key in why they are indeed not made in the shape of conventional maps.

41   You have to turn the rounded object to see the backside of it, and as you do so, you let go of the initial perspective. Conventional maps, too, carry similar traits. Area, distance, shape, direction and bearing are all relevant characteristics of the conventional map, but you cannot map them all at once; you have to let go of some traits to be able to embrace others. A globe, as we know, combines most such features in one visual representation. The globe, however, is in this context a materialized map since the globe is prominently an object with a rounded form and fields out of sight, rather than a map with full oversight.

map or the universal reading of it, would make way for the most immaterial aspects, such as kinship, social relations, and what Derrida calls the ghost, magic or superstition (Derrida, interviewed by Tellez/Mazzoldi 2007: 380-382) to gain presence in map-making and map-reading. The map-object itself becomes the teller in relation to the onlooker. It becomes a part of the social relation itself.

So, just once more, imagine being there on the cliff. Imagine feeling the connectedness, the intimate kin relations even within your very own being, while the world thinks that for the Hadza, for you, kin relations do not really matter. You know that this is the prevalent story, even in this situation where you behold these impressive matters of kin before you: the mountains that you know as powerful gods and that are abodes for your forebears. The forebears whose names you carry forward in time with your breathing and carnal being. For generations the Hadza have created power objects, these name-matters as connectors of relations, that testify to the sheer importance of social relations for the Hadza – especially kin relations. So, I do not have a complete answer to the question of how to draw, paint, sculpt or carve such maps, but to fashion a kinship diagram – this one-lined, visual chart of relations of different kinds and of time – could be a starting-point, a hodological first thread, in the weave of how to graphically start to chart landscapes encompassing social relationships, non-human agents and the dimension of time.

References

Apicella, Coren L. (2018): "High levels of rule-bending in a minimally religious and largely egalitarian forager population." In: Religion, Brain & Behavior, 8/2, pp. 133-148 (DOI: 10.1080/2153599X.2016.1267034).

Apicella, Coren L./Marlowe, Frank W./Fowler, James H./Christakis, Nicholas A. (2012): "Social Networks and Cooperation in Hunter-Gatherers." In: Nature 481/7382, pp. 497-50.

Appadurai, Arjun (1996): Modernity at large: cultural dimensions of globalization, Minneapolis: University of Minnesota Press.

Barnard, Alan/Woodburn, James (1988): "Introduction." In: Timothy Ingold/David Riches/James Woodburn (eds.), Hunters and Gatherers – Property, Power and Ideology, Oxford and Herndon: Berg, pp. 4-31.

Basso, Keith (1988): "'Speaking with Names': Language and Landscape among the Western Apache." In: Cultural Anthropology 3/2, pp. 99-130.

Bird-David, Nurit (1999): "Introduction: South Asia." In: Richard Lee/Richard Daly (eds.), The Cambridge Encyclopedia of Hunters and Gatherers, Cambridge University Press, pp. 231-237.

Bird-David, Nurit (2018): "The kinship infrastructure of the hunter-gatherer world: or, paradoxes in hunter-gatherer studies and how to overcome them." Keynote address, CHAGS12, Penang, Malaysia.

Bird-David, Nurit (2019): "Kinship and scale. On paradoxes in hunter-gatherer studies and how to overcome them." In: Hunter Gatherer Research 4/2, pp. 177-192 (DOI: https://doi.org/10.3828/hgr.2018.9).

Bohannan, Paul (1959): "The Impact of money on an African subsistence economy". In: The Journal of Economic History 19/4, pp. 491-503 (DOI: 10.1017/S0022050700085946).

Bourdieu, Pierre (1984): Distinction: a social critique of the judgement of taste, London: Routledge.

The British Museum (2013): Power objects. Exhibition text for display case in the Africa exhibition, London: December 2013.

Du Plessis, Pierre L. (2018): Gathering the Kalahari: Tracking Landscapes in Motion, PhD Dissertation, Aarhus University and UC Santa Cruz (https://escholarship.org/uc/item/7b98v9k6, last accessed February 24, 2020).

Evans-Pritchard, Edward E. (1940): The Nuer, London: Oxford University Press.

Evans-Pritchard, Edward E. (1953): "The Nuer Conception of Spirit in its relation to the social order." In: American Anthropologist 55/2, pp. 201-214.

Evans-Pritchard, Edward E. (1956): Nuer Religion, Oxford: Clarendon Press.

Grimes, Ron (1990): "Breaking the glass barrier: The power of display." In: Journal of Ritual Studies 4/2, pp. 239-261.

Guardiola-Rivera, Oscar (2007): "Return of the fetish: a plea for a new materialism." In: Law and Critique 18/3, pp. 275-307.

Guardiola-Rivera, Oscar (2009): Being against the World: Rebellion and Constitution, New York: Birkbeck Law Press.

Guenther, Mathias (1999): Tricksters and Trancers. Bushman religion and society. Indiana University Press and Bloomington and Indianapolis.

Guenther, Mathias (2020): Human-Animal Relationships in San and Hunter-Gatherer Cosmology, Vol. I and II, Palgrave Macmillan.

Guillaume-Pey, Cécile (2018): "From Ritual Images to Animated Movies: The Transformative Journey of the Sora Paintings (Central-Eastern India)." In: Uwe Skoda/Birgit Lettmann (eds.), India and its Visual Cultures. Community, Class and Gender in a Symbolic Landscape, New Delhi, California, London and Singapore: Sage Publications, pp. 142-169.

Hawkes, Kristen/O'Connell, James F./Blurton Jones Nicholas G. (1997): "Hadza Women's Time Allocation, Offspring Provisioning, and the Evolution of long postmenopausal Life Spans." In: Current Anthropology 38/4, pp. 551-577.

Haraway, Donna (1991): "Situated Knowledges: The Science Question in Feminism and the Privilege of Partial Perspective." In: Haraway, Donna (ed.), Simians, Cyborgs and Women: The Reinvention of Nature, London: Routledge, pp. 183-201.

Henare, Amiria/Holbraad, Martin/Wastell, Sari (2007): "Introduction." In: Thinking Through Things: Theorising Artefacts Ethnographically, London: Routledge, pp. 1-31.

Hirsch, Eric/O'Hanlon, Michael (1995): Anthropology of landscape: perspectives on place and space, Oxford: Clarendon Press.

Hoskins, Janet (1998): Biographical Objects: How Things Tell the Stories of People's Lives, New York and London: Routledge.

Ingold, Timothy (1993): "The Temporality of the Landscape." In: World Archaeology 25/2, pp. 24-174.

Lee, Richard B. (2005): "Power and Property in Twenty-First Century Foragers: A critical examination." In: Thomas Widlok/Wolde G. Tadasse (eds.), Property and Equality, Vol. II: Encapsulation, Commercialisation, Discrimination, New York and Oxford: Berghahn Books, pp. 16-31.

Lee, Richard B./Devore, Irwin (1968): Man the Hunter, New Brunswick and London: Aldine Transaction.

Lévi-Strauss, Claude (1962): Totemism, London: Merlin Press.

Malamoud, Charles (1989): Cuire le monde, rite et pensée dans l'Inde ancienne, Paris: La Découverte.

Markham, Annette (2012): Lecture. 'Cultural Methods, Methods of Culture', at Aarhus University, Fall 2012.

Marlowe, Frank W. (2010): The Hadza. Hunter-Gatherers of Tanzania, University of California Press.

Mguni, Siyakha (2006): "Iconography of Termites' Nests and Termites: Symbolic Nuances of Formlings in Southern African San Rock Art". In: Cambridge Archaeological Journal 16/1, pp. 53-71.

Morgan, Lewis Henry (1871): Systems of Consanguinity and Affinity of the Human Family, Washington: Smithsonian Institute.

Murdock, George Peter (1981): Atlas of World Cultures, University of Pittsburgh Press.

Parkington, John (2003): "Eland and Therianthropes in Southern African Rock Art: When Is a Person an Animal?" In: African Archaeological Review 20/3, pp. 135-147.

Pietz, William (1985): "The problem of the fetish I." In: RES: Journal Of Anthropology And Aesthetics 9, pp. 5-17.

Pontzer, Herman/Raichlen, David A./Wood, Brian M./Thompson, Melissa E./Rachette, Susan B./Mabulla, Audax Z.P./Marlowe, Frank (2015): "Energy Expenditure and Activity among Hadza Hunter-Gatherers." In: American Journal of Human Biology 27/5, pp. 628-637 (DOI: 10.1002/ajhb.22711).

Power, Camilla (2015): "Hadza gender rituals – epeme and maitoko – considered as counterparts." In: Hunter Gatherer Research 1/3, pp. 333-358 (DOI:10.3828/hgr.2015.18).

Power, Camilla (2017): "Reconstructing a Source Cosmology for African Hunter-gatherers." In: Camilla Power/Morna Finnegan/Hilary Callan (eds.), Human Origins: Contributions from Social Anthropology, New York and Oxford: Berghahn Books, pp. 180-203.

Power, Camilla/Watts, Ian (1997): "The Woman with the Zebra's Penis: Gender, Mutability and Performance." In: The Journal of the Royal Anthropological Institute 3/3, pp. 537-560.

Purzycki, Benjamin G./Henrich, Joseph/Apicella, Coren/Baimel, Adam/Cohen, Emma/McNamara, Rita A./Willard, Aiyana K./Xygalatas, Dimitris/Norenzayan, Ara (2017): "The evolution of religion and morality: a synthesis of ethnographic and experimental evidence from eight societies." In: Religion, Brain & Behavior, 2017, pp. 101-132 (DOI:10.1080/2153599X.2016.1267027).

Sahlins, Marshall (1968): "9b. Notes on the Original Affluent Society." In: Lee, Richard B./Devore, Irwin (eds.), Man the Hunter, New Brunswick and London: Aldine Transaction, pp. 85-89.

Sahlins, Marshall (1972): Stone Age Economics, Chicago and New York: Aldine, Atherton, INC.

Sands, Bonny (1998): "The Linguistic Relationship between Hadza and Khoisan." In: Schladt, Mathias (ed.), Language, identity, and conceptualization among the Khoisan, Köln: Rüdiger Köppe, pp. 265-283.

Scott, James C. (1998): Seeing like a State. How Certain Schemes to Improve the Human Condition Have Failed, New Haven and London: Yale University Press.

Skaanes, Thea (2015): "Notes on Hadza Cosmology: Epeme, objects and rituals." In: Hunter Gatherer Research 1/2, pp. 247-267.

Skaanes, Thea (2017a): Cosmology Matters. Power objects, rituals, and meat-sharing among the Hadza of Tanzania. PhD Dissertation. Aarhus University (unpublished).

Skaanes, Thea (2017b): "Sounds in the Night. Ritual bells, therianthropes and eland relations among the Hadza." In: Camilla Power/Morna Finnegan/Hilary Callan (eds.), Human Origins: Contributions from Social Anthropology, New York and Oxford: Berghahn Books, pp. 204-223.

Skaanes, Thea (2018, unpublished manuscript): "The life and death of Masako. A clay doll's kinship relations and ritual futurity among the Hadza." Paper delivered at Panel #32: The material correlates of kinship processes in hunter-gatherer societies, CHAGS12, Penang, Malaysia.

Skaanes, Thea (2019): "Kødkraft. En historie om køddeling fra feltarbejde blandt hadza i Tanzania." In: Jordens Folk 2, Danish Ethnographic Association, pp. 17-29.

Skaanes, Thea/Lehrmann, Malthe B. (2019): "Mongoliet. Pastoralnomader på Djengis Khans stepper." Educational research communication. UNESCO Samlingerne, Moesgaard Museum (www.unescosamlingerne.dk/Mongol iet, last accessed July 23,2020.

Sullivan, Sian/Low, Chris (2014): "Shades of the Rainbow Serpent? A KhoeSān Animal Between Myth and Landscape in Southern Africa – Ethnographic Contextualisations of Rock Art Representations." In: Arts 3/2, pp. 215-244.

Tellez, Freddy/Mazzoldi, Bruno (2007): "The Pocket-Size Interview with Jacques Derrida". In: Critical Inquiry 33/2, pp. 362-388.

Turnbull, David (2007): "Maps Narratives and Trails: Performativity, Hodology and Distributed Knowledges in Complex Adaptive Systems – an Approach to Emergent Mapping." In: Geographical Research 45/2, pp. 140-149 (DOI: 10.1111/j.1745-5871.2007.00447.x).

Widlok, Thomas/Tadesse, Wolde G. (2005): Property and Equality, Vol. I and II, New York and Oxford: Berghahn Books.

Widlok, Thomas (2017): Anthropology and the Economy of Sharing, London and New York: Routledge.

Woodburn, James (1968a): "An Introduction to Hadza Ecology." In: Richard Lee/Irven Devore (eds.), Man the Hunter, Chicago: Aldine Publishing Company, pp. 49-55.

Woodburn, James (1968b): "9c. Does hunting bring happiness?" In: Richard Lee/Irven Devore (eds.), Man the Hunter, Chicago: Aldine Publishing Company, pp. 89-92.

Woodburn, James (1970): Hunters and Gatherers. The material culture of the nomadic Hadza, London: The British Museum.

Woodburn, James (1979): "Minimal politics: The political organization of the Hadza of North Tanzania." In: William A. Shacks/Percy S. Cohen (eds.), Politics in leadership: A comparative perspective, Oxford: Clarendon Press, pp. 244-266.

Woodburn, James (1982a): "Social dimensions of death in four African hunting and gathering societies." In: Maurice Bloch/Jonathan Parry (eds.), Death and the Regeneration of Life, Cambridge University Press, pp. 187-210.

Woodburn, James (1982b): "Egalitarian Societies." In: Man, New Series, 17/3, pp. 431-451.

Woodburn, James (1998): " 'Sharing is not a form of exchange': an analysis of property sharing in immediate-return hunter-gatherer societies". In: Chris M. Hann (ed.), Property Relations, Cambridge: Cambridge University Press, pp. 48-63.

Canvases as legal maps in native title claims

Saskia Vermeylen

Introduction

In this chapter I look into the relationship between law and maps. I explore the extent to which maps can be perceived as an aesthetic representation of space. I use the metaphor 'maps as an aesthetic practice' to interrogate the relationship between paintings and maps within the context of Aboriginal land claims. This is part of a wider enquiry that seeks to explore the meaning of space in law. This is a question that has been of interest for quite some time now in legal geography (see e.g. Blomley 1994; Holder/Harrison 2003; Blomley et al. 2001; Delaney 1998; Braverman et al. 2014), drawing attention to the spatial aspects of relevant legal concepts within the context of evidence in native title claims, such as territory (see e.g. Elden 2013; Mohr 2003), legal pluralism (see e.g. Falk Moore 1978; Merry 1988, 2000; Mellisaris 2004) and *terra nullius* (see e.g. Banner 2007). In addition to studying the social aspects of legal spaces, legal geography also refers to the spatial role of law, the importance of how law is spatially represented (see e.g. Manderson 2005), and also how spaces can disrupt and subvert legal meaning in positivist law (see e.g. de Sousa Santos 2018).

Just like other disciplines, law is engaging with the material turn in the social sciences and humanities (see e.g. Davies 2017; Vermeylen 2017). Law is seeking to extend legal personhood to, for example, the non-human through the recognition of rights of nature (see e.g. Vermeylen 2017). This is particularly relevant when thinking about indigenous peoples' land claims; the legal requirements for evidence in ancestral land claims have so far only recognized a predominantly western worldview in terms of the relationship with the land. Other relations between humans, non-humans and more-than-humans are slowly being recognized in native title claims (see e.g. Anker 2014). How to represent these relations on maps, however, as a part of providing visual evidence of how a group of people are relationally connected to a specific piece of land, remains underexplored. This requires redressing a traumatic legal history where spatial legal concepts, defined by colonial and settler legal authorities, continue to haunt indigenous peoples.

I am particularly interested in the relationship between cartography and the dispossession of indigenous peoples' land and the overlaps of spatial metaphors that can be applied to law and mapping. Both physical and cartographic representations of colonial land claims and subsequent dispossessions have left epistemological and ontological traces in the physical and legal landscape that continue to haunt indigenous peoples in their battles to get their claims over land recognized on the basis of their own spatio-legal concepts.

As part of the ontological turn in cartography (see e.g. Kitchin et al. 2013) and law (see e.g. Davies 2017; Vermeylen 2017), I am looking for alternative representations of the legal landscape that include indigenous peoples' laws which embody the ontological relationship between indigenous peoples and their wider environment. This also includes reflecting on how the connection between the human, the non-human and the more-than-human can be represented in the context of spatio-legal mapping in native title claims.

Indigenous peoples have used maps as a technology in courts to provide evidence of their enduring occupation of land (see Brody, this volume). However, the cartographic convention impedes a culturally appropriate mapping process and outcome. What is conveyed as a neutral mapping process and outcome of indigenous land claims often turns out to be implicated in the colonial project, which misrepresents indigenous peoples' belonging to land and its wider environment (Anker 2018: 14). Despite a raft of counter-mapping projects, it remains questionable to what extent the master's tool can convey indigenous peoples' ways of being (see Introduction and Dieckmann, this volume). In this chapter, I analyze two examples of indigenous mapping projects that are different from conventional topographic mapping: the bark paintings that supported the Blue Mud Bay sea ownership claim in Arnhem Land and the *Ngurrara Canvas II* that was presented in a preliminary hearing before the Native Title Tribunal. Both are examples of relational representations of the link between people, land, sea (in the Blue Mud Case) and law. The cultural understanding of the relationship between the environment and people is more than just a representation of property rights, it also depicts the landscape "as a determinant of or as an active component of people's lives" (Morphy/Morphy 2006: 68). In this chapter, I explore, through these two case studies, whether indigenous 'artistic' representations of belonging and walking the landscape may provide a better canvas on which ontological belonging and its legal expression can be mapped than conventional mapping processes. Before I turn my attention to the two case studies, I first sketch the joint history of law and mapping, followed by a reflection on how this problematic positivist connection between mapping and lawmaking haunts indigenous peoples when they are asked to provide evidence of their ancestral connection to land in court cases. Problematizing conventional cartography as a technical ploy for legal dispossession, I explore whether visual arts theory may provide the language to start thinking differently about how to map the ontological belonging of indigenous peoples in a particular landscape.

Cartography and law

Establishing legal title in the common law tradition is intricately linked to the concept of memories of how the land was being used. In preliterate times, this could be done through specific – often embodied – rituals. Local knowledge about the relationship between land and legal title was bound up in knowing the rituals that recorded the cultural events that demarcated property (Pottage 1994: 361). "The functional locus of title was in the local knowledge about boundaries and transfers; the ritual of transfer merely underlines the accumulated practice of neighbors and past owners as to who held what rights and where" (Anker 2005: 109). However, establishing legal title through performative practices (like turning the turf) was replaced with the arrival of maps, which removed memory of the rituals and substituted them with a homogenizing and linear grid (ibid.). Proof of title in common law is now established through the logic of exchange on paper and through abstraction (ibid: 108). Cartography has played a role in the dephysicalization of real property in common law (ibid.).

The relationship between maps, law and colonialism has been criticized extensively by critical geographers as the map "renders the land legible through its reduction of the world to boundaries and surface areas, profitable tree species or types of land use, recording only what the state deems valuable" (Anker 2018: 15). The law of property has been affected by a gradual process of dephysicalization; the 'reality' on the ground is not necessarily reflected in securing legal rights or even getting secure access to land (see e.g. Graham 2011).

Despite the somewhat problematic relationship between law and cartography, indigenous peoples have used maps to challenge the dominant legal idea of vacant or empty land, or so-called *terra nullius* (Anker 2018: 14). The attempt to map indigenous land rights, using new technologies such as participatory geographical information systems, is not without its own risks and problems. Maps and cartography in general are part of the colonial process of creating boundaries and containing peoples in pre-conceived spaces. Indigenous peoples' understanding of land and ways of being have often been under- or misrepresented in these mapping exercises (Anker 2018: 14; see e.g. Vermeylen et al. 2012; Dieckmann, this volume).

The use of maps in indigenous peoples' quests to reclaim their lands is part of a wider discussion around acceptable evidence in native title claims. One of the most emblematic encounters between indigenous and universalized western legal systems is reflected in Chief Justice McEachern's famous words: "This is a trial, not a performance", in *Delgamuukw v. R.* (1991). When the Gitksan and the Wet'suwet'en defended their native title claim in British Colombia in the Canadian Court, their evidence was presented in a performance consisting of dances, songs, oral histories and the retelling of collective memories. Chief Justice McEachern dismissed cultural practices as legal evidence but the Court of Appeal later accepted oral evidence (1993, 1997).[1]

Canada has now built a reputation around the admissibility of indigenous evidence in court cases, including songs, dances, regalia and wampum belts (Anker 2018: 14). However, the way oral evidence has been used in court cases is still constrained by a hegemonic legal system of common law that treats alternative evidence as legal facts and that does not really grasp the cultural context and other ways-of-being of indigenous peoples (Anker 2018: 14). The way evidence is being theorized and practiced is now being challenged through the ontological turn in anthropology, which has opened up the debate about the role of natural entities, such as the non-human and beyond-the-human, as legal evidence, including how they are represented on maps (see e.g. Vermeylen 2017).

The way law and cartography depict relations to land is still very much embedded in a colonial discourse of property rights. There is hardly any acknowledgment of the importance of non-human or more-than-human beings. Neither is there awareness that there are other ways to relate to property. At the risk of over-generalizing, property in non-Eurocentric societies is an

---

1   See also Brody, this volume.

institution or process that builds networks of responsibilities and generosity between humans and non-humans which is very different from a Eurocentric property system that is based on exclusive private rights (see e.g. Borrows 2010; Black 2011). This obviously raises questions about (i) how to map these relationships in a more inclusive and culturally respectful manner, and (ii) how to give legal meaning to these non-hegemonic mapping practices.

Exploring these issues also raises further queries about the role of legal pluralism within the context of providing evidence in land rights claims. A hierarchical approach has often been favored when multiple and often ontologically very different legal systems meet and clash in the court (Vermeylen 2013). State law is still favored as the main body of legal rules, while what has been perceived as informal and unofficial law is tested for its legality against formal state law. Both cartography and law are defined by a positivist approach that characterizes space and law from a dominant worldview that fails to recognize spatial and legal pluralism (Mohr 2003: 54). This mutually reinforcing positivist relationship between space and law can be best demonstrated through the well-known colonial construct of a close and intimate connection between territorial exclusivity and the legal determinacy of the nation-state (ibid: 55). A good example of this spatio-legal construct is the idea of *terra nullius*, which has been used throughout history and across continents to dispossess indigenous peoples. As widely accepted by critical geographers, however, space is fluid and this plurality should also be reflected in the acceptance of law as a fluid body that can represent different legal orders and identities (see e.g. Manderson 2005; Fitzpatrick 2001; Mohr 2003). Concretely, this means that in most cases any territory or land is legally determined by different legal orders that cannot be fixed nor can their legality be decided by formal state law.

One of the main discourses that were used to justify colonization was the idea that spaces outside Europe were empty. These vacant spaces were waiting to be cultivated, Christianized and legalized by white European men. The idea of emptiness was spatially reflected through the perfection of the Roman practice of a Roman grid system consisting of two axes. The coordinates of *cardo* (north-south) and *decumanus* (east-west) became popularized as the Cartesian idea that any point could be projected as a two-dimensional space that could be represented on a map. However, the colonial powers' hegemony was not just limited to a spatial representation of mapping emptiness with coordinates. They also needed to establish political and legal power in these places. This was done through the notion of jurisdiction, whereby state power coincided with the territory of the state, which was spatially expressed through borders and gridlines when mapping. In other words, Cartesian maps were multifunctional in the sense that they could "map the possibility of emptiness", but simultaneously, could also map "boundaries that may be filled with a legal regime" (Mohr 2003: 60).

Cartography and its accompanying Cartesian grid system contributed to the silencing of the plurality of legal systems that once resided in a particular area. During medieval times distinct groups shared a specific piece of land, each with their own tribal laws which travelled with them when they moved to other parts of a region. Each land thus had multiple jurisdictions. But with modernity and Enlightenment ideas, citizenship was increasingly linked to territorial absolutism, which eventually led to the formation of an "absolute state as a compulsory institution" (ibid: 61). In other words, "the undifferentiated legal space of a state's jurisdiction meets Cartesian space in the homogeneity of its subjects and of its space" (ibid.). It is against this background of a spatio-legal homogeneity that centralizes the power of the state by only recognizing the exclusive jurisdictional boundaries of state law that indigenous peoples are seeking to redress past injustices. One of the many challenges that arise from this situation is a rather prescriptive notion of what can count as legal evidence in indigenous peoples' legal attempts to regain access to and control over their ancestral land.

Evidence of legal title and the use of maps

Indigenous peoples need to be able to access their own laws when they need to provide evidence of their claims to land. For example, in the settler court system, Aboriginal peoples in Australia must provide evidence on two matters: their traditions and customs and their connection to the land claimed (Schreiner 2013: 170). It was only after the famous *Mabo* decisions of the High Court of Australia in 1988 and 1992 that the Native Title Act 1993 came into existence. Before that, Aboriginal peoples were subject to Australian legislation. Under the Native Title Act, Aboriginal peoples had to file everything that could serve as native title, which, according to the Native Title Act of 1993 is:

> "The expression 'native title' or 'native title rights and interests' means the communal, group or individual rights and interests of Aboriginal peoples [...] in relation to land or waters, where: (a) the rights and interests are possessed

under the traditional laws acknowledged, and the traditional customs observed, by the Aboriginal peoples [...] and (b) the Aboriginal peoples [...] by
those laws and customs, have a connection with the land or waters; and (c)
the rights and interests are recognised by the common law of Australia" (Native Title Act 1993 – s. 233).

The Native Title Act thus adds a very specific legal requirement. It must be
demonstrated that there is substantial maintenance of the continuous connection between the laws and customs of contemporary claimants and their
ancestors at the time of establishment of British sovereignty (Asche/Trigger
2011: 219). Or, in other words, the law and customs that were once practiced
must still be practiced today. This raises the question of how indigenous peoples can present their laws that can prove connection to the land. This is a
particularly thorny issue as indigenous peoples' laws are different from the
Eurocentric legal system, with the added complexity that indigenous laws
are often mistranslated and misrepresented in Eurocentric law (see e.g. Vermeylen 2013, 2015; Schreiner 2013; Teubner 1998). Australia has acknowledged,
arguably more so than other jurisdictions, the fluid characteristics of Aboriginal laws and has accepted the idea that "traditional laws" should not be
reduced to something that is ancient, sound and authentic (Schreiner 2013:
170).

As part of the process of demonstrating a continuing relationship with
the land under Aboriginal peoples' laws and customs, claimants to native title
provide oral evidence. Oral testimonials are often corroborated through what
are perceived as expert witness statements and evidence from, for example,
anthropologists, linguists, archaeologists and historians (see e.g. Reilly 2003;
Palmer 2011). Increasingly, the oral testimonies are part of a wider performative process of giving evidence as a way of avoiding the need to seek expert
evidence and of establishing Aboriginal law as a source of law on an equal
footing with Australian law (Morphy 2007: 31). However, the process of native
title claims is still haunted by a colonizing force where the main objective is to
enact the sovereignty of a colonizing society over its colonized subjects (ibid.).
Courts still struggle with the interpretation of the performative elements of
indigenous laws.

The case study of the Yolŋu Blue Mud Bay (which I will discuss in further
detail below) is testimony to a growing awareness among Aboriginal peoples
that although their indigenous laws and institutions may have been eclipsed
by colonial processes, this does not mean that they are a colonized people,

despite the fact that their land has been appropriated. As far as the Yolŋu are concerned, when the colonizers sought access to the Yolŋu heartlands, the ancestors never concluded that the first missions of the colonizers extinguished their sovereignty over their own homelands (Morphy 2007: 31). For the Yolŋu, Mawalan, the head of the land-owning Rirratjingu clan, granted the permission to establish a mission station at Yirrkala in 1935. From a spatial perspective, native title claims embody a meeting place in the courts of different and divergent perspectives on sovereignty. Despite the coming together of European law and Aboriginal law in the physical space of the court, it is still mainly European law that is perceived to be the main or only legitimate source of law in the court, despite the attempt to recognize customs in native title claims. *Rom* or Yolŋu laws are customs that have no legal force within the context of native title claims. Within the context of the court, the intricacies of *Rom* are reduced to performative acts, even though they represent for the Yolŋu people expressions of sovereignty (ibid: 33-34).

Within this context of proving the sovereignty of Aboriginal law, the cartographic representation of rights over land and waters is gaining importance (see e.g. Reilly 2003). Mapping has been used as a way of providing evidence for indigenous peoples' use and belonging to the land. As required by section 62 of the Native Title Act, the external boundaries of the claim and the boundaries of the existing land tenures within the claimed area must be represented on a map (ibid.). Claimants map their relationship to the land. Defendants map improvements to the land under statutory grants as part of their argument that native title must be extinguished within the claim area. In native title claims, two very different spatio-legal descriptions of the land come together on the map that is used in the courts. Dreaming tracks are mapped alongside other spatio-legal symbols in the landscape, such as fences, roads and homesteads representing distinctive ways of viewing the world that can be associated with Aboriginal versus Australian law respectively (see e.g. Reilly 2003). This results in "an epistemological gap between the foundation of native title in Indigenous laws and customs and its cartographic representation" (Reilly 2003: 4). The map's colonial and imperial roots are reflected in the representation of new conquered spaces as blank canvases. This raises the issue of the extent to which maps can actually be used as an inclusive and respectful form of representing Aboriginal law as long as they are embedded and part of a colonial history that has used the idea of *terra nullius* to establish British sovereignty in Australia. Historically, mapping has been used as a tool to convey the message that Aboriginal peoples had no legal rights to the land, as their relationship to the land did not bear any legal significance. Since *Mabo v Queensland* [No 2] and the Native Title Act, using maps solely to indoctrinate the idea of *terra* and *res nullius* has come under scrutiny and a new form of indigenous mapping has found traction.

This has developed into a practice that can broadly be labelled as indigenous cartography and is sometimes part of a wider movement around critical cartography. "Indigenous cartography is based on relational epistemology that works within a system where 'place' and 'ways of knowing' are intimately linked to Native communities' notions of kinship, oral traditions, and traditional ecological knowledge acquired over the millennia" (Richard 2015: 13). This links to a wider awareness that mapping should also reflect ontological relations as there is a need to map peoples' relationship with land more actively, but also, following Barbara Bender's proposition, to visualize "the active representation of landscapes" (1992: 735).

The two case studies that are the focal point in this chapter reflect the interrelationship between a decolonized approach to mapping and the recognition of Aboriginal law and its representation on the maps that are used as part of the evidence in native title claims. As I have already mentioned above, indigenous cartography is part of a wider critical cartographic movement which addresses some of the by now well-known reservations regarding cartography as a positivist exercise in mapping land ownership.

Instead of repeating the well-rehearsed storyline of critical cartography, spearheaded by the work of John Brian Harley and Denis Wood, who used the concept of deconstructing the map as a political and legal activity (see e.g. Vermeylen et al. 2012), I am telling this story through the artwork of the Canadian artist Landon Mackenzie (for an overview of her artwork see Harmon 2009: 66-71).

I turn to the idea of fusing maps and arts for two specific reasons. First, as Claire Reddleman (2018) has argued, representing the arguments of critical cartography through art opens up a new avenue for critical engagement, which is the role of perspectivism and the relationship with the viewer. As I have argued elsewhere (Vermeylen 2013), the problem that indigenous laws face in native title court cases is the unwillingness of the judges and the judiciary to accept oral histories and narratives as a legal source. Even when indigenous peoples can give evidence through a close narration of their pathways, dreams and visions of their ancestors, the listener – i.e. the judge – struggles to understand the legal merit of these stories. Often, the uniqueness of indigenous legal systems is translated into a legal epistemology that is part of a positivist legal understanding. Therefore, a study of the friction that occurs when different legal systems and cultures meet in court must also include an analysis of perception and perspectivism (Anker 2018). The knowledge and language to do this can be found in the artistic expression and abstraction of maps.

Second, Aboriginal art is also an expression of indigenous laws and the ontological connection between law and landscape on maps (see e.g. Watson 1994). In the Australian context of art and mapping, Howard Morphy defines art as "a way of acting in the world" (2009: 117). "Art is a way of expressing knowledge – a means of expressing the experience of being-in-the-world and a means of communicating ideas and values" (ibid.). Aboriginal art is revelatory in nature; it "stands for a repertoire of designs and stories (dreamings), depicting shared and sacred knowledge of the world" (Schreiner 2013: 168). Aboriginal art and Aboriginal law must "give evidence of their history and continuity up until today to be in the position to claim the future in separate ways" (ibid: 171). For Aboriginal peoples they are not separate things; "art, law, land and ceremony are all part of a long history" (ibid.). This link between aesthetic practices and law in native title claims has already been expressed through other art practices such as songs, treaty ceremonies and wampum belts (Anker 2014: 141) Some of these artistic expressions of belonging to the land have also been accepted in courts as evidence, of which *R v Van Der Peet* (1996) is a good example.

Maps as art and art as maps

As illustrated through the examples of the Canadian artist Landon Mackenzie, approaching maps as art allows a more immersive and performative perspective that, in addition, also subverts the gaze. Landon Mackenzie started to think about the relationship between her art practice and the politics of land when First Nations' rights were being hotly debated in Canada. Mackenzie questioned the practice of her own landscape paintings and became increasingly interested in overlaying geographical terrain with socio-political ideologies; she started to explore "the complex relationship between politics and how land is visually represented" (Harmon 2009: 66).

The series of Saskatchewan Paintings from 1993 represented her journey into Saskatchewan, where she visited archives and studied old maps from the nineteenth century. That material was not just represented in a map, but instead she used the old maps as a starting point that she overlaid with her own interpretation of those spaces, including other iconography and stories in those 'maps'. MacKenzie's artwork is a visual representation of Harley's critique of the map, which silences certain histories (Harley 2001) and experiences that can be found in the landscape (see e.g. Vermeylen et al. 2012). MacKenzie represented in her paintings both the gaps she found in the archival material but also how maps depict "tricks of the pens" when they deliberately falsify information to mislead competing explorers (Harmon 2009: 69). She wanted to illustrate in the paintings how records and maps both reveal and conceal history.

This led her onto another project, *Tracking Athabasca: Macke It to Thy Other Side* (Land of Little Sticks), where she sat with a friend of Cree, Chipewyan and Scottish descent on the canvas talking while her friend drew the layout of her childhood village. MacKenzie kept adding more stories onto the canvas as map and in particular added white shapes that squirt over the canvas. As the story goes, her friend was a descendent of the Scottish Governor Simpson, who had allegedly fathered 200 children. Mackenzie represented the traces of this European DNA as part of Canada's history and represented it on the map as trails of white sperm shapes which also symbolized meteorological systems of "whirls and bursts of wind, rain or snow on an aerial weather map" (Harmon 2009: 69). Other cartographic metaphors were also added, such as blue beadwork, to signify the relatively worthless goods that white traders used to exchange for furs with First Peoples (Harmon 2009: 71).

These artworks capture visually some of the developments and critiques in critical cartography. As I have already established in the previous section, cartography and law share a positivistic and objectivist epistemology that has been criticized in critical cartography and critical legal studies (see e.g. de Sousa Santos 1987). The critical perspectives in cartography and law are driven by the same group of scholars that have inspired their respective critical movements; these include, most notably, Michel Foucault and his work on power and knowledge and Jacques Derrida's on deconstruction. Denis Wood (1992) and John Brian Harley (1989; 1992; Harley/Lexton 2001) are the most well-known critical cartographers, applying a Derridean approach to deconstruction and a Foucauldian emphasis on power-knowledge relations to the analysis of cartographic imagery and its history (Reddleman 2018: 3). It is beyond the scope of this chapter to provide an overview of the many approaches in critical cartography, but one of their main contributions is, in the words of Harley, an awareness that "through [...] maps a social order is communicated, reproduced, experienced and explored. Maps do not simply reproduce a topographical reality; they also interpret it" (Harley/Laxton 2001: 45). This makes maps communicative devices that have attracted the attention of artists for their ability to represent and affect behavior (Wood 2006: 5). What makes the relationship between maps and art particularly conducive to be more progressive and inclusive is the fact that art allows the power relations that are embedded in maps to be exposed. Despite widespread beliefs that maps are neutral and represent an objective depiction of a terrain, artists reveal the entangled power relations. They "strip the map from its so-called neutral mask" (Wood 2006: 5) and show the true nature of the map's political prowess. Art therefore becomes a useful conduit through which to critique mapmaking practices (see e.g. Reddleman 2018). Arguably, art deepens the reflective aspect of critical cartography, as it allows the focus to shift from mapmaking practices to the reading and viewing of maps (see e.g. Reddleman 2018; see also von Reumont, this volume).

Conceptualizing maps as artistic expressions helps to shift the perspective to establish a relationship between the viewer (i.e. the court and its judges) and the viewed (i.e. indigenous communities). What is important for indigenous mapping projects is that the viewer gets this sense of being immersed in the landscape so that the viewer can understand indigenous peoples' worldviews and how they relate to a specific place. Indigenous places must not be experienced through a bird's eye view representation as it may distort the landscape and not represent indigenous peoples' relational being-in-the-world (Anker 2018: 27). Instead, representing indigenous places must allow the viewer to feel immersed in the landscape, to feel the connections with other humans, non-humans and more-than-humans. The person-in-place perspective allows an embodied experience of what it means to dwell in a particular landscape. It is only through an embodied being, situated in a landscape, that law and how it is linked to specific landscapes and places can be experienced (see e.g. Anker 2018). It is difficult to convey the performative element of indigenous law through the conventional bird's eye view perspective, as it represents a Eurocentric property regime that uses maps to demarcate boundaries around exclusive claims (see e.g. Anker 2018).

The indigenous maps that are being produced for native title claims are in a sense a cartographic practice in circulation, meaning that we not only have to be aware how the maps have been produced and the different epistemological approaches and worldviews that underpin the production of these maps (see also Introduction, this volume). We also need to think about the kinds of contexts in which maps are used and the kind of readership or 'viewship' they are exposed to. We must not forget that there is often a hegemonic relationship between space and law reinforcing the idea that positivist Eurocentric law is the only legitimate source of law, regardless of other laws also to be found in that particular space. Therefore, Claire Reddleman (2018) argues that maps as art may offer the potential to act as sites of resistance that go above and beyond counter mapping practices. As I will illustrate with the two case studies of Aboriginal mapping, when producing and seeing maps as art a more immersive and embodied relationship with the viewer may be elicited on the map. The maps that I discuss below share with Mackenzie's map, *Tracking Athabasca: Macke It to Thy Other Side*, the idea that an embodied experience of the map may draw the viewer closer into the world and the experience of the mapmaker. It is through the narratives that are performed on the map that another way of being-in-the-world unfolds on the map, illustrating a more relational approach towards law making and ties to the land.

The *Ngurrara Canvas*[2]

The first case study to be discussed is the *Ngurrara Canvas*. Fifty artists belonging to the Walmajarri, Wangkajunga, Mangala and Juwaliny peoples painted the *Ngurrara Canvas* (an 8x10 meter painting) over a period of 10 days as part of the evidence they provided in the National Native Title Tribunal in 1997. In the 1960s and 1970s, the people belonging to the area of the Great Sandy Desert in the southern Kimberley region had left their land as a result of European invasion, but kept links with their 'country' through ceremonies (Wildburger 2013). Following the *Mabo* High Court decision, the Walmajarri, Wangkajunga, Mangala and Juwaliny peoples claimed title to their land in 1996. In 1997, the Native Title Tribunal set up camp in the homeland of these peoples to start collecting information and data in order to make a decision about whether the claim could be heard in court. It became obvious that there was a discrepancy between the Tribunal officials' high English and the claimants' Aboriginal languages. The variance in language was symbolic of the underlying differences between laws and worldviews; an issue that seemed impossible to bridge (ibid.). To surmount this problem, the idea of *painting* the claimants'

---

2   The canvas can be viewed at https://www.nma.gov.au/exhibitions/ngurrara (last accessed May 24, 2020).

belonging to their homeland was born. The canvas became a collaborative work and each of the claimants painted their own piece of the land they belonged to and for which they had a responsibility.[3]

The canvas represents the area each artist had responsibility for in terms of land and lore (Anker 2014: 141). In addition to depicting the spiritual places in the landscape, such as the waterholes or *jila*, the relationship between the spiritual places and the artists themselves is also represented on the canvas. The canvas also symbolizes the lore of the Aboriginal peoples in North Western Australia. As one of the claimants and artists, Ngarralja Tommy May, explains, native title claims are about 'blackfella law' (i.e. Aboriginal law) and the painting for him is evidence of that law (Chance 2001: 38). Evidence for Ngarralja Tommy May is not something that refers to static facts and truths, but the painting shows the relation between landscape and knowledge, including Aboriginal law, that is embedded in the landscape. The evidence on the canvas is thus about different ways of knowing and relational ways of being. It depicts different ways of interpreting the relationship between law and landscape; it portrays 'blackfella' law (Anker 2005: 92-93). Besides departing from a common law perspective on property and land, the canvas also subverts a colonial representation of maps and challenges the Western hegemonic dominance of space, property and memory (Hershey et al. 2014: 3). As I have discussed in the first part of this chapter, both maps and law share the tradition of embodying colonial hegemonies (de Sousa Santos 1987). The *Ngurrara Canvas* demonstrates that the law is embedded in the stories that belong to the landscape. This makes the canvas a "legal document that proved and re-established land-ownership" (Wildburger 2013: 205).

As Aboriginal lawyer and writer Larissa Behrendt confirmed:

> The dominant legal culture has an emphasis on the written word, on economic rights and is focused on the individual. By stark contrast, Aboriginal law has an emphasis on oral transmission, the preservation and maintenance of culture and is communally owned. The Ngurrara canvas, by bridging an embodiment of Aboriginal law into the court for consideration by the dominant culture, communicated across the divide. (Behrendt 2008, n.p.)

As I have already alluded to earlier in this chapter, for Aboriginal law to be validated, the hegemonic relationship between Aboriginal law and its view-

---

3   For more details see https://www.nma.gov.au/exhibitions/ngurrara (last accessed May 24, 2020).

ers, who only know Australian law, must change so that Aboriginal law gets recognized on its own terms without the need for translating it into positivist law. Conventional mapping practices that topographically allocate places on gridlike systems may struggle to depict the relational and embodied aspects of Aboriginal land claims. A different approach of representing perspective between two divergent and in some cases opposing legal systems must be visually depicted in mapping projects. Through its artistic practice, the *Ngurrara Canvas* manages to subvert the colonial practices of perspective. The painting draws the viewer into the canvas so that the non-Aboriginal viewer who is not familiar with the legal meaning of the landscape can become immersed in the worldviews and belief systems of the Aboriginal claimants. One of the claimants, Chuguna Walmajarri Elder, refers specifically to the importance of the viewer when talking about the canvas:

> We're painting so that the non-Aboriginal people from far away, from the city can see that our claim is true. The place is a long way from town in the sandhill desert. There's no rivers here, it's billabong country. It's a big country, with sandhills. We're painting the living waterholes; we are painting them all in one painting, so that the government can look at it, and so that the non-Aboriginal people see whether it's true what we're painting. (Chuguna Walmajarri, quoted in Mohr 2003: 56)

The painting presents the land and its law, and the canvas bridges the topographical representation of a western map and the oral tradition of the claimants (Mohr 2003: 56). The painting represents a performance of the relationship between people and land, and therefore becomes an embodied expression of the law. Unlike any other map before, the canvas distilled a wealth of information that illustrated the connection with the country and became an important source for providing 'legitimate' evidence (Dayman 2016). Unfortunately, the stories on the canvas were still translated onto a 'traditional' map as in the European sense. The claimants described their attachment to the land through stories on the canvas but these were subsequently pinpointed to places on a map to give the claims 'European' reference (Mohr 2003). Non-Aboriginal peoples and lawyers thus located the points on the canvas to specific locations on the map; however, in such a translation process from canvas to map the specific meaning of the places may get lost. As Mohr spells it out: "the law of the land that can be deciphered by an Aboriginal initiate is in no way the same as that which is imagined by a common law judge" (2003: 56). So, although the places may be the same, in terms of their legal language, the relationship between the place and identity and the legal discourse around property will differ. The different ownership relations, the different identities and laws cannot be mapped using the same set of cultural referents (ibid.). There remains an uncomfortable jarring between the multiple, overlapping and complementary responsibilities for land in Aboriginal laws and the singular and exclusive claims required under common law, including e.g. the Native Title Act. Western law and spatial conceptions still define land with exclusive boundaries and unambiguous coordinates through the translation process from canvas to conventional map (ibid: 57).

This tension between common and indigenous law became particularly poignant in the subsequent development around the Ngurrara claim when the Martu people also lodged a claim to the area called Warla (or on the Western map called the Percival Lakes district), which adjoins and partially overlaps with the Ngurrara claim. While the overlapping claims were not an issue in indigenous law as it allows overlapping relations between land and people, this was more problematic for the common law as the latter still translates native titles to a principle of singular and exclusive claims (see McNamara/Grattan 1999 in Mohr 2003: 57). The so-called overlapping claims were solved by the Federal Court, which enforced its solution that the Ngurrara would drop their claim over the Warla area and the Martu would include Ngurrara claimants in their claim to that area. So despite the canvas being accepted as evidence in the court, western law was still enforcing specific ideas around the relationship between space, law and land that were rooted in Western legal and spatial traditions of exclusive boundaries and unambiguous coordinates. Despite these shortcomings, the canvas still carries, in addition to its artistic significance, a political and legal importance (Dayman 2016: 267). What makes the canvas remarkable is that it exceeds its cartographic function and clearly expresses the legal geography of the landscape (Dayman 2016: 185-186). By owning the process of painting their relationships in the landscape, the Ngurrara artists confirmed their legal affirmation of their ownership of country. The canvas debunked the idea of non-Aboriginals that the Great Sandy Desert is an empty space. But the canvas also conveys the idea that Aboriginal law is performative. Given the vast scale of the canvas, reading the work and soaking up the enormity of its claims can only be experienced by walking on the surface of the canvas. The act of standing and walking the canvas was a purposeful reflection that the claim included individual tracts (as each artist painted their own claim), as well as the interrelation between the broader claims of the group (Dayman 2016: 274). As Dayman explains:

The most logical exhibition of *Ngurrara Canvas II* happens when the artists are present and sitting or walking over it. The painted surface marks clearly the living waterholes around which there are many such stories but much comes from the dialogue of the artists about the work. From the production, where the artists were spread across the length and breadth of the desert, to the determination ceremony where Justice Gilmour from the Federal Court of Australia traversed the work as he handed out legal tenure documents to the named applicants, the larger canvas in particular has been underfoot regularly. (Dayman 2016: 274-275)

This performative element makes the canvas unique and distinct from other indigenous mapping practices. The legal geography and land tenure are literally discovered when walking through the landscape on the canvas. The *Ngurrara Canvas* task of claiming title came to an end in 2007 when Justice Gilmour handed down the title deeds to the Ngurrara people, confirming that the Court had determined that native title already existed as established by the traditional laws and customs (Dayman 2016: 286). For Anker (2005), this makes the canvas a triptych of proof, truth and map. While these elements may have their own significance for the artists, they also have special meaning in Western law.

The *Saltwater Collection*[4] (Blue Mud Decision)

For Aboriginal peoples, art can be used to mediate the impact of European colonization and empower people to take back control as active agents over their land who control their own destiny (Morphy 2009: 117). This is particularly effectively communicated in what is known as the *Saltwater Collection*, painted by the Yolŋu as part of their native title rights to their seas in Blue Mud Bay. The *Saltwater Collection* is arguably even more interesting to analyze from a legal perspective than the *Ngurrara Canvas* for two reasons. First, the paintings represent the spiritual relationship between the Saltwater People (Aboriginal people and Torres Strait Islanders) and the water. The canvases show ritual performances that relate to the social mechanisms through which the Saltwater Peoples manage and control the seas (McNiven 2004: 329). Expressing

---

4   The bark painting can be viewed on https://hyperallergic.com/412659/sea-rights-bark-paintings-australia/ (last accessed May 24, 2020).

spiritual attachments to the sea forms an important part of these canvases. Unlike cartographic sea maps, *the Saltwater collection* is unique because of the ability of the paintings to communicate the ontological relationships between peoples and the sea (ibid: 330). Therefore, *the Saltwater Collection* represents an ontological meaning of the laws that relate to the sea (and the land) and provides insights into customary marine tenure of the Saltwater Peoples (ibid: 332).

Second, the *Saltwater Collection* also challenges the meaning of tenure in positivist law, and particularly the Law of the Sea (The United Nations Convention on the Law of the Sea, UNCLOS, 1982). This makes the collection particularly useful to study. Aboriginal art not only embodies Aboriginal law, it also queries and criticizes Eurocentric and international law. Furthermore, one of the biggest challenges Aboriginal law faces is to expose the hegemonic power of Eurocentric property law. The *Saltwater Collection* excels in pushing property theory in new directions by exposing the distinction that has been made between land and water and the rigid boundaries that are drawn between land and sea and in areas that are actually fluid, open and adaptive.

On July 31, 2008, Australia's High Court[5] decided that the Northern Territory Fisheries Act could no longer issue licenses for fishing in waters that fell within the boundaries of land covered by the Aboriginal Land Rights Act. Since this landmark case only the Aboriginal Land Council is entitled to grant fishing licenses. Commercial fishing fleets can no longer enter Aboriginal waters without asking permission. In particular, extending the traditional owners' exclusive native title rights to the intertidal zone was an important victory for Aboriginal peoples in Australia.[6] They had lamented for many years that the Native Title Act 1993 did not recognize the *exclusive possession* of Aboriginal sea estates, despite the recognition of native title rights to water as well as land. Neither did it recognize the *exclusive use* of the resources (mainly fish) of native title in a small part of the sea (Dillon 2002: 15). This is part of a wider legal shortcoming in native title approaches that generally leads to Aboriginal participation in resource management being neglected or ignored (Tan/Jackson 2013: 140). It is widely commented upon that under the Native Title Act

---

5   Northern Territory of Australia v Arnhem Land Aboriginal Land Trust (2008) 236 CLR 24.

6   For a concise overview of the case and other native title claims in Australia see https://www.creativespirits.info/aboriginalculture/land/blue-mud-bay-high-court-decision#fnref6 (last accessed March 10, 2020).

1993, Aboriginal peoples gained some recognition of their rights in the sea, but these rights were far more limited than the rights in fee simple granted over the land under the Aboriginal Land Rights Act 1976, which left the question of sea ownership open (Morphy/Morphy 2006: 70). Under the Land Rights Act, the Yolŋu people were only granted ownership over land down to the low water mark, which for coastal hunters was insufficient security of tenure as their life centers on the sea (Morphy/Morphy 2006).

When, in 1996, a group of Aboriginal peoples discovered an illegal fishing camp hidden in mangroves on their sacred land in Blue Mud Bay, in northeast Arnhem Land, they decided to create a series of bark paintings to document their history. In particular, finding a severed head of a crocodile, which in Yolŋu culture is their ancestor *Baru*, prompted 46 Yolŋu artists under the leadership of Djambawa Marawili to paint 50 artworks to illustrate in court their rules, philosophies and the stories that link the Yolŋu peoples to the coast, rivers and oceans. As the clan leader Djambawa Marawili testified: "It is time for non-Aboriginal people to learn about this land, learn about the waters. So if we are living the way of reconciliation, you must learn about Native Title and Sea Right."[7] For the Yolŋu people, the bark paintings epitomized the title deeds to the sea rights of coastal waters.

Even more so than the *Ngurrara Canvas*, the *Saltwater Collection* has become a symbol of two divergent cultural traditions of the sea and how they have informed different legal cultures.[8] The cornerstone of the Eurocentric tradition of the sea is captured in UNCLOS 1982, an international legal mechanism that has created boundaries and allocated extensions to territorial zones with sovereign rights. The Law of the Sea represents a revolutionary change in the legal regime which has governed the seas for most of the time since Hugo Grotius published his *Mare Liberum* (open sea) in 1609. The legal scholar Grotius championed the legal principle of the freedom of the seas as he lobbied for the Dutch East India Company in support of their zeal for territorial expansion that required crossing seas. The Law of the Sea moved away from the principles of freedom of the seas and the Convention embraced the idea of the closed sea, which John Selden, Grotius' opponent, argued for in 1635 in his *Mare Clausum* (closed sea). In UNCLOS, coastal states are given sovereign

---

7   See https://hyperallergic.com/412659/sea-rights-bark-paintings-australia/ (last accessed March 10, 2020).

8   For a detailed anthropological account of the Saltwater Peoples and the Blue Mud Bay, see Barber (2005) and Sharp (2002).

rights to marine resources, which, under conventional international law, were either *res communis* (i.e. belonging to everyone) or *res nullius* (i.e. no owner) (Logue 1982: 28). The Convention is thus a rejection of the Grotian and pre-Grotian view that oceans and their resources should be regarded as *res nullius* or as *res communis*.

Aboriginals' perception of the sea is in stark contrast to this. Using the example of the Yolŋu, the anthropologists Nonie Sharp (2002), Howard Morphy and Frances Morphy (2006) explain in great detail these different traditions of property relations in the sea and how they translate into very different ideas around sea mapping. They explain how Saltwater people have strong conceptions of seawater property and how they own areas of salt water in the same way as they own land, namely on behalf of a clan. This joint ownership with or on behalf of others (which is mainly a link to the ancestors) is very different from conceptions of ownership in common law and the International Law of the Sea. While Grotius and Selden had an opposing view, what they did agree upon was the extension of the principle of state sovereignty over territorial waters. Coastal European states claimed power over the waters adjacent to their territories. Beaches, estuaries, inlets, reefs and fishing grounds, often held in customary ownership by groups of local inhabitants, were absorbed into seas belonging to territorial states (Sharp 2002). This was a process that was accompanied by the portrayal and mapping of seas as vast and empty spaces that were ready to be delineated through the drawing of boundaries.

The *Saltwater Collection* must be interpreted against the background of an ocean politics that has imperialistic and colonial roots. The ocean has mainly been used by a political elite using a historical discourse that was part of an ideology that assumed that European imperial powers were superior on the presumption that they were civilized, which gave them the authority to use the ocean to colonize others perceived as inferior and primitive. As such, "ideational force creates material force that then reinforces the ideational origins and the Western ontology of mechanistic exclusion of people from nature, like the ocean, creating a master ontological narrative about how to live with the sea and those anchored to the sea" (Peter 2009: 61).

While the sea of the Saltwater peoples is full of memory and patterns of belonging (Morphy/Morphy 2006), the sea in Eurocentric thought is emptied of its sentient and spiritual character. It is part of the wider distinction between culture and nature. Detachment from nature and purported objectivity produces a sea that is free from stories and memory, allowing the imposition of base lines and limits in a linear manner. Philip Steinberg (2009) argues that the objectification of the sea was part of a market-based view of the sea in which possessive individualism became the central cultural value. Before the 19th century there was another history and relationship with the sea, but that changed in the 19th century to one that was part of a European attitude of detachment, precision and measurement linked to a "mercantilist-era ide-ology" (Steinberg 2009: 480).

A historical look at sea mapping reveals quite an interesting history of the relationship between land and sea prior to the 19th century. Looking at 16th century ocean maps, Steinberg (2009) discovers that the artistic embellish-ments on the maps, like the dots in the sea and the drawings of sea monsters, were more than just artistic decoration. They represented the view of what the ocean was; most cartographers in the early 16th century made little distinction between land and sea. The ocean was typically represented as a material and textured space through techniques such as stippling and drawing waves. But increasingly this material depiction of the ocean became problematic and pro-voked a crisis of representation, as ideally the ocean should be depicted as a vast and empty space, an external void, because a material representation of the ocean would be perceived as an obstacle to movement. As Steinberg (2009) further explains, the depiction of the ocean as a textured and material space of nature did not resonate with the emerging ideas around capitalism that wanted to annihilate spaces that were perceived as being empty. Increasingly, cartographers turned away from depicting the ocean as a material space or the ocean as land-like. From 1700 onwards, the ocean is represented as a space of trade routes. The trade routes served the purpose of spreading the idea that the emptiness of the ocean was a space that could be navigated by construct-ing routes through that empty space. Soon generic commercial routes were depicted, such as the route to the East Indies. As we know the story all too well:

> [B]y depicting the ocean as a space of differentiated and functional routes, the ocean was cartographically represented in a manner that closely paral-leled its legal designation during the same time as *mare liberum* or *res extra commercium* (Steinberg 2009: 483).

The bark paintings represent the strong ontological connections between the Yolŋu and the creative forces of their ancestral beings (human and non-hu-man) (Morphy/Morphy 2006: 68). The system of ownership of the Yolŋu is linked to their society and how it is divided into two moieties, the *Dhuwa* and the *Yirritje*. Each moiety (which is patrilineal and exogamous) incorporates a number of separate clans, denoting the primary level of ownership. What is remarkable and signifies the ontological difference between Eurocentric and Yolŋu ownership is the fact that the distinction between the two moieties also extends into the natural world, with "plants, animals, fish and birds belonging to one moiety or the other" (ibid.). Furthermore, each moiety also has its own spiritual identity and set of ancestors (ibid.).

The bark paintings demonstrate how the Yolŋu's sea rights originate from creator beings who shaped the seas and who gave the Yolŋu rights over them. The creator beings gave Yolŋu people rights and responsibilities for the beaches, reefs, seabed, seal life and waters adjoining their lands. Those waters have spiritual power and the shimmering waters (that are clearly depicted on the bark paintings) speak ancestral power to the Yolŋu, who recreate the spiritual shimmering in the most sacred paintings (Sharp 2002: 11). The intricate knowledge that the Yolŋu have about the geography and geology of the reefs, the channels and the currents are stored in the Yolŋu people's memories, in the stories they tell about the sea and its inhabitants of turtles and fish and about how they are all connected through their life cycles, seasons and sea tides (ibid.). As the bark paintings testify, for the Yolŋu the law is written on the reefs and waters, the channels and passages, the rocks and the beaches. The bark paintings are like a tapestry of their laws (ibid.). Sacred designs or *miny'tji* from each clan, represented through crosshatched patterns on the bark, give the bark paintings a distinct texture. Each visual detail, whether relating to fishing or cultural heritage, is steeped in the Yolŋu people's traditional and spiritual relationship to the coast and etched into their law.[9]

As Yolŋu elders testify, although the bark paintings may give the appearance of being representational, they are far more complex:

> An icon might show a creature, a cloud, a rock, fire, a spear, or a rope. This can denote an ancestral being as well as its actions, and it may be a code for relations between people, places, and things.[10]

It is in these relations that the bark paintings become political and legal statements. The objects that are illustrated on the bark paintings, relating to either

---

9   See https://hyperallergic.com/412659/sea-rights-bark-paintings-australia/ (last accessed March 11, 2020).

10 See https://hyperallergic.com/412659/sea-rights-bark-paintings-australia/ (last accessed March 11, 2020).

a natural or a cultural heritage, symbolize traditional and spiritual relation-ships to the coast. The depiction of these relationships has ultimately sup-ported the court case, as reflected in the High Court's opinion that:

> Aboriginal Land when used in s70(1), should be understood as extending to so much of the fluid (water or atmosphere) as may lie above the land surface within the boundaries of the grant and is ordinarily capable of use by an owner of land.[11]

The High Court thus recognized Yolŋu ownership of the intertidal zone on the edge of the Yolŋu's lands.

I would like to end this section by drawing on the reflections of Helen Watson, on the work she has done around Aboriginal bark paintings and how they relate to maps even though they do not look like maps. (Watson 1994[12]). Watson refers to the bark paintings as *dhulaŋ*, which is the name that the Yolŋu have given to the paintings. *Dhulaŋ* represents *djalkiri*, or the footprints of the ancestors, representing how time, space, personhood and community are constructed in Yolŋu life (Watson 1994). The ancestors left their footprints in the landscape and these can be found in the songlines that depict the time when the two great ancestors created the landscapes of *Dhuwa* and *Yirritja* by living in it. When a clan or a person refers to their *djalkiri*, they refer si-multaneously to the country and to the songs, dances, stories and graphic representations that belong to that 'country'. *Djalkiri* refers thus to owner-ship over country that is represented in the 'Dreaming', or to songlines that are left behind by the ancestors. *Dhulaŋ* is a map that not only depicts sig-nificant places for Yolŋu peoples but also invites an embodied and relational experience of the songlines that reflect the relations between humans, non-humans and more-than-humans.

Conclusion

The use of maps as evidence in native title claims has been problematized in this chapter. Native title claims need to recognize Aboriginal law and arguably

---

11   *Northern Territory of Australia v Arnhem Land Aboriginal Trust* [2008] HCA 29 30 July 2008 D7/2007.

12   See http://territories.indigenousknowledge.org/exhibit-5.html (last accessed May 21, 2020).

also extinguish the hegemonic power of Eurocentric and positivist law in order to be successful. This is where conventional cartographic practices fail to subvert Eurocentric law. Conventional mapping practices are still too much focused on claiming boundaries and exclusive rights over specific territories. As such, they reinforce the imposition of a legal culture that has dispossessed indigenous peoples from their land but, importantly, they also silence other ways of being in the landscape and their expression in the law (see also Dieckmann, this volume). For mapping practices to be helpful in native title claims, they need to show at the very least the tension between the different legal cultures that come together and expose the problematic history of non-recognition of Aboriginal rights.

Conventional cartographic practices share the same epistemological and ontological history as positivist Eurocentric law. Yet there is a danger that, by reprocessing a historiography that has used boundaries on the map and in the law, we are enforcing a specific order on indigenous peoples yet again. Representations of country on the map become the country (Reilly 2003: 12-13). A more subversive language and practice must be expressed on the map. The examples that have been discussed in this chapter explicitly break with the Eurocentric tradition of mapping and law making. It is in their artistic performance that we see a clear manifestation of a specific legal culture that is rooted in a different epistemological and ontological context.

The indigenous maps that have been discussed in this chapter are a good example of a relational approach towards mapping and they express an embodied movement in the landscape. But as the maps are also part of another way of being and moving in the landscape they can also be interpreted as sites of resistance against hegemonic depictions of spaces on maps. They include elements of a political manifesto that seeks to unshackle conventional and colonial representations of land, sea and ownership. By letting the ancestors speak through 'mapping' the cultural and natural objects and subjects, we can follow the paths they have carved in the landscapes. Together with the animals, spirits and all other relational objects and subjects, we are embarking on a journey through time and space. This is what we could refer to as the ontological turn in mapping. The way Yolŋu relate to the natural, cultural and spiritual world is clearly reflected in their mapping practices and in their maps themselves. It is this relationship that also needs to be reflected and incorporated in the law.

For mapping to be useful in native title claims, the map needs to represent the material turn of the law. The coming together of different legal orders that co-exist in the landscape needs to be expressed on the map. Both the bark paintings and the *Ngurrara Canvas* illustrate the materiality of the law by showing, through, for example, waterholes, songlines, rituals and sacred places, how the law is grounded and contextualized in the sea and on the land, how beings are connected to the ancestors. The relationship with the ancestors that is aesthetically reproduced on the map symbolizes more than just a factual dating of how long these people have resided on a specific piece of land. A waterhole is not just a geo-legal fact that can provide evidence in the court of how long people have resided in a specific area. The waterhole is a relational embodiment of the law; law is *djalkiri*.

The theme of this edited collection is to explore how to map different ways of being. I would like to add that from a legal point of view the law is also an ontology and being. The law's ontology is all about keeping order and maintaining that order by minimizing change. Therefore, the law marginalizes or even distinguishes uncertainty by maintaining an image of solidity, linearity and universality. As legal theorists know (whether or not you agree with this principle), the law needs a *Grundnorm* (see e.g. Kelsen 1949). Hans Kelsen (1881–1973), Austrian jurist and philosopher of law, developed the most rigorous form of positivist theory of law, arguing that the core (*Grundnorm*) of the law can only be found in what is referred to in legal jargon as black letter law. To simplify a complex and abstract debate, the *Grundnorm* is situated in the abstract norms of the law itself. For example, when a judge is adjudicating, his judgement becomes a norm, but in order to come to a legal decision the judge will be relying on higher norms, such as the constitution or statutes. In other words, every norm is based on a higher authority of norms that have been constituted earlier.

What the two case studies have shown, though, is that the *Grundnorm* can also be located in the physicality and materiality of the land and the sea. The maps that were used to illustrate the belonging to the land or the sea are doing more than just claiming ownership over specific geographical areas. The waterholes, the intertidal zones, the paths in the landscape, are all part of the fabric of Aboriginal life; they embody the multiple relationships in the landscapes which have legal significance. Law for Aboriginals is not about the constitution or a statute on a piece of paper. Law is something that is part of the daily rhythms of life. Therefore, the relationship between law and mapping must go beyond positivist Eurocentric cartographic coordinates on the map. It is in the paintbrushes and the performativity of applying the acrylics that the law appears on the canvas, not as a boundary or a point on the map but as a dialogue, a point of reference with other ways of being.

References

Aboriginal Land Rights (Northern Territory) Act 1976. (Cth., No. 191), Canberra: Parliament of Australia.

Anker, Kirsten (2005): "The Truth in painting: Cultural artefacts as proof of native title." In: Law Text Culture 9, pp. 91-124.

Anker, Kirsten (2014): Declarations of Interdependence: A Legal Pluralist Approach to Indigenous Rights. Farnham: Ashgate

Anker, Kirsten (2018): "Aboriginal Title and Alternative Cartographies." In: Erasmus Law Review 11, pp. 14-30.

Asche, Wendy/Trigger, David (2011): "Native Title Research in Australian Anthropology." In: Anthropological Forum 21, pp. 219-232.

Banner, Stuart (2007): Possessing the Pacific: Land, Settlers, and Indigenous People from Australia to Alaska, Cambridge: Harvard University Press.

Barber, Marcus (2005): Where the Clouds Stand: Australian Aboriginal Relationships to Water, Place and the Marine Environment in Blue Mud Bay, Northern Territory, Unpublished PhD Thesis, The Australian National University.

Barnes, Trevor J./Duncan, James S., eds. (1992): Writing Worlds: Discourse, Text and Metaphor in the Representation of Landscape, London: Routledge.

Behrendt, Larissa (2008): "Ngurrara: The Great Sandy Desert Canvas." In: Aboriginal Art Directory. (https://www.aboriginalartdirectory.com/news/feature/ngurrara-the-great-sandy-desert-canvas.php, last accessed March 9, 2020).

Bender, Barbara (1992): "Theorising landscapes and the Prehistoric Landscapes of Stonehenge." In: Man 27, pp. 735-55.

Blomley, Nicholas (1994): Law Space and the Geographies of Power, New York: Guildford Press.

Blomley, Nicholas/Delaney, David/Ford, Richard, eds. (2001): Legal Geographies Reader: Law, Power and Space, Oxford: Blackwell.

Borrows, John (2010): Drawing out Law: A Spirit's Guide, Toronto: University of Toronto Press.

Braverman, Irus/Blomley, Nicholas/Delaney, David/Kedar, Alexandre (2014): The expanding Spaces of Law: A Timely Legal Geography, Stanford: Stanford University Press.

Chance, Ian (2001): Kaltja Now, Adelaide: Wakefield Press.

Davies, Margaret (2017): Law Unlimited: Materialism, Pluralism, and Legal Theory, London: Routledge.

Dayman, Karen (2016): The Ngurrara Artists of the Great Sandy Desert: Painting to Claim Native Title, Unpublished PhD Thesis, Faculty of Arts and Social Sciences, University of Sydney.

de Sousa Santos, Boaventura (1987): "Law: A map of misreading: toward a postmodern conception of law." In: Journal of Law and Society 14, pp. 279-302.

de Sousa Santos, Boaventura (2018): The End of Cognitive Empire: The Coming of Age of Epistemologies of the South, Durham: Duke University Press.

Delaney, David (1998): Race, Place, and the Law, Austin: University of Texas Press.

Delgamuukw v. British Colombia (1991), 79 D.L.R. (4th) 185 (B.C.S.C.).

Delgamuukw v. British Colombia (1993), 104 D.L.R. (4th) 470.

Delgamuukw v. British Colombia [1997] 3 S.C.R 1010.

Dillon, Rodney (2002): "Seeing the Sea: Science, Change and Indigenous Sea Rights." In: Maritime Studies 123, pp. 12-16.

Elden, Stuart (2013): The Birth of Territory, Chicago: The University of Chicago Press.

Falk Moore, Sally (1978): Law as Process: An Anthropological Approach, London: Routledge & Kegan Paul.

Fitzpatrick, Peter (2001): Modernism and the Grounds of Law, Cambridge: Cambridge University Press.

Harley, John B. (1989): "Deconstructing the Map." In: Cartographica 26, pp. 1-20.

Harley, John B. (1992). "Deconstructing the Map" In: Trevor J. Barnes/James S. Duncan (eds.): Writing Worlds: Discourse, Text and Metaphor in the Representation of Landscape, London: Routledge, pp. 231-47.

Harley, John B./Laxton Paul, eds. (2001): The New Nature of Maps: Essays in the History of Cartography, Baltimore, Maryland: Johns Hopkins University Press.

Hershey, Alan/McCormack, Jennifer/Newell, Gillian (2014) "Mapping Intergenerational Memories (Part I): Proving the Contemporary Truth of the Indigenous Past." In: Arizona Legal Studies 14–01, pp. 1-26.

Holder, Jane/Harrison Carolyn, eds. (2003): Law and Geography, Oxford: Oxford University Press.

Kelsen, Hans (1949): General Theory of Law and State, Harvard University Press.

Kitchin, Rob G. J./Dodge, Martin (2013): 'Unfolding mapping practices: A new epistemology for cartography." In: Transactions of the Institute of British Geographers 38, pp. 480-496.

Kütting, Gabriela/Lipschutz, Ronnie eds. (2009): Environmental Governance: Power and Knowledge in a Local-Global World, London: Routledge.

Logue, John (1982): "The revenge of John Selden: The Draft Convention on the Law of the Sea in the light of Hugo Grotius' Mare Liberum". In: Grotiana 3/1, pp. 27-56.

Mabo and Others v Queensland (No.2) [1992] 175 CLR 1, [1992] HCA 23

Mabo v Queensland (No.1) [1988] 166 CLR 186.

Manderson, Desmond (2005): "Interstices: New work on legal spaces." In: Law Text Culture 9, pp. 1-10.

McNamara, Luke/Grattan, Scott (1999): "The Recognition of Indigenous Land Rights as 'Native Title': Continuity and Transformation." In: Flinders Journal of Law Reform 3, pp. 137-162.

McNiven, Ian (2004): "Saltwater People: Spiritscapes, maritime rituals and the archaeology of Australian Indigenous Seascapes". In: World Archaeology 35, pp. 329-349.

Mellisaris, Emmanuel (2004): "The More the Merrier? A New Take on Legal Pluralism." In: Social and Legal Studies 13/1, pp. 57-79.

Merry, Sally (1988): "Legal Pluralism." In: Law and Society Review 22/5, pp. 869-896.

Merry, Sally (2000): Colonizing Hawaii: The Cultural Power of Law. Princeton New Jersey: Princeton University Press.

Mohr, Richard (2003): "Law and Identity in Spatial Contests" In: National Identities 5, pp. 53-66.

Morphy, Frances (2007): "Performing Law: The Yolŋu of Blue Mud Bay meet the native title process." In: Benjamin R. Smith/Frances Morphy (eds.), The Social Effects of Native Title: Recognition, Translation, Coexistence, Canberra: The Australian National University E Press, pp. 31-57.

Morphy, Howard (2009): "Acting in a Community: Art and Social Cohesion in Indigenous Australia." In: Humanities Research XV, pp. 115-131.

Morphy, Howard/Morphy Frances (2006): 'Tasting the Waters: Discriminating Identities in the Waters of the Blue Mud Bay. In: Journal of Material Culture 11, pp. 67-85.

Native Title Act 1993. (Cth., No. 111), Canberra: Parliament of Australia

Northern Territory of Australia v Arnhem Land Aboriginal Land Trust (2008) 236 CLR 24.

Northern Territory of Australia v Arnhem Land Aboriginal Trust [2008] HCA 29 30 July 2008 D7/2007.

Palmer, Kingsley (2011): "Piety, Fact and the Oral Account in Native Title Claims." In: Anthropological Forum 21, pp. 269-286.

Peter, Jacques (2009): "The Power and Death of the Sea." In: Gabriela Kütting/Ronnie Lipschutz, (eds.), Environmental Governance: Power and Knowledge in a Local-Global World, London: Routledge, pp. 60-79.

R v Van der Peet [1996] 2 SCR 507.

Reddleman, Claire (2018): Cartographic Abstraction in Contemporary Art: Seeing with Maps, Abingdon: Routledge.

Reilly, Alexander (2003): "Cartography and native title." In: Journal of Australian Studies 27, pp. 1-14.

Richard, Gina (2015): Radical Cartographies: Relational Epistemologies and Principles for Successful Indigenous Cartographic Praxis, Unpublished PhD Thesis, Faculty of the Department of American Indian Studies, The University of Arizona.

Sharp, Nonie (2002): Saltwater People: The Waves of Memory. Crows Nest: Allen & Unwin.

Smith Benjamin R./Morphy, Frances, eds. (2007): The Social Effects of Native Title: Recognition, Translation, Coexistence, Canberra: The Australian National University E Press.

Steinberg, Philip (2009): "Sovereignty, Territory, and the Mapping of Mobility: A View from the Outside." In: Annals of the Association of American Geographers99, pp. 467-495.

Tan, Poh-Ling/Jackson, Sue (2013): "Impossible Dreaming – does Australia's Water Law and Policy Fulfill Indigenous Aspirations?" In: Environment and Planning Law Journal 30, pp. 132-149.

Teubner, Guenther (1998) "Legal Irritants: Good Faith in British Law or How Unifying Law Ends Up in New Divergences." In: Modern Law Review 61, pp 11-32.

Turnbull, David, ed. (1994): Maps are Territories: Science is an Atlas, Chicago: University of Chicago Press.

Vermeylen Saskia/Davies, Gemma/van der Horst, Dan (2012): 'Deconstructing the conservancy map; hxaro, n!ore and rhizomes in the Kalahari'. In: Cartographica 46/2, pp. 121-134.

Vermeylen, Saskia (2013): "The Nagoya Protocol and Customary Law: The Paradox of Narratives in the Law." In: Law, Environment and Development Journal 9/2, pp. 187-201 (available at http://www.lead-journal.org/content/13185.pdf, last accessed August 12, 2020).

Vermeylen, Saskia (2015): "Comparative Environmental Law and Orientalism: Reading beyond the 'Text' of Traditional Knowledge Protection." In: Review of Environmental Comparative International and European Law 24, pp 304-317.

Vermeylen, Saskia (2017): "Materiality and the Ontological Turn in the Anthropocene: Establishing a Dialogue between Law, Anthropology and Eco-Philosophy." In: Louis J. Kotzé (ed.), Law and Governance for the Anthropocene, Oxford: Hart Publishing, pp. 137-162.

Watson, Helen (1994): "Aboriginal-Australian Maps." In: David Turnbull (ed.) Maps are Territories: Science is an Atlas, Chicago: University of Chicago Press.

Wildburger, Eleonore (2013): "Indigenous Australian Art in Practice and Theory." In: Coolabah 10, pp. 202-212.

Wood, David (1992): The Power of Maps, New York: Guilford.

Wood, David (2006): "Map Art." In: Cartographic Perspectives 53, pp.5-14.

Mapping meaning with comics – Enhancing Maps with visual art and narrative

Frederik von Reumont

Introduction

This chapter looks at possibilities of using maps as tools to communicate meaning of places and spatiality.

I suggest enhancing maps with visual art and narrative, i.e. comics, in particular, in order to map the meaning of places. I will first take a closer look at the emergence of meaning and the role of experience using a phenomenological approach. I will briefly outline contact theory as a useful concept recently put forward by Hubert Dreyfus and Charles Taylor in their book *Retrieving Realism*. Afterwards, I will explore possibilities of sharing experience and communicating meaning based on the works of Achille Mbembe and Felwine Sarr, two prominent thinkers in the post-colonial discourse. I will then present some empirical research on communication from cognitive as well as neuropsychological perspectives on the effects of narratives, complemented by a narratological stance. This research supports Mbembe and Sarr's theoretical considerations. Then I will discuss the advantages of visual art in maps. I argue for the integration of narrative and visual art in the comic form within maps in order to capture the meaning of places. Against this backdrop I will discuss the potential of comics in maps, including in indigenous mapping projects.

Meaning through experience

When we attempt to map the meaning of places for human beings, we have to assume that there is some kind of relationship between the conscious mind of living beings and the physical world. Strongly influenced by Descartes, this relationship has been described as constructed through means of each individual mind. This view claims a strict division between the mind and the body in which the mind only receives signals from the senses, but has no direct contact with the world 'out there'. This dualist sorting implies that the mind receives information only through the mediation of the senses. The mind's task is then to make sense of the impressions by forming concepts, which in turn requires language. This conception of mind and body isolates the mind from the outer world and no real contact seems to be possible. Everything is interpretation. However, it seems very hard to uphold this "mediational picture" (Dreyfus/Taylor, 2015), and not only in recent philosophical terms. Findings from the fields of cognitive psychology, brain research and linguistics, among others, rather support a theory of an embodied cognition rooted in a shared physical world.

My approach builds in large parts on the contact theory put forward by Charles Taylor and Hubert Dreyfus (2015). They establish a picture that is not mediational, but allows for the human corporeal self to be firmly embedded in the real world and society.

Dreyfus and Taylor (2015) reject the strict division between body and mind as two radically different entities, building on the thoughts of Wittgenstein, Husserl, Merleau-Ponty, Heidegger, Gadamer and others. They argue instead for the possibility of a direct or un-mediated and prelinguistic contact between the living being and the world. In their terms, the relationship of living beings with the world is characterized as "… the contact of living active beings, whose life form involves acting in and on a world which also acts on them. These beings are at grips with a world and with each other" (Dreyfus/Taylor 2015: 18). They argue that all our beliefs and thus our meaning making are formed through this "more original, 'primordial' (*ursprünglich*) epistemically fruitful contact with the world, which is prepropositional and in part even preconceptual" (Dreyfus/Taylor 2015: 72, original emphasis).

Knowledge arises from the interaction of the corporeal self with the world and thus depends on the existence of both. "My ability to get around this city, this house comes out only in getting around this city and house" (Dreyfus/Taylor 2015: 47). My knowledge of the world is "a 'coproduction' of me and the world" (ibid: 93) which in turn produces "unshakeable, incorrigible" (ibid.) takes on the world, such as 'I can use this goblet to drink from it.' This knowledge arises from a personal or subjective perspective on the world. However, this perspective is not "simply one constructed or determined by me". Rather, "our grasp of things lies in the way we are in contact with the world" (ibid.).

The "primordial" experience in interaction with the world reveals the meaning of things to us as humans ("human meaning"; ibid: 108).

The different stages of forming beliefs in this way are based in the causal contact between the body and the world. The senses are activated by physical objects to perceive some of their characteristics. This allows for interaction between the perceiver and the identified object. The interaction then produces an understanding of the object. Certain beliefs about the object can be formed. These beliefs can but don't need to be expressed in terms of language. Only this process "can allow for a coherent account relating perception and action, understanding, language and belief" (ibid: 90). Following this theory, we arrive at a picture of the human being as "an embodied agent, embedded in a society, and at grips with the world" (ibid: 91).

In this way, we are in contact with the world by perceiving and interacting with the objects within it. This creates a unique subjective and conscious experience of our surrounding reality. This raw experience, which is prelinguistic and preconceptual, does not stand alone, however. We are "psychological and historical structure[s]" resulting in a personal "style" of being-in-the-world, which is our "means of communication" with the world around us (Merleau-Ponty 1962: 455), maybe comparable to a lens through which we see the world. We almost immediately contextualize our experiences, and in doing so make sense of the world. This is influenced by a range of factors. Experiences are always accompanied, for instance, by emotional responses, which can be overwhelmingly strong. But even subliminal emotions can influence our interpretation of an experience. As social beings we are exposed to preexisting imaginations of the world. These imaginations influence our ideas of how to interact with the world's objects. We internalize attitudes informed by the values, beliefs and spirituality of the society we are born into, which were formed by others long before we could have our own experiences. The conscious embodied experience cannot be separated from this conglomerated way of interpreting it with all its feedback loops. But such an interpretation or construal of the world is in response "to what is actually there, and in this sense causally dependent on it" (Dreyfus/Taylor 2015: 99). In effect, from this clutter of subjective, embodied, interpreted and conscious experience emerges meanings which might be practical, emotional, or even spiritual, moral or ethical. I believe that in the same sense the interpreted experience of the objects that open up space constitutes the meaning of a place. At the base of the immaterial realm of meaning lies the human experience of the material world.

If we want to communicate meaning, we have to think about how we can express our own personal experiences and how we can come to understand somebody else's experience. In order to understand the meaning of a particular place for somebody other than ourselves, we have to see that place 'through the eyes of' that person, or come as close as possible to their personal perspective.[1] How can we use our contact theory to access other views of reality, e.g. non-European ones, 'indigenous' ones, etc.? Achille Mbembe and Felwine Sarr shed light on phenomenological approaches in a post-colonial context. When setting out their ideas of understanding and expressing African perspectives, both Mbembe and Sarr emphasize the experiential character of our being-in-the-world and our meaning making through our relations to the material realm.

When asked personally how we could teach German students about the meaning that a place like the city of Lagos, Nigeria has for its inhabitants, Mbembe (2019a) replied that the best way would be to take them there, so they can experience the city themselves. Sarr (2019), too, emphasizes the subjective experience of place when trying to grasp life in African cities such as Lagos, Abidjan, Cairo or Dakar. He uses an almost poetic narrative description of what to expect when walking through certain cities to illustrate this. However, we have to be aware of our biased interpretations of reality and how our imaginations influence our experiences. Mbembe (2019a) differentiates between a colonized and an un-colonized way of seeing the world. He sees a need for a true change of perspective in order to decolonize ourselves and understand each other. This means that in order to truly understand perspectives that differ from our own, we have to openly explore different epistemic traditions, exploit new and unfamiliar cognitive assemblages, and establish new bodies of thought, memory and different layers of the real (Mbembe 2019a: no pagination). These new bodies of thought include categories of being, matter, time and agency. To grasp this view on reality we should focus on its processual and relational nature. Mbembe (2019b) shows how objects in many African philosophies are more than just objects. Objects are "depositories of a vital force" and "repositories of energies" (min. 35). African cultural objects are often meant to represent the relation of human beings and the objects in the same "assemblage" (min. 68). This is in contrast to a more European approach of seeing objects and humans as fundamentally detached from each other. Mbembe calls for the development of a broader understanding of objects and

---

1   See Skaanes, this volume.

non-objects alike, which he calls "the entirety of the living" (min. 59). Objects, he suggests, are important for conveying different ways of seeing, for "imagining different ways of living" (Mbembe 2019b, min. 68). Similarly, Sarr (2019) argues that we need other descriptions of reality than those utilized by traditional 'western' science in order to understand "African realities" (in Sarr's terms).

He calls for a new epistemology to better understand African realities (ibid: 112-113) and emphasizes that life itself cannot be measured since it is an experience. This is important in the context of expressing our being-in-the-world. I suggest extending this call to better understand reality everywhere. More modes of description are needed. Sarr (2019: 40-41) suggests developing new frameworks for integrating realities that exceed the purely factual, i.e. purely measurable and categorized descriptions. He refers to a wide range of expressional modes to express reality, meaning and vision, including thought, literature, visual art, fashion, song and music, and many more (ibid: 131). The African novel, to him, is the place where Africa's reality is best expressed.

Let us return to the meaning of place. The meaning of a place is not only determined by present purposes or events, but also by historical events or the remembrance of them. Mbembe suggests a multimodal way of expression. He also elaborates on contemporary African literature as examples of truth telling in remembrance of places. For Mbembe (2014), time does not exist per se, but is constituted by our contingent ambiguous and inconsistent relation to things, the world and the body. In African literature for instance, time is experienced with senses like smell, touch, hearing, taste. In this embodied experience of time, the human body is at the center of the experience with all its organs, nervous system and emotional responses. Memory is always expressed in the sensory world. Mbembe (ibid.) refers to contemporary African literature as reporting a scene where a person remembers a time of destruction (war) by seeing the destructed and severed buildings. He states that remembering literally means seeing the trails an event has impressed on the "body of a place". Time is experienced within a landscape. In this example from an African novel, we can see the close connection between body, world and meaning.

According to this line of thought, accessing perspectives by sharing experiences and thus understanding meaning is possible. It is possible because we share one world on the basis of being human. Sharing one world with its affordances and necessities gives us a common ground in which the human condition finds its roots. In the course of the ontological turn, as proposed e.g. by Viveiros de Castro, the existence of one single world is often denied in favor of the idea of there being multiple worlds and realities. But even the strongest representatives of that concept would not actually go as far as "arguing that there are parts of the world where water runs uphill, there are three-headed flying monkeys, or pi calculates to 3.15", as Graeber (2015: 20) puts it in a reply to de Castro. Mbembe (2014), too, insists on a shared world with a shared ecology and a shared history, and we all share a wish to be fully human (ibid: 330). Based on this shared humanity we can share and compare experiences. Communication and understanding is possible, no matter how different our ways of life seem to be, since all belief is built on experiencing the world around us. As Dreyfus and Taylor put it: "We are not imprisoned, because language- and world making are not arbitrary; they are in response to something" (2015: 129).

Experiencing stories – communicating meaning

Mapping the meaning of places means sharing experiences that were had at specific locations at a certain time. In order to share, we need to transfer the experience to another location and time by means of media such as texts, maps and other symbols. One of the most effective ways to share experiences is narrative. This view is supported by Mbembe and Sarr, providing examples from African novels. Emphasizing that experience is key to understanding. Mbembe and Sarr underline the importance of modes of expression that capture and convey more than factual accounts. In the present context, I define narrative in the simplest terms as an account of actions while taking (implicitly or explicitly) the perspective of an agent or agents. In this way, the term "narrative" is quite similar if not identical to the term "story". In stories, we can not only share experiences but re-experience them as if they were our own. Different points of view can be deployed in story-telling to orient the reader in the story world (first person, third person, objective, omniscient, and so on). But these are devices to situate the audience in the best place to understand what is driving the agent or agents. Authors use a specific narrative perspective as a tool to enable the recipients of the story to best follow the experiences of different characters in the story. How this works can be explained by theories of embodied cognition and confirmed by empirical tests. Neuropsychological studies argue that while perceiving stories the brain is in nearly the same state as it is when experiencing social interaction or trying to make sense of other beings (Theory-of-Mind).[2] In this sense, narrative can be interpreted as a simulation of experiences. This is also true for the experience of space, as we will see below. This is, in my view, an indication that we as human beings are equipped with the capacity to share experiences in a profound way. In the following, I will briefly outline some recent findings in (neuro-)psychological research, complemented by cognitive narratology and an evolutionary perspective.[3] This kind of research anchors the comprehension of story-telling deeply in the corporeal self of embodied beings.

Story-telling and thus narrative can be considered a deeply human activity that has been part of many aspects of life in every culture throughout human existence. But why do humans engage in storytelling? One reason is that it is a way of making sense of the world by extending one's horizon. Cognitive narratologist Marie-Jaure Ryan states, for instance, that narrative is widely recognized as "a way to give meaning to our being-in-the-world, to our interpersonal relations, and to the temporality of our existence" (2010: 469). With the help of stories we can emotionally and cognitively relive other persons' experiences. Stories function like simulations (Oatley/Djikic 2018: 162). Our brains lack the capability to grasp and connect complex multi-causal settings quickly and effectively in 'objective' descriptions lacking overt perspective. Stories are, however, easily comprehensible, because "as depictions of imaginary lives narrative form runs closely parallel to the self-narratives and simulations constructed in the brain's default mode network" (Carroll 2018: 142). According to Carroll "[t]hrough imaginative virtual worlds people envision the present in relation to the past and future, associate behavior with

---

2   Although studies exist indicating that seeing a landscape is fundamentally different from being in it, see e.g. Rowland/Yanovich/Kentros (2011), the applicability of this particular study to the human condition is problematic. This study was conducted on rats, and it is more than dubious to transfer these findings to humans, although the authors do this at the very end of the article. But we do not know anything about the rats' capacities of imagination. To me it is one of the big differences that make humans human: the extreme power of imagination, which allows us to plan the future, remember the past, and construct all sorts of ideas.

3   Some of the articles cited were published in a special issue on "The Psychology of Fiction", edited by Keith Oatley amongst others. Oatley has been researching fiction in terms of cognitive psychology for a long time. He has also worked together with Raymond A. Mar, director of the Mar Lab (www.yorku.ca/mar/), examining e.g. how fiction relates to simulation in terms of cognition. Oatley has also influenced the work of the cognitive narratologist Marie-Laure Ryan, who borrowed from him the "concept of mental simulation" (Ryan 2010: 470).

abstract norms, locate events within narratives of individual and group identity and encompass present reality within cosmic visions imbued with human meaning" (2018: 142). Stories trigger (mental) simulation, through which recipients gain access to what is otherwise beyond their horizon of experience (ibid.); we can "enter [a] character's circumstances" (Oatley/Djikic 2018: 162). Through this, "stories model and abstract the human social world" (Mar/Oatley 2008: 173). They "enable us to enter into the minds of others and enable us to engage with, and perhaps get better at the making of such models" (Oatley/Djikic 2018: 165). In this way, narrative driven from the perspective of an agent can point to truth, i.e. the true meaning of something for a specific person, which is sometimes better than factual text (ibid: 166). These theories about the empathic effects of narrative have been well confirmed in a number of empirical psychological studies, as summarized by Koopman (2018: 169-175). This includes the general "effects of narrativity, that is to say, of imagining the feelings, thoughts, and actions of a character (perspective-taking)" (ibid.), which ultimately lead to a better understanding of the whole group the character belongs to (ibid: 172). Whether literary texts work better than unambitious narrations in respect to empathy effects has not been determined yet (ibid: 175).

Meaning consists of experiences in individual minds, sensations, emotions, perceptions and thoughts (Carroll 2018: 135). This raises the question of whether we can willfully evoke the specific sensations, emotions etc. in others, that allow us to convey meaning by simulating another person's experience. How can we hope that what we want to say is actually what is understood? The relationship between author and audience sheds light on the issue. Characters in stories act out of a certain set of motivations, just like real persons. Thus, characters are convincing when comprehensible motives make actions credible. The evolutionary sociologist Joseph Carroll explains this in terms of neurology, building on evolutionary theory. When we acknowledge the existence of our material bodies in a material world which is shared by us humans, we also expect these bodies to have evolved similarly through evolutionary adaptation. This body then produces a "species-typical suite of behaviors" (ibid: 137) driven by a set of motives. Moving between biological needs and human nature as "social animals" (ibid: 138), a complex system of different motivations comes into being. Motives, in turn, "make themselves felt through emotions" (ibid.). Creating emotions in response to a fictional character's interaction with the world is thus a "simulation of social experience" (ibid.). These experiences can be deliberately created by authors (at least those that aim at being understood by their audience), supposing a common set of cognitive capacities that have evolved similarly across the human species (ibid: 139). Carroll (ibid.) locates the ability to comprehend stories and take perspectives in the "default mode network" of the brain: its imaginative capacities are "key to large scale structures of meaning in the minds of authors and readers." This physical likeness seems to enable us to read and also to elicit specific emotions in others. Story-telling following the rules of genres shows that this works in general. Horror stories induce fear, comedy induces laughter. The functionality of the story-telling techniques hinge on the credibility of the protagonists – and the antagonists as well. Or as Ryan puts it: to enable recipients "to understand a plot, it is necessary to construct the mental states that motivate agents. These mental states consist of desires, goals, beliefs, and plans" (2010: 477). If they are credible, they move us, just like real people would. Ryan sees it as "undeniable that without the ability to construct representations of other people's minds we would be unable to understand, and much less to appreciate stories" (ibid: 478). This theory is further supported by neuro-scientists who locate the ability to understand stories and characters within the human brain (Mar 2011: 103) (which is a bodily organ) and thus within our corporeal being-in-the-world. In a meta-analysis of studies of the human brain, Mar (2011) concludes that very similar networks in the brain are active during story comprehension and when reading the emotions of real persons. This links the two processes in terms of our embodied being-in -the-world. The strong overlap between Theory-of-Mind and narrative comprehension could mean that "people can treat fictional persons as if they were real" (ibid: 123).[4]

For the purpose of mapping meaning in an understandable way, character-driven narrative thus seems to be a useful tool. It is understandable and enables us through (mental) simulation to experience events that are otherwise out of reach. Expanding this notion to the experience of space, Ryan states that, "[f]or readers to get immersed, there must be an environment to be immersed in, and [...] this environment is [...] a world populated with objects and characters who attract the reader's interest" (Ryan 2018: 6). Narrative

---

4   Admittedly, most if not all of these studies have a strong cultural bias, as they have been conducted by 'western' scientists with 'western' subjects. However, the main conclusion of these studies in the present context, namely that narratives (verbal and textual) and direct experience have similar effects on humans, should be valid for humans from other cultural backgrounds too.

and the imagination of space and place are strongly connected. Readers experience these worlds in some way as real space. This becomes evident when they map these worlds. In fan art, we see a lot of these maps that are created by readers after having read the story, e.g. of a fantasy world, as in the Harry Potter stories, as recounted in the introduction of this book. Ryan states:

> [A]ll narratives imply a world with spatial extension, even when spatial information is withheld. [...] Mental maps [...] are both dynamically constructed in the course of reading and consulted by the reader to orient himself in the narrative world. The various landmarks shown or mentioned in the story are made into a coherent world through an awareness of the relations that situate them with respect to each other. (Ryan 2014: no pagination)

> The process of mapping storyworlds bears some analogies with the formation of cognitive maps of the real world. A cognitive map is a mental representation that enables people to orient themselves in real space; it is based on a person's embodied experience. [...] Cognitive maps of storyworlds differ from cognitive maps of real space in that they are built on the basis of selected textual information [...]. (Ryan 2018: 8)

She continues that "these worlds become habitats where we want to return over and over again, spaces of exploration, and sources of collective experiences that create cultural bonds" (ibid: 13).

We have seen that even relatively short narratives can evoke strong effects (even when the authors are not award-winning literary figures, as shown e.g. by the experiments conducted by Koopman (2018)). Before we consider the question of the relationship between maps and narrative and how we can integrate both into one meaningful whole, we have to think about the modes of narration. What if our language lacks the terms for specific new experiences of both unfamiliar places and unknown ways of being-in-the-world? Building on the thoughts of Dreyfus and Taylor, Mbembe and Sarr, we will have to expand our language by combining different modes of expression, exceeding the purely verbal to produce a narrative that more fully allows us to experience space and the realm of meaning.

A multimodal approach to communicating meaning

How can we communicate most effectively? Are there more channels than just verbal expressions to convey the meaning of a narration? The phenomenological approach outlined above allows us to look for communication devices beyond language alone. The concept of a corporeal being in direct contact with the world offers more modalities than just text with which to capture – and express – meaning. In the following, I would like to suggest moving beyond words to communicate meaning.

As I have outlined above, the meaning of a place can be conveyed with narrative techniques. Narrative techniques, though, don't need to be limited to words. Visual representations are at times more powerful, one of the reasons why maps are very popular. Acknowledging our embodied being in the world, experience is the basis of knowledge. A lot of knowledge can only be expressed non-verbally. I suggest using a broader array of communicative means in combination in order to access meanings of unfamiliar experiences. Human communication is fundamentally multimodal, putting our entire body to work, e.g. in gesture, posture and interaction with objects while talking. Bodily expressions are a place where meaning is constructed. This can be used in certain visual art forms like comics. As a medium combining text and image, comics can accommodate a wide range of means of communication in an integrated and portable fashion.

According to Dreyfus and Taylor (2015), meaning is constituted by language. But this language might include a broad range of modes of expression resulting from our embodied nature of being in the world. It includes "declarative speech, story, symbol, [...] rules and [...] habitus" (Dreyfus/Taylor 2015: 119). This view can be complemented by recent empirical studies broadening the definition of language to include non-verbal expressions that are nonetheless essential in communication. Researchers from the fields of communication and ethnographic linguistics have made inquiries into the entanglement of speech and bodily action, social interaction, and interaction with objects (Streeck et al. 2011: 2). Many case studies show how, in the interaction of the human body with objects, a sense of meaning emerges. Face to face communication is a concerted effort involving speech, pointing and other gestures, the positioning of bodies in respect to other persons and the objects that they talk about, etc. By communicating with our whole bodies and interacting with objects, "precision and flexibility become [...] possible" (ibid.) where words alone would be useless, especially when describing patterns, exact positions, or orientation of objects. This is especially true for meaning making in spatial contexts. "Through meaning imbued residence in the world ..., we read our environment, as revealed in the ways we respond to it." (Enfield 2011: 60) Streeck et al. "insist that embodied interaction in the material world, which includes material objects and environments in the process of meaning making and action formation, is primary" (2011: 9). They build their argument on a number of empirical studies showing how the body and objects are used in meaning making and communication. Thus, we can observe the emergence of meaning by observing the interaction of humans with the world. Describing meaning, then, requires a holistic approach. To understand a gesture, we have to consider the context in which it was made. "We have survived by means of our multiple and heterogeneous objectivations, which include language and artifacts such as tools, skilled practices, rituals, and institutions. These objectivations can only be understood and explained in relation to one another." (ibid: 6)

The human body itself can therefore be considered as a communication device, since it is the carrier of gesture, posture and prosodic features; even the position and orientation of the body in space expresses meaning (for a linguistic perspective see Streeck et al. 2011; Enfield 2011; Hutchins/Nomura 2011). The body plays a crucial role in interacting with the physical world and thus it plays a crucial role in making sense of it. Words and gesture are often used in interplay to express meaning. This is why Enfield suggests that we "capture this broad flexibility of form in communicative formulation" (2011: 59). To 'read' the body it usually has to be in sight. Thus, we have to "rethink the putative primacy of [purely verbal] language in meaning making" (ibid: 64) in favor of a more pictorial vocabulary displaying the human body and its interaction with the environment and any object therein.

Analysts of meaning-making processes "should consider visible phenomena from the outset" (Streeck et al. 2011: 12). With the help of recordings, we can permanently visualize the non-permanent modes of expression like gesture, facial expression, and intonation of spoken word, through visual representations of the human body and the symbolization of sound.

When mapping the meaning of places, words alone are not sufficient to represent the experiences or events that constitute this meaning. Mbembe states that memory exists only where an event meets words, symbols and images. This strong connection between words, symbols and images allows us not only to express an event but to make it appear, as in an "epiphany" (Mbembe 2014: 230).

Multimodal maps comprising narrative and visual art

When mapping the meaning of places, it is useful to focus on the map as a mode of expression. It has distinct advantages for communicating spatial patterns, relations and scales, such as measurability, strict geometric reference in a well described coordinate system, and so forth.[5] A traditional 'western' map has a highly specialized set of symbols to express a view point in as impersonal a way as possible. Although mapmakers have tried hard to remove personal experience from the map they have never quite succeeded. Rather, they have concealed the subjective aspects of maps. As a result, current cartographic language has to be re-enhanced in order to express meaning in its full scope, which necessitates the expression of subjective experience, as we have seen earlier. Cartographic language is flexible and ever evolving. The symbols which compose the map can be applied in differing degrees of abstraction and complexity, which gives us the possibility of using the cartographic grammar while enhancing the vocabulary.[6] Maps are communicative devices. We want them to be understood. So we have to target the user of the map, the person attributing meaning to what they see. "The interpreter drives the process" (Enfield 2011: 60). We can provide the users of our maps with a set of signs which they can understand. We can extend the modality of maps by adding narrative and visual art to them.

For some time now, Cartwright, for example, has called for a recognition of art in maps (2009; 2010). Art enables the map user to "read between the lines" (Cartwright 2010: 294) by introducing vagueness, interpretation and impressions into the map. Cartwright considers art as an equally important component; alongside science and technology, "[a]rt is also necessary to ensure that the map can be understood" (ibid: 299). In this sense, art refers to the experience of emotions, affections and critical readings, and can thus point to the uncertainty and ambiguity of data. Crampton (2010: 3) calls the separation of art and maps a myth, anyway, that was introduced in an attempt to make cartography scientific, but was never truly achieved.

The combination of visual art/narrative and science in maps is a unique opportunity. There are several possibilities for placing art in the map. We can consider the map as art in itself (see Vermeylen, this volume). Another way

---

5   I use the term "map" here in a rather strict sense. For definitions of map, see Eide, this volume; for a broader use of the concept, see Vermeylen, this volume.

6   See Pearce, this volume.

is to frame the map with art, to use its surroundings to place all kinds of additional material, like images and text, in the immediate vicinity of the map. I focus on the latter.

Critical cartographers point out that the map has to be considered as an interplay between creator, artifact and audience. Post-representationalists argue that the map cannot be separated from the social, 'cultural' and psychological processes underlying its production and interpretation, for the meaning of a map lies in the context it was made in. Wood and Fels have established the term "paramap" (2008: 192), referring to everything that surrounds the actual map but is not the map itself, like the quality of its paper, the website it is embedded in, or a complementing text or article referring to the map. The paramap can be used for at least two different purposes. First, it can be used to deconstruct the map as an authoritative tool by disclosing its making. Second, it can help to communicate the meaning of places for individuals, communities, etc. Adding reflective elements to the paramap means deconstructing the map as a representation of reality. The paramap can become a place where we can reveal the purpose of the map, for instance, whether it is an attempt to convey 'facts' about the world, whether it aims to communicate the relationship of the inhabitants with their environment, or whether the map is intended to serve as a political tool. With regard to the second point – the communication of the meaning of places for specific people – the metrics usually used in maps show location, distribution, spread, etc. They hardly tell us anything about impressions, emotions, experience and the like, which also constitute meaning. Visual art and narrative integrated into the paramap can help to convey experience and thus the meaning of place.

Art is able to give a more complete rendering of the landscape, as Crampton (2010: 110), for example, shows by mentioning many examples where mapping is combined with photos, poems, etc. to convey a "sense of the landscape" (ibid.). In this sense, art can be considered as another, nonetheless equally important approach to dealing with "questions of truth" (ibid: 174). Caquard and Cartwright emphasize the need to introduce emotions into the map. They consider this a major challenge because of the "dehumanizing" characteristics of conventional 'western' maps, which aim at achieving an impersonal view of the world (Caquard/Cartwright 2014: 103). They (ibid.) suggest using stories to meet that challenge. We should connect "maps with other media and modes of expression to better capture the profound emotional link that some stories have developed with places" (ibid: 104). Caquard and Cartwright (ibid.) recognize two main types of relationships between maps and narrative. First, maps are used to visualize the spatial aspects of a given story. Second, maps induce storytelling (but apparently do not tell a story of their own) through their display of data and places. I would like to introduce a third way of merging map and story by using comics. I essentially envision an artifact that pools together the expressional modes of both media. Comics are, in their sequential storytelling, the translation of time into space (McCloud 1993: 7). They have achieved the use of a static carrier medium to show the passing of time. Essentially, they are the combination of visual art and narrative. The combination of map, narrative and visual art will help us in mapping the immaterial realm of meaning by making personal perspectives accessible in a multimodal way.

The relation of maps and comics

Visual art broadens what can be expressed and can help us to escape the prison of language. Language, on the other hand, can help interpret or even explain what is seen (Sousanis 2015: 52). This can enhance the cartographic language of maps. In parallel, narratives can evoke empathy and support perspective taking while descriptions can support the forming of one's own opinion about the facts. A hidden strength lies in the combination of both picture and text, visual and narrative art in the description of the map. Taylor and Dreyfus call this approach "a multimedia grasp on meanings. This interweaving of the bodily, the symbolic, and the narrative and propositional illustrates [...] the inseparability of the life and human meanings in the stream of human existence." (Taylor/Dreyfus 2015: 117) This is what comics do. Comics can portray propositional as well as non-propositional meanings expressed through the body and its environment, e.g. by depicting habitus, position in space, or facial expressions.

The way comics express meaning through a combination of text and visuals and the extensive use of symbols is very similar to that of maps. Just like maps, comics can convey their stories in non-linear ways. Both media give the possibility of making use of the space of the page (or screen) to meaningfully arrange narrative elements in a representation of geographic space. They offer the use of frames and borders, icons, symbols and pictograms, and the color and type of font as meaningful parts, just as maps do.[7] In comics, the

---

7   See Pearce, this volume.

speech balloon allocates text in a pictorial display of a spatial scene. Maps, in turn, can efficiently make use of this language of comics, e.g. in the form of pop-up windows in webmaps, corresponding to speech balloons in comics.

From a comic artist's perspective, maps and comic art are close relatives. In his comic book *Atlas*, Dylan Horrocks, one of New Zealand's most prominent comic artists, even refers to maps and comics as being "the same thing" (2001: 26). Although I would not go quite this far, I argue that the multimodal language of comics makes an especially promising candidate for enhancing the language of maps. The similarities of maps and comics in their respective expressional modes allow a close-knit combination or even a fusion of the two forms to convey a more sophisticated view of meaning, the material and the immaterial world. For Horrocks, the primary goal of comics is "world building": "it's about making a place in which to explore ideas and experiences and their meanings" (2004: no pagination). World building, in this sense, seems to be very close to the aim of maps. Generally, comic artists are not trying to draw realistic representations of real-world phenomena. They rather create symbols that are easily recognizable and that speak for themselves. Yet the degree of abstraction is fluid and can thus be used according to context. Due to the similar approaches of mapmakers and comic authors, symbols used in the map could reappear in the comic. This bridges the gap between the two media and would fuse comic and legend. A legend could still be used in the same way as a glossary for background information about certain important terms or objects appearing in both comic and map.

In contrast with maps, comics can express time by arranging panels in a certain order. Space is converted to time. They can produce "plurivectorial narration", a kind of storytelling that moves in different directions at the same time, and shows different time slices simultaneously (Dittmer 2010: 231), each panel representing a moment in time. Comics can use visual perspective freely; they usually deploy a close to human scale and an expressionist use of color. Comics can (re)embed humans into maps and integrate emotions, chain of thoughts, reasoning and perceptions. In his doctoral thesis on "learning in many dimensions", published in comic form, Sousanis (2015: 53) promotes the use of comics to achieve a bigger variety of modes of expression, enabling authors to "unflatten" the map, because "not even the most expansive mapping can convey everything" (ibid: 57). One of the reasons comics are so good at "unflattening" is the dual nature of comics, not only in their combination of text and image, but also in the "spatial interplay of sequential and simultaneous" (ibid: 62), the possibility to read a comic layout panel by panel in a temporal alignment and at the same time in its entirety, holding its own meaning.

Fusing maps and comics offers a wide range of advantages over conventional 'western' maps without relinquishing their benefits, namely describing the world through spatial and statistical metrics. Meanwhile, comics can illustrate interaction, personal experience and perspective, and thereby construct and verbalize meaning. Comics can display and ideally also evoke emotions and thus reactions. We can use the narrational capacities of comics to tell stories of spirituality, morality or ethics. We can report on change, pointing out processes and displaying the passage of time. We can convey all of this with a broad palette of expressive means provided for us in the combination of visual art and written text.

It has become clear that perspective taking plays a crucial role in mapping meaning. But whose perspective can we hope to portray in an artifact such as a map? One problem with maps about certain communities authored by an outsider is the acquisition of an authentic perspective. This is why Caquard and Cartwright (2014) formulate a shift of importance from the map towards the narrative of the mapmaking process. These narratives should shed a critical light on the cartographic process and the persons 'behind' the map. One way of dealing with this problem is to make the author's voice explicit, ideally within the map itself. With the integration of comics into the map we can do two things. Emotional storytelling is possible by establishing a perspective *within* the map. At the same time, we can establish a perspective *on* the map, by introducing map viewers and authors as commenting agents into the map itself. With elements of graphic narrative, as found and perfected in comics, we can establish a meta-communication. By portraying characters looking from an outside perspective at the map, we can make explicit the voice of an onlooker or commenting map author. In interactive web maps, this technique could even induce a dialog, utilizing web 2.0's commenting functions.

How can we practically enhance the mapping language to map the immaterial realm of meaning with comics? Figures 1 and 2 illustrate two ways that show how maps and comics can be fused into one multimodal form of expression. In Figure 1, the classic map is placed in the center of the display. Comic stories are then arranged in the space around the map. They are anchored to the map by lines pointing to the locations where the stories take place. In combination with the map, the stories are readily available at first glance and can be accessed at any time in any order. The map user can mentally integrate the stories with the rest of the map, because we can easily switch between map and stories, both of which share a similar 'language'. The comic stories are thus part of the map and function like any other map symbol. Of course, they are highly complex symbolizations as they are composed of text and many other symbols. Of all the symbols the rose is an especially striking one, as it is the only colored one. This eye-catcher appears in the map, as well as in the comic stories, producing a reciprocal effect. It brings the story around the rose into the map. At the same time, it places the object of the stories in the world and creates (spatial) relations between them.

Figure 1: Different perspectives within a map can be represented using comic stories, indicating what is happening where through the eyes of the stakeholders. The figure shows an example of an artifact treating an exemplary globalization process, which is explained in the map and filled with meaning in the comic stories (Comic by von Reumont).

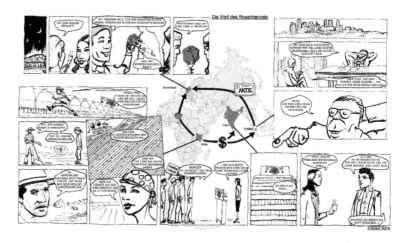

Whereas Figure 1 has shown how stories can be arranged around the map, Figure 2 illustrates how maps can be inserted into a comic story. It is an excerpt of an atlas, which uses maps to navigate through ten different stories of climate change and action. The stories tell of the different encounters people around the world have with the conditions of a changing climate, how they feel about it and how they react to it. It tells the stories of what the climatological metrics of change really mean for the livelihoods of everyday people.

Figure 2: Different perspectives on a map can be represented with comic storytelling techniques. A meta-level can be established using image composition, coloring, differing degrees of realism, speech bubbles, etc.(Comic by von Reumont).

The comic is intended to inform about climate change from the perspectives of affected persons. This is explicitly revealed in several parts of the story, e.g. by having the characters look at a satellite map and comment on it, uttering their construal of the facts presented in the map (Figure 2).

Discussion

Mapping meaning, comics and indigenous communities

As I have argued, in order to include meaning in maps, narratives and visual art, - especially in combination as comics - are promising additional media to consider. From my point of view, the fusion of maps and comics in mapping projects with and by indigenous peoples has a lot of potential, which I would like to briefly outline below.

One goal of mapping with indigenous communities is the documentation and promotion of indigenous knowledge and cultural heritage (see Introduction, this volume) and therefore the meaning of the environment and the places for indigenous communities. As outlined above, comics have a lot of potential in conveying meaning. They are able to integrate personal perspective, experience of place, 'invisible' agents and relations to land (as, for example, dealt with by Dieckmann, Sullivan, Skaanes, Vermeylen, this volume) in maps.

Furthermore, one of the issues often encountered in participatory mapping methodology (see e.g. Roth 2006; 2009), used with and by indigenous communities, is the need for highly specialized skills in order to truly participate in map making (see Rambaldi et al. 2007). Often, 'participation' is therefore restricted to the contribution of knowledge. Integrating comics drawn by the participants can strengthen their participation in the actual map making. The combination of pictures and words is not unfamiliar in most cultures and the skills for drawing comics can easily be acquired. The participants could then use their own repertoire of pictorial expression and explain it to the outsider. Both parties could engage in an intense dialogue that could be captured and distributed for further use. Tony Chavarria, the curator of Ethnology at Santa Fe's Museum of Indian Arts and Culture gives examples of how Native Americans "articulate identity, politics, and culture using the unique dynamics of comic art" (Chavarria 2019: 48). He sees a connection between the 'traditional' story telling of Native art techniques and the visual language of comics and thus calls it "a natural step that [Native] artists would delve into the art of comics" as they "recognize the power of cultural symbols to speak about their past, present, and future" (Chavarria 2009: 4-5). Having compiled an annotated bibliography of indigenous comics, Callison and Rifkind believe that "visual representation [in comics] can influence and inform our understanding of a particular person, place, or cultural group" and hope "that visual texts might [...] assist with the ongoing efforts toward reconciliation and decolonization" (2019: 153).

Additionally, participatory mapping is a conglomerate of many different participatory techniques. The mapping itself, for example, is often accompanied by other activities such as group discussions, interviews and direct observation (e.g. Njounan Tegomem et al. 2012: 50; Dieckmann, Sullivan, Goldman, this volume). However, the maps themselves remain mostly silent on the process of mapmaking, the methodology, the authors and the kind of participation which took place. With comics, these processes of mapmaking can be made visible on indigenous maps (and on any other map).

Comic-maps in the light of other media

When designing maps, the question of the medium of choice is of great importance. The use of high-tech interactive multimedia maps is very promising and seems to be a good approach to bring us closer to the embodied experience of space in the real world, as demonstrated by Pearce and Louis (2008), who created a multimedia map including animations, virtual 3D models and different layers of maps. What are missing here, in my view, are subjective perspectives conveyed by narrative. These perspectives are accessible in the paper, explaining the concepts and reasons behind the map design (so in a way they are part of the distant paramap). But without the stories about how Hawaiians have used and lived in the places, the map remains mute. In her paper maps, Pearce has implemented perspective narrative in a most impressive and effective way, e.g. in her map of Champlain's travels. Her paper map on Canadian place names is also an impressive example of how perspective can be formed in maps. Her current mapping project is also about forming an indigenous perspective on large-format map panels, rather than using interactive digital media (see Pearce, this volume, for an outline of her various projects). It is most likely that the choice of the medium has influenced the story telling techniques used in maps. However, convincing examples of good story maps are rare in digital formats. Moore et al. (2018) describe a technique that effectively integrates narrative in the comic form directly into an interactive 3D map. This allows for a very close relationship between the space of the map and the time line of the comic story. They have, however, met many constraints, some of which are typical of 3D maps, such as cluttering. The stories are organized in 'walls' along time lines. These walls are depicted as such in the 3D model and hide a lot of the information in the maps behind them.

Moore et al. (ibid.) concede that only rather simple stories can be mapped in this way.

Too many possibilities for interaction can quickly become confusing and even tiring to a person who wants to engage with a map. If information and narrative are exposed only by clicking a certain icon, the question is, what is the motivation for me to click that icon? This is especially relevant when the map user does not even know what it is that she or he is looking for. This is why the program manager of ESRI-storymaps, Allen Carroll, recommends avoiding deploying interaction as a condition of understanding the storyline. It might interrupt the flow and thus the immersion of the audience in the narrative, meaning that they miss the point of what the author is trying to convey.[8]

Film is a very strong medium that comes fairly close to the actual embodied experience of a place. As demonstrated for example by Roberts (2014), a simple walk along a certain route can raise strong emotions if embedded in a narrative context. In the video shot by Roberts, he follows the route of an abduction, in the course of events of which a two-year old boy was tortured and killed. This technique, however, is very distant from the way conventional maps are expected to function. Only embedded in the background narrative of the abduction and in conjunction with other mappings can the emotional impact of this video fully unfold in relation to its specific location. A multimodal approach, bringing the two media closer to each other in a single form, seems to be necessary. Solutions exist e.g. in the form of Neatlines[9], an internet platform that allows its users to create multimodal maps for the web. In times of the internet, multimedia access does not seem to be a great obstacle. However, with regard to indigenous peoples' mapping projects, access to the internet might indeed be an obstacle, and one needs to weigh up the benefits, costs and obstacles of this option. Furthermore, digital mapping in the sense outlined requires even more technical skills than the production of analog maps and might run the risk of decreasing the "participation" even further towards mere contribution of knowledge. Therefore, analog media not requiring electricity, projection devices and highly sophisticated IT knowledge for their production and maintenance, etc., might be preferable in the communication, bridging a given digital divide in order to continue the dialogue.

---

8   See https://storymaps.esri.com/stories/2018/maps-minds-stories-3/index.html (last accessed June 20, 2020).

9   See https://neatline.org/showcase/ (last accessed June 20, 2020).

Comics in analog maps offer some benefits for the map maker and map user in general. The possibility of visually connecting story and map, the portability and ease of use and production, and the non-linearity paired with the simultaneity of information are all arguments for the use of the comic form on paper maps in preference to film and computer.

References

Callison, Camille/Rifkind, Candida (2019): "Introduction: 'Indigenous Comics and Graphic Novels: An Annotated Bibliography'". In: Jeunesse: Young People, Texts, Cultures 11/1, pp. 139-155 (DOI: 10.1353/jeu.2019.0006).

Caquard, Sébastien/Cartwright, William (2014): "Narrative Cartography: From Mapping Stories to the Narrative of Maps and Mapping." In: The Cartographic Journal, 51/2, pp. 101-106 (DOI: 10.1179/0008704114Z.000000000130).

Carroll, Joseph (2018): "Minds and Meaning in Fictional Narratives: An Evolutionary Perspective." In: Review of General Psychology, 22/2, pp. 135-146 (DOI: 10.1037/gpr0000104).

Cartwright, William (2009): "Art and Cartographic Communication." In: William Cartwright/Georg Gartner/Liqiu Meng/Michael P. Peterson (eds.), Cartography and Art. Lecture Notes in Geoinformation and Cartography, Berlin: Springer, pp. 9-22 (DOI: 10.1007/978-3-540-68569-2_2).

Cartwright, William (2010): "Addressing the value of art in cartographic communication." In: ISPRS Journal of Photogrammetry and Remote Sensing 65/3, pp. 294-299.

Chavarria, Tony (2009): "Indigenous Comics in the United States." In: World Literature Today, May-June, pp. 47-49.

Crampton, Jeremy (2010): Mapping. A Critical Introduction to Cartography and GIS, Oxford: Wiley-Blackwell.

Dreyfus, Hubert/Taylor, Charles (2015): Retrieving Realism, Cambridge, Massachusetts: Harvard University Press.

Dittmer, Jason (2010): "Comic book visualities: a methodological manifesto on geography, montage and narration." In: Transactions of the Institute of British Geographers 35, pp. 222-236.

Enfield, Nick (2011): "Elements of Formulation." In: Jürgen Streeck/Curtis Goodwin/Charles LeBaron, (eds.): Embodied Interaction, New York: Cambridge University Press, pp. 59-66.

Graeber, David (2015): "Radical alterity is just another way of saying 'reality'."
In: HAU: Journal of Ethnographic Theory 5/2, pp. 1-41.

Horrocks, Dylan (2001): Atlas. Vol. 1, Montréal: Drawn and Quarterly.

Horrocks, Dylan (2004): "The Perfect Planet. Comics, Games and World-Building." (www.hicksville.co.nz/PerfectPlanet.htm, last accessed August 4, 2020).

Hühn, Peter/Meister, Jan Christoph/Pier John/Schmid, Wolf, eds., (2004): the living handbook of narratology, Hamburg: Hamburg University (http://www.lhn.uni-hamburg.de/, last accessed May 15, 2020).

Hutchins, Edwin/Nomura, Saeko (2011): "Collaborative Construction of Multi-modal Utterances." In: Jürgen Streeck/Curtis Goodwin/Charles LeBaron, (eds.): Embodied Interaction, New York: Cambridge University Press, pp. 29-43.

Koopman, Eva Maria (2018): "Does Originality Evoke Understanding? The Relation between Literary Reading and Empathy." In: Review of General Psychology, 22/2, pp. 169-177 (DOI: 10.1037/gpr0000107).

Mar, Raymond (2011): "The Neural Bases of Social Cognition and Story Comprehension." In: Annual Review of Psychology, 62, pp. 103-134 (DOI: 10.1146/annurev-psych-120709-145406).

Mar, Raymond/Oatley, Keith (2008): "The Function of Fiction is the Abstraction and Simulation of Social Experience." In: Perspectives on Psychological Science 3/3, pp. 173-192 (DOI: 10.1111/j.1745-6924.2008.00073.x).

Mbembe, Achille (2014): Kritik der schwarzen Vernunft, Berlin: Suhrkamp.

Mbembe, Achille (2019a): University of Cologne Graduate Seminar 21.06.2019. Cologne, Germany.

Mbembe, Achille (2019b): Memory and Restitution – Museumsgespräch 18.06.2019 (https://amp.phil-fak.uni-koeln.de/40320.html, last accessed July 24, 2020).

McCloud, Scott (1993): Understanding Comics, New York: Harper Perennial.

Merleau-Ponty, Maurice (1962): Phenomenology of Perception, London: Routledge.

Moore, Antony/Nowostawski, Mariusz/Frantz, Christopher/Hulbe, Christina (2018): "Comic Strip Narratives in Time Geography." In: ISPRS Int. J. Geo-Inf. 7/245/, pp. 1-20 (DOI:10.3390/ijgi7070245).

Njounan Tegomo, Olivier/Defo, Louis/Usongo, Leonard (2012): "Mapping of resource use area by the Baka Pygmies inside and around Boumba-Bek National Park in Southeast Cameroon, with special reference to Baka's customary rights." In: African Study Monographs 43, pp. 45-49.

Oatley, Keith/Djikic, Maja (2018): "Psychology of Narrative Art." In: Review of General Psychology 22/2, pp. 161-168 (DOI: 10.1037/gpr0000113).

Pearce, Margaret W./Louis, Renee (2008): "Mapping Indigenous depth of place." In: American Indian Culture & Research Journal 32/3, pp. 107-126.

Rambaldi, Giacomo/Muchemi, Julius/Crawhall, Nigel/Monaci, Laura (2007): "Through the Eyes of Hunter-Gatherers: participatory 3D modelling among Ogiek indigenous peoples in Kenya." In: Information Development, 23/2-3, pp. 113-128 (DOI: 10.1177/0266666907078592).

Ryan, Marie-Laure (2010): "Narrative Representation in Art, Cognition, and Social Interaction." In: Style, 44/4, pp. 469-495 (https://www.jstor.org/stable/10.5325/style.44.4.469).

Ryan, Marie-Laure (2014): "Space." In: Peter Hühn/Jan Christoph Meister/John Pier/Wolf Schmid (eds.), the living handbook of narratology, Hamburg: Hamburg University (http://www.lhn.uni-hamburg.de/, last accessed May 15, 2020).

Ryan, Marie-Laure (2018): "Narrative mapping as cognitive activity and as active participation in storyworlds." In: Frontiers of Narrative Studies 4/2, pp. 223-247 (DOI:10.1515/fns-2018-0020).

Roberts, Les (2014): "The Bulger Case: A Spatial Story." In: The Cartographic Journal 51/2, 141-151 (DOI: 10.1179/1743277413Y.0000000075).

Roth, Robin (2006): "Two-dimensional maps in multi-dimensional worlds: A case of community-based mapping in Northern Thailand." In: Geoforum 38, pp. 49-59 (DOI:10.1016/j.geoforum.2006.05.005).

Roth, Robin (2009): "The challenges of mapping complex indigenous spatiality: from abstract space to dwelling space." In: cultural geographies, 16, pp. 207-227 (DOI: 10.1177/1474474008101517).

Rowland, David/Yanovich, Yelizeveta/Kentros, Clifford G. (2011): "A stable hippocampal representation of a space requires its direct experience." In: Proceedings of the National Academy of Sciences 108/35, pp. 14654-14658.

Sarr, Felwine (2019): Afrotopia, Berlin: Matthes und Seitz.

Sousanis, Nick (2015): Unflattening, Harvard University Press: Cambridge.

Streeck, Jürgen/Goodwin, Curtis/LeBaron, Charles (2011): "Embodied Interaction in the Material World: An Introduction." In: Jürgen Streeck/Curtis Goodwin/Charles LeBaron, (eds.): Embodied Interaction, New York: Cambridge University Press, pp. 1-26.

Streeck, Jürgen/Goodwin, Curtis/LeBaron, Charles, eds. (2011): Embodied Interaction, New York: Cambridge University Press.

Wood, Dennis/Fels, John (2008): "The Natures of Maps: Cartographic Constructions of the Natural World." In: Cartographica 43/3, pp. 189-202 (DOI:10.3138/carto.43.3.189).

What shall we map next? Expressing Indigenous geographies with cartographic language

Margaret Wickens Pearce

The question of whether something is mappable has been an ongoing presence in my life, or rather, a persistent thorn in my side, as so often when I undertake a project, people say to me, "you will never be able to map that." Would they say to another artist – you will never be able to film that, or paint that, or tell that story in a novel? Why cast doubt only where maps are involved? My experience tells me it might have something to do with societal assumptions and expectations about the content, appearance, and function of cartography: how maps are obligated to look and what they are obligated to include and achieve, and their capacity and potential to do more. When someone then further elucidates, "you will never be able to include everything," I know they assume the map is an inventory, a definition for map with its roots in the information extraction industry of colonial economies. When someone tells me, "a printed map can only take you so far; you need to add video and interactive features," I know they assume the map is essentially a digital technology, improvable by increasing the presence and functionality of additional technological features.

Another way to think about maps is to assume cartography is a mode of creative expression structured like language, akin to the creative languages of music and architecture, and sharing qualities with speech and writing. These assumptions have always felt natural and logical to me because I came to cartography from writing, lured by the way cartographers describe the form as made of graphic marks (functioning like words), combined together in symbols (functioning like phrases), and mapped according to rule systems such as projection, classification, and layout design (functioning like grammar) (MacEachren 1995: 269–309). A form whose grammar can be intentionally broken at certain times, for particular reasons. Like the other expressive languages, such a cartography is not a universal language; it is culturally constructed (Pearce 2009). Indeed, as Lisa Brooks and others have demonstrated, cartography more closely resembles North American Indigenous traditional expression than written words arranged in typed lines on the pages of a book, because of its relationality to traditional Indigenous inscriptive languages, its utility as a mnemonic device, and its power to represent situated narratives, and so must be given equal consideration for telling Indigenous stories (Brooks 2008; Pyne/Taylor 2012: 92-104; Goeman 2013).

If we begin that way, by assuming cartography is language, we can expect it to be capable of infinite creative expansion if we have the courage, craft, patience, and dedicated practice to imagine it so. That is, the same expectations and discipline we already bring to words. How often do we say it's hard to use words to convey differences in the ways we experience time and space, yet we still try? Spoken conversations are capable of leading us to insights and understandings that can only arise from that dialogical exchange, and we can hope we find our inner capacity and conversation skills to arrive at those understandings. Indeed, some of our most profound understandings of ontological differences may have come from speech or writing.

I remember exactly where I was standing when I first picked up Hugh Brody's *Maps and Dreams*, in the now defunct Globe Bookstore in Northampton, Massachusetts. I remember the aisle, I remember it was on the top shelf in the middle of a short bookcase, slightly to the right of my gaze. I must have bought it, because my next memory is of reading it back on my college campus. As I read, I came to a gradual understanding of the differences between two ways of mapping, because of what he said, and also, because of the way he said it: the interleaved structure of numerical evidence and stories about peoples' lives, and the tone he sets. The book has been with me pretty much ever since. Re-reading it many times with students over the years, different aspects of the story became important to me as my own research experiences changed which questions were foremost on my mind.

Maybe you had the same experience with this book, or maybe another writer comes to mind, whose effectiveness on paper is not because they write with a particular typewriter or software. It is because of what is said, and how they say it, with a structure that shapes an emergent feeling of understanding in the reader's consciousness.

In their 2017 workshop and edited volume *Crumpled Paper Boat*, a team of anthropologists came together to reimagine ethnographic writing to "convey more elusive truths in experience," ontological truths, through new ways of working with language. Each had decided to respond to "problems of understanding" through a "deflection" to, for example, narrative prose fiction and other forms of writing that foreground feeling, intimacy, and uncertainty, forms resistant to closure. "Writing with the force of passage is what equips us to think otherwise, to bend our concepts to the concepts of others" (Pandian/McLean 2017: 4-5).

In her research on Maasai wildlife conservation, Mara Jill Goldman demonstrated that the *structure* of these new forms of writing must necessarily follow the expressive structures of the people whom she writes about. To convey the ways that Maasai people engage multiplicity in decision-making dialogues moving towards consensus, Goldman's "deflection" is to undertake their *enkiguena* as the conceptual structure for both her research method and her writing structure, to bend closer to the traditional ontologies of her subject. Such an approach by definition requires the tools of narrative prose fiction (in her case, theatrical dialogue), to imagine an *enkiguena* onto the page, creating an environment for building respect and cooperation across knowledge worlds, and for knowledge production itself (Goldman 2020: 22, 26, 242; see also Goldman 2011).

I agree, and look to cartographic language for my deflective form. Cartographic narratives work on us over time, making ruminative spaces to visit and re-visit in our minds, as we move towards new understandings and insights, including insights for what Ute Dieckmann highlights as the places where conventional settler[1] cartography is weak and Indigenous geographies strong: the presences of humans, beyond-humans, dreams, spirits, and sounds, and the qualities of relationality, perspectivism, situatedness, temporal fluidity, ambiguity, and humans as part of an integrated ecology.

But how to get there? In my experience, Indigenous presences and qualities do not manifest in the map as *things, for instance, as a palette of symbols or other objects* to place at locations in the map. As markers for Indigenous ontologies, they coalesce in the map when a cartographer Indigenizes the mapmaking process by incorporating Indigenous methodologies, pedagogies, and epistemologies.[2]

---

1   I use the term "settler" throughout this article to refer to non-Indigenous people in states created by settler colonialism.

2   There are a range of other approaches in use by Indigenous communities and their collaborators, including the design of culturally-relevant symbols (Tobias 2000), the use of film and animation to cartographically explain change over time (Remy 2018), painting place name sites in collaboration with Elders (Enote/McLerran 2011), hand-drawn maps (Stephansen 2017) and development of interactive online maps

Their coalescence also depends on our attention to the mapping process as one of translation, and our awareness of the translator's tools for mediating when a translation should feel familiar, and when it should feel unfamiliar (Venuti 2008). Like all translations, not everything can be re-expressed; the translation is always partial and provisional. Our responsibility is to learn what must be kept and what let go, for one map moment in time. The goal of this Indigenized map translation is not to duplicate what can already be said with words, but instead to *parallel those words in a complementary way*, focusing on what maps do so well, that is: to draw our attention to the situatedness, the relationality, and the categories present in geographical narratives. All qualities essential to understanding ontological differences. With such an approach, I believe ontologically expressive vocabularies can reveal themselves.

Emotion, place, and the reader

The first time I decided to take cartographic language apart to make room for new structures was not for Indigenous geography. The project was to map the journey of North West Company clerk John Macdonell into the Pays d'en Haut in 1793, in a way that would evoke the emotional depths of a clerk's recollected journey as he travels into a world utterly unknown to him (Pearce (as Journey Cake) 2005; Pearce 2008). I created a six-foot base map of the rivers, lakes, and streams of his trip by tracing the water features from digital scans of paper maps and printing this base on a single long roll of paper. Then I read his diary carefully and in tandem with other Canadian canoe memoirs, and drew in each place he mentioned for each day.

Tracing is slow, meditative, and can be as intimate as reading. Tim Ingold writes of tracing, of "re-tracing", as a way of inhabiting the page or paper as one inhabits a landscape (Ingold 2007), and this has been true for me. Repeated readings of Macdonell's diary entries gave me the rhythm of his story, one of extreme brevity as he wrote notes where and when possible. The process of drawing while reading encouraged me to imagine the places and motion more specifically than just reading, and gave me a body memory for the stories as I marked each place in pencil, while showing me the visual, locational

---

(Thom/Colombi/Degai 2016; McGurk/Caquard 2020), to name a few. I respect these projects while also taking a different approach, as you will see in the article.

rhythm of his memories as a whole. While working, I was guided by writings on the way place and narrative are co-constitutive (Entrikin 1991; Casey 1993), and techniques for generating that condition in collaboration with the reader (Iser 1974; Casey 1993; Berlant 1998). And then there was this six feet of map in my house, always present, like a family member. This project was not an Indigenous map project, yet I look to it as a turning point for what have become significant aspects of my process: the pace and intimacy that comes from tracing, the deeper attention levels and engagement that come from drawing while reading, and the necessity of dwelling with the map on paper until it enters into dialogue with the environment it resides in.

These methods moved me towards a new way of mapping (Figure 1). To convey the feeling of looking back on a journey, I translated narrative techniques of focalization, voice, and brevity into cartographic technique to create intimacy, ambiguity, and sense of place in the map. There is little in the way of explanation in the map overall; instead, I used brevity to create ambiguity about the meanings of those palettes, which the reader must then resolve by drawing on their own travel memories. Outside the palette of his daily joys and fears, the map is mostly empty.

Figure 1: Pearce 2005

As I circulated my drafts, and my intentions for the work gradually became known, people (cartographers and other colleagues) began to tell me how these techniques would be untenable: that readers would not understand the reasons for the changing hues, and more information would need to be supplied; that it would be confusing not to include familiar geographical markers outside the route frames; and that in general too much was left without explanation along the route. These objections arise from assumptions that the map is an explanatory, scientific document, and the reader is a passive consumer. But the purpose of this map was to convey an emotional landscape.

Heteroglossia

A few years later, Michal Hermann and I collaborated on a map commissioned on the occasion of the 400th anniversary of Samuel de Champlain's founding of Quebec City (Pearce/Hermann 2008; Pearce/Hermann 2010). Champlain was an explorer, colonizer, and cartographer whose ability to travel and survive depended on the knowledge, diplomacy, assistance, and advice of many Indigenous people over time, especially Wendat, Innu, and Algonquin leadership. Our purpose was to map Champlain's travels during the years he was scouting and then building the city, by drawing on his published journals, and to make room for Indigenous voices and intentions in the context of those reported travels.

Again, cartographers and other colleagues told us those Indigenous voices would be unmappable, as there are no corresponding Indigenous published journals from that same context. People also objected that, whereas the voyageur map followed one person's journey in a single direction at a fixed geographical scale, Champlain's travels could not be mapped similarly because they extended over many years, with multiple directions and at multiple scales. To develop any visual alternative to a line for expressing these multiplicities would only be confusing. These objections assume that maps are diagrams that exist independently of the theoretical debates and breakthroughs of colonial and Indigenous histories, and that lines on a map are clarifying.

Assuming cartography is language, the presence of dialogue is logical and sometimes expected, and Mikhail Bakhtin's approach to history through dialogism is relevant to addressing these skepticisms. In Bakhtin's concept of heteroglossia, or speech diversity, history is conceived as "a system of intersecting planes" composed of multiple languages, styles, and voices. Heteroglossia is then a narrative structure where an author gives unity to the form, but not to the voices themselves (Bakhtin 1981: 48). It was a quality to pursue in the project.

We printed a large base map of rivers and lakes, and over four days, read the journals out loud from start to finish, and marked by hand everything that seemed important. The process of close listening to Champlain's journals drew our attention to when, where, and how Indigenous people were mentioned, as well as emotional landscapes Champlain allowed to be visible. Whereas in the voyageur map, my awareness of all the voyageur ignored or missed led me to seek a fidelity with the narrowness of his experience in the map, with Champlain, the obstinate myopia and judgemental tone of his narrative felt unconscionable. We were obligated to speak out.

When we finished the journals, we spent three snowy weeks retracing by car the route Champlain traveled by boat or on foot over the course of years. Cartographers often speak of fieldwork as a locational fact-check and clarification stage of the mapping process, but it is also a way of getting a body feeling for the map. It is another kind of tracing, as important to dwelling in the project as tracing on paper. Though we were not traveling at the same pace, our ability to stand in place, look in the same direction, and imagine, made all the difference. Tracing on the ground showed us the relative sizes of places and stories and the distances between them, while also connecting us to how Canadians were interpreting the same stories. The Quebec anniversary was getting underway, with tributes to Champlain already in the museums and bookstores. These public histories broadcasted repeating tropes that taught us which stories loomed large in the public imagination, and which ignored. This was a new kind of untenable myopia, compounding Champlain's narrow account with contemporary prejudice and reaffirming the cartographers' obligation to intervene.

The trip also yielded a trove of photographs, videos, and post cards recording the colors, textures, and sounds to be brought back to the studio, none of which directly contributed to the composition. Instead, like the novelist who keeps a map of their story without including the map in the book itself, our research and collections of impressions formed deeper images of place held in mind while we found a visual rhythm for marks and stories on the map. They gave a certainty to the map's marks that could not have been there otherwise.

In the resulting map (Figure 2), dialogism describes route direction on the ground, and dialogical layouts translate conflicting perspectives (individual and collective, Indigenous and European) on the same events, with cartographer's voice interjecting to comment. To place Indigenous voices in equal exchange with Champlain, we drew on Indigenous oral history, ethnohistory, and archaeology to create imagined voice, in the same typeface. All three voices take different positions with respect to the reader, sometimes addressing them directly and sometimes speaking around them; the reader, meanwhile, is free to explore a map with designated point of beginning but no specific path from that point. The multiple directions and ambiguities of Champlain's route are further described by a shifting route ribbon, rather than a line (Figure 2).

Like Frederik von Reumont (this volume), I too look to the language of sequential art for its potential to transform cartographic structures, a way of inserting new spaces with different visual grammars in the space of the map. In the Champlain map, we created a device called sequential insets (Figure 3), blending the detail function of the inset map with the temporal, scalar, and heteroglossia possibilities of sequential design. Sequential insets opened flexible spaces for following narratives across time in a particular place, for following the scale-changes of those narratives, for interjecting Indigenous commentary and cartographers' commentary, for blending emotional and environmental qualities with color, and for blending dreamed and imagined geographies with those of the world as lived during the day. We also incorporated the presence of multiple cartographic languages, translating the grammar of Champlain's cartography into the main map, insets, and map elements, a heteroglossia of cartographic narratives of the same events in space.

Indigenous ontologies

Meanwhile, Renee Pualani Louis, Ev Wingert, and I collaborated to re-map the Na Pali cliffs on the island of Kaua'i in Hawai'i (Pearce/Louis 2008). We were inspired by David Turnbull's idea that technoscience (including digital cartographies and GIS) must be reframed through the transmodern, that is, in a middle ground of practices from Indigenous and non-Indigenous map traditions (Turnbull 2000: 3). We set out to demonstrate that Indigenous ontologies could be expressed through U.S. federal digital data if we only pay attention to the ways that data expressed time and space. Our process was to examine which aspects of a U.S. Geological Survey map were inconsistent with Indigenous Hawaiian ontologies, and correct for some of those inconsistencies by changing only the discursive structures in the map and not the data itself. To guide us on the qualities of Hawaiian ontologies, we looked to the *ahupua'a*, the units of land at the foundation of their traditional land division and governance. *Ahupua'a* are marked on the land but not fixed in

Figure 2: Pearce and Hermann 2008

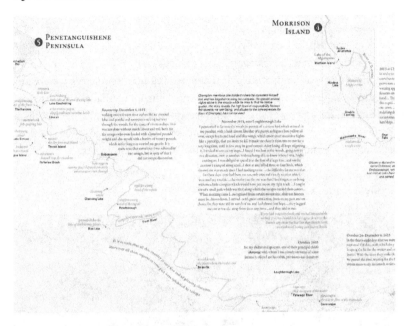

Figure 3: Pearce and Hermann 2008

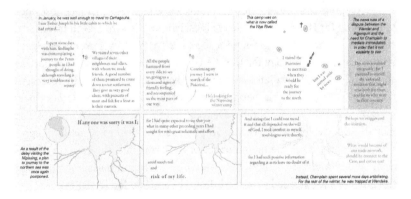

place; their edges expand or contract to follow seasonal and diurnal changes in the microclimates enfolded within the steep, mountainous terrain. So, too, then, must the map also follow seasonal and diurnal change, moving with the environment and the families and governance structures interwoven in that environment.

Like the voyageur map, this project was also a narrowing down, in order to focus on one aspect: demystifying ontological difference by reimagining cartographic grammar. The *ahupua'a* led us to focus on light angle, viewing angle, and viewing position as ontological agents. The map sequences we created (Figure 4) explore the portrayal of sensory elements of shadow and season, specifically, the agency of shadow and season to shape *ahupua'a* boundaries at Kaua'i. The sequences also explore the importance of shifting viewer positions and angles as foundational to Indigenous Hawaiian ontologies.

Figure 4: Pearce and Louis 2008: 121-122

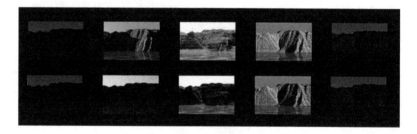

In keeping with our intention to uncover a transmodern technoscience of mapping for Hawai'i, that is, a technoscience woven from both traditional Hawaiian science and Anglo-American science, the maps don't entirely substitute Hawaiian ontology for U.S. Geological Survey ontology. They portray some Indigenous Hawaiian assumptions about how to accurately represent time and space, including boundary ecologies, respectful protocols of perspective, and the priority of tides over the concept of coastline. The maps also include U.S. Geological Survey assumptions about how to accurately represent space on a map: the maintenance of uniform scale, the absence of sentient beings, and the portrayal of elevation as a series of measured points on the ground, the so-called bare earth Digital Elevation Model (DEM).

Indigenous methodologies

Soon after the Kaua'i project, I had the opportunity to collaborate with Penobscot Cultural & Historic Preservation for a new map of the place names of their territory encompassing the Penobscot River watershed in Maine (Pearce/Penobscot Cultural & Historic Preservation Department, 2015; Pearce 2014). The purpose was to support language revitalization in a community with few speakers of the language, to clearly convey Penobscot territory and sovereignty to outsiders, and to collaborate with community members to express the ways traditional place names emote culturally, politically, and spiritually. One way people (colleagues and friends, both Penobscot and non-Penobscot) told me the intentions were unmappable related to tribal members themselves: if there are few speakers of the language, how will you involve the Penobscot community if they don't know the traditional place names (the assumption that Indigenous tradition lies only in an authentic past)? Other people commented that a paper map was a weak choice for conveying the depth of place names' meanings, in need of augmentation from video storytelling and online interactivity (the now-familiar technology assumption).

Our process was guided by Indigenous methodologies prioritizing values of respect, reciprocity, and responsibility in how we worked together, how we worked with community members, and how the map took shape (Wilson 2008; Smith 2012). Penobscot traditional pedagogies for teaching and learning language through immersion, and place names through story, also guided the structure and content of the map. Just as *ahupua'a* comprise a genre of Indigenous cartography at Kaua'i, so too does the web of place names and story comprise a genre of Penobscot traditional cartography. Translating traditional, land-based pedagogy into the map thus becomes translating Indigenous cartographic language into non-Indigenous cartographic language, blending cartographic grammar from both traditions.

One way we worked on the names with community members was to organize an Elders' cafe open to all ages, with food and maps, to start the conversation. At the cafe, people began remembering the names they grew up with, names constructed mostly from "English" words but which are only used by Penobscot people, appearing in no US Geological Survey map nor Google database. To widen the conversation, we then left the map on the wall in the Council Chambers and in the Elders' lunchroom so people could add to it themselves whenever they remembered a name, with the result in the map that the Penobscot side includes all Penobscot place names irrespective of which languages they draw on. As William Meadows (2008) shows us in his work with Kiowa place names, all of the names, no matter which time scale they come from, are Penobscot names; all name the land together, and all form the basis of identity.

The format we chose for the resulting map also acknowledged Penobscot tradition across time (Figure 5). We made the map two-sided, separating Penobscot names from English translations, to facilitate language learning and to mimic Penobscot pedagogies: one side expresses what is heard, the other side expresses the meanings of what is heard when one speaks the language. This separation extends to all aspects of the map, from descriptive text to place names and grid labels. We sized the map to fit Penobscot people's bodies, as wide as an armspan in a truck or a canoe, and sized an accompanying gazetteer to fit in their hands or pockets, as a personal, intimate portal into the map. The gazetteer connects the content of the two sides, serves as a handheld rubric for memorizing language, and invites rumination about the connectivities between places, as names with the same stem naturally group together alphabetically.

Traditional pedagogies showed us that stories are central to learning and inextricable from the place names. But how to respectfully share that in the map? At first, I tried to make graphic symbols to represent story events in the map with pictures, rather than words. But Indigenous story events are not 'things', objects to be located in the discourse of settler cartography. They are inextricable from voice, the Penobscot speakers whose words are quoted for the stories, and the ancestors whose words are quoted for the place names. These spoken stories produce places, in the literal sense by enacting the creation of landforms, and in the wider sense by producing imagined geographies in the minds of listeners. The voices would have to bring the names into the map.

In Figure 6 is an example from the English-language side of how that was done, with a story about their ancestral hero Gluscabe, threaded through and including the place names. Reading from the translated meanings, we learn that the place names teach where to do something ("handiest"), and what the landscape looks like ("half standing"), and form pools of associations ("kettle" names). We learn that the story teaches how to do something (get flint stone at kkineo, kill and eat a moose), and itself forms a map by telling events in sequence that refer to directions on the land. The cartographic force of the story is reinforced by an adapted north arrow, a "story arrow" centered on a

Figure 5: Pearce and Penobscot Cultural and Historic Preservation Department 2015

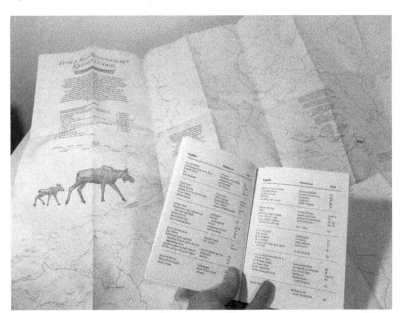

moose head, which orients us not to the cardinal directions but instead, to the locations of story events. None of this structure is explained elsewhere in the map, but instead, again following pedagogy, revealed in context to the reader who assembles the concepts in their mind. The map only includes two stories, but we don't have to include every story for the reader to understand that there are many stories.

The stories bring with them the presence of spirits (in this case, their ancestral hero Gluscabe), not as graphic pictures on the map, but as graphic pictures in the reader's mind as they listen and interpret what they hear. The stories heighten the reader's awareness of the same presences in the place names' translated meanings, along with other ontological differences revealed there, including the presence of all time scales, and traveling as a kind of witnessing of Gluscabe's landform creations. Translating structures of Indigenous pedagogies in this way, the map enacts epistemological difference by demonstrating how place names are traditionally taught in a Penobscot way (using the two sides of the map, incorporating story, and leaving closure of meaning

Figure 6: Pearce and Penobscot Cultural and Historic Preservation Department 2015

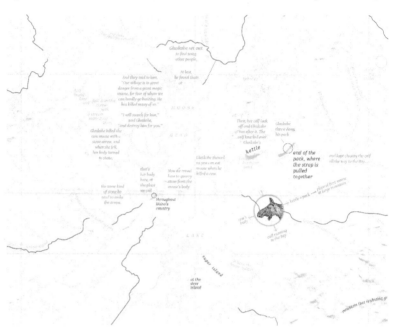

to the reader), and how they are traditionally taught in a non-Penobscot way (the presence of the map itself, and the device of an accompanying gazetteer).

Self-determination

I again had the opportunity to work entirely in Indigenous place names on the occasion of the recent celebration of Canadian confederation known as Canada 150 (Pearce 2017; Pearce/Hornsby 2020). The purpose of the map was to honor Indigenous sovereignties in the year that Canada celebrated its sovereignty, by remapping Canada only in Indigenous place names, by permission of the communities to whom the place names belong. This time, cartographers and other colleagues had many things to say about why it was both impossible and a bad idea. Their objections focused on my inability to ever "fill it" with names (the inventory assumption), that no one agrees on what the names are (the assumption that there must be agreement within and between Nations), that it would be ridiculous to ask permission for so many names (the assumption that Indigenous methodologies do not scale up, that they are "extras"), the impossibility of portraying which names were "first" because people move around so much (the assumption that linear time is relevant), and the impossibility of determining "correct" territory boundaries (the assumption that Indigenous territories would be represented by lines).

Assuming cartography is a spatial language for telling stories, there is no inherent need to fill it with anything (nor can all stories be shared at once), nor is there a requirement to express time and space in any particular way. In previous projects, I had experimented with new grammatical structures to encode narrative in the map, but this project required a specific grammar for reasons of power and political context. I set the size, scale, and projection of the map to match exactly with the same parameters used by Natural Resources Canada for their national map posters, in order for the two maps to converse on equal footing.

The task of looking for place names involved hundreds. of communities, yet included no travel funds for visiting even a small number of those communities. I worked by researching communities one by one, then emailing or calling to present the project and ask permission, and ask if they would be interested to contribute. And then followed person to person, asking each to share a list of names, or even one name, and listening to what people told me. About half of the communities or individuals I connected with declined to participate, and for many dozens more, I was never able to make that initial connection.

The grammatical constraints and possibilities of the cartographic language (scale, size, projection parameters) and the particular, contributive nature of the mapping process both influenced the ways Indigenous ontologies manifested in the final map. Indigenous permissions encircle the map in a font size larger than the place names, offset by their own hue, to indicate that respect for these permissions is the first order of the map (Figure 7). The permissions form portals from each of four directions through which to enter into the place names. Their protocols are not uniform, and include individuals, councils, Nations, and cultural organizations. Their diversity teaches that everyone is in a different place with how they work on their names, and what or who constitutes authority in the protocols surrounding the names.

The density of diverse Nations at the limited scale of the map, and the nature of contributing and building trust at a distance, made it impossible and inappropriate for stories to be present as spoken narratives, as in previous projects. Yet story is present nonetheless, referenced in the place name translations themselves. Sometimes these stories are evident to outsiders, but oftentimes not, when the translated meaning sounds deceptively generic ("Like a lake") yet figures prominently in their literatures. The brevity of the meanings and their locations protects cultural property from extraction by outsiders, while simultaneously building intimacy for those who understand their references, knowing the names are speaking to them and them only. So, too, do translated meanings bring dialogism into the composition, when ancestors' voices speak to each other and to the map reader, and the reader responds by repeating the names. The presence of ancestral voices is particularly strong when they tell us unambiguously to pay attention ("Place to take a wrong turn," and "Shallow. Hazardous", Figure 7).

There are several regions where the map continues without the presence of place names, where neither contributing project partners nor cultural property permissions allowed place names to be reproduced. In solidarity with the work of Audra Simpson, Eve Tuck, and K. Wayne Wang, I honor those refusals as part of the narrative whole, which is itself inextricable from self-determination (Simpson 2007; Tuck/Wang 2014). They are not missing information, they are part of the lesson. I speak to these silences in the map introduction by indicating the names are not all of the names, nor the Nations all of the Nations. In this way, the silences constitute one of the many places in the map where readers must close the gap with curiosity and personal responsibility.

Sometimes people told me stories as a way of telling me about the names, and this sensibility influenced the way the names are placed, and the type styles I chose. At first, I differentiated the names only by whether they were primarily about the water (blue) or the land (black). Gradually, I understood I must also ligature all the names, an extension of honor and affection to the smallest scale, though invisible to most readers. Rather than use the lines formed by the digital data, I re-drew by tracing all of the land, water, and road lines, for a softness and fluidity that digital data lines cannot achieve, and for the inhabiting that tracing generates. This network of intimate highways places the names in a web of responsibility by indicating our obligations to visit, and fusing time scales of the past and present as always simultaneously relevant to Indigenous ontologies.

Figure 7: Pearce 2017

By excluding story as narrative between names, the map reveals the power and agency of place names to bring dialogism and ontological fluidity into the map. The names tell us the sounds, feelings, wind, and textures of places in the voices of the ancestors, forming pictures in our minds. They direct our attention to the presence of spirits and multiple time scales. And they ask the reader to dwell on them by the brevity and ambiguity of their translated meanings. Each name is like a puzzle, the way a poem is a puzzle, a concept or message to be taken up for consideration by the reader.

On first glance, the result is a highly conventional map. With reading, and the accumulation of meaning that comes from that reading, the map gradually reveals ontologies erased by conventions of settler cartography.

Reflection

The point of all this is to demonstrate that, in my experience, there are no universal techniques for translating the presences and qualities of relational ontologies into cartographic language.[3] The cartographic manifestation of those qualities arises from particular projects, situated in time and place. Each is a chronotope, a unique assemblage of time and space generative of its own narrative character (Basso 1996, 62; Bakhtin 1981: 84).

Intimacy in one map comes from typeface and ligature; in another, from a palette of emotional hues. An aerial viewing angle in one map might signify detachment, but if paired with voices becomes intimacy, or authorial empowerment. Likewise, an oblique angle can be used in one map as a sign of respect, then in another map as a sign of confusion. Motion may arise in stepped surfaces, or the fluctuations and rhythm of a ribbon-like route, or a line tapering to white to indicate something rushing through the composition. Time may manifest in the cadence of sequential comic panels, in the direction of story across the page, or in the temporal scales referenced by place names.

Yet when I look back on these projects, I see qualities in common to all: the presence of situated stories, the resistance to closure, the incorporation of the reader into the narrative structure and story, and the agency of stories as portals to relational ontologies. There is also an empty space where a new project must sit: a project in search of a heteroglossia of Indigenous and settler ontologies leading not to conflict and mistrust, but to consensus made from (and respecting divergences among) multiple voices. A map expressing relational ontologies (Alberti 2013; Blaser 2013) as though our lives depend on it, because they do.

Moving forward: relational ontologies

Which brings me to my work in progress, Mississippi Dialogues. The project is to portray public opinion about flood management in an Indigenized map of the Mississippi River. The larger intention is to move seemingly intractable debates about Mississippi flood management out of spaces shaped by settler assumptions about space, time, and relations between humans and beyond-humans. In keeping with methods from previous maps, I work towards no predetermined outcome, but instead seek to learn what becomes possible. The destination is a series of large-format map panels installed at publicly-

---

3   For more details about the methods, setbacks, and lessons of each project, read Pearce 2008; Pearce/Louis 2008; Pearce/Hermann 2010; Pearce 2014; and Pearce/Hornsby 2020.

accessible sites along the river, with accompanying guidebook, supported by public programming. I began this work in late 2018, with hope to launch it in 2022.

By "Indigenized" river I mean a river defined as Indigenous place names and their meanings; Indigenous ways of thinking and talking about water, flooding, and living with the river; Indigenous visual grammars from each region of the river; and the shorelines, wetlands, sand, mud, rocks, islands, and flooded forest lands from before the major public works projects of the U.S. Army Corps of Engineers. How can we talk about living with the river, when it is defined only as a series of locks, dams, spillways, pools, levees, and floodways? My project moves away from maps assuming human control of the river, and moves towards maps assuming human collaboration with and obligations to a beyond-human river to create a space for a shared vision about flood management.

You can see from this description how the project builds on and expands the theories, processes, techniques, insights, and lessons of previous work. My projects have moved from mapping place names as archival sources for Indigenous historical voices, to mapping names for language revitalization, to mapping names as evidence of political and cultural obligations and territories, and now to the current project, to map the names as agents of lessons critical to our ability to understand our individual and collective responsibilities for climate action. The work follows Jean-Sébastien Boutet's inquiry into the multiplicity of Indigenous ontologies in play in every region, and Caroline Desbiens and Étienne Rivard's demonstration of the ways that Indigenous and settler ontologies are co-constructed. It is particularly inspired by the work of Julian S. Yates et al., who show us that, "if we take seriously the possibility of multiple water worlds" (2017: 807), then the site of ontological analyses must be on the waters themselves (Boutet 2014; Desbiens/Rivard 2014; Yates/Harris/Wilson 2017).

All kinds of people tell me my intentions are unmappable. Some of their reasons are familiar, including, that I will never get permission from "everyone", and what will I do if some communities decline to participate, or have no names to share? Some of the unmappable reasons are new, related to concerns that the project does not reflect the interests of communities along the river, that the scale and expense of the project are too great, and that multiple ontologies of water is too much to ask of one map design.

I share these concerns, but they don't lead me to conclude the project is unmappable. The cartography I know is language. With an Indigenized translation process, I can feel my way forward to a map whose appearance I cannot yet know. You can guess which qualities are on my mind: dialogism, intimacy, brevity, heteroglossia, affection, fluidity of space and time, and categories and relationalities of human and beyond-human. I trust the design process to show the way.

Closing

Cartography as language moves away from the map as inventory, the imposition of uniformity, the binary of map as art or science, the focus on an 'authentic' past, and the mandate of explaining at the reader. Cartography as language moves towards narrative, dialogue, intimacy, ontological fluidity, focus on discursive structures (within or across communities), activating the reader's imagination, memory, and responsibility, and the possibilities for expressing relational ontologies. Indigenizing the mapping process leads to insights regarding how to articulate ontological differences critical to the readers' understandings. And Indigenous place names and voices activate relational ontologies, dialogism, and intimacy, simply through speaking.

This mode of working is not a 'solution' for every context. I present it as a way of working that I enjoy, one that is inseparable from my identity as an artist living in the world, just as a novelist or poet may feel inextricable from their ways of writing. The more I work, the more I feel cartography remains a nascent form. We must use our courage to ignore those who tell us it can't be done, our imaginations to explore possibilities, our perseverance to practice technique, and our patience to refine through revision, to nurture and expand this form. We must learn to say with a map what we feel to be falling through the cracks between words, yet which we know must be said.

What shall we map next, together?

Acknowledgements

Igwien, I'm grateful to the Elders, language keepers, and Nations who kindly contributed some names to make the Coming Home map possible; to Carol Dana, James Francis, Gabe Paul, and the community members of Penobscot Nation; to Stephen Hornsby, Stephanie Crosby, and Michael Hermann of the Canadian-American Center, University of Maine; to Renee Pualani Louis and in memory of Ev Wingert; to Ute Dieckmann and Øyvind Eide for their invaluable comments; and to everyone from the Köln workshop, may we stay connected.

References

Alberti, Benjamin (2013): "Relational Ontologies." In: Benjamin Alberti/Andrew Meirion Jones/Joshua Pollard (eds.), Archaeology After Interpretation: Returning Materials to Archaeological Theory, New York: Routledge, pp. 37-42.

Bakhtin, Mikhail M. (1981): The Dialogic Imagination, Austin: University of Texas Press.

Basso, Keith H. (1996): Wisdom Sits in Places: Landscape and Language Among the Western Apache, Albuquerque: University of New Mexico Press.

Berlant, Lauren (1998): "Intimacy: A Special Issue." In: Critical Inquiry 24, pp. 281-288.

Blaser, Mario (2013): "Ontological Conflicts and the Stories of Peoples in Spite of Europe: Toward a Conversation on Political Ontology." In: Current Anthropology 54, pp. 547-568.

Boutet, Jean-Sébastien (2014): "Opening Ungava to Industry: A Decentring Approach to Indigenous History in Subarctic Québec, 1937–54." In: Cultural Geographies 21/1, pp. 79-97.

Brody, Hugh (1982): Maps and Dreams. New York: Pantheon.

Brooks, Lisa (2008): The Common Pot: The Recovery of Native Space in the Northeast, Minneapolis: University of Minnesota Press.

Casey, Edward S. (1993): Getting Back into Place: Toward a Renewed Understanding of the Place-World, Bloomington: Indiana University Press.

Desbiens, Caroline/Rivard, Étienne (2014): "From Passive to Active Dialogue? Aboriginal Lands, Development and Métissage in Québec, Canada." In: Cultural Geographies 21/1, pp. 99-114.

Enote, Jim/McLerran, Jennifer (eds.) (2011): A:shiwi A:wan Ulohnanne / The Zuni World, Zuni: A:shiwi A:wan Museum & Heritage Center, and Museum of Northern Arizona.

Entrikin, J. Nicholas (1991): The Betweenness of Place: Towards a Geography of Modernity, Baltimore: Johns Hopkins University Press.

Goeman, Mishuana (2013): Mark My Words / Native Women Mapping Our Nations, Minneapolis: University of Minnesota Press.

Goldman, Mara J. (2011): "Keeping the Rhythm, Encouraging Dialogue, and Renegotiating Environmental Truths: Writing in the Oral Tradition of a Maasai Enkiguena." In: Byron Caminero-Santangelo/Garth A. Myers (eds.), Environment at the Margins: Literary and Environmental Studies in Africa, Athens, Ohio: Ohio University Press, pp. 95-120.

Goldman, Mara J. (2020): Narrating Nature: Wildlife Conservation and Maasai Ways of Knowing, Tucson: University of Arizona Press.

Ingold, Tim (2007): Lines: A Brief History, New York: Routledge.

Iser, Wolfgang (1974): The Implied Reader: Patterns of Communication in Prose Fiction from Bunyan to Beckett, Baltimore: Johns Hopkins University Press.

MacEachren, Alan M. (1995): How Maps Work: Representation, Visualization, and Design, New York: Guilford.

McGurk, Thomas J./Caquard, Sébastien (2020): "To What Extent Can Online Mapping Be Decolonial? A Journey Throughout Indigenous Cartography in Canada," In: The Canadian Geographer 64/1, pp. 49-64.

Meadows, William C. (2008): Kiowa Ethnogeography, Austin: University of Texas Press.

Pandian, Anand/McLean, Stuart J. (2017): "Prologue." In: Anand Pandian/Stuart J. McLean (eds.), Crumpled Paper Boat: Experiments in Ethnographic Writing, Durham, NC: Duke University Press, pp. 1-10.

Pandian, Anand/McLean, Stuart J., eds. (2017): Crumpled Paper Boat: Experiments in Ethnographic Writing, Durham, NC: Duke University Press.

Pearce, Margaret W. (2008): "Framing the Days: Place and Narrative in Cartography," In: Cartography and Geographic Information Science 35/1, pp. 17-32.

Pearce, Margaret W. (2009): "Non-western mapping," In: Rob Kitchin/Nigel Thrift (eds.), International Encyclopedia of Human Geography, New York: Elsevier.

Pearce, Margaret W. (2014): "The Last Piece is You," In: Cartographic Journal, Special issue on Cartographic Narrative 51/2, pp. 107-22.

Pearce, Margaret W. (2017): Coming Home to Indigenous Place Names in Canada, Orono, Me.: Canadian-American Center, University of Maine.

Pearce, Margaret W. (as Journey Cake) (2005): The Intricacy of These Turns and Windings: A Voyageur's Map, Marshall, Mich.: Journey Cake.

Pearce, Margaret W./Hermann, Michael J. (2008): They Would Not Take Me There: People, Places, and Stories from Champlain's Travels in Canada, 1603–1616, Orono, Me.: Canadian American Center, University of Maine.

Pearce, Margaret W./Hermann, Michael J. (2010): "Mapping Champlain's Travels: Restorative Techniques for Historical Cartography," In: Cartographica 45/1, pp. 33-48.

Pearce, Margaret W./Hornsby, Stephen J. (2020): "Making the Coming Home Map," In: Cartographica 55/3, Special issue on Decolonizing the Map.

Pearce, Margaret W./Louis, Renee Pualani (2008): "Mapping Indigenous Depth of Place," In: American Indian Culture & Research Journal 32/3, pp. 107-26.

Pearce, Margaret W./Penobscot Cultural & Historic Preservation Department (2015): Iyoka Eli-Wihtamakw Ktahkinawal / This Is How We Name Our Lands, Indian Island, Me.: Penobscot CHP, Penobscot Nation.

Pyne, Stephanie/ Taylor, D. R. F. (2012): "Mapping Indigenous Perspectives in the Making of the Cybercartographic Atlas of the Lake Huron Treaty Relationship Process: A Performance Approach in a Reconciliation Context," In: Cartographica, Special issue on Indigenous Cartography and Counter Mapping, 47/2, pp. 92-104.

Remy, Lola (2018): "Making the Map Speak: Indigenous Animated Cartographies as Contrapuntal Spatial Representations," European Journal of Media Studies 7/2, pp. 183-203.

Simpson, Audra (2007): "On ethnographic refusal: Indigeneity, 'voice' and colonial citizenship," In: Junctures: The Journal for Thematic Dialogue 9, pp. 67-80.

Smith, Linda Tuhiwai (2012): Decolonizing Methodologies: Research and Indigenous Peoples, 2nd edition, London: Zed Books.

Stephansen, Maria Therese (2017): "A Hand-drawn Map as a Decolonising Document: Keviselie (Hans Ragnar Mathisen) and the Artistic Empowerment of the Sami Movement," In: Afterall: A Journal of Art, Context and Enquiry 44, pp. 112-121.

Thom, Brian/Colombi, Benedict J./Degai, Tatiana (2016): "Bringing indigenous Kamchatka to Google Earth: Collaborative digital mapping with the Itelmen peoples," In: Sibirica 15/3, pp. 1-30.

Tobias, Terry N. (2000): Chief Kerry's Moose: A Guidebook to Land Use and Occupancy Mapping, Research Design and Data Collection, Vancouver: Union of BC Indian Chiefs and Ecotrust Canada.

Tuck, Eve/Wang, K. Wayne (2014): "R-Words: Refusing Research." In: Django Paris/Maisha T. Winn (eds.), Humanizing Research: Decolonizing qualitative inquiry with youth and communities, Thousand Oaks: SAGE Publications, pp. 223-47.

Turnbull, David (2000): Masons, Tricksters and Cartographers: Comparative Studies in the Sociology of Scientific and Indigenous Knowledge, London: Routledge.

Venuti, Lawrence (2008): The Translator's Invisibility: A History of Translation, New York: Routledge.

Wilson, Shawn (2008): Research Is Ceremony: Indigenous Research Methods, Halifax: Fernwood Publishing.

Yates, Julian S./Harris Leila M./Wilson, Nicole J. (2017): "Multiple Ontologies of Water: Politics, Conflict and Implications for Governance." In: Environment and Planning D: Society and Space 35/5, pp. 797-815.

About the authors

Hugh Brody is an anthropologist, film-maker and writer. He has carried out cultural mapping projects and worked on documentary films with Indigenous peoples in Arctic and Subarctic Canada, on the North Pacific Coast and in South Africa's southern Kalahari. He was also a member of the Morse Commission, working in western India. His books include *The People's Land, Maps and Dreams, Living Arctic* and *The Other Side of Eden*. He is an Honorary Associate of the Scott Polar Research Institute at the University of Cambridge and Honorary Professor of Anthropology at the University of Kent, Canterbury. From 2004–18 he held the Canada Research Chair in Aboriginal Studies at the University of the Fraser Valley in British Colombia.

Ute Dieckmann is an anthropologist at the University of Cologne and currently German Principal Investigator for *Etosha-Kunene Histories* (www.etosha-kunene-histories.net), supported by the German Research Foundation and the UK's Arts and Humanities Research Council. Over the last three years, she was senior researcher within the E3 Project (*Anthropological Models for a Reconstruction of the First African Frontier*) of the Collaborative Research Centre 806. For many years, she has worked at the Legal Assistance Centre in Windhoek, doing research with and advocacy for marginalized and indigenous communities in Namibia.

Øyvind Eide is a professor in Digital Humanities at the University of Cologne. He holds a PhD in Digital Humanities from King's College London (2013). He was the chair of the European Association for Digital Humanities (EADH) from 2016–19 and is also actively engaged in several other international organizations. His research interests are focused on modelling and media differences, especially the relationships between texts and maps. He is also engaged in theoretical studies of modelling in the humanities and beyond.

Welhemina Suro Ganuses is a resident of Sesfontein / !Nani|aus, north-west Namibia, and an administrator for the NGO Save the Rhino Trust (Namibia). Since 2014 she has been a collaborator on the research project *Future Pasts* (ww w.futurepasts.net), which explores the conservation and cultural landscapes of west Namibia. With Sian Sullivan she has recently contributed a chapter on 'Understanding Damara / ǂNūkhoen and Ubun indigeneity and marginalisation in Namibia' for a major review on *Indigeneity, Marginalisation and Land Rights in Post-independence Namibia*, published in 2020 by the Legal Assistance Centre, Windhoek, Namibia.

Mara Jill Goldman is an associate professor of Geography and a fellow in the Institute for Behavioral science at the University of Colorado, Boulder, where she teaches environment-society, development, and African geographies. She is an affiliate of the Gender and Women's Studies program and the Center for Native American and Indigenous Studies. She has worked with Maasai communities in Tanzania and Kenya for over two decades on the politics of knowledge surrounding wildlife conservation, rangeland management, development, and climate change adaptation. She co-edited *Knowing Nature: Conversations at the Intersection of Political Ecology and Science Studies* (2011, University of Chicago Press) and authored *Narrating Nature: Wildlife Conservation and Maasai Ways of Knowing* (2020, University of Arizona Press).

Margaret Wickens Pearce is a cartographer and writer, and an enrolled member of Citizen Potawatomi Nation. She grew up on Seneca territory at Ga'sgöhsagöh, At the Waterfall (Rochester, NY, USA), and today lives as a guest on Penobscot territory at Catawamkeag, the Great Landing Place (Rockland, Maine). Her work has been exhibited nationally and internationally, and awarded support by Yaddo, ART Omi, A Studio in the Woods, the Landes Fund, the Center for Native American and Indigenous Research at Northwestern University, and the American Council of Learned Societies (ACLS), among others, and she has received two national cartographic design awards. She has taught at Humboldt State University, Ohio University, and the University of Kansas, and holds a PhD in geography from Clark University.

Thea Skaanes is an experienced ethnographer and social anthropologist and since 2008 has been the head of the ethnographic UNESCO Collections at Moesgaard Museum, Denmark. Her doctoral research (Aarhus University,

2018) is on cosmology, rituals, power objects, human-animal relations and meat-sharing among the hunter-gathering Hadza of Northern Tanzania. While still working in this field, her present research is within the areas of religion, materiality and time. Since 2011, alongside doing fieldwork among the Hadza, she has examined different ethnographic museum collections on Hadza material culture on site and has collected a material collection on Hadza cosmology for Moesgaard Museum.

Sian Sullivan is Professor of Environment and Culture at Bath Spa University and UK Principal Investigator for *Etosha-Kunene Histories* (www.et osha-kunene-histories.net), supported by the UK's Arts and Humanities Research Council and Germany's Deutsche Forschungsgemeinschaft. She is an environmental anthropologist, cultural geographer and political ecologist concerned about better understanding diversity in cultural understandings and representations of the natural world, amidst contemporary concern over climate change and species decline. Over the last few years, she has led a research project called *Future Pasts* (www.futurepasts.net), which explores the conservation and cultural landscapes of west Namibia. She has also researched the 'financialisation of nature' – see the Natural Capital Myth (www.the-natural-capital-myth.net).

Saskia Vermeylen is a socio-legal property theorist, and Chancellor's Fellow in the law school at the University of Strathclyde, Scotland. She is also the recipient of a Leverhulme Trust fellowship, studying utopian literatures and outer space law. Her work focuses on the critical socio-legal and philosophical dimensions of property frontiers.

Frederik von Reumont is currently working as a cartographer for the Institute of Geography Education at the University of Cologne. He holds both a Master of Arts in Geography from the University of Aachen and a Master of Science in Cartography and Geoinformation from the University of Vienna. Since 2016 he has been engaged in his PhD thesis with the working title: "Using the Potential of Comics and Maps for Conveying Geographical Meaning". His research interests include maps and comics in education, paleo vegetation modeling, geovisualization, and virtual field trips. His publications focus on both the potential of maps and comics to convey meaningful information, and on interactive geo-visualizations for the web.

Social and Cultural Studies

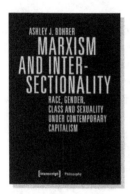

Ashley J. Bohrer
Marxism and Intersectionality
Race, Gender, Class and Sexuality
under Contemporary Capitalism

2019, 280 p., pb.
29,99 € (DE), 978-3-8376-4160-8
E-Book: 26,99 € (DE), ISBN 978-3-8394-4160-2

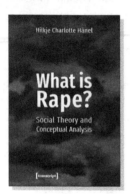

Hilkje Charlotte Hänel
What is Rape?
Social Theory and Conceptual Analysis

2018, 282 p., hardcover
99,99 € (DE), 978-3-8376-4434-0
E-Book: 99,99 € (DE), ISBN 978-3-8394-4434-4

Jasper van Buuren
Body and Reality
An Examination of the Relationships
between the Body Proper, Physical Reality,
and the Phenomenal World Starting from Plessner
and Merleau-Ponty

2018, 312 p., pb., ill.
39,99 € (DE), 978-3-8376-4163-9
E-Book: 39,99 € (DE), ISBN 978-3-8394-4163-3

**All print, e-book and open access versions of the titles in our list
are available in our online shop www.transcript-verlag.de/en!**

Social and Cultural Studies

Sabine Klotz, Heiner Bielefeldt,
Martina Schmidhuber, Andreas Frewer (eds.)
Healthcare as a Human Rights Issue
Normative Profile, Conflicts and Implementation

2017, 426 p., pb., ill.
39,99 € (DE), 978-3-8376-4054-0
E-Book: available as free open access publication
E-Book: ISBN 978-3-8394-4054-4

Michael Bray
Powers of the Mind
Mental and Manual Labor
in the Contemporary Political Crisis

2019, 208 p., hardcover
99,99 € (DE), 978-3-8376-4147-9
E-Book: 99,99 € (DE), ISBN 978-3-8394-4147-3

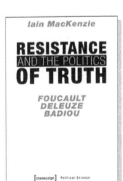

Iain MacKenzie
Resistance and the Politics of Truth
Foucault, Deleuze, Badiou

2018, 148 p., pb.
29,99 € (DE), 978-3-8376-3907-0
E-Book: 26,99 € (DE), ISBN 978-3-8394-3907-4
EPUB: 26,99 € (DE), ISBN 978-3-7328-3907-0

**All print, e-book and open access versions of the titles in our list
are available in our online shop www.transcript-verlag.de/en!**

CPSIA information can be obtained
at www.ICGtesting.com
Printed in the USA
JSHW050747020123
35616JS00004B/44

9 783837 652413